Modern Enthusiast

The New Step-by-Step Training Handbook

William (Sil) Sanders

Rime Publications
Stanwood, WA
2017

Rime Publications
33101 44th Ave NW, Stanwood, WA 98292
Sil@WestiesNW.com
www.EnthusiasticTracking.com
360-708-4665

Copyright © 2017, All rights reserved.

No part of this publication may be reprinted, reproduced, stored in a retrieval system, or transmitted, in any form or by any electronic, mechanical or other means, now known or hereafter invented, without the prior written permission of the author, except in the case of brief quotations embodied in critical reviews.

Sanders, William R.
   Modern Enthusiastic Tracking: The New Step-by-Step Training Handbook / William R. (Sil) Sanders.
   432 p. 28 cm.
   Includes bibliographical references and index.

ISBN-13: 978-1-892119-21-6 (paper)

1. Tracking dog training.   I. Title.   II. Title: Dog Training

Library of Congress Control Number: 2017941531
LC Call No.: SF428.75.S26 2017
Dewey No.: 636.7/0886 21

Second Printing, 2020.

Printed in the United States of America on acid free paper.
Published 2017.

To Alicia, Mr. Q, Dessa, QT, and Twizzle, my very best teachers,

&

to Maureen, an exceptional friend, tracking student, and teacher herself,

&

to Anne, for accepting my passion for tracking in preference to other possible vices.

Sil's Westie Honor Roll

CH Rime's Alicia Aquena CDX TDX CG (Alicia)
CH Rime's Quonquering Hero VCD3 UDX MX JE (Mr. Q)
CH Rime's Off To See The Wizard TD JE (Wizard)
CH Rime's Game Goddess TDX (Dessa)
CH CT Camcrest-Rime Q'd Up For Trouble VCD1 RAE TDU MXP AJP OFP ME EE RATS (QT)
GChB Camcrest-Rime Twizzle On Ice BN RA TDX TDU SWE SCM SEM SHDE NW3 NW3-I NW3-E NW3-V NJP NFP ME RATCH (Twizzle)
Ch Rime-Camcrest Hat Trick TD (Gretzky)

Contents

Contents v
Preface vii
Acknowledgments ix
Introduction to Tracking 1
Part I — Basic Tracking Training for the TD and TDU 13
    Phase 1. Introducing your dog to Tracking 14
    Phase 2. Developing Straight-Line Tracking Skills 34
    Phase 3. Crosswind Tracking and Preparing for Corners 49
    Phase 4. Introducing Corners 56
    Phase 4GT.X — Gradual Corners (Optional Remediation) 70
    Phase 5. Multiple Corners 73
    Phase 6. Reading Your Dog 87
    Phase 7. Track Age 107
    Phase 8. Perfecting Skills 128
    Phase 9. Preparing for the TD or TDU Test 148
Part II — Advanced Tracking towards the TDX 159
    Phase X1. Aging the Track to Three Hours 166
    Phase X2. Age Again and Crosstracks 179
    Phase X3. More Crosstracks, and Age Progression Once Again 199
    Phase X4. Skill Improvement 214
    Phase X5. Preparing for the TDX Test 245
Part III — Urban Tracking Foundations: Training for the TDU 255
    Phase U1. Lawn Contamination and Hard-Surface Tracks 262
    Phase U2. Contamination, Surface Transitions, and Hard Surface Skills 275
    Phase U3. Preparing for the TDU, and Foundations of the VST Journey. .. 286
Part IV — Advanced Urban Training for the VST, UTD, and UTDX 301
    Phase V1. VST Hard-Surface Corners 309
    Phase V1S UTD Supplement — Preparing for the CKC UTD 329
    Phase V2. Non-Vegetated Corners Developed. 337
    Phase V3. Putting the Pieces Together. 357
    Phase V4. Preparing for the VST Test — Special Situations and Blind Tracks. 378
Appendix A — Advanced Training Exercises 401
Bibliography 419
Index 421

Preface

The purpose of this book is to lay out a step-by-step training plan for those starting a dog with the aim of earning the TD, the TDU, or both titles. This training also provides a solid foundation for the team to subsequently train for and earn the TDX, the VST, or both to become an esteemed Champion Tracker. Also included is a recommended plan to transition a TD or TDX dog to the TDU and VST.

In addition to these American Kennel Club (AKC) titles, preparation is included for the similar Canadian Kennel Club (CKC) tests. The Canadian TD, UTD, TDX, and UTDX are similar to the AKC tests, but the CKC UTD is more complex than AKC TDU while the CKC TDX is typically simpler than the AKC TDX. The Australian Shepherd Club of America (ASCA) also has a tracking titling program similar to the AKC TD, TDX, and TDU tests, but with their own interesting and fun variations.

Almost all dog trainers and dogs learn best when they follow a plan even if they adapt it. For this reason, the training plan is organized as a fairly linear stream of sessions and exercises. The user should follow the plan in as step-by-step fashion as possible but keep their eyes and minds open, as many dogs and handlers will require more work on specific skills, as well as perhaps some different work. So don't be afraid to drop back and redo a section of material if your dog is not performing in the expected way. And don't be afraid to try techniques you learn from other experienced tracking resources.

For those who are familiar with my 1998 tracking book *Enthusiastic Tracking*, each training phase in it is replicated here with additional sessions so the dog learns to track in urban situations in parallel while learning to track in the fields. The sessions are laid out explicitly in a step-by-step fashion, so the trainer has a clear plan to follow while the dog has the structure that promotes his skill development.

This book is divided into four parts.
  I. The first part parallels and expands Part I of *Enthusiastic Tracking*. In particular, Part I now prepares a dog for the urban TDU test as well as the traditional field TD test.
  II. Part II continues field tracking training by focusing strictly on the TDX. To make the training process simpler and more straightforward than the 1998 book, additional material on crosstracks and additional step-by-step schedules were added.
  III. Part III is a completely new section on preparing the previously field-only or field-mostly tracking dog for the urban TDU test. It also serves as a foundational review for the dog who did the Part I urban work.
  IV. Part IV takes the TDU trained dog and prepares him for the additional complexities of the VST.

Each part in further divided into chapters called phases because they represent different phases of training.

If you have little background in canine tracking, do follow the step-by-step program as directly as possible. Your dog and you will have fun and learn a lot.

While this book presents a coherent step-by-step plan to develop your dog into a highly-skilled tracking dog and to develop your own handling and training skills, no single plan of this scope can be exhaustively complete. There are many good ways to teach your dog to track and to teach yourself to be an excellent handler. I know the techniques and step-by-step program described here are one of the good ways to accomplish your tracking goals. But, there are others. The further you go in your tracking training, particularly for the advanced TDX and VST tests, the more likely you will find other techniques that complement this plan.

If you are an experienced tracking trainer, take from this book techniques that you find valuable for skill development and problem solving. Or use the book as a baseline that you adapt to the needs of your own dog or your students' dogs. You can also use other techniques that have worked for you in the past, integrating them sensibly with the **Modern Enthusiastic Tracking** techniques.

As in the 1998 book, in this book I refer to all dogs as male and all people as female to reduce pronoun ambiguity.

Comments Welcome

I always appreciate your comments on this book so I can improve it. Send your comments to me at 33101 44th Ave NW, Stanwood, WA 98292-7106; 360-708-4665; Sil@WestiesNW.com. So that I know which version your comments apply to, please reference the date below in any correspondence.

March 2020   *Sil Sanders*

Acknowledgments

No one becomes knowledgeable about any endeavor without learning from others. Shirley Hammond was my first tracking instructor and longtime tracking mentor. Her deep knowledge of scent, training methods, and handling techniques built the strong foundation upon which all my current knowledge is based. And her recognition that non-conventional breeds can become excellent tracking dogs provided the environment for my Westie to earn the first TDX in the breed at a time when others thought Westies too small and too distractible to do advanced tracking.

I have been lucky enough to see many dogs track and to discuss tracking with many of their handlers. Laying a track for someone else is so rewarding because the dog loves tracking, the owner appreciates your help, you get to see how another dog tracks, and you get to learn how another person trains their dog.

Helping or spectating at many tracking tests in Northern California allowed me to gain a wider perspective on training and handling from the judges, other tracklayers, and exhibitors that were invaluable in refining and extending these training techniques. Since starting to judge in 1992, I have had the benefit of working with numerous expert tracking judges and have been able to see many excellent tracking teams pass their tests.

I acknowledge and sincerely appreciate the techniques I have learned from tracking authors and seminar presenters:

- Glen Johnson, Tracking Dog – Theory and Methods Seminar, 1980. In particular, his overall training structure is an ongoing influence on my techniques. I continue to see the value of using logical step-by-step training techniques.
- Curbs and curbed-island tracks from Steven Ripley, author of **Making Scents of the Urban Jungle**, 2nd ed., 2011 and seminar presenter.
- Intentional contamination from Terri Everwine, AKC judge, tracking instructor, and seminar presenter, (~2010). See blogs at http://www.morainetrackingclub.org/articles.
- Advanced lawn serpentines from Debbi Best, tracking instructor, (2011).
- The use of SIAB and Hydration by Steve White. See page 8.
- Other techniques indirectly reported to me by seminar attendees (various).

Many of their techniques have been extended substantially from what was described at the seminars and worked into an overall step-by-step program to develop dog and handler skills in a rational and clear way.

Several tracking friends have recently shown me interesting techniques that are included in this book. For example, Nancy Skinner's use of straws to make flags invisible from a distance and Maureen Fielding's liberal use of small pieces of freeze-dried lamb lung on advanced urban tracks.

As valuable as each and everyone else have been to my education, my best teachers have been my own dogs. Alicia suffered my many novice training mistakes and kept patiently guiding me because she loved to track so much. Mr. Q, who is the best natural footstep-tracking Westie I ever expect to see, solidified the importance I place on enthusiastic tracking and, through his expressive behavior at scent transitions, taught me a great deal about scent. Mr. Q had the honor of enjoying my many initially misdirected attempts to teach an excellent field tracking dog to track on the urban lawns and parking lots of VST. Dorie, Aura, and Belle's difficulty understanding corners taught me to separate the issues of corners from the issue of crosswind tracking. Dessa helped me understand and refine the techniques to leave ground animals and return to the good track. Another excellent field tracking dog, QT, enjoyed years of experiments to encourage him to transfer his field excellence to urban lawns and parking lots. He earned his VST and CT at age 9 a full seven years after his TDX. More recently Twizzle has been teaching me that she can be a great tracker if I am willing to let her have the freedom to do it her way, which is often a little farther from the track than I otherwise prefer.

I was able to learn a great deal by observing Shirley's other students and their dogs. Trouble, BJ, Foxie, Arusha, Blossom, Bishop, Joy, Gamble, Bonnie, Bridie, Pogo, and their owners all taught me valuable tracking lessons that I could not have learned alone.

Once I moved to the Seattle area, Jessie, Seja, Margarita, Diva, Mandy, Chaz, Alena, Hari, Treasure, Keegan, and their owners allowed me to continue my tracking education.

In the last fifteen years these dogs helped me refine training techniques and expand them to urban environments: Orrin, Tusk, Connor, Annie, Kramer, Thomas, Frank, Derby, Tink, Fonzie, Mochi, Maddie, Billy, Ziggy, Spike, Tiki, Wrangler, Stuka, Raven, Max, Griz, Ray, Kazuki Aki, Kate, Merry, Pix, Gustav, Safari, Ray, Gino, Humphrey, Charlotte, Griffin, Quigley, Jake, Joey, Tocai, Virgil, Isaac, Casey, Rusty, Solo, Ethan, Rosey, Koa, Luna, Zoe, Quinn, Tazra, Qiss, Jet, Ellie Mae, Dusty, Gimme, Tippet, Louie, Dante, Shyre, BonnieB, Bella, Bacchus, Rody, Knight, Skookum, Gus, Star, Cleo, Tazzle, Butter, Burk, Cherry, Heidi, Truffle, Willow, Cyd, Dori, Hawk, Doyle, Alice, Troy, Scout, and many others along with their dedicated handlers. Apologies to those students whose dogs I have failed to mention.

I also wish to thank:
- Google's licensing policies for allowing use of images from Google Earth in limited printed works like this.
- Arner Publications, Inc for permission to use the excerpt from page 114 of Glen Johnson's book.
- The late Mario Salacone for permission to use his cartoon artwork of dogs tracking.

Pictures of dogs tracking on the cover are used with the kind permission of their owners and photographers (Matt Uhry photographer for the third and fourth):
- Ch CT CKC-Ch Camcrest-Rime Q'd Up for Trouble VCD1 RAE TDU TDX2 AX OAJ MXP AJP NF OFP EE NW2 RATS CKC-TDX UTD SE (QT, Sil and Anne Sanders & Sandy Campbell)
- Ch Rime-Camcrest Hat Trick TD (Gretzky, Sil and Anne Sanders & Sandy Campbell)
- CT Hob Nob Super Hawk CGC TKN NW2 K9SAR (Hawk, Sheigh Crabtree & Matt Uhry)
- CT Hall's Doyle Twinkie Toes CGC TKI ELT1 K9SAR (Doyle, Matt Uhry & Sheigh Crabtree)

Other photographs are by the author.

I also greatly appreciate the dedication and hard work the people who offered suggestions, made substantive recommendations, and provided copy-edits on advanced copies of this book including: Jill Jones, editor par excellence, Maureen Fielding, Carla Baker, personal writing coach and extraordinary copy-editor, Marsha Skewis, Deb Van Emmerik, Lori Daniels, Deborah Dowd, and Sandra Gould. Maureen, Deb, and Christina Bunn also field-tested several exercise types and provided valuable feedback that improved them.

Introduction to Tracking

Tracking is a fun activity for a dog and handler to enjoy together. The general idea is for the dog to follow the scent left by a person walking through an area and to find an article dropped by that person. It turns out dogs are quite good at this and naturally enjoy using their noses. We do not teach the dog how to use his nose; he is naturally thousands of times better at using his nose than we are at using ours. We are going to teach the dog to stay close to the track until he finds the article. We teach this by showing him that it is always lots of fun to do so!

The major premise behind the **Modern Enthusiastic Tracking** training technique can be summarized by listing the three most important issues in successful dog tracking: motivation, motivation, and motivation. This analogy to the old real-estate joke reminds us that no matter how well-trained our dog is, he will only follow a scent (which we cannot smell ourselves), lead us down the track (which we cannot see ourselves), solve the scenting problems along the way (which we can at best only vaguely understand), and find the article at the end, if he is strongly motivated to do so.

Tracking is nearly unique in AKC companion dog sports in that the dog knows what to do and the handler must read her dog and follow him. Although we carefully structure our initial training tracks so the handler does know exactly where the track is located; before her dog is tested, he must be prepared to assume the leadership role.

In addition to the supreme importance of motivation, the dog must master numerous scenting and problem-solving skills before he will be successful. This training method provides ample opportunity for the dog to learn and master these skills.

Tracking is a team sport in the truest sense of the concept. Although the dog is the master of scent and the team leader, the handler has a critical support role to play for the team to be successful. The first important aspect of this support role is for the handler to trust and believe her dog when the dog is committed to a track. The second aspect is when a scenting problem causes a dog to lose the track, then the handler may need to organize the dog's search and encourage him to search nearby quadrants or areas that he has not yet covered.

This training method first develops basic scenting skills in the dog while building motivation to stay committed to the track. Then the method develops handler skills in reading the dog and organizing searches for lost tracks. Finally, the method refines the basic skills of the dog and handler until they are fully prepared to handle the situations they are likely to face in a test.

AKC and CKC both offer two types of tracking tests. The field type uses farm fields and open-space meadows to test the dog and handler in a natural rural setting. The urban type uses campuses and parks to test the dog and handler in urban settings. Part I of this book develops these two types of tracking in parallel, so the dog becomes a balanced tracker, equally facile working in both environments. As the dog and handler approach being ready to enter a particular test, they may specialize for the particular test.

Some trainers will want to specialize in either field or urban from the start if their access to practice tracking land or their interests are primarily focused on one or the other. Each phase in Part I has special instructions and sessions to allow for either specialization.

Field tracking is the original type and is typically considered easier to learn, but many city/suburban dwellers lack easy access to wild-open meadows and farmers' fields, so they choose urban first or urban mostly.

If you and your dog are well prepared, you and your dog will pass the TD/TDU test and have the foundation to go on to the TDX and VST. Once you pass a particular test, it is unlikely you will get additional opportunities to be tested since most tracking tests are full. So, enjoy your training! It will account for 99% of your tracking experience. Make every training session fun for you and your dog. Focus on that fun and success at the tests will follow.

In this introduction, I discuss an overview of scent, how a dog works scent, some aspects of important training philosophy, equipment, and access to suitable land. The remaining chapters deal with specific schedules of training activities that are designed to mold you and your dog into a confident tracking team.

Scent

There are more opportunities to enjoy scent sports with your dog now than ever before. In addition to tracking that has been an AKC sport since the late fifties, we now have opportunities in Barn Hunt, Scent Work, and Nose Work, all of which were added in the last decade. Furthermore, scent and olfaction have become an established academic research topic in both biology and robotics.

In 1994 with the introduction of urban tracking (AKC's Variable Surface Tracking Test), tracking people had to expand their understanding of scent beyond the basics in order to understand how the dogs behaved following scent in urban environments. What we knew about scent in 1998 when I wrote Enthusiastic Tracking remains true, but there is much more to understand to be successful tracking in parks and campuses.

So this is an introduction to how I think about scent for the purpose of tracking. I'll explain additional phenomena about scent and how it moves in Phase 5 on page 78 and also in Part IV on page 302.

Dog olfaction is very sensitive, and dogs are able to detect and observe very small differences in the chemical composition of scent for long periods of time without olfactory fatigue. Their nasal passages simultaneously detect the concentrations of many different individual volatile chemicals.

Since the strength of scent found on most tracks is too faint for human detection, we have to observe how a dog reacts to scent to learn how scent is affected by various conditions. We can never directly know the experience of scenting a two-hour-old track. However, by careful observation of many dogs tracking, we can learn much about scent and about a dog's detection of scent.

When a person walks through a field, he or she leaves five different types of scent. By understanding these types of scent, we can better understand how to train our dogs to track.

1. **Personal Odors:** A person is constantly giving off particles or rafts from their skin, their hair, and their breath. Skin Rafts are "heavy" clumps of skin and bacteria. They fall to the ground within about 10' to 15' of the track. Volatile chemicals evaporate off of them over many hours. If your nose is sensitive enough, these particles must smell like the person. They float through

the air and leave scent over a wide area to each side of the walker's path. Wind and air turbulence distributes the scent in a very complex way. Typical scenting behavior indicates that there is a distinct change in scent about 10–15' to each side of the walker's path. The personal odor is also called tracklayer scent.

2. **Crushed Vegetation:** As a person walks through a vegetated area, each foot crushes and bruises the grass or weeds underneath it. The damaged stalks and leaves give off odor particles much like a freshly mowed lawn gives off odor. I imagine each footprint as a miniature mowed lawn that is as obvious to the dog's sensitive nose as a big mowed lawn is to my nose. This strong flow of crushed vegetation scent flows up out of the footprint and floats downwind. The odor particles are influenced by similar wind and air turbulence that affect the personal scent. These footprints keep emitting scent until the plant damage heals, so crushed vegetation scent is detectable to the dog for quite a long time.

3. **Disturbed Dirt:** Each footstep also disturbs the soil beneath it. The microbes busily working in the soil constantly out-gas particles that give fresh-turned dirt its strong odor. The footfall breaks open the surface that is holding in this gas allowing it to escape and flow out of the footprint along with the crushed vegetation scent. This scent continues to flow until the soil surface reseals the cracks made by the footstep.

4. **Shoe Scent:** Each footstep also rubs off some particles of the shoe sole. This scent must smell exactly like the walker's shoe soles. Although apparently weaker than the first three types of scent, some dogs learn to detect and follow it if the other normally stronger scents are unavailable.

5. **Article Scent:** In tracking, the walker leaves one or more articles along the track. The article scent comes from the material itself and from the personal odor particles transferred to the article while the tracklayer carried it. Many materials, like leather, have quite strong intrinsic odors. In addition, many articles appear to absorb the tracklayer's personal scent quite effectively; therefore the articles smell both like themselves and like their owner. The scent from most articles is quite strong and is spread out by the wind and air-currents over a wide area.

The volatile chemicals directly off of the person and from all these secondary sources drift in the air for considerable time. They may condense on or pool near vertical surfaces like bushes, trees, fences, buildings, and curbs. These condensed chemicals may later re-evaporate creating additional off-track sources of scent for the dog.

Skin rafts may also be directly detected by the dog by licking them off the surface using the vomeronasal organ in the roof of the dog's mouth.

The dog must distinguish the track scent (all the five component scents) from other competing scents that are also present in the field. For example, the scent of the undisturbed dirt, the scent of various weeds and other vegetation, and the scent left by the numerous small animals that use the field must be distinguished from the main-track scent. And of course, the scents left by other people and animals walking in the area must be distinguished as well.

Introduction to Tracking

Tracking has its jargon, and a few special words are worth knowing. The scent cone is the area of strong scent close to the track. It often extends ten to fifteen feet or more to each side of the track. The distinct drop-off or change in scent at the edge of this scent cone is called the fringe. Dogs who range from side-to-side of the track in a constrained way are said to be casting or quartering. Dogs who wander widely in the general vicinity of the track may be said to be fringing.

There is much more that can be discussed about how scent moves in the wind, how scent is affected by age, humidity, and other environmental factors, and how the dog perceives it. The five-part model above is an adequate basis for starting your dog tracking. As your dog's training progresses, you can learn a great deal about scent by observing your dog's behavior.

Styles of Scent Work

There are numerous ways that dogs use their nose. Although this book focuses on tracking human scent, the dog's ability to do this work is related to its ability to do other scent work. It can be helpful to keep these other scenting work styles in mind when observing and understanding a dog on a track.

Air scenting is a scenting style that is often used by dogs in search and rescue. Highly trained search and rescue dogs may be able to detect the scent of a victim over long distances under the right wind conditions. Some of these dogs can also switch into tracking mode when a track is available. These dogs and handlers choose the best method to reliably and quickly find the victim, as conditions dictate. Although air scenting is a valuable skill, it is not encouraged in the AKC and CKC tracking tests that are the focus of this book. Bloodhounds do have a trailing test where the dogs are encouraged to follow the air scent near a human trail.

Tracking prey was an obvious evolutionary selection pressure that encouraged the dog to develop his excellent scenting ability. Many of today's suburban dogs show excellent natural scenting skill when given the opportunity to track prey. Since animals may cross the tracks in AKC and CKC tracking tests, we train the dog to stay on the original track and to ignore animal tracks. However, tracking dogs also excel in hunt tests and hunting trials when given the opportunity to do so.

Discrimination of articles touched by different people is a skill that is used in obedience as well as police work. Dogs can be trained to distinguish many different scents and to find articles discarded by a lost person in search and rescue as well as those discarded by fleeing suspects.

Detection of known scents is another valuable skill used by police and military dogs to find drugs and explosives. It has been turned into a sport for all dogs called Nose Work that dogs find a lot of fun. Several organizations host trials including the founding National Association of Canine Scent Work, the AKC Scent Work program, and others.

Detection of vermin is another new sport called Barn Hunt that requires the dog to locate live rats in PVC tubes while ignoring similar PVC tubes filled with just rat litter. Specifically, the dog has to alert on the live-rat smells rather than the lingering rat odor of the litter.

As your dog's tracking training progresses, it will be important to encourage the dog to follow the original track scent closely, rather than allowing him to adopt broad-ranging air-scenting behaviors or allowing him to follow animals that may have crossed his track. Trying to adopt such strategies is a very natural mistake for the dog to make. He should be gently guided toward the style of tracking that allows him to develop into an expert tracker that you can trust and be able to follow with confidence.

Training Philosophy

Motivation is the key factor in successful tracking because a dog must lead us down the test track that is obvious to him no matter how invisible it is to us. Limp tracking line is a poor tool for pushing a dog twenty feet ahead of us, so we must develop and maintain a keen sense of joy in the dog when he is on the track. It is much easier to develop this relish for tracking on simple tracks that are known to the handler than to try to develop it on more difficult and complex tracks. Moreover, it is always better and more efficient to maintain this enthusiasm than it is to lose it and try to redevelop it later.

We build motivation and enthusiasm by rewarding the dog frequently in the beginning and withdrawing those rewards slowly and randomly. We maintain motivation in all dogs by continuing them on an intermittent schedule of random rewards.

Because motivation is the key factor in successful tracking, we avoid using any harsh corrections. Harsh corrections are likely to demotivate the dog. We also structure the progression of the training so that at each step in the training, the dog is much more likely to succeed than fail. Ongoing failure is likely to demotivate the dog, so we always find something good about the dog's performance to compliment.

Although we avoid corrections, we will mold the dog's tracking behavior by gentle adjustments in line tension as well as by the use of food, play and praise rewards. This combination of reward and varying line tension encourages the dog to rapidly learn what is needed to find the rewards.

Whenever we have to help the dog, we adopt a very happy and positive attitude. We gladly show the dog what is the fun thing to do! A forty-acre tracking field is too small a space for frustration.

From the dog's point of view, staying right on the track should always be the easiest, the most fun, and the most rewarding thing to do. It should still be fun to be near the track, just a little more work to get to the goodies. In those rare instances when the track gets too confusing, the handler happily shows the way to rewards. The dog should never know anything about failure, his handler being frustrated, or strong corrections on the tracking field.

Equipment

You will need a tracking harness. Use a non-restrictive harness — one that does not have any straps across the sides of the shoulders and one that does not choke the front of the dog's neck when his head dips all the way to the ground. Premier Sure-Fit Harnesses work well and are widely available in pet supply stores and online. J & J also has nice nylon and leather harnesses (800) 642-2050. Several other vendors carry suitable harnesses as well.

Other basic equipment:
- Articles like an old leather glove and a cotton sock. In the beginning, one glove will do. Just a little way into training, the tracklayer will need 3 socks and 3 gloves.
- Forty-foot tracking line (1/8" mountaineering cord, 1/8" nylon parachute cord, 1/4" to 1" biothane or 1" flat webbed cotton line for large, strong dogs who like to pull). For CKC, use a 49' tracking line.
- 8–12 tall tracking stakes.
    - 36" wire stakes with 4"x5" fluorescent flagging work well for field tracks. They are available

online at http://www.forestry-suppliers.com inexpensively in bundles of 100.
- Old ski poles with their webs removed work well as do driveway markers. Attach colorful surveyor's tape or flagging to each stake so it will be visible from a distance.
- 8–20 short tracking stakes for urban sites. 12–15" marking flags are available at most hardware stores and online.
- Sidewalk chalk for marking concrete and asphalt.
- A container of water you carry with you in a fanny pack for the dog's hydration.
- Yummy food treats like hot dogs sliced into small pieces.
- A detailed tracking log or journal.

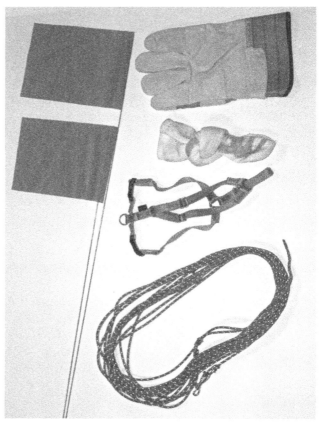

The figure at the right shows some typical equipment for TD training: two flags, a leather glove, a sock, a harness, and a tracking line.

Avoid using just a thirty-foot tracking line. It is the most common length available in 1" flat webbing and so many people start out with the thirty-foot length. This shortcut will hurt your ability to handle difficult corners. So get that fifty-foot line and cut it down to length! If you track exclusively in Canada, you can use a 49' line, so you don't even have to cut it down to AKC length.

Food Rewards

Because I always train with food rewards, the schedule shows the food drops on the track maps. I highly recommend using grab-and-go food drops on the track if at all possible. If the food drive is not strong, consider delaying his morning meal until the end of the track. If you have a dog that is not motivated by food at all but loves toys, consider using one or two toys along each leg and then switch to a cloth article on the track for which you quickly produce a toy. If fire ants or birds block your use of food drops, consider putting each drop in a small pill case, but then you will need to quickly run up and open the case for the dog.

While hot dogs are easy to use and most dogs love them, other food treats work well. The treat should be moist, easy to munch down, and shouldn't crumble — fallen crumbs entice a dog to stay where the food drop was and find all the crumbs. While not moist like hot dogs, small ¼" pieces of freeze-dried lamb lung work well on urban lawns and sidewalks and are less likely to get stolen by savvy birds as your track ages. Be sure to cut them up into small pieces at home where the crumbs can find another use and not get on the track itself.

There is a minor art in slicing hot dogs for food drops. A dog senses as much reward from a small piece of food as a large one. For medium and large dogs, slices of hot dog the shape and thickness of a nickel or two work very well. They are large enough to be easily found and not too large to fill the dog. For small and toy dogs and puppies of all breeds, slice the hot dog lengthwise in half or quarter before slicing crosswise into nickel thickness. You must make the drop small enough that the dog is hungry enough to be rewarded after finding lots of them on a track. Slicing the hot dog thinner than a nickel causes them to dry out and be less appealing. Freshly cut moist hot dog nickels, or half-nickels, or quarter-nickels are the magic treat that I recommend.

Operant conditioning research indicates that the ideal reward size is 1/40th the dog's daily food intake. So if you want to use that as a guide, you will have a lot of research behind your choice. I have found the sizes I recommend above fairly close to their recommendation and they work well in the context of tracking.

Tracking Journal

It is useful to keep a detailed log or journal of each tracking session. The detailed log format on pages 31 or 32 can be photocopied to allow you to conveniently record the details of each track. The 3"x5" index card format shown on page 32 is suitable for printing on Avery 5388 3"x5" Index Card stock. The format can also be used as a model for the pages in a field book like ***Rite in the Rain All Weather Field Book*** (#350) that I personally use — the left page for the details and evaluation and the right page for the track map. A typical log entry for Phase 1 is shown on page 28. Sample journal entries are included throughout the book on pages 68, 147, 191, 211, 221, 299, and 395.

In addition to the detailed journal entry, it is useful to keep a summary log for each phase that tersely shows just enough information to make a quick overview of the dog's progress. This view can be useful for seeing patterns developing that may need to be emphasized or de-emphasized as appropriate. Summary logs suitable for copying are provided at the end of each phase.

> An electronic workbook is available for Part I of this book showing every session map individually with exact yardage and recommended treat placements. You can take it out into the field on your mobile device or print individual session pages and take them along. See ***Modern Enthusiastic Tracking Workbook 1, TD & TDU Field Maps*** on www.enthusiastic-tracking.com/store.

Suitable Land

While I still give a new dog his first set of tracks on pristine meadows or silage fields, the second session (or set of tracks) is on urban lawn (a sports field or park lawn). Urban lawns have lots of contaminating smells from other people and their dogs recently crisscrossing the lawn. These other people and dogs disturb the dirt, crush the vegetation, and emit their own skin rafts and volatile chemicals. So the crushed vegetation and disturbed dirt become less valuable indicators of the direction to the next hot dog, and the tracklayer's personal scent becomes the only reliable indicator of track location and direction. This helps the dog focus primarily on the human scent right at the start of his training.

The third type of location we use to introduce the dog to tracking is hard surface. Find a large parking lot with minimal car activity and with long curbs and islands at the end of the parking rows. Stadium lots, shopping mall parking lots, churches, and vacant businesses provide examples.

To build the specific foundational skills needed by the dog throughout his tracking career, the training alternates between "pristine" wild meadows or farmed fields with few conflicting tracks, well-used park or sports lawns, and asphalt parking lots or concrete plazas.

With the last 70 years of urban and suburban sprawl, many of us live in areas where there are no readily accessible "pristine" fields suitable for field tracking. These people may use less popular sports fields and parks in the early morning for their natural-field sessions while using popular sports fields and parks in the middle of the day or early evening for the urban-lawn sessions. When school is out, the school play-yards may also work if dogs are permitted on them. If you do primarily use lightly-contaminated sports fields in place of wild meadows and farmed grass fields to train for the TD, be sure you occasionally get your dog out into real nature and track him in the kind of places where he will be tested for his TD.

So even if your only goal initially is a traditional field-based TD, you may find it is easier to find nearby training areas if you start out using pristine fields, sports fields, and parking lots in your initial training. This will build a solid foundation and you will have plenty of opportunity to specialize on one type of tracking further along in your training, if you wish to specialize later.

Hard-Surface Tracking

Throughout your tracking training you will be tracking on a variety of terrain and surfaces. TD tracks are typically on farmed-grass fields or wild-grass fields with a variety of weeds mixed in. Urban tracks, on the other hand, are primarily on lawn grass and non-vegetated surfaces like concrete or brick sidewalks and plazas, asphalt driveways and parking lots, and sand, gravel and mulch areas. I use the term hard surface to refer to asphalt, concrete, brick and stone that predominates in typical urban environments. I also use it casually to refer to any non-vegetated surface like sand, gravel, and mulch. All kinds of non-vegetated surfaces should be used from time to time for both TDU and VST training.

Asphalt (aka blacktop) can quickly get quite hot in the summer sun, which dries out the scent quickly as well as becoming too hot on which to work. Even in the morning sun, asphalt can be 20–30 °F hotter than the air temperature while it can be 60 °F degrees hotter at noon. So for your dog's safety, avoid asking him to track when the asphalt gets too hot. My rule of thumb is to put my hand on the asphalt and hold it there comfortably for 10 seconds. If it takes an act of will to hold it there, it is too hot to track your dog.

Even when the asphalt is not too hot, it dries out or ages the scent quickly. Scent intensifiers are useful in the dog's early training as well as later in his career whenever the dog seems to struggle to find the scent on a hard surface. Scent intensifiers include Bare Feet, Sandals, Scent-In-A-Bottle (SIAB), Hydration, Hand Swipes, and Short Steps. Using food drags or scuffing your feet have not worked for me as my dogs have not continued to be interested in the track once they are no longer used. Another technique is to double or triple lay a track, but that technique leads to dogs who no longer care about track direction and so is avoided — track direction is an important skill that the dog will need in TDX and VST tracks.

- **Bare Feet** tracklaying can be challenging when there are stones or gravel that your feet may find uncomfortable. One thing I always do is carry a pair of flip-flops to slip on if a particular section of the track hurts my feet.
- **Sandal** tracklaying is straightforward. It allows more foot scent to fall close to the track, even more than airy tennis shoes.

- **Short Stepping** tracklaying is also straightforward, although one must be careful not to adopt a scuffing action. Scuffing roughs up the hard surface too much, releasing strong scents, which later will not be there with normal footsteps.
- **Scent-in-a-Bottle** is a technique that uses a 1-gallon garden sprayer filled with distilled or well water that smells like the tracklayer. The tracklayer makes the smells-like water by taking off her tee-shirt about 20 minutes before laying the track and putting it in a gallon of well or distilled water to soak. Right before laying the track, she wrings-out the tee shirt and adds all the water to the garden sprayer. She then sprays the water in a narrow stream in front of her as she lays the track. It helps if she only uses the gentlest soaps to wash her tee shirt so there are no chemicals in the shirt to contaminate her scent. To withdraw SIAB over many sessions, slowly widen the spray pattern then make the spray intermittent.
- **Hydration** is a simplification of Scent-in-a-Bottle. Steve White, who apparently invented both methods, prefers hydration. I find Scent-in-a-Bottle more effective but only if you use distilled or well water, freshly worn clothes and make it right before you use it. Regardless, hydration works by wetting the hard surface that allows the skin rafts to stick more easily and also promotes the evaporation of their volatile chemicals.
- **Hand Swipes** require some flexibility on the part of the tracklayer who bends over periodically and swipes her hand on the hard surface. It is mostly used to intensify the scent in places like corners or transitions — but the other methods can be used in a similar way. It can also be used by the tracklayer swiping her hand along a wall, railing or similar vertical surface.

This book uses food drops even on hard surfaces until the dog is fairly advanced. Be on the lookout for ants or wasps on the food when the dog gets to it, or for birds stealing the food. If they are prevalent, switch to tiny pieces of freeze-dried lamb lung. If that does not work, you will have to switch to using small intermediate articles instead of food drops. I like to use food drops because they are grab-and-goes that reward the dog without disrupting his tracking very much. At an article, your dog needs to indicate it, and then you need to reward him for finding it, so it breaks up the tracking more than a grab-and-go. If you need to use intermediate articles instead of grab-and-go rewards, use small articles so they are less visibly obvious — small pieces of dark leather or dark cloth work well as they hold the tracklayer's scent and are easy for the dog to find.

Training Goals and Time Commitment

Although it is generally best to have a clear goal in mind when starting a new venture, you may or may not know enough about tracking at this point to set a clear goal. Your goal may be as general as learning about tracking to as specific as having your new puppy earn all available tracking titles. Whatever your goal, this book and your own diligent work can help you reach that goal.

AKC offers four tracking tests leading to five titles: Tracking Dog (TD), Tracking Dog Excellent (TDX), Tracking Dog Urban (TDU), Variable Surface Tracker (VST), and Champion Tracker (CT). A dog must first earn his TD or TDU and then may work towards the TDX, the VST or both. A dog with both a TDX and a VST becomes a CT. The CKC offers TD and TDX titles for passing tests that are similar to their AKC counterparts. The CKC basic urban test UTD and their advanced test UTDX roughly parallel AKC urban tests. And, having both a TDX and a UTDX earns the dog his TC (Tracking Champion).

The TD is typically earned on a 45-minute-old track that is 470 yards long with four corners. There is a flag at the start and one at 30 yards, so the handler knows the initial direction of the track.

The Canadian version of the test is very similar. Almost any dog and handler team that can walk through a meadow can learn to pass either of these tests by following the instructions in this book.

The TDU test is very similar to the TD test except it takes place in a campus-like setting on lawns and crosses sidewalks, driveways and parking lots but has a restriction to not turn on a hard surface. The CKC UTD is similar but includes one hard-surface turn.

The TDX is earned on a 3+ hour-old track that is about 900 yards long and has about six corners. The main track will be crossed by two people about 90 minutes after the track was laid. The track will contain at least two obstacles that will challenge the dog's scenting ability and the handler's skill in reading her dog. It is a difficult test with a low passing rate. The Canadian version of this test is similar, although it uses a single person to cross the track and it typically uses less challenging obstacles. The first part of this book focuses on building a firm foundation for tracking; the second uses that foundation to support advanced training toward a TDX.

The VST is typically earned on a 3-hour-old track through an urban or suburban setting like a college campus or business park. The track is on land that many other people typically traverse and will use non-vegetated surfaces like gravel, concrete, and blacktop for much of its length, and it will pass near large buildings. It uses lawns rather than wild meadows for most of its vegetated surfaces. Like the TDX, it is a difficult test that requires extensive preparation and training.

It is fair to wonder how long it might take to train a dog to his TD tracking degree. The time depends on your dog's natural love of using his nose and learning to do 'things' for you, your prior knowledge and skill in dog training, whether you focus on field tracking only and the focus you bring to bear on achieving your goals. The time also depends on how quickly you get into a test.

In spite of this variation, we can estimate the length of time based on the number of times per week you are able to track. So the chart below shows a range of months of training where the smaller number applies to the quick-to-learn dog-handler teams and the larger number applies to more typical dog-handler teams. I do want to emphasize that there is nothing inherently better about quick-to-learn teams than typical teams except they learn faster. Teams that are more typical can definitely learn as well and can end up performing as well or better than the quick-to-learn teams.

Training Months to earn a TD if solely focused on the TD			... Both TD and TDU
Sessions Per Week	Months for Quick-to-Learn Dog-Handler Teams	Months for Typical Dog-Handler Teams	Months for Typical Dog-Handler Teams
7	2	4	5–6
5	3	5	7–9
3	5	8	11–13
2	7	12	15–18

Many trainers are successful if they train the first two or three phases as rapidly as possible and then settle back into a less frequent schedule. Although this works for many people and dogs, it is more important to adopt a schedule that fits your and your dog's energy level and ability to dedicate time to this fun activity. At various times, I have successfully trained dogs using different schedules. One dog was successfully trained 7 days a week for the first four phases of training where we dropped down to 3 days a week. Another was trained less than once a week.

Personally, my own most comfortable training schedule is three times a week. Experiment a little and see what works for you and your dog.

Whatever your level of training and your long-term goals, setting short-term goals and keeping them will give you and your dog a sense of immediate success and add to your motivation to continue. Practicing with a friend allows you to keep one another going when you might not feel like going out on your own.

Tracking is one sport that you can and should practice in all types of weather. Heavy rain does not wash away the scent, and strong wind does not blow it away. Nevertheless, they do affect the scent conditions and you and your dog should be used to working in them. When it comes time to be tested, a gale force squall is not going to cancel the test, so be prepared. You will enjoy (or at least tell yourself you enjoy) being out in the fresh air amidst nature's wonders. I certainly have seen more rainbows while tracking than while sitting in an office, so dress for the weather and enjoy it.

Most of us do most of our training in temperate conditions and avoid very hot and very cold weather. However, people have trained dogs to track in the summer in the desert and the winter in the North Country. If you do attempt to train in very hot or very cold conditions, contact someone in your area that already does it to learn the local tricks to make it successful.

Some people who followed *Enthusiastic Tracking (1998)* skipped sessions because they felt their dog was clever and ready for more advanced work. I do not skip with my own dogs as I find I spend more time later doing remedial work if I don't make the fundamentals solid. So I certainly recommend following this schedule step-by-step. If you have a natural tracking dog (quite rare) and are already a good tracking handler and trainer, you may be successful doing less than the full curriculum. You are your dog's trainer, so it is up to you.

Other Resources

The focus of this book is on a particular training method that I have found to produce excellent tracking dogs of many different breeds and personality types. I hope it is complete enough to stand on its own. However, much can be learned from the other treatments of tracking and scent work found in several excellent books. I encourage you to add to your knowledge by also reading these tracking books. Several additional books are listed in the bibliography for those who want an extended library of tracking knowledge.

I recommend Glen R. Johnson's *Tracking Dog — Theory And Methods,* Arner Publications, Inc., Canastota, NY, 1977. This was the bible of sport tracking for many years. His tracking schedule and many of his techniques served as the basis from which I evolved the method described in this book. Much has been learned about tracking since Johnson's book was published. In particular, the introduction of TDX in this country in the early eighties led many of us to discard his double and triple laid tracking techniques that lead to confusion about track direction. In addition, we learned that many more dogs and handlers could succeed by avoiding as stressful a training schedule as he advocated. I strongly recommend to all serious tracking students the first three general chapters as well as the chapter on problem solving.

A book that combines a scientific approach to scent with practical dog training techniques is Milo Pearsall and Hugo Verbruggen, M.D., *Scent — Training to Track, Search, and Rescue,* Alpine Publications, Loveland, Colorado, 1982. Anyone who wants to extend their knowledge of scent beyond the basics should be aware of the extensive knowledge presented in this book.

A very informative book on scent and how dogs use it to find what they are seeking is Michael R. Conover's **Predator-Prey Dynamics, the Role of Olfaction,** CRC Press (2007). This updates Pearsall (1982) and while not about tracking people's scent, his insights and diagrams are enlightening to those of us who follow our dog while he follows a human scent trail.

You will need a rulebook for the tests you intend to enter. The American Kennel Club's Tracking Regulations covers all four tracking tests and is available from them online at http://www.akc.org/rules/ titled "Tracking Regulations." The Australian Shepherd Club of America has an active tracking program similar to AKC's program and allows all breeds to enter. Other registries in the USA, like the American Mixed Breed Owners Association, basically follow AKC's rules. The rules for tests in Canada are available from the Canadian Kennel Club.

If you are new to tracking, try to find a local class to attend. A good knowledgeable instructor can make a big difference in noticing your imperfections and your dog's imperfections in a timely fashion and suggesting corrections. Ideally, find an instructor who is willing to work with you as you follow this schedule. If no instructor is available to you, track in a small group every week or two. Your tracking friends can offer their observations that you might fail to see yourself. You can learn a lot by observing your friends and their dogs. If no one else in your area is interested in tracking, just go do it yourself. See page 16 for additional information on training alone. Do spend a little extra time reflecting on your performance and your dog's performance. Keep a detailed journal and review it regularly.

You can join an email tracking list. I currently monitor several of these lists. You can expect to get answers to your questions from a variety of tracking people from around the country and the world. To subscribe to one of the major email tracking lists, access:
    www.groups.io/g/TrackingDog
    http://groups.google.com/group/trackingdogs
    https://groups.yahoo.com/neo/groups/ckc-tracking/info
and, of course:
    www.groups.io/g/enthusiastictracking

I also created a group on Facebook called "Modern Enthusiastic Tracking Group" for discussions about any aspect of **Enthusiastic Tracking** or **Modern Enthusiastic Tracking**. See
    http://www.facebook.com/groups/ModernEnthusiasticTracking.

Or join one of the other tracking groups on Facebook. There is a broad tracking discussion group called "AKC, CKC, ASCA Tracking" that is active and not restricted to my training techniques.

Use a search engine to find web sites dedicated to tracking. There are quite a few good sites with lots of interesting information about tracking.

Part I — Basic Tracking Training for the TD and TDU

This part will show you how to train your dog for both the TD and the TDU in parallel, developing both your and your dog's fundamental tracking skills for both field and urban tracking. If you only want to focus on the field TD or the urban TDU to begin your tracking adventure, each phase has specific instructions for the specialized trainer.

The specific goals of Part I are four-fold:
1. Teach the dog and handler the necessary skills to be successful in TD and TDU tests.
2. Teach the dog and handler the foundation skills for later work towards the TDX and VST.
3. Do so in a step-by-step fashion so most dogs and most handlers can be successful by intelligently following the explicit instructions in the training progression.
4. Have fun all along the way since enthusiastic performance is best built with fun and rewards for both the dog and the trainer.

Our initial goal is to mold the dog to stay close to the track so he will be easy to read. We use frequent rewards along simple tracks combined with varying line tension so the dog learns that following close to the track is the most fun place to be, the best place to be, and the most rewarding place to be.

To achieve this initial goal, we will do lots of straight tracks, first upwind so the scent of the track and the scent of the hot dogs encourage the dog forward and then straight downwind to encourage the dog to track with his nose fairly low and close to the ground.

Then we will introduce crosswind legs and corners so our dog learns to indicate loss of scent at the corner, to search for the new leg, and to confidently commit to the new leg.

Up through Phase 5 of our training, all the tracks are clearly marked so the handler knows exactly where the track is located. This enables her to adjust line tension and make sure her dog does not venture too far off the track. This clear marking of the tracks is a key part of training the dog to stay close to the track.

Then in Phase 6, we take away the obvious flags and focus on training the handler to read her dog. This is a key training transition that some handlers find scary but which turns out to be enjoyable as the handler learns to read her dog on the track.

Through Phase 6 we keep the tracks under 30 minutes old to facilitate training the dog and the handler. Then in Phase 7 we introduce age up to about 75 minutes while continuing to help the handler become better at reading her dog.

Phase 8 provides alternate paths to tune up the dog and handler for their upcoming test by resolving any weak skills or loose ends the team may have. And finally, Phase 9 provides a "peaking" procedure to put the team at the top of their game for test day.

In addition to the combined field and urban training plan detailed in each phase, there is a separate schedule for field-only training near the end of each phase as well as instructions for adapting for an urban-only plan.

Phase 1. Introducing your dog to Tracking

Purpose:
- Introduce your dog to tracking.
- Teach your dog that when he is given the command to track, there is something to find and his nose helps him find it.
- Teach your dog that tracking is fun.
- Teach the handler how to use the line to communicate with her dog.

Strategy:
- Entice and tease your dog while laying the track so he is excited and anxious to follow the track.
- Start out with very short tracks where your dog will be frequently rewarded and will find the article quickly.
- Extend the length of the tracks and the distance between the rewards gradually.
- Rotate the session locations between natural fields, urban lawns, and hard surfaces to help your dog understand he can track on all these surfaces.
- Start out with the tracks going into the wind so your dog smells the track and hot dogs ahead of him.
- Switch so the tracks go downwind, which helps him bring his nose down onto the track.
- Gradually increase the line length as your dog starts to stay right on the track.
- Keep your dog unstressed and happy.

How to use this chapter:
- Look through the table on the next page, which summarizes the training structure of this phase.
- Read the discussion section that follows.
- Start with session 1.0, which is on line handling and is detailed on page 21.
- Then do each of the following 12 sessions that rotate between natural fields, urban lawns, and parking lots.
  - They introduce your dog to tracking in these three critically important environments.
  - Before each session, carefully review the detailed tracklaying and handling instructions for natural fields on page 22, urban lawns on page 25, or parking-lot curbs on page 26.
  - You may find it convenient to copy the session detail pages so your tracklayer has the details she needs to lay the desired tracks.
- Keep a detailed log of each session using a format like the one shown on page 31 and keep a summary log like the one shown on page 33.
- Finally, do the review session on page 28 to evaluate your dog's progress and your own training-skill development

> The alternative Field-Only Schedule is on page 27.
>
> The alternative Urban-Only Schedule is the same as the combined schedule on page 15 except the sessions labeled for Natural Fields should be done on Urban Lawns with as little natural contamination as possible (early morning sessions for example).

Phase 1 Session Schedule:

Sesn	Location	Track Shape	Wind	Age Min.	Track 1 Length Yards	Track 2 Length Yards	Track 3 Length Yards	Short Hard Steps	Follow
1.0		Line Handling (Handler and Tracklayer only, no dog)							
1.1	Natural Field	Straight	into	5	10	20	30	Full	6'
1.2	Urban Lawns	Straight	into	5	15	30	50	Full	6'
1.3	Parking Lot	Along Curb	into	5	15	30	40	Full	6'
1.4	Natural Field	Straight	into	8	20	40	80	Full	10'
1.5	Urban Lawns	Straight	into	8	30	60	120	Full	10'
1.6	Parking Lot	Along Curb	into	8	20	40	75	Full	10'
1.7	Natural Field	Straight	with	8	40	80	160	First 80	10'
1.8	Urban Lawns	Straight	with	8	50	100	200	First 80	10'
1.9	Parking Lot	Along Curb	with	10	30	50	90	First 80	10'
1.10	Natural Field	Straight	with	10	120	240		First 50	15'
1.11	Urban Lawns	Straight	with	10	150	300		First 50	15'
1.12	Parking Lot	Along Curb	with	10	60	100		First 50	15'
1.13		Review							

Discussion:

Take the time at the outset to become thoroughly familiar with the procedure so you can feel confident about what you are doing when you are training your dog. You and the tracklayer will need to convincingly communicate to your dog your overwhelming enthusiasm for tracking. That is hard to do when you are uncertain what you are supposed to do.

Before starting a tracking session, make sure you have all your equipment (page 5), and that you and the tracklayer understand your roles as described in detail on page 21. If the tracklayer is new to tracking, show her how to lay a short straight track without the dog nearby. If both of you are new to tracking, both should practice tracklaying and handling without the dog. There is much detail in the description of the first session of tracks. The detail is there to help you visualize the best way to teach your dog, so you avoid problems in the future.

Note that tracklayers should always provide their own articles. We want the articles to smell like the tracklayer and not be a mix of the tracklayer and someone else.

Training Alone. If you want to teach your dog all by yourself, you can be both the tracklayer and the handler. In this first phase, you can leave your dog in a crate at the start while you lay the track. For people with breeds that require large crates that are hard to carry into the training field, using a crate may be difficult. Starting all tracks from the edge of the field by a parking spot may be possible. If you are comfortable staking your dog out in the field, then doing so for the short period you are laying these tracks may be appropriate. In any case, just be sure your dog can see the track as you lay it.

Finding **suitable locations** for each session can be a challenge. You will rotate your tracking locations first going to a "natural field" like a farmer's grass field or a wild meadow, then going to an urban-lawn like a sports field or park lawn, then going to a parking lot, and then repeating the cycle. This helps your dog generalize the tracking game and learn that the best place to be and the most rewarding place to be is near the track regardless of the terrain, environment, or conditions. Doing so from the beginning also helps him understand that the personal tracklayer scent rather than the crushed vegetation and disturbed dirt is the most valuable scent to follow and reduces the possibility he will become fixated on or dependent on the other two available scents.

In your personal situation, you may not be able to get to each type of location in strict rotation, and that is OK. Doing two or three of one type of location in a row is OK as is missing two or three. Just don't get too far out of balance; you should try to do all the sessions in a phase before moving on to the next phase.

Article Indication. It is important that your dog indicates articles clearly and reliably, although in his early training we are happy to gradually shape his indication as we train. Dogs will indicate an article in many ways. You want to teach your dog to indicate it in a way that is easy for you to see. People have their dog touch the article, pick up the article, retrieve the article, sit at the article, down at the article, or just stop at the article. Any of these methods work well. For the first few sessions, accept any behavior by the dog that demonstrates the dog notices the article. Gradually raise your standards and mold a particular article indication of your choice. For dog breeds that resist obedience-like controlled behaviors, accepting a stop at the article will avoid a good deal of dog-handler tension on the track at the article.

Handling. The handler should not try to control the dog as in obedience. The dog needs the freedom and self-confidence to find the track himself. In training, the handler restrains the dog when he is too far off the track but does not correct the dog for being off the track. That restraint is achieved by increasing the tension on the line until the dog stops moving away from the track.

Line handling is very important. When the dog is exactly on the track, keep a light-firm tension on the line with your hand at belly level. As the dog moves to the side, raise your hand gradually until it is over your head and increase the tension on the line. The farther off the track the dog is, the higher your hand and the greater the tension. When the dog gets six to ten feet off the track, your hand should be over your head, and you should not be moving. Wait until the dog swings back toward the track, lowering your arm and the tension as he approaches the track and take a step forward as he comes to the track or attempts to parallel it. You are making it easy for the dog to stay on the track and hard to stray from the track.

Keep your line hand directly in front of you. Do not move your hand back and forth to steer the dog because the dog will learn to take steering directions from you and will not learn to be responsible for finding the track himself. You are raising and lowering your hand to make it harder or easier for your dog to track, not to steer him. If you have a very large dog that pulls strongly off the track, raise your hand to the side of your head and keep your arm close to your body. This way you can use your full weight against the dog going off the track without moving your hand very far from the center.

Another way some people find to get this raising-lowering effect is to hold their elbow close to their body and pivot their forearm up toward their shoulder like curling a dumbbell.

Note the column marked "Follow" refers to how far back you should generally work from your dog. Always use your full forty-foot line and let the rest trail behind you.

Handling Tip — if your dog becomes confused at any time in his training, he may look to you for help. Be patient and express your confidence that he can do it. If he really cannot, then help him in a light-positive way, like pointing at the track and asking him "Is that your track?" Only if he really struggles or seems to quit will you get down, touch the track, and express your love for the track itself. In this case, you don't ask or beg your dog to track; you tell the track itself how much you love it. Your dog will be intrigued by your interest in the track and move ahead to investigate what you find so wonderful. It takes a little play-acting but think of yourself as Juliet and the track as Romeo (see details on pages 59–60).

Being supportive of your dog and positive about the track will help keep the dog from learning that anytime he struggles, Mom will fix things and make everything better. You want to avoid that because the dog will learn to just quit when the track gets tough until you help him — and you won't be able to help him on a blind test track.

See "Helping — a Delicate Balance" on page 59 for a detailed description of the progressive steps of helping a dog so he learns his skills without learning to be dependent on his mom to solve the problem.

Handler's Key Behaviors:
- As the dog gets the idea and stays close to the track on his own, extend the distance between you and the dog as indicated in the schedule.
- Make a big deal when your dog finds an article; play with your dog enthusiastically so the articles become very important to the dog.
- Watch for the dog's nose coming down closer to the track on downwind tracks.
- Long tracks may cross changes in cover like a change from grass to weeds. Watch how the dog works at a change in cover. He may break off and have to find the track in the new cover.
- Watch and listen to your dog so you can learn how to tell when the dog is using his nose and when he is not.

Handler Attitude. It is easy for a new handler to be optimistic for her dog and become frustrated if the dog does not get the idea immediately. Such expectations and frustrations are out of place. Most dogs will get the idea during the first phase, but it does not matter when during this phase he gains this knowledge, or even if he does not really figure out how much fun this is until Phase 2. Just keep to the schedule and he will pick it up along the way.

Since the dog can easily sense your frustration, keep such emotions completely blocked by being genuinely happy the whole time you are on the tracking field. At the end of each track after the play and rewards, it is a good idea to mentally list the three things you liked about your dog's tracking and your own handling. Do this throughout your dog's tracking career. Don't think about what went wrong or what needs to be improved until you get back to your car.

Puppies and Toy Breeds: Start puppies as early as you want. As young as seven weeks is OK for many puppies since the work is fun and there are no corrections. Don't expect a young puppy to stay focused on the task as well as an older puppy or an adult. Make sure the puppy is enjoying it. If not, do something else with the puppy until he is a little older and can better understand what you want.

For puppies, use the same schedule but scale all distances in half in Phase 1. So the first session will have tracks of 5 yards, 10 yards, and 20 yards with hot dogs every 2–3 yards along the track. For a young puppy, skip sessions 1.10 to 1.12. If the young puppy gets physically or mentally tired, skip the longest track of the session. See page 24 for an explicit puppy schedule. If the distances still seem long for your young puppy, scale the distances to a third. What is important to do is to start short and progress to longer tracks, not to follow any arbitrary distance schedule.

Physically small breeds, very low-energy breeds, and low-energy handlers should adapt the schedule by scaling all distances in half in Phase 1, see page 24. It is better for your dog to succeed at shorter distances than to complete a longer track that exhausts him.

Tips for Phase 1 Training Sessions. In each phase of training we will use several different exercise types. In this Phase 1, some sessions have three straight tracks laid and run one at a time in a natural field, others have the same pattern of tracks on a urban lawn, and a third type of session has the same pattern of tracks laid on asphalt/concrete right along a curb.

The Phase 1 session schedule on page 15 summarizes the training schedule with a row for each session in the phase. For each type of tracking session within the phase, there are detailed diagrams and the track parameters like length, age, wind direction, hot dog placement, article placement, and specific tracklayer instructions. *Owners of this book are, of course, allowed to make personal-use copies of these session diagrams for their tracklayers, perhaps highlighting the parameters for today's particular session.* In addition to the summary, detailed procedures for each session type are shown later in the phase, specifically pages 22–26. An eBook with each session in Part I given a separate diagram is available on www.enthusiastictracking.com/store.

The flag symbol indicates where the tracklayer places each flag. The circles indicate the general location of the hot dogs, but the exact placement and number of hot dogs is shown in the table for each session. The star with a circle inside indicates the glove at the end of the track with some hot dogs in the palm of the glove. In this phase, we do not bother with a start article as it is not necessary and is sometimes distracting. A hot dog at the start is all that is needed. Later we will add a start article so the dog has an opportunity to take the tracklayer's scent — something that will be very useful when there is a lot of contamination in the start area.

The **wind direction** is important. Do your best to lay the tracks into the wind or downwind as directed in the schedule (upwind for the first six sessions and downwind for the next six). If there is no detectable wind, use the prevailing wind direction in case it comes up. Sometimes the wind can shift direction between when you start to lay the track and when you run it. If the wind shifts from being along the track to blowing across the track on one track in a session, go ahead and run the track. Keep the dog on a short line and keep him on the track. Don't let it happen too often, because the dog can learn some bad habits by tracking in crosswinds at this early stage. It is better to re-lay a track that has been messed up by the wind than to lay many tracks in the future to correct a bad habit.

The age of the tracks is shown in the schedule. The handler shouldn't start until the tracklayer gets back because the tracklayer returning will be an unnecessary distraction for the dog.

Tracklayer's Key Behaviors:
- Use distant landmarks to keep the tracks straight and into the wind.
- Leave a second flag at 30 yards on every track that is longer than 30 yards.
- As the tracks get longer, use intermediate flags every 50–75 yards.
- If the field is too short for the long tracks, either bend putting a flag at the bend, or stop early.
- Keep up the enthusiasm; excite the dog while laying the tracks even if the dog ignores you.

Those of you familiar with *Enthusiastic Tracking (1998)* may notice the placement of hot dogs on the longer tracks is different. For longer tracks, the separation of hot dogs got wider and wider throughout the track, but now it gets wider during the first half and starts to narrow down in the second half. This helps less active dogs and dogs with shorter attention spans to keep motivated as they learn to track long distances.

Intentional Contamination will be needed for urban-lawn tracks that do not have enough very recent natural contamination. If your dog seldom has trouble sorting out the good track from the contamination, he is not getting enough practice in the skill at this stage. Have someone besides the tracklayer cross the track right as it is being laid. Feel free to have them take along their dog to make the contamination even more interesting to your dog. We want your dog to experience and sort out a wide variety of contamination throughout all the phases of training. Have the contamination layer(s) cross the track anywhere after the directional flag at this level, crossing each track once, twice or three times.

If you are tracking without a partner to lay either the track itself or the contamination, you can make do with natural contamination. I use the Frisbee Golf courses found in many parks — they are ideal for providing quite a bit of natural contamination in somewhat predictable patterns even in wet weather. Any area that gets a fair number of people walking on the lawns will work.

Shaping or Molding. Dog trainers who are familiar with positive training methods, sometimes known as clicker training, may recognize the Phase 1 training process as one of 'shaping' or (perhaps less politically correct) one of 'molding'. Instead of clicking and treating, we place the hot dogs along the track where we think they will be helpful and let the dog be rewarded right on the track. We avoid click and treat because that brings the dog's attention back to us and we want his attention forward on the track. The molding occurs when the handlers vary the tension on the line making it easier or harder for the dog to move forward, depending on how close he is to the track. This is in contrast to free shaping where we might just let the dog magically discover the track leads to the line of treats without any guidance from us.

Track Direction Relative to the Wind

An upwind track is laid moving directly into the wind. A downwind track is laid with the wind hitting your back. A crosswind track is laid with the wind to one side or the other. See the diagrams on page 77 for an illustration.

Phase 1. Introducing your dog to Tracking

A Dog's First Track

Mom has been talking about tracking all week and at long last we're going to see what this is all about. After a long wait, Mom gets me out of the car and we walk out into a field along with a rather nice man who smells faintly of hot dogs. The man keeps talking to me like we are bosom buddies, but I'm really paying more attention to the fresh wet grass underfoot.

Before we have gone very far, the man stops, and Mom starts putting that funny harness on me. She practiced putting it on me yesterday and to hear her tell it, she's the *World's Greatest Engineer* for getting it buckled around me.

Now the man starts calling me in a cutesy kind of way and holds out his hand to my nose. Sniff, Sniff! There seems to be something good in his hand! Yes, a most delectable morsel of hot dog comes my way, because, he says, I am a good girl (which is, of course, ever so true). The man waves another morsel under my nose and plops it into a glove. I strain against the harness to get some, but Mom holds me back as the man adds two more morsels to the glove.

He waves the glove in front of my face while saying silly things like "Watch the glove!" Of course, I'm watching the glove, it's full of goodies! Instead of giving it to me, he turns around and walks away. "Hey Mister, did you forget to give it to me?" I wonder. Nevertheless, he keeps talking to me in a loud excited voice as he walks away. Pretty quick, he spins around, waves the glove over his head, yells to me to watch him, and then lays the glove to the ground. He turns again and quickly walks away from the spot, then circles back to Mom and me.

As soon as he is back, Mom allows me into his footstep and tells me to "Find it!" That should be simple enough; it's right out ahead here someplace. If I just scamper out there, I'll find it for sure. Off I go, but Mom keeps my harness on a short line.

As I tug her from side to side, I run into a hot dog on the ground. Wow, I never knew that hot dogs grew in the meadow — we should come here more often. Well, I'd better check for more hot dog plants nearby. Mom keeps saying "Find it!" and keeps me on a short line. This keeps my scampers crossing the path that, by the smell of it, the glove-man made. Pretty soon, we come across another hot dog plant that is oh so yummy to find. This field of hot dogs must be the greatest natural wonder of the world, so we are off again to find some more.

We continue to cross the glove man's footprints as I search for more hot dog plants. Sniff sniff! — Sniff sniff! — I think the morsel laden glove must be nearby — just over to the left — Oh yes, here it is — Yummy! Mom comes up and tells me what a Super Girl I am and plays with me and the glove. I think this tracking is going to be fun, but I wonder why they don't call it hot-dogging.

Session 1.0 — Practice being a Tracklayer and being a Handler.

Purpose:
- Introduce the tracklayer and handler to tracklaying.
- Introduce the handler to line handling.

Tracklayer:
- Study the tracklayer's instructions for session 1.1.
- Lay a pretend track like track 1.1.3 (the third track of phase 1, session 1), without a dog.
- Make sure you pick out a distant landmark to walk towards when laying the track. This will help you walk in a straight line.
- Study the handler's instructions for session 1.1 so you can remind the handler what to do.
- Help the handler with the line-handling lesson below (you get to play the part of the dog).

Handler:
- Study the tracklayer's instructions for session 1.1 so you can be sure the tracklayer is laying the track correctly and so you can learn to lay tracks yourself.
- Lay a pretend track like track 1.1.3 without a dog.
- Make sure you pick out a distant landmark to walk towards when laying the track. This will help you walk in a straight line.
- Study the handler's instructions for session 1.1.
- Have the tracklayer act the part of a dog. Clip a 40' line onto her belt and have her walk down a road in front of you. Try different tensions until you know how good a firm-gentle tension feels like. Your line should not flop around in the breeze, and the "dog" should not have to strain to get you to follow along behind her. Have the "dog" move off the track. Raise your arm and increase the tension. Have the "dog" move from side to side as you practice your line handling.
- Switch roles. You be the "dog" and let the tracklayer handle. Feel what firm-gentle tension is like. Move off the track and have the handler raise her arm. Feel the tendency to swing back to the track as her arm goes up and the tension increases.
- Make sure you have all your equipment ready for the next session.

Dog Actor:
- Hook the line onto your belt or around your waist.
- Agree to a visual track direction, then establish with the handler what light-comfortable tension is like.
- Walk down the track at a steady pace, then gently move from side to side so the handler gets to practice her linework. Give her verbal feedback like "too light", "too heavy", "felt like a correction", etc.
- Try to move more than 10' to the side to allow the handler to stop you, then move closer to the track paralleling it to make sure she moves forward with you within the 6-10' range.

Evaluation:
- Even though you probably felt stupid doing all this without a real dog, it is better to feel a little stupid and learn how to do something correctly, than either to not learn it at all or to confuse your dog as you are learning it later.

Sessions 1.x Natural Fields

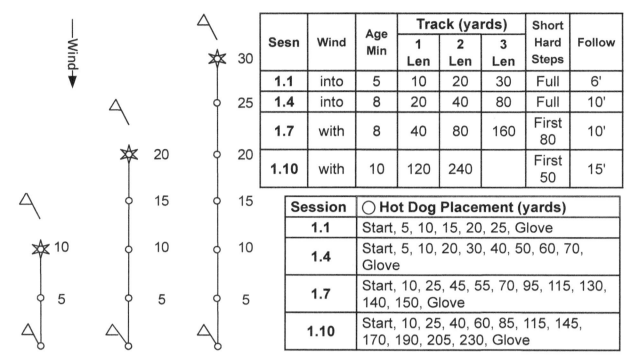

Track 1.1.1   Track 1.1.2   Track 1.1.3

Sesn	Wind	Age Min	Track (yards) 1 Len	2 Len	3 Len	Short Hard Steps	Follow
1.1	into	5	10	20	30	Full	6'
1.4	into	8	20	40	80	Full	10'
1.7	with	8	40	80	160	First 80	10'
1.10	with	10	120	240		First 50	15'

Session	◯ Hot Dog Placement (yards)
1.1	Start, 5, 10, 15, 20, 25, Glove
1.4	Start, 5, 10, 20, 30, 40, 50, 60, 70, Glove
1.7	Start, 10, 25, 45, 55, 70, 95, 115, 130, 140, 150, Glove
1.10	Start, 10, 25, 40, 60, 85, 115, 145, 170, 190, 205, 230, Glove

* For sessions 1.4, 1.7, 1.10, scale the diagram appropriately per the charts above and add a 30 yard flag for tracks over 30 yards long.

Purpose:
- Introduce the dog to tracking.
- Introduce the idea that when you give the command to track, there is something to find.
- Introduce the dog to the fun of tracking.
- Familiarize your dog with tracking in natural fields or minimally-contaminated urban lawns.

Tracklayer:
- Note the diagrams above are representative but not to scale for any particular session. The chart of hot dog placements shows where to place the hot dogs, but on the shorter tracks in a session not all hot dogs are put down.
- At the start, place the first flag and choose the direction of the track directly into the wind (1.1 & 1.4) or directly downwind (1.7 & 1.10).
- Note a distance landmark in the track direction to use for reference.
- Turn 180° to face the dog.
- Ask in a happy voice if he wants to find the goodies today.
- While the handler restrains the dog, give him one piece of food.
- Have him watch you place three pieces of food into the article (place them in the article in a way to make it easy for him to get the food out of the article without help).
- Excite the dog with the article (don't worry if he does not act excited).
- Turn to face the direction of the track.

- Leave a piece of food at the start between your feet.
- Make hard short steps (heel to toe) for 5 yards (1.1 & 1.4) or for 10 yards (1.7 & 1.10), all the while talking excitedly to the dog.
- Make a small footprint pad on the track, place a piece of food directly in the footprint pad and tell the dog there are goodies out here. The footprint pad is just to make it easy for the dog to find the treat and is made by stomping the grass down so the hot dog is easy to get.
- Proceed using hard short steps as before, continuing to talk to the dog and placing the hot dogs per the schedule shown.
- As tracks get longer, put a flag just to the side of the track every 50 yards or so.
- At the end, make a small footprint pad, place the article with food in the footprint pad and tell the dog that there is something exciting to find out here.
- Put a flag 5 yards past the article.
- Quietly walk a couple more paces in the same direction, then start circling back to the dog. Stay 20 or more yards to the side of the track as you return.
- Walk behind the handler. Remind her to stay on the track and to keep good tension.

Handler:

- When you get to the start, put on your dog's harness and a long line, although you will only use the first 6–15' in these sessions. Note the "Follow" column in the charts indicates how far back on the line you should be, not the total length of the line (always 40' for AKC or 49' for CKC).
- Position your dog a few feet from the start so he will look directly down the track.
- Restrain your dog so he cannot quite get to the tracklayer but so the tracklayer can reach him.
- Don't worry if your dog is not very interested in the proceedings, since he does not know what is going on yet.
- Try to gently keep your dog's attention on the tracklayer as the track is being laid.
- When the tracklayer returns, bring your dog up to the start holding onto the harness directly.
- Gently hold your dog at the start; sit or down him only if he is comfortable with it.
- Restrain him at the start until he smells and finds the food drop.
- Continue to restrain him at the start for a few seconds to give him a chance to start to sniff the footprints at the start.
- When he starts to sniff the footprints (or after a few seconds if he isn't going to actively sniff), give him your tracking command (like "Find it!") and give him about 3' of line.
- When he moves forward directly on the track, take a step.
- He is likely to cast widely from side to side. Don't worry at this stage but only step along the track when he is on the track or paralleling it within 6–10', at most.
- Raise your hand with the line over your head whenever your dog is off the track. Lower it whenever your dog is directly on the track. The height of your hand should be proportional to the distance your dog is off the track. Your hand should be belly high when he is right on the track.
- If he tends to move directly along track, let out more line (up to 6–15' per the Follow column).
- If he happens to go over a middle drop without eating it, restrain him there until he finds it. You do not need to praise him for finding the food drops.
- If he takes several steps straight down the track, praise quietly without distracting him.
- When he gets to the article, praise him wildly as soon as his nose comes close to the article.
- Help him get the food out of the article if necessary, play excitedly with him and the article and give him some more food.

Phase 1. Introducing your dog to Tracking

- Toss the article a very short distance and encourage him to go touch it or pick it up. Give him more food (on the article is good) and lots of praise. After the last track, play the article toss and touch game six to ten times.
- He should feel happy and proud of himself at the end of the track no matter what happened along the way! It is up to you to make him feel that way.
- Proceed to the next track to watch it being laid. Offer him water between tracks. After the third track, take off the harness before returning to the car.

Evaluation:

- Note in your detailed tracking log (page 31) and Summary Log (page 33) how he reacted to the proceedings. Did he sniff at the start or on the track? Did he smell, indicate, or play with the article? Did he stay on the track some of the time? Did he enjoy the food drops? Did anything happen to discourage him? Was he happy?
- If he used his nose at all, even for just an instant, you have had a very successful session. If not, don't worry. Many good tracking dogs take several sessions to get the idea. He may have used his nose without you being aware of it.
- Some dogs may get highly excited watching the tracklayer tease them while she lays the track. So when finally allowed to start, they can be wild and go every which way for a while. Keep using your line-handling techniques of raising and lowering your hand and the level of tension. Be patient and your dog will settle down and start to focus on the track. Take a tiny step forward along the track as you are being patient so your dog has a chance to run into the next hot dog.

Young Puppy Distances for Phase 1

All distances for small or young puppies are cut in half compared to the page 18 schedule.

Sesn	Location	Track Shape	Wind	Age Min.	Track 1 Length Yards	Track 2 Length Yards	Track 3 Length Yards	Short Hard Steps	Follow
1.1	Field	Straight	into	5	5	10	15	Full	3–5'
1.2	Lawns	Straight	into	5	5	15	25	Full	3–5'
1.3	P. Lot	Curb	into	5	5	10	20	Full	3–5'
1.4	Field	Straight	into	8	10	20	40	Full	5–7'
1.5	Lawns	Straight	into	8	15	30	60	Full	5–7'
1.6	P. Lot	Curb	into	8	10	20	35	Full	5–7'
1.7	Field	Straight	with	8	20	40	80	First 40	5–7'
1.8	Lawns	Straight	with	8	25	50	100	First 40	5–7'
1.9	P. Lot	Curb	with	10	15	25	45	Full	5–7'

- Keep your puppy within 3–6' of the track on each side.
- For particularly young puppies, do only the first two tracks per session or the first and the third, depending on their energy level and attention span.
- Hot dog distances should be reduced at least in half as well. See pages 22, 25, and 26.

Sessions 1.x Urban Lawns

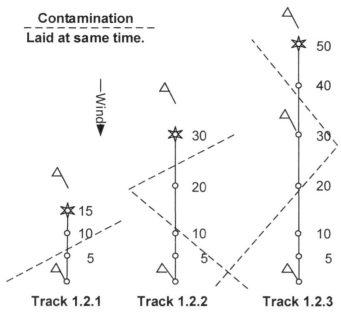

Ses.	Wind	Age Min	Track (Yards) 1	2	3	Short Hard Steps	Fol-low
1.2	into	5	15	30	50	Full	6'
1.5	into	8	30	60	120	Full	10'
1.8	with	8	50	100	200	First 80	10'
1.11	with	10	150	300		First 50	15'

Session	○ Hot Dog Placement
1.2	Start, 5, 10, 20, 30, 40, Glove
1.5	Start, 10, 20, 30, 40, 50, 60, 70, 80, 90, 100, 110, Glove
1.8	Start, 10, 25, 45, 55, 70, 100, 130, 155, 175, 190, Glove
1.11	Start, 10, 25, 45, 70, 100, 135, 175, 210, 240, 265, 285, Glove

* Scale other sessions appropriately per the charts above.

Purpose:
- Introduce the dog to tracking on contaminated lawns.

Tracklayer:
- Tracklayer lays these just like the natural-field tracks including exciting the dog while laying the track.

Contamination Tracklayer (see page 19):
- The contamination tracklayer may be anyone other than the tracklayer including the handler.
- If no contamination layer is available, use a lawn where people have been walking recently.
- If the dog is tracking nicely and handling the contamination quickly, the contamination layer can bring along a leashed dog to give a more realistic experience to the tracking team.

Handler:
- Handle as in natural-field tracks on page 22.
- Your dog will notice the natural and intentional contamination and have to sort out which he should follow. Be patient and try to let him sort it out. Help well before he gets frustrated.

Evaluation:
- Note in your detailed tracking log (page 31) and Summary Log (page 33) how he reacted to the proceedings. Did he sniff at the start or on the track? Did he smell, indicate, or play with the article? Did he stay on the track some of the time?
- If he used his nose at all, even for just an instant, you have had a very successful session. If not, don't worry. Many good tracking dogs take several sessions to get the idea.

Phase 1. Introducing your dog to Tracking

Sessions 1.x Parking-Lot Curbs

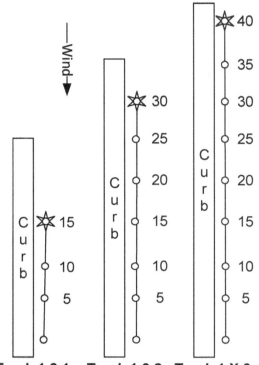

Sesn	Wind	Age Min	Track (yards)			Short Hard Steps	Fol-low
			1	2	3		
1.3	into	5	15	30	40	Full	6'
1.6	into	8	20	40	75	Full	10'
1.9	with	10	30	50	90	First 80	10'
1.12	with	10	60	100		First 50	15'

Session	◯ Hot Dog Placement
1.3	Start, 5, 10, 15, 20, 25, 30, 35, Glove
1.6	Start, 5, 10, 20, 30, 40, 50, 60, 70, Glove
1.9	Start, 10, 25, 45, 65, 80, Glove
1.12	Start, 10, 25, 45, 65, 80, 90, Glove

* Scale other sessions appropriately per the charts above

Track 1.3.1   Track 1.3.2   Track 1.X.3

Purpose:
- Introduce the dog to tracking on hard surfaces.

Tracklayer:
- Lay these tracks right alongside the bottom of the curb.
- Excite the dog as you lay the track just like the field and lawn tracks.
- Choose a relatively long and mostly straight curb. It is OK if it bends.
- You don't need flags as the article and hot dogs indicate where the track is located.
- Use chalk marks on the curb if the handler needs them.

Handler:
- If there is grass on the other side of the curb, your dog may want to investigate it. Don't move forward when your dog is beyond the curb.
- Your dog needs to be close to the curb to succeed (be able to move forward and get the hot dogs). Be patient and let your dog figure it out.
- Be willing to help and encourage your dog, if needed, to avoid him getting frustrated.

Evaluation:
- Note in your detailed tracking log (page 31) and Summary Log (page 33) how he reacted to the proceedings.
- If he used his nose at all, even for just an instant, you have had a very successful session. If not, don't worry.

Field-Only Sessions 1.1f–1.8f Natural Fields

If you are only interested in training for the field TD and perhaps eventually the TDX, follow this schedule for all of Phase 1. For detailed tracklayer, handler and evaluation instructions for sessions 1.1f–1.8f, see page 22.

Session (Info)	Track Shape	Wind	Age Min.	Track 1 Yards	Track 2 Yards	Track 3 Yards	Short Hard Steps	Line Length
1.0f	Line Handling — See 1.0 on page 21.							
1.1f (1.1)	Straight	into	5	10	20	30	Full	6'
1.2f (1.2)	Straight	into	5	15	30	50	Full	6'
1.3f (1.4)	Straight	into	8	20	40	80	Full	10'
1.4f (1.5)	Straight	into	8	30	60	120	Full	10'
1.5f (1.7)	Straight	with	8	40	80	160	First 80	10'
1.6f (1.8)	Straight	with	8	50	100	200	First 80	10'
1.7f (1.10)	Straight	with	10	120	240		First 50	15'
1.8f (1.11)	Straight	with	10	150	300		First 50	15'
1.9f	Review and Evaluation — see 1.13 on page 28.							

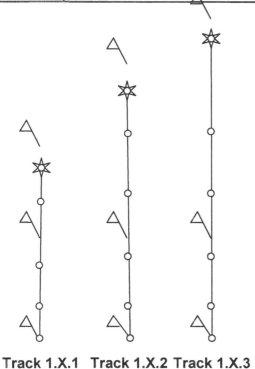

Track 1.X.1   Track 1.X.2   Track 1.X.3

Session	See Page	○ Hot Dog Placement
1.0f	21	
1.1f		Start, 5, 10, 15, 20, 25, Glove
1.2f		Start, 5, 10, 20, 30, 40, Glove
1.3f		Start, 5, 10, 20, 30, 40, 50, 60, 70, Glove
1.4f		Start, 10, 20, 30, 40, 50, 60, 70, 80, 90, 100, 110, Glove
1.5f		Start, 10, 25, 45, 55, 70, 95, 115, 130, 140, 150, Glove
1.6f		Start, 10, 25, 45, 55, 70, 100, 130, 155, 175, 190, Glove
1.7f	22	Start, 10, 25, 40, 60, 85, 115, 145, 170, 190, 205, 230, Glove
1.8f		Start, 10, 25, 45, 70, 100, 135, 175, 210, 240, 265, 285, Glove
1.9f	28	

Phase 1. Introducing your dog to Tracking

Session 1.13 Review and Evaluation

Purpose:
- Review your dog's progress and summarize his accomplishments.

Evaluation:
- Don't expect either you or your dog to be perfect at this stage of your training.
- Write a summary of how your dog has tracked during this phase in your logbook.
- If your dog is not indicating the article by now, start play training him with articles on non-tracking days in your backyard. Throw the article, excitedly tell him to find it and give him a treat as soon as his nose touches it. Repeat. Keep it fun!
- Write a review of his enthusiasm to start, his enthusiasm during the track, how close to the track he stays, how he reacts to changes in cover, and how he indicates the articles.
- Write down what you can do to encourage him to do better.
- Write a review of how well you show your enthusiasm for tracking during the training sessions, your line handling ability, how the line feels when your dog is tracking, how the line feels when your dog is off the track, and how well you can read your dog when he is on or off the track.

Your dog does not need to be perfect, so proceed directly to Phase 2 from Phase 1. Phase 2 will help develop his enthusiasm and his skill.

Sample Journal Log Entry — Phase 1

Session: *1.5*
Dog: *Haute*
Date: *8/30/14*
Layer: *Sil*
CXT Layer: *Orci Urna*
Location: *Skagit River Park*
Weather: *Warm, Sunny*
Wind: *1-3*
Length: *30, 60, 150*
Age: *5-10*
XT Age: *Same*

Evaluation: *Very Good.*

She was wild on all three starts, but settled down.
She noticed contamination, but was focused and willing to be guided.
She came back for most hot dogs.

Hot dogs every 10.

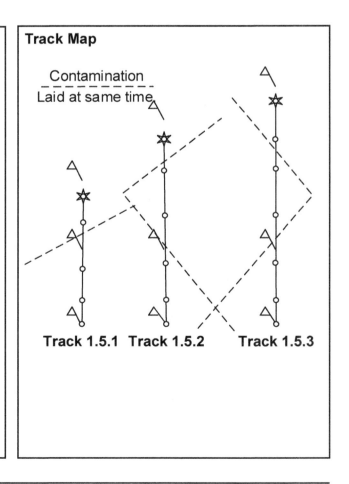

Track Map

Contamination
Laid at same time

Track 1.5.1   Track 1.5.2   Track 1.5.3

Fast Dogs — an Interlude

The big dog that loves to pull and loves to run fast can present a dilemma to the handler. How can the tension be light and comfortable when the handler has to hold on for dear life? One part of the answer is that comfortable refers to the comfort of the dog and not the comfort of the handler. Sorry!

On the other hand, a handler should never let the dog run so fast or pull so hard that the handler is in danger of falling or getting hurt. If the dog wants to go faster than the handler can safely follow, the handler must increase tension to slow the dog down and give the dog an "Easy" command. "Easy" means to slow down but to continue tracking. In slowing the dog down while he is on the track, you want to do so evenly without jerking or stopping the dog. It will be helpful to teach an "Easy" command on-lead in a non-tracking situation; then the dog will understand what "Easy" means as you transfer it to the track.

When a handler cannot safely keep up, some big-fast dogs adopt a circling behavior to pass the time as the handler catches up and allows them to continue. Every 20 to 50 yards along the track, the dog breaks off tracking for no apparent reason and starts to circle wildly. This may be due to some jerking on the line, boredom, or just playfulness on the part of the dog. Treat it as an indication that your line handling should improve — you want the dog tracking steadily down the track. So, work on your "Easy" command and work on making your line handling smooth and even. Your dog will be much easier to read and the two of you will be a more successful team.

Impulsive Dogs — Fast and Quick

When a fast dog also changes direction rapidly, the handler must try to be as quick as her dog to reel-in the line, change tension, or let out the line.

Gloves like workout gloves can help prevent the rope burn for some people. For others, not so much.

While your reaction time may be slower than your dog's changes in direction, work to reel-in the line, change the tension, or let out the line as quickly as you can. Luckily, most such impulsive dogs do not take offense at the inevitable jerks and pops that occur while they change direction rapidly.

Phase 1. Introducing your dog to Tracking

Light-Comfortable Tension — an Interlude

It may be unclear what is meant by the phrase "light-comfortable tension." The use of the phrase "firm tension" in the charts should be taken as synonymous with "light-comfortable tension." Because tension is very important to your success as a dog-handler team, you need to establish good tension now that will provide the proper foundation for your teamwork in phases 3 and above.

Individual dogs will consider different tensions "light" and "comfortable." Picture what a 5-pound toy dog might consider as light-comfortable tension. Then picture what a 90-pound sled dog might consider as light-comfortable tension. These tensions are probably very different. The handler of the toy dog has the line daintily between two fingers and there will be a slight arc in the line between the handler and the dog. The handler of the sled dog must wear gloves and is holding on to the line with all her might. She might even have the line wrapped around her waist (not recommended). There is no arc in the line as the dog pulls the handler down the track. However, both of these tensions are light-comfortable tensions for those individual teams. Your own dog is probably somewhere between these two extremes. So you will have to discover what your dog considers light-comfortable tension.

In all cases, light-comfortable tension involves tension! The line can never drag along the ground between the handler and the dog. The dog must be able to feel the presence of the handler by the tension in the line at all times. Any time the line goes slack or arcs too much, the dog loses contact with the handler and will either (1) look back to see what happened to the handler or (2) lose confidence and slow down. Neither of these actions is desirable. When the slack is taken up, the dog will feel a pop much like an obedience correction; a few of those will cause the dog to lose confidence. So train yourself to maintain a light-comfortable tension at all times.

In no case should the normal tension while the dog is right on the track be as high as to make the dog fight just to move forward. The comfortable part means that the tension is comfortable for the dog. The light part is important because you will increase the tension when the dog moves off the track.

Detailed Log   **4" x 6" Index Cards**

Session: _____ **Evaluation:**
Dog: _____
Date: _____
Layer: _____
Location: _____
Weather: _____
Wind: _____
Length: _____
Age: _____
XT Layer: _____
XT Age: _____
XT Age: _____

_ See other side for track map.

See the template at www.EnthusiasticTracking.com

Detailed Log **Avery 5388 3"x5" Index Cards**

Session: _____ **Evaluation:**
Dog: _____
Date: _____
Layer: _____
Location: _____
Weather: _____
Wind: _____
Length: _____
Age: _____
XT Layer: _____
XT Age: _____
XT Age: _____

__ See other side for track map.

Session: _____ **Evaluation:**
Dog: _____
Date: _____
Layer: _____
Location: _____
Weather: _____
Wind: _____
Length: _____
Age: _____
XT Layer: _____
XT Age: _____
XT Age: _____

__ See other side for track map.

Session: _____ **Evaluation:**
Dog: _____
Date: _____
Layer: _____
Location: _____
Weather: _____
Wind: _____
Length: _____
Age: _____
XT Layer: _____
XT Age: _____
XT Age: _____

__ See other side for track map.

See the template at www.EnthusiasticTracking.com

Phase 1 — Summary Log.

Session	Location	Date	Actual Track Age	Evaluation
1.1	Natural Field			
1.2	Urban Lawn			
1.3	Parking Lot			
1.4	Natural Field			
1.5	Urban Lawn			
1.6	Parking Lot			
1.7	Natural Field			
1.8	Urban Lawn			
1.9	Parking Lot			
1.10	Natural Field			
1.11	Urban Lawn			
1.12	Parking Lot			

Phase 1. Introducing your dog to Tracking

Phase 2. Developing Straight-Line Tracking Skills

Purpose:
- Mold the dog to prefer to stay very close to the track.
- Skill improvement for the dog and the handler.
- Age scent to 15 minutes.

Strategy:
- Threefold:
    - On natural fields, return to very short tracks where the dog is frequently rewarded and finds the article quickly.
    - On urban lawns, use a serpentine track shape to teach the dog to focus on the track more closely.
    - In parking lots, start to cross narrow gaps in the curbs.
- Extend the length of the tracks and the distance between the rewards gradually.
- All tracks are laid generally downwind, so the dog will stay on the track and do less ranging from side to side over the track.
- Over the course of these sessions, gradually increase the distance you follow the dog when he is right on the track, but dynamically shorten the follow distance whenever the dog is to the side of the track.
- Gradually increase the track age.
- Keep the dog unstressed and happy.

How to use this chapter:
- Look through the table on the next page, which summarizes the training structure of this phase.
- Read the discussion section that follows.
- Do each of the 12 sessions that rotate between natural fields, urban lawns and parking lots:
    - Before each session, carefully review the detailed tracklaying and handling instructions for natural fields on page 40, urban lawns on page 41, or parking lots on page 43.
    - You may find it convenient to copy the session detail pages so your tracklayer has the details she needs to lay the desired tracks.
- Keep a detailed log of each session using a format like the one shown on page 31 and keep a summary log like the one shown on page 47.
- Finally, do the review session on page 46 to evaluate your dog's progress and your own training-skill development.

The alternative **field-only schedule** is on page 45.

The alternative **urban-only schedule** is the same as the combined schedule on page 35 except the sessions labeled for natural fields should be done on urban lawns with as little natural contamination as possible (early morning sessions for example).

Phase 2 Session Schedule:

Session	Location	Track Shape	Wind	Age Min	Trk 1 Len. Yards	Trk 2 Len. Yards	Trk 3 Len. Yards	Follow	Short Hard Steps
2.1	Natural Field	Straight	with	10	20	40	80	6'	5 yds
2.2	Urban Lawn	Flagged Serpentine	with	10	60	90		10'	5 yds
2.3	Parking Lot	Island-to-Island Gaps	with	10	40	60		10'	5 yds
2.4	Natural Field	Straight	with	10	40	80	160	15'	5 yds
2.5	Urban Lawn	Flagged Serpentine	with	10	90	120		10'	5 yds
2.6	Parking Lot	Island-to-Island Gaps	with	10	60	80		10'	5 yds
2.7	Natural Field	Straight	with	10	60	120	240	20'	
2.8	Urban Lawn	Flagged Serpentine	with	10	120	150		15'	
2.9	Parking Lot	Island-to-Island Gaps	with	10	80	100		15'	
2.10	Natural Field	Straight	with	15	160	320		20'	
2.11	Urban Lawn	Flagged Serpentine	with	15	150	210		20'	
2.12	Parking Lot	Island-to-Island Gaps	with	15	100	120		15'	
2.13		Review							

Discussion:

The **tracklaying** procedures are similar to those of Phase 1 except:
- The dog should be kept away from the start of the track while it is being laid. The dog is not to be excited by the tracklayer.
- A sock is left at the start. For the first six sessions, place a hot dog on top of the sock. From 2.7 on, no treats on any article — reward your dog for finding the article by itself.
- The end article, a glove, has a hot dog in its palm through session 2.6. For 2.7 or later, bait is not used in gloves and other articles. The dog needs to transition to indicating the article first and then being immediately and amply rewarded by the handler.
- The tracklayer can lay two or three of these tracks in a row before returning to the start for a timely start for the dog.
- The tracklayer should use whatever treats are provided by the handler, typically hot dog pieces or tiny treats like ¼" freeze-dried lamb lung pieces. While the lamb lung is dry, it works well in urban lawns and hard surfaces since it does not tend to be stolen by birds who watch you lay your track.

The **handling** procedures are similar to Phase 1 with very few exceptions:
- Your dog is kept away from the tracks while they are laid.
- You should be close to your dog when he finds articles without food so you can quickly provide rewards once he has noticed the article.
- Line handling is the same, although you can be a little farther back on the line if your dog is doing well on his own.

Line Handling is very important and is worth reviewing. When your dog is exactly on the track, keep a light-comfortable but firm tension on the line with your hand at belly level. Stay fairly close to your dog as indicated in the schedule as well as the detailed session diagrams. As your dog moves to the side, raise your hand gradually until it is over your head and increase the tension on the line. The farther off the track your dog is, the higher your hand and the greater the tension. When your dog gets six to ten feet off the track, your hand should be over your head and you should not be moving. Wait until your dog swings back toward the track, lowering your arm and the tension as he approaches the track, and step forward as he begins to parallel or converge with the track within 6–10'. You are making it easy for your dog to stay on the track, somewhat harder to track to the side and very hard to stray more than 6'-10' from the track.

You should have practiced that up and down line handling all during phase 1. A further refinement will improve your technique and your dog's training: whenever you hold the line at belly level, use your arm as a shock absorber by holding your elbow out away from your body and your forearm square across your belly. As your dog suddenly pulls forward, your hand can automatically go forward with him keeping the light-firm tension constant. As your hand is going forward, your body has an extra split second to speed up and stay with your dog. And as your dog suddenly slows down or stops, your hand can automatically pull back in to your belly keeping the light-firm tension constant. Your other hand holds the trailing line and can feed line forward or reel-in the line as the distance between you and your dog dynamically varies on the track. (Most right-handed people, like me, use their right hand as the line hand. Left-handed people, I am told, always use the appropriate hand without needing advice.)

For smaller people with larger dogs, the same effect can be achieved by holding the elbow down next to your side and using your forearm as a lever to raise the level and increase the tension.

On straight tracks, you need only to remember to raise and lower your hand as your dog moves to the side of the track and to use your arm as a shock absorber to maintain a steady light-firm tension of the line. Remember the "Follow" column refers to how far back on the line you should generally follow your dog. Always use your full 40' line on all AKC practice tracks and your 49' line for all CKC practice tracks.

Some people with very fast moving dogs, very slow moving dogs, very big dogs, or very small dogs think that they can be less careful about line handling than other people. All this discussion about line handling must be for someone else. In fact, careful line handling is required for all dogs. Of course, the tension level for a big fast moving dog that loves to pull will be higher than the tension level for a small slow moving toy dog. All dogs should have a steady tension without the line flopping around in the breeze, without the line touching the ground between the dog and handler, and without the dog being jerked inadvertently by rapid changes in tension.

Handlers of small dogs may be able to handle the tracking line between their thumb and forefinger. Handlers of large dogs may have to wear thin gloves and wrap the line around the palm of their hand to hold the proper tension. Handlers of fast moving dogs may have to adjust to changes in speed more quickly to avoid slack and jerk. Handlers of all types of dogs will be better handlers if they adopt the line handling style described above. It takes practice, but it is worth the effort.

Clear-Confident-Commitment refers to the way a dog focuses on the track — clearly, confidently, and with his full commitment. You may well see your dog being Clear-Confident-Committed to portions or all of Phase 2 tracks. That achievement is something you should note in your session evaluation as it indicates your dog truly understands his job in this tracking game.

Session Design. Some people might ask why not do just a single longer track rather than the three separate tracks indicated. The answer: both you and your dog will learn better by playing with the first and second glove for a while, decompressing, and having a chance to consider what you should do to be better for the next track.

Some students have noted that the tracks at the end of the first phase were older than five minutes, so perhaps they should age these tracks longer or even skip most of this phase. I applaud such creative thinkers, but it turns out to be a bad idea. Follow the program as closely as you can. Your dog will be a better and more successful tracker as a result.

Start Articles: AKC introduced a cloth start article to the TD test in 2005. Phase 2 is an excellent time to introduce your dog to a sock or cloth glove at the start of each track. Use food in it for the first half of the phase, then no food. Don't force your dog to smell it specifically. Do pick it up as you start your dog or after he leaves the start, so you will have it with you if you want to re-scent him somewhere later in the track.

Re-Scenting: Use the start article to remind your dog of the scent of the tracklayer. Gently hold it under or in-front of his nose and let him sniff or breathe in the scent. Don't stuff it into his muzzle — many dogs will consider that a correction.

Scent Pads: CKC uses a one-meter square scent pad instead of a start article. The scent square is made by the tracklayer tromping the grass in a square near the start for 60 seconds before leaving the flag. Phase 2 is an excellent time to introduce scent pads for Canadian dogs.

Puppies: If you started a young puppy or a toy breed and scaled all distances in the first phase, you may choose to scale distances in this phase also. A high-energy puppy that is barreling his way down the track may well be old enough now to do full distances. A low-energy puppy or one who is not yet sure of himself should benefit from shorter distances. Do all the tracks in this phase. See page 44 for a sample half-distance puppy schedule.

In Phase 3 and beyond, you will work up to full distances with all dogs.

Tracklaying Serpentines. The urban lawn tracks in this phase have a curved shape called a serpentine. Two serpentines are diagrammed below.

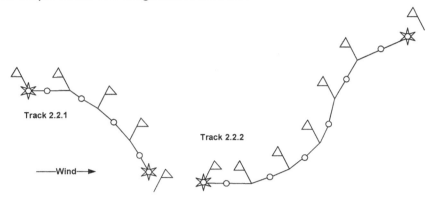

Laying a good serpentine requires a certain amount of care and the use of many landmarks. The general procedure is:
1. Pick a landmark directly downwind of your starting location, put in a flag and drop the sock.
2. Walk 7 yards toward your landmark, drop a hot dog, and continue on another 8 yards.
3. Put in a flag. Then look at your landmark, scan your eyes 15–30° to the right, and pick out a new landmark.
4. Repeat steps 2 & 3 four to eight times to complete an approximate semi-circle. Then switch to scanning your eyes to the left instead of the right. See the diagram on page 41.
5. Repeat this overall sequence of scanning your eyes to the right for several legs and then scanning to the left for several legs until you have reached the total desired length.

This requires finding and using many landmarks. The landscape picture below shows a typical sports field near a school and spans a little more than a 60° view.

The arrow heads along the bottom indicate landmarks about 15° apart. The landmarks are easier to see in real life than in the picture, but the picture still shows the kinds of landmarks you can look for when laying these serpentines. Starting from the left, they are:
1. The right post of the scoreboard,
2. the right edge of outfield fence,
3. the fifth tall backstop pole,
4. about midway between the three firs and the leafless deciduous tree,
5. the left seam in the soccer goal net.

Large-fast dogs can benefit from longer segments, for example, 15 yards each half segment.

Suitable Parking Lot Locations. It is important to identify suitable locations to use that have several islands in a row each with a single-width gap and a time of day with minimal traffic activity. Some parking lots, particularly for shopping malls, use an alternating pattern of islands that makes for much too wide a gap for a beginner dog. You are looking for parking lots with islands at the end of each single or double row of parking spaces. Typical driveway width is 7–10 yards and typical double-parking-row to double-parking-row spacing is 20 yards.

The parking lot picture below shows the islands often found at the end of double rows of parking places. The island gaps are suitable when laying the track horizontally but would be considered big-gaps if the roadway was crossed vertically. The gaps from the middle row of islands to the row at the very bottom are very wide gaps.

1. *Image © 2016 Google*

Light-Comfortable Line Tension

Maintaining an even light-comfortable line tension is important for developing your dog's skill to stay close to the track and move in a straight line. Once your dog masters that skill, you will find following and handling your dog on a blind track with no flags is much easier.

Sessions 2.x Natural-Field Straight Tracks

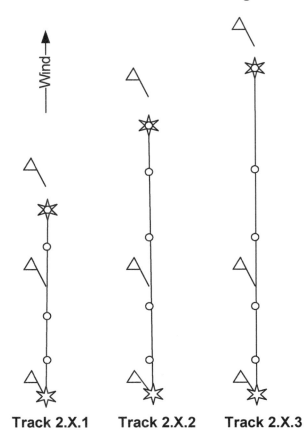

Sesn	Age Min	Track (yards) 1	Track (yards) 2	Track (yards) 3	Short Hard Steps	Fol-low
2.1	10	20	40	80	5	6'
2.4	10	40	80	160	5	15'
2.7	10	60	120	240		20'
2.10	15	160	320			20'

Session	Hot Dog Placement and Instructions
2.1	Start, 10, 25, 45, 60, 70, Glove
2.4	Start, 15, 35, 60, 90, 115, 135, 150, Glove
2.7	15, 35, 60, 90, 125. 155, 180, 200, 215, 225, Not in Glove.
2.10	15, 35, 60, 90, 125, 165, 200, 230, 255, 275, 290, 305, Not in Glove.

Track 2.X.1   Track 2.X.2   Track 2.X.3

Diagram is general for all sessions and not to scale for any of them. Use lengths in charts above.

Purpose:
- Give the dog some easy tracks to increase motivation after the long tracks ending Phase 1.
- Introduce the dog to following tracks he has not seen laid.

Tracklayer:
- Place a sock at the start as a start article with food on it for 2.1 & 2.4 and no food for others.
- Short hard steps only the first 5 yards through 2.6. No food in the end article after 2.6.
- Lay out two or three tracks in a row, then circle back to meet the dog and handler at the start.
- Walk behind the handler on the track.

Handler:
- Keep the dog away from tracks until they are laid.
- The handler should move up the line as the dog approaches articles without food and immediately give food and wild praise as soon as the dog indicates the article. Don't let the dog walk over the article; do restrain at the article until the dog indicates it in any way.
- Show lots of enthusiasm when the dog finds the article. Play with the dog. Have a party!

Evaluation:
- In your journal (page 31) and summary log (page 47) note how your dog tracks, indicates the article, and level of enthusiasm for the tracks.
- Note how often your dog demonstrates clear-confident-commitment on these tracks.

Sessions 2.x Urban-Lawn Serpentines

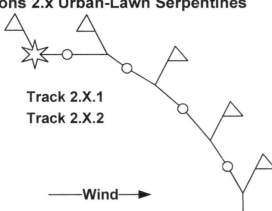

Track 2.X.1
Track 2.X.2

⟶ Wind ⟶

Sesn	Age Min	Track (yards) 1	Track (yards) 2	Follow	Short Hard Steps
2.2	10	60	90	6'	5
2.5	10	90	120	6'	5
2.8	10	120	150	10'	
2.11	15	150	210	10'	

Session	Hot Dog Placement and Instructions
2.2, 2.5	Flag & gentle bend every 15 yards. Hot dogs at the start & half way in between each bend.
2.8, 2.11	Flag & gentle bend every 15 yards. Hot dogs half way in between each bend.

Diagram is general for all sessions and not to scale for any of them. Use lengths in charts above.

Purpose:
- The curving track helps teach the dog the track might not go straight ahead and that he needs to focus on it carefully.

Tracklayer:
- Laying a serpentine takes more tracklayer skill than laying a straight track. Here is the technique I use:
  1. Pick a landmark directly downwind of your starting location, put in a flag and drop the sock.
  2. Walk 7 yards toward your landmark, drop a hot dog and continue another 8 yards.
  3. Put in a flag. Then look at your landmark, scan your eyes 15–30° to the right and pick out a new landmark.
  4. Repeat steps 2 & 3 four to eight times. Then switch to scanning your eyes to the left instead of the right.
  5. Repeat this overall sequence of scanning your eyes to the right for several legs and then scanning to the left for several legs until you have reached the total desired length.
- Write down a sketch of each landmark. This will help you follow the track as the dog runs it and also help develop your map-making skills. The flags at each bend will do most of the work.

Phase 2. Developing Straight-Line Tracking Skills

- Your early serpentines will be shorter than what is shown and your longer ones will have more bends. As they get longer, you'll continue this pattern across the lawn.
- Use hot dogs or tiny treats (¼" freeze-dried lamb lung) along the track as provided by the handler.
- Place a treat on the start article for 2.2 and 2.5. Then no treats on any article.
- Walk behind the handler on the track.

Handler:
- Keep the dog away from these tracks until they are laid.
- The handler wants her dog to stay close to the track. It is OK for the dog to investigate a little beyond the bends up to a body length. Ideally, we want him bending right by the flag. Use a combination of patience, restraint and gentle encouragement to help the dog understand how to notice these bends quickly and to bend right at the change in direction.
- On the straight sections, gradually raise your arm when the dog moves off the track and increase the tension. Use the same 6–10' criteria you use elsewhere.
- At the bend, tighten your tolerance to about a body length. We want the dog to be focused right on the track.
- Distractions are common in these urban-lawn environments. Let your dog spend a few seconds focusing on the distraction and then ask him, or help him, get back to work.
- Show lots of enthusiasm when the dog finds the article. Play with the dog and article at the end of each track. Have a big party!

Evaluation:
- Note how your dog tracks, indicates the article, how he investigates and sorts out the bends, and his level of enthusiasm for the tracks.
- Note how often your dog demonstrates clear-confident-commitment on these tracks.

Reminder — No more Treats in the Glove

Treats are most meaningful for the dog as a reward for doing the right thing or for solving a problem.
- Use them until about midway through this phase. Then no more food in the glove.
- Using them in the glove beyond midway through this phase will not provide the right experience for the dog.
- The dog should indicate the article (glove) and earn his reward from you. He no longer needs to be lured to the glove by the smell of food in it.
- Continuing to use food in the glove may lure the dog to the glove but is no longer necessary. We must withdraw the lure of food in the glove and require the dog to indicate the glove to earn his big-fun party.

Sessions 2.x Parking-Lot Curbed-Island Serpentines

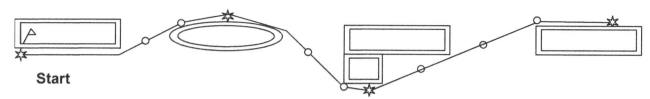

Start

Sesn	Age	Track 1 Yards	Track 2 Yards	Short Hard Steps
2.3	10	40	60	5
2.6	10	60	80	5
2.9	10	80	100	
2.12	15	100	120	

- **Hot Dogs** or Tiny Treats mid-gap & where tracklayer lands on next island.
- **Diagram** is generic for all sessions and not to scale for any of them. Use lengths in chart to the left.

Purpose:
- The third type of track uses a sequence of curbed islands in a parking lot to provide short flat areas between the islands for the dog to learn to put his nose down on flat asphalt even when the curb is no longer right there to hold the scent.

Tracklayer:
- Laying these serpentines is much easier than laying the ones out on urban lawns. You will need to find a suitable location as discussed on page 39.
- On these tracks, it is useful to use sidewalk chalk to mark the direction of the track crossing each gap.
- At the end of each island, the tracklayer randomly decides to go to the left or right side of the next island.
- Use either hot dogs or tiny treats (¼" pieces of freeze-dried lamb lung) on these tracks as directed by the handler.
  - Ants or bees may have swarmed the hot dog by the dog arrives. Freeze-dried treats typically do not attract as much attention from ants or bees.
- Make a mark on the asphalt with colored chalk, then proceed halfway across where you drop a treat, proceed across to the curb, place another treat there, mark the curb with the chalk, and then proceed along the island and drop an article a short way down that curb.
- Take short steps but don't scuff your feet.
- Place a treat on the start article for 2.3 and 2.6. Then no more treats on any article.
- Walk behind the handler on the track. Warn the handler if any traffic approaches or if her line might be run over by a passing car.

Handler:
- The handler's job is to patiently let the dog investigate the gaps so he can discover that the footprints lead to hot dogs and to the correct side of the next island.
- Don't rush the dog at the gaps. Let your line out keeping very light-comfortable tension and be patient.
- In this phase, if your dog dips his nose in the vicinity of the track in the flat and moves roughly parallel to it, encourage him and follow along to support him across.
  - On the first few sessions, after a minute or two, be willing to hint or help your dog rather than let him wander aimlessly. As the dog gets the idea, be more patient.
- If the dog wants to go down the next island on the wrong side, let him go a ways, but then gently restrain him so he continues to investigate and finds the hot dogs on the correct side.
- Distractions are common in these urban-lawn environments. Let your dog spend a few seconds focusing on the distraction and then ask him, or help him, to get back to work.
- At every article, the handler should have a big party, giving treats and playing with her dog before restarting her dog down the curb.

Evaluation:
- Note how your dog tracks, indicates the articles, how he investigates and sorts out the gaps and the next island, and his level of enthusiasm for the tracks.
- Note how often your dog demonstrates clear-confident-commitment on these tracks.

Puppy Schedule for Phase 2

If your puppy is still young, you may want to continue to use half-distance tracks.

Sesn	Location	Track Shape	Wind	Age Min	Trk 1 Yards	Trk 2 Yards	Trk 3 Yards	Follow	Short Steps
2.1	Field	Straight	with	10	10	20	40	3–5'	5 yds
2.2	Lawn	Serpentine	with	10	30	45		3–6'	5 yds
2.3	P. Lot	Island Gaps	with	10	20	30		3–6'	5 yds
2.4	Field	Straight	with	10	20	40	80	5–10'	5 yds
2.5	Lawn	Serpentine	with	10	45	60		5–10'	5 yds
2.6	P. Lot	Island Gaps	with	10	30	40		5–10'	5 yds
2.7	Field	Straight	with	10	30	60	120	5–10'	
2.8	Lawn	Serpentine	with	10	60	75		5–10'	
2.9	P. Lot	Island Gaps	with	10	40	50		5–10'	
2.10	Field	Straight	with	15	80	160		10–15'	
2.11	Lawn	Flagged Serpentine	with	15	75	105		10–15'	
2.12	P. Lot	Island Gaps	with	15	50	60		10–15'	

- As your puppy ages, he may be able to transition to longer tracks closer to the regular lengths.
- Keep your puppy within 3–6' of the track on each side.
- For particularly young puppies, do only the first two tracks per session or the first and the third, depending on their energy level and attention span.
- Hot dog distances should be reduced at least in half as well. See pages 40, 41, and 43.

Field-Only Sessions 2.1f–2.8f

Straight tracks and Flagged Serpentines are both done in natural fields or on uncontaminated sports fields. For detailed tracklayer, handler and evaluation instructions see pages 40 and 41. Then do the review and evaluation 2.13 on page 46.

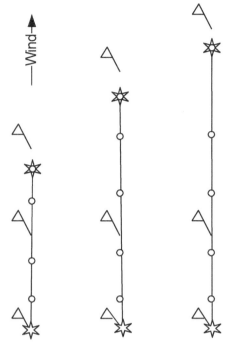

Session (Info)	Age	T. 1 Yard	T. 2 Yard	T. 3 Yard	Follow
2.1f (2.1)	10	20	40	80	6'
2.3f (2.4)	10	40	80	160	10'
2.5f (2.7)	10	60	120	240	15'
2.7f (2.10)	15	160	320		20'

Session	○ Hot Dog Placement
2.1f	Start, 10, 25, 45, 60, 70, Glove
2.3f	Start, 15, 35, 60, 90, 115, 135, 150, Glove
2.5f	15, 35, 60, 90, 125. 155, 180, 200, 215, 225. Not in glove.
2.7f	15, 35, 60, 90, 125, 165, 200, 230, 255, 275, 290, 305

Track 2.Xf.1 Track 2.Xf.2 Track 2.Xf.3

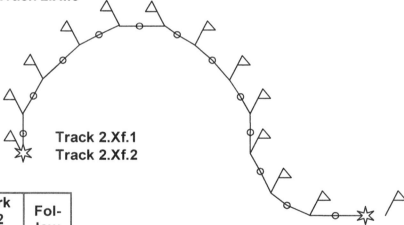

Track 2.Xf.1
Track 2.Xf.2

- Flag and gentle bend every 15;
- Hot dog at the start of 2.2 & 2.4.
- Hot dog halfway in between each bend.

Session	Age	Trk 1 Yard	Trk 2 Yard	Follow
2.2f (2.2)	10	60	90	10'
2.4f (2.5)	10	90	120	10
2.6f (2.8)	10	120	150	15'
2.8f (2.11)	15	150	210	20'

Phase 2. Developing Straight-Line Tracking Skills

Session 2.13 — Review

Purpose:
- Review the dog's progress and summarize his accomplishments.

Evaluation:
- Ideally, you want your dog to be Clear-Confident-Committed to the tracks in Phase 2 for their whole length (see page 37 for an explanation of clear-confident-commitment).
- Don't expect either you or the dog to be perfect at this stage of the training. However, your dog should be attentively tracking most of the length of each of the tracks.
- Write a summary of how your dog has tracked during this phase in your logbook.
- Write a review of his enthusiasm to start, his enthusiasm during the track, how close to the track he stays, how he reacts to changes in cover, and how he indicates the articles.
- Write down what you can do to encourage him to do better.
- Write a review of how well you show your enthusiasm for tracking during the training sessions, your line handling ability, how the line feels when your dog is tracking, how the line feels when your dog is off the track, and how well you can read your dog when he is on or off the track.

Progress Decision:

If the dog is following the natural-field and urban-lawn tracks fairly closely and mostly on his own, go to Phase 3. If he is not following fairly closely to the track, consider repeating 2.7–2.12. Strive to combine better line-tension adjustments to the dog's position relative to the track. Combine with good timing on giving occasional quiet positive feedback to the dog when he is right on the track.

There will be plenty of additional work on hard surface, so don't expect perfection on hard surfaces yet and go on to Phase 3.

Phase 2 Summary Log

Session	Location	Date	Actual Track Ages	Evaluation
2.1	Natural Field			
2.2	Urban Lawn			
2.3	Parking Lot			
2.4	Natural Field			
2.5	Urban Lawn			
2.6	Parking Lot			
2.7	Natural Field			
2.8	Urban Lawn			
2.9	Parking Lot			
2.10	Natural Field			
2.11	Urban Lawn			
2.12	Parking Lot			

Walking in a Straight Line — A Tracklayer's Interlude

When laying some of the long tracks in the first two phases, you will have noticed how hard it is to walk in a straight line for several hundred yards. The straighter you walk, the easier time you will have if the dog loses the track necessitating you to need to help the handler find the track. Also, if you walk in a straight line, the dog and handler will have an easier time and will be more successful — so you will be a popular tracklayer.

The easiest way to walk in a "perfectly" straight line is to notice two landmarks in the distance that are lined up with the direction you want to go, which are also well separated from each other. Say you are going to lay a 200-yard straight track in a field — at the far edge of the field is a large fence post, and directly behind that fence post is a telephone pole in the far distance. If you keep these two landmarks lined up as you walk towards them, you will walk in a straight line.

Often you will be unable to find such convenient landmarks in the direction you want to go. Perhaps you can find one, but there is no second landmark in line with the first. If you look carefully, you may notice a tuft of grass or a unique weed in the foreground that lines up with the main landmark. Use this foreground landmark until you get close to it, and then find another clump of grass or weed that is in line with the main landmark. This technique is more difficult because you have to use several landmarks along the one straight leg, but it can keep you in a relatively straight line.

Finally, on hilly terrain, you may lose sight of your landmarks as you go up and down the slopes. Use several intermediate landmarks on this type of leg, choosing your next landmark before you get to the current landmark or before it goes out of view. If you have to bend a leg that the handler expects to be straight, put in an extra flag at the bend to avoid confusion and to help the handler as she follows her dog.

Improvisation — Another Tracklayer's Interlude

Always try to do exactly what the handler asks you to do. Get the handler to write down exactly what you should do and clarify any issue before you start to lay the track. No matter how careful you are, unexpected situations will arise as you are laying the track, and you will be called upon to improvise. Here are some rules you should keep in mind as you are improvising:

- If the situation seems hopeless, drop an article, put in a flag, return to the handler, and tell her what happened. If the handler does not want to run the dog on the track as laid, someone else might have a dog ready for it or you can always enjoy walking the track again to pick up the flags and the article.
- If you have a choice between two or more alternatives, choose the simplest alternative that will make the track easier rather than harder for the dog and handler. Tell the handler what you did.
- If anything about the track makes it more difficult than the handler expects, put down additional food treats 5 to 10 yards past the difficulty to reward the dog for getting past the obstacle. Tell the handler what you did.
- If you do not have an article, use a sock, a hat, a handkerchief, a tee shirt, a belt, or whatever you can spare. Do not use your keys, your wallet, your eyeglasses, or anything valuable since it might be stolen by a passerby, damaged by the dog when he finds it, or never found again.

Phase 3. Crosswind Tracking and Preparing for Corners

Purpose:
- Teach crosswind tracking.
- Prepare the dog for corners with angled approaches to the start flag, more hard-surface curbed-island serpentines, and more urban-lawn flagged serpentines.

Strategy:
- Keep the dog on the track on crosswind legs.

How to use this chapter:
- Look through the table below, which summarizes the training structure of this phase, and read the discussion section that follows.
- Do each of the 8 sessions that rotate between natural fields, urban lawns, and parking lots.
    - For the alternative field-only session schedule, see page 54.
    - For alternative urban-only training, use this schedule below using urban lawns with minimal contamination for the natural-field sessions.
- Before each session, carefully review the detailed tracklaying and handling instructions for each session type starting on page 52.
- Keep a detailed log of each session using a format like the one shown on page 31 and keep a summary log like the one shown on page 55.
- Finally, do the review session on page 54 to evaluate your dog's progress and your own training-skill development.

Phase 3 Session Schedule:

Session	Location	Configuration	Wind	Age Min	Trk 1 Yard	Trk 2 Yard	Trk 3 Yard	Trk 4 Yard
3.1	Natural Field	Four Square	All	15	75	75	75	75
3.2	Urban Lawn	Four Square	All	15	75	100	75	100
3.3	Parking Lot	Curbed-Island Serpentine	Ignore	15	90	120		
3.4	Field or Lawn	Article Oval	Ignore	15	120	120		
3.5	Natural Field	Four Square	All	15	100	100	100	100
3.6	Urban Lawn	Four Square	All	15	100	125	100	125
3.7	Parking Lot	Article Oval	Ignore	15	120	120		
3.8	Urban Lawn	Flagged Serpentine	Ignore	15	150	180		

Discussion:

After Phase 2 your dog should be pretty good at closely following a straight track and at least OK following tracks with gentle bends. To prepare for introducing sharp 90° corners, we need to introduce the dog to crosswinds — since both the leg coming into a 90° corner and the one going out cannot both be downwind. Of course, for serpentines only the general trend is downwind, and some of the segments are at various quartering angles downwind. Regardless, before introducing corners, we need to carefully introduce the dog to crosswind tracking.

Also, to further prepare the dog for corners, we introduce the dog to the idea the track might not be straight ahead. We do this by the handler approaching each start flag at an angle so the dog needs to search at the start for the correct direction. Vary the angle randomly between 30°, 45°, and 60° both from the right and the left. Expect the dog to burst forward when you release him at the start. Because of the angle, he is likely to diverge from the track. Increase the tension, keep the dog from diverging more than 6–10', and remind him to find it. Give him a few seconds to circle over to find the track. If he doesn't, point to the track and happily encourage him to find the track.

The third way we prepare the dog for corners is to do another urban-lawn flagged serpentine.

We will also do a couple of article ovals to improve the dog's response to articles as this is a good place to improve his article recognition skills.

Use the tracks in this phase to study your dog's posture and body language while he is tracking. Over the next several phases, you will improve your ability to read your dog as he is tracking and searching for the track. When the flags disappear in Phase 6, you'll be glad you studied your dog when the tracks were simple and well-marked.

Crosswind Tracking. We introduce wind variation by putting in four separate tracks, one in each of four directions. Lay one straight track, move ahead 20–30 yards, turn 90°, move ahead 10–20 yards, and lay the next track. Repeat until all four tracks are laid. While I prefer to lay the first track directly downwind, that order requires access to the field on the upwind side, which is not always possible. It is OK to lay the first leg in any wind direction if the downwind choice is inconvenient.

In a crosswind, the dog may tend to track a few feet downwind of the footsteps. This is natural but can easily become a bad habit. The handler should raise her arm and increase the tension in proportion to how far he is off the track. If he stays off the track, she can move upwind of the footsteps up to 3' to increase the torque helping to bring him back on the track. Now is a critical time to keep the dog close to the footsteps. Care now can avoid problems later. Remember, our strategy is to make it easiest for the dog to move forward directly over the footsteps and to make it more difficult but not impossible, to move forward when the dog is off the track up to 6–10'.

Don't expect the dog to be perfect in the crosswind on his first track. How far he wants to track off the footsteps depends on the wind strength, track age (15 minutes), weather, and his experience. As he gains positive experience tracking in a crosswind, he will become a solid crosswind tracker. He will be doing well in the first few tracks if he moves parallel to the track within 3' of the footsteps. He must be under increased tension while off the footsteps any distance, so keep your arm up and a nice firm tension. By the middle of this phase, he may be happily tracking right on the footprints with only an occasional diversion downwind.

Avoiding Problems. The food drops become less frequent in this phase. You may notice your dog picks up speed and stays closer to the track after the drops. That's why they are there. You may notice him going off the track downwind a few yards before the drops. This is normal since there is a lot of scent pooling near the drops. If you cross a cover change or other slight obstacle that your dog has not experienced before, place a drop five to ten paces past the obstacle. The food drop will reward your dog for getting past the cover change.

If he is not starting well, go back to putting a drop at the start and another at 15 yards. Withdraw these two extra drops slowly and randomly once his enthusiasm returns.

If your dog is losing enthusiasm near the end of the session, do three things: a) condition him on non-tracking days to improve his stamina, b) increase the number of food drops on the last half of the track, and c) have hugely fun parties at the glove.

Puppies: If he is a toy dog or a young puppy losing enthusiasm, and you used half-length tracks in Phase 2, you can continue to constrain the total length of his tracks in this phase, although you will gradually need to motivate him and condition him so he is happily tracking full-length 500 yard tracks by Phase 5.

Handling Tips. On the straight legs of the four square sessions, you can be 15'-20' behind your dog unless he wants to be too far to the side of the track, in which case you'll reduce your following distance to help keep him closer to the track.

On the serpentines, you should stay closer to your dog, perhaps 10' or even closer. This will allow you to have the fine control needed to show your dog he can stay very close to the track.

Tracklaying. The exact length of the tracks you lay is not critical, but it is a good idea to get a general idea of how many steps you need to take to walk 10 yards. I typically take 11 steps to 10 yards so when I am counting my steps, I double count all the 10 numbers as in "1, 2, 3, 4, 5, 6, 7, 8, 9, **10, 10**, 11, 12, 13, 14, 15, 16, 17, 18, 19, **20, 20**, 21, 21, 23, 24, 25, ..." You may find the length of your stride is different on smooth flat lawns and asphalt parking lot than out in the rougher terrain of natural fields.

I like to occasionally check the length of my stride and that of my students. Using a 100' tape measure, I put out flags 100 yards apart in a natural field. Or if I want my lawn stride, I can just use the yard-lines on a sports field. I count my steps to the one-hundred-yard mark and that gives me my ratio of steps to yards.

Note that in tracking and this book, numbers are often stated without units for brevity. It is generally understood that numbers relating to track distances are stated in yards for AKC or meters for CKC. And that numbers relating to line length or the distance between you and your dog are stated in feet.

Sessions 3.x Four Square

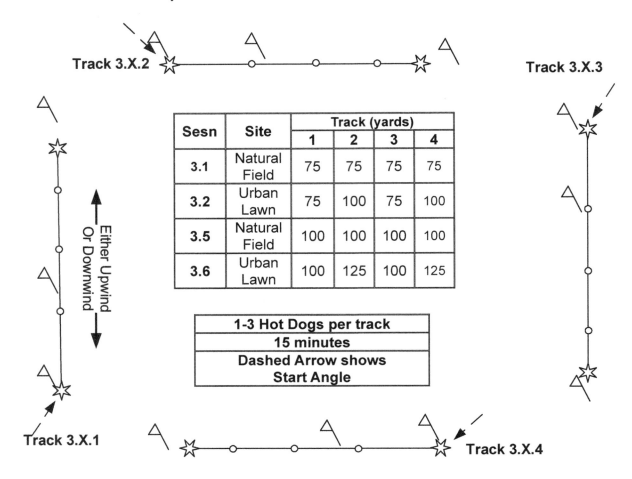

Sesn	Site	Track (yards)			
		1	2	3	4
3.1	Natural Field	75	75	75	75
3.2	Urban Lawn	75	100	75	100
3.5	Natural Field	100	100	100	100
3.6	Urban Lawn	100	125	100	125

1-3 Hot Dogs per track
15 minutes
Dashed Arrow shows Start Angle

Purpose:
- Introduce crosswind legs.

Tracklayer:
- Lay four tracks in a big square; the first one directly downwind (or upwind).
- Lay all the tracks one after the other; keep them 25–50 yards apart.

Handler:
- The handler should approach each start flag at an angle, so your dog needs to search at the start for the correct direction. Vary the angle randomly between 30°, 45°, and 60°, and from both the right and left. Dashed arrows suggest approach angles.
- The handler should pay particular attention to her line handling on crosswinds since your dog is liable to want to track to the side of the actual track. Stay 15'-20' behind your dog. Raise your hand and increase tension when your dog moves to the side but continue to walk forward with him so long as he stays pretty close (say 6–10') to the track.

Evaluation:
- In your journal and summary log (page 55) note how your dog tracks, indicates articles, and his level of enthusiasm for the tracks. Note how enthusiastically you are playing at articles.

Sessions 3.x Article Ovals

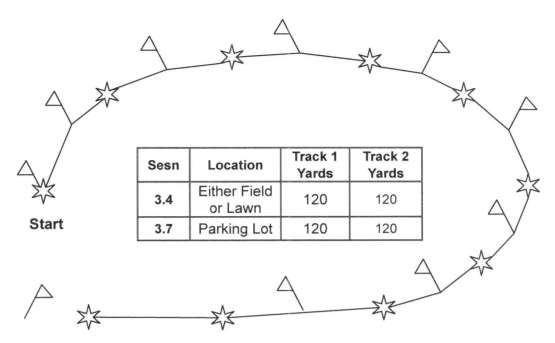

Sesn	Location	Track 1 Yards	Track 2 Yards
3.4	Either Field or Lawn	120	120
3.7	Parking Lot	120	120

Purpose:
- Build value for articles and introduce additional article types.
- Practice a sincere, enthusiastic fun "glove game" at each article.
-

Tracklayer:
- For 3.4, use an urban lawn or a grass field with short mowed grass.
- Use socks, gloves, pieces of cloth and leather. There is no need to include plastic or metal at this early stage.
- These tracks are laid in a big oval or circle with an article every 10–15 yards along the track.
- You only need to lay one of these; the dog and handler can go around more than once.
- On grass, put 8 or more flags along the track to help show where the oval is located.
- For 3.7, use a flat parking lot without nearby curbs; the articles will be their own track markers.

Handler:
- This is a game so keep it fun for the dog.
- Keep the dog fairly close to the track and make sure the dog stops at each article where you reward the dog with food and fun play for 20 to 60 seconds before restarting the dog.
- Unlike any other track, you can take your dog around the oval more than once if you drop the articles in place as your dog starts tracking toward the next article.
- Show real enthusiasm for your dog finding each and every article. Each individual article must be very-very special to you so it is very-very special to the dog.

Evaluation:
- In your journal and summary log (page 55) note how the dog indicates the articles and whether their level of enthusiasm increases.

Session 3.3 Curbed-Island Serpentines are just like Phase 2.x curbed serpentines on page 43. However, in this phase, you want to hesitate and let your dog cross the gaps without you close behind him. After he fully commits across the gap, follow him and climb back up your line.

Session 3.8 Urban-Lawn Flagged Serpentines are just like Phase 2.x lawn serpentines on page 41.

Session 3.9 Review

Once you have completed the 8 sessions, move right on to Phase 4. If some things did not work perfectly during this phase, like no wind on the four square sessions, just remember to continue to hold your dog fairly close to the crosswind legs on the more complex tracks with corners.

Field-Only Sessions 3.1f–3.3f

The four straight tracks are done in natural fields or on uncontaminated sports fields. For detailed tracklayer, handler and evaluation instructions see page 52. Then proceed directly to Phase 4.

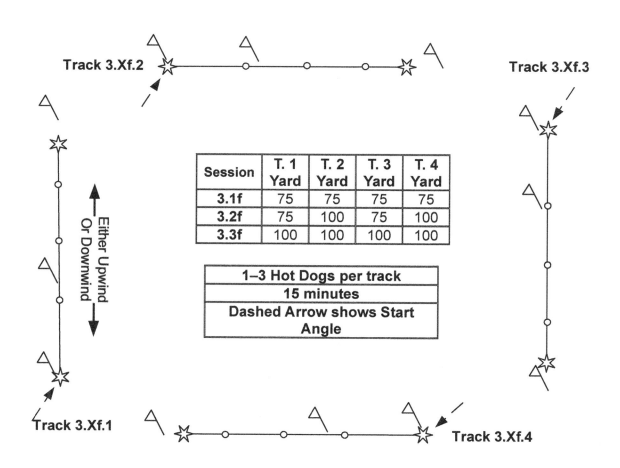

Session	T. 1 Yard	T. 2 Yard	T. 3 Yard	T. 4 Yard
3.1f	75	75	75	75
3.2f	75	100	75	100
3.3f	100	100	100	100

1–3 Hot Dogs per track
15 minutes
Dashed Arrow shows Start Angle

Phase 3 Summary Log

Session	Site	Track Config.	Date	Evaluation
3.1	Natural Field	Four Square		
3.2	Urban Lawn	Four Square		
3.3	Parking Lot	Island Serpentine		
3.4	Natural Field or Urban Lawn	Article Oval		
3.5	Natural Field	Four Square		
3.6	Urban Lawn	Four Square		
3.7	Parking Lot	Article Oval		
3.8	Urban Lawn	Flagged Serpentine		

Phase 3. Crosswind Tracking and Preparing for Corners

Phase 4. Introducing Corners

Purpose:
- Teach right and left turns on grass fields and park lawns as well as along curbs.

Strategy:
- Keep the dog on track on crosswind legs.
- Allow the dog to overshoot the corner a little, then investigate and search the corner area.
- Encourage the dog to take the new leg happily when he finds it.

How to use this chapter:
- Look through the table below, which summarizes the training structure of this phase, and read the discussion section that follows.
- Practice your line handling on corners as described in session 4.0 on page 62.
- Do the 11 sessions that rotate between natural fields, urban lawns, and parking lots. Make sure you and the tracklayer review the detailed session instructions that start on page 63.
  - The alternative field-only schedule is on page 67.
  - For urban-only training, do natural-field sessions on urban lawns.
- Keep a detailed log of each session (page 31) and keep a summary log (page 69).
- Finally, do the review session on page 68 to evaluate your dog's and your own progress.

Phase 4 Session Schedule:

Session	Location	Configuration	Wind	Track 1 Leg 1	Track 1 Leg 2	Track 2 Leg 1	Track 2 Leg 2
4.0		Practice Corner Linework					
4.1	Natural Field	Left, Right 135°	into	100	30	100	60
4.2	Urban Lawn	Right, Left 135°	into	100	30	100	60
4.3	Parking Lot	Right, Left Curbs	into	60	20	60	40
4.4	Natural Field	Right, Left	into	100	80	100	100
4.5	Urban Lawn	Left, Right	into	100	80	100	100
4.6	Parking Lot	Right, Left Curbs	with	80	45	80	75
4.7	Natural Field	Left, Right	with	120	80	120	120
4.8	Urban Lawn	Right, Left	with	120	80	120	120
4.9	Parking Lot	Right, Left Curbs	with	100	60	100	90
4.10	Natural Field	Right, Left	with	120	100	120	120
4.11	Urban Lawn	Left, Right	with	120	100	120	120
4.12	Review	Review					

Discussion:

The Ideal Corner. Before discussing what a dog is going to do on his very first corner, let's understand what we would like him to do once he is thoroughly experienced with corners. Ideally, when a dog comes to a corner, he immediately turns his head down the new leg and marches around the corner like a cartoon character bending around a corner. Alternatively, if he is moving down the leg quickly when he comes to the corner, he should nod his head down the direction of the new leg, put on the brakes, and quickly come to a stop within a few feet of the corner. When he does pass the corner, the ideal dog will immediately and actively search for the new direction by circling until he intersects and takes the new leg.

Many dogs, including those who nod in the direction of the new leg as they go past the corner, seem to want to check out the opposite direction before taking the new leg. They may circle to the opposite direction, then come up to the corner and proceed down the new leg. Let the dog search however he wants to search, so long as it is active and purposeful. How a dog circles may be influenced by his innate tendency to turn right or left, the wind direction, tracking conditions, and his drive to continue on the track.

Tracklayer Tips. Whether laying the open corners of 4.1 and 4.2 or the 90° corners of the remaining field and lawn tracks, some planning before setting out is desirable. Sessions 4.1, 4.2, 4.4 & 4.5 all need to have the second leg going straight upwind. The remaining sessions all have the second leg straight downwind. See the diagrams on pages 63 & 65. That means you need to determine the wind direction and set your first leg so the corner will be the correct angle and the second leg will be at the desired angle to the wind. I generally put the track diagram flat in front of me and align the second leg drawn there with the wind, which means I am facing in the desired direction for the first leg.

While some trainers recommend putting a hot dog right at the corner or a series of hot dogs in each step of the second leg, I recommend keeping treats at least 25 yards from before or after a corner. You want the hot dogs to be a reward for doing the right thing, not a lure to make the dog look like he is doing the right thing. So help the dog learn to do corners without nearby food lures and he will understand them much better than the dog who is lured.

The natural-field sessions show using two tracks per session. Some high-energy dog and handler teams may enjoy a third track each session. Do it for fun but still do each of the sessions.

Some dogs are very visual and will beeline to a visible fluttering flag rather than go to all the work of using their nose to follow the track. This can become obvious on tracks with corners where the dog departs the first leg somewhere in the middle and heads directly to the end flag or the flag of another track in the field. I do want the handler to have flags so she is sure where the track is located. Instead of just getting rid of the fluttering flags, you can make them invisible from a distance by taking a length of straw to act as a sheath for the rolled up flag material. If a straw is too small, two or three rubber bands may work. You want to be able to see the flags when you are close, but you don't want your dog to pay attention to them from a distance.

The Dog and Handler's First Corner — one of the things we accomplished in the first three phases is to develop a strong drive to complete the track so the dog is now ready to handle corners.

Every dog is different, but you should expect to see some typical behavior when the dog reaches his first few corners. Since the dog has been tracking the footprints or just to the side of them and has always found a glove, he has never run out of scent before. So expect him to continue down the line of the first leg for several feet before realizing the track has been lost. Two to three body lengths past the corner might be typical for some dogs while 20–40' might be typical for very fast moving dogs. At the instant he runs out of scent, he may look back at you with a puzzled expression. As if to say, "No fair, you've changed the rules of the game!"

Some dogs immediately start to look for the track while others are less sure what to do. The work we did with serpentines on sports lawns will help the dog know he should search. Even if the dog does not realize searching is the right thing to do, we will teach the dog to search for the track by our actions at the corner. Since we are about 15' behind the dog when the typical dog notices the loss of track, we are not quite to the corner flag when we stop. If the dog does not stop within 10' past the corner, increase the tension until the dog stops and stop yourself before the corner.

Stay where you stopped, keep light-comfortable tension with the dog even if that means quickly reeling in the line if the dog comes back closer to you. While you may need to raise your arm to avoid getting the line tangled with the dog, or the stake, or vegetation, primarily keep the line in both hands at chest level, constantly adjusting the line length to control the dog's distance and raising your arm only when it is necessary to avoid tangling the line. As the dog circles, pivot to stay facing the dog so you can see him. Don't walk around; stay at the pivot point.

Until the dog circles, continue to face the direction of the first leg while noting the footprints and flags of the second leg. You want to encourage the dog to find the direction of the second leg without, if possible, helping him find it. By keeping your body facing down the direction of the first leg, you avoid giving the dog clues about what direction to search. You want him to understand he is the one doing the searching. Keep a steady comfortable tension on the line and occasionally quietly encourage the dog to "Find it. Go ahead. You can do it. That's right, find it." But otherwise don't interfere.

Watch how the dog's nose works as he searches for and approaches the new leg (or directly downwind of the new leg). When the dog reaches the second leg, he will generally start right out on the upwind leg. Some dogs seem to notice the second leg but are reluctant to take it. An upwind leg probably smells a little different than a crosswind leg, so he may not be sure it is the same track. At this early stage, feel free to encourage him to take the leg if he does not take it or even show him the new leg if he cannot find it. Just give him a chance to find it himself before helping him.

If the dog needs help, first encourage him with your voice and use your body language to go in the correct direction. If he still needs help, reach down and tickle the grass right on the track right in front of his nose as you happily encourage him to find it. Walk forward with him down the track tickling the track until he takes off ahead of you. It is very important to maintain a happy attitude whenever you help your dog.

See the Corner Problems section on page 60 for a discussion of how to train dogs who tend to overshoot the corners, who want to play on the corner, and dogs who want to quit on a corner.

The Second Leg — when the dog takes the second leg, you may notice him weaving from side to side. This is natural on an upwind leg. A dog that weaved on the upwind legs of Phase 1 will probably weave on these upwind legs also. Of course, you want to encourage him to stay right on the track by raising your arm and increasing the tension in proportion to how far off the track he is.

On subsequent corners in this phase's tracks, your dog will gain understanding about corners and how to work them. Keep the image of the ideal corner in your mind and encourage his behavior that is close to the ideal.

Helping, a Delicate Balance — A few really rare dogs might exist who never need help on any training track, but I have never met such a wonderful natural tracker. Don't assume your dog is a natural tracker who innately knows all tracking skills. Helping your dog offers him the opportunity to learn what is correct in this scenting situation and to develop his skills so he can behave in a way you can read him and follow him on blind tracks.

When your dog encounters a scenting problem, first let him try to solve it himself. Be patient and don't rush him. Before he gets frustrated and starts to think about quitting, you should help him. Always try to help as little and as gently as possible.

The **"Be Patient"** part is very important to avoid some common training problems. Handler impatience leads to:
- Training your dog to grab whatever contamination track is near his nose.
- Training your dog to give up responsibility and just go wherever you want to go.

Here is a hierarchy of help levels from least to most:
1. **Face in the Correct Direction** — dogs are very aware of our body posture and turning your body to face the new leg suggests to your dog what is correct.
2. **Restraint** — restrain your dog when he is at the end of his line and wanting to search farther out in the wrong direction or commit to a contamination track out there.
3. **Reel-in and Re-Scent** — by bringing your dog back, you have the opportunity to re-scent your dog and get him focused on what you want him to follow.
4. **Make it Easy** for him to follow the good track. Lowering the tension on the line as he approaches the track or taking a few steps in the correct direction helps him commit to the track without explicit direction from you.
5. **Reel-in and Point** to the correct track and direction.
6. **Reel-in and Love the Track** on your knees, moving forward slowly on the track speaking lovingly to the footprints until he moves forward in front of you focused on this interesting thing. Aka "You are Juliet, the track is Romeo, and we ignore the audience (your dog)."

> If your only image of **Romeo and Juliet** is stilted high-school renditions, what is important here is to express your love of the track with genuine heartfelt passion. Become a bit of an actress and make the track in the grass believe you so your dog will believe you as well.
>
> The words you say don't matter, but how you say them does — emotionally love the track itself and forget about the dog — he will get interested in what you find so interesting. If you need a script, the following might help you feel the love of the track:
>
>> *Oh! The sweet bouquet of these footsteps in fresh spring grass. I do so cherish you, sweet track. I desperately, tenderly, passionately, completely love you. I want to savor each of your leaves and yearn to taste your dew-drops with my tongue. If you only knew how I crave your fragrance. I long to scent the length and breadth and depth of you, the very essence of you. I want to inhale you forever. I'll remember every fragrance you share with me. I love you, beautiful track.*

Catching Corner Problems Early. You can avoid problem-solving later by watching for and intervening when you first see consistent signs of a corner problem.

1. **Overshooting Corners or Line Tracking.** Some dogs tend to track a considerable distance past the corner. We call these dogs "line trackers" since they like to keep going in a line. To discourage this behavior from developing, don't let the dog get 20' past the corner. Stop when you are 5' from the corner and increase the tension until the dog stops within 20' of the corner. Proceed as described on page 58. If the problem persists, build tracking drive by putting drops at 25, 30, and 35 yards past each corner. Escalate to drops at 25, 30, 35, 40, and 45, if needed.

2. **Fooling Around or Playing.** Some dogs want to play at the corner — as soon as they run out of scent, they take it as permission to run wildly about having a good time. We try to keep this from happening by building tracking drive in the dog during the first three phases, using quiet encouragement for the dog to search on the corner and using steady tension on the line at the corner. Dogs that start to play should have the line tension increased and have drops at 25, 30, and 35 yards past each corner. A dog that persists in playing should have several remedial straight tracks in various wind conditions until he is a happy tracker in all wind directions. You can repeat session 3.1 with four straight 75 yard tracks that make a box shape by laying one track into the wind, the next crosswind, the next downwind, and the next back crosswind. Start each track about 10 yards from the end of the previous track. Then try a corner session again. If the dog plays on the corners again, do several more four-square sessions. This time use a motivational food pattern to encourage the dog to complete the track. On a 75-yard track, put food at the start, 15, 40, 55, 65, and 70 yards.

3. **Quitting.** Some dogs may become perplexed when they lose the scent at the corner. They may stop, look at you and not actively search. Alternatively, they may search for a while and then become discouraged when they cannot immediately find it. (Dogs that lack self-confidence are prone to this behavior). Wait a moment when the dog first stops to see if he will restart on his own. If not, repeat your tracking command "Find it". Then use an encouraging tracking monologue like "Search for it. Go ahead. You can do it. Find it". Be happy, take a few steps toward the corner and repeat the extended monologue.

If the dog does not get started again, reduce the line length to a few feet and walk down the second leg with the dog while pointing at the footsteps and happily and excitedly saying "Look over here. Here it is. You can do it. You can find it." Encourage the dog down the track until he moves out in front of you. He will soon find a drop and the article, so he will quickly understand these new legs are OK.

If the dog really struggles or seems to quit, get down, touch the track and express your love for the track itself. Specifically, you don't ask or beg your dog to track; you tell the track itself how much you love it. Your dog will be intrigued by your interest in the track and move ahead to investigate what you find so wonderful. It takes a little play-acting, but think of yourself as Juliet and the track as Romeo.

Dogs who quit also can benefit from the gradual-turn schedule included at the end of this phase (See page 70). These sessions are used to build confidence and help the dog understand the concept of corner.

While it is important to look for and catch corner problems early, remember this is your dog's introduction to corners. Your primary handling approach is to shape the dog to break off when the scent changes at or just after the corner, and then to search diligently for the new leg, which might smell a little different than the incoming leg. As described on page 58, gently restrain your dog when he gets several feet past the corner if he does not break off himself. Keep light-comfortable tension on the line 100% of the time he searches for the new leg. Most important, make it easy for your dog to follow and commit to the new leg, so he gets the treat and is rewarded for his cleverness.

Phase 4. Introducing Corners

Session 4.0 Practice Corner Linework

At last, you are ready to practice your corner line handling, where your friend plays the dog, and you practice handling the dog on a corner (much as you did in session 1.0 for straight tracks). Your friend can give you verbal feedback about what your line handling feels like, and the exercise is very valuable experience for both the handler and the person playing the dog.

Dog Actor:
- For the first 2–3 practice corners, be a good dog — search and find the new leg quickly.
- For the next corner track, try to keep going in a straight line past the corner.
- For the next practice corner, search only on the side away from the new leg until the handler faces in the new direction or encourages you to go search over there.

Handler:
- Keep 15' behind the 'dog' as you approach the corner.
- Stop yourself before the corner, perhaps 5–10' before.
- Encourage the 'dog' to search and find new the leg.
- On a corner where the "dog" does not find the new leg quickly, face down the direction of the first leg until the 'dog' commits to the next leg, or you have to help (see page 59).

Sessions 4.1 & 4.2 Single Open Corner Tracks in Natural Fields and Urban Lawns.

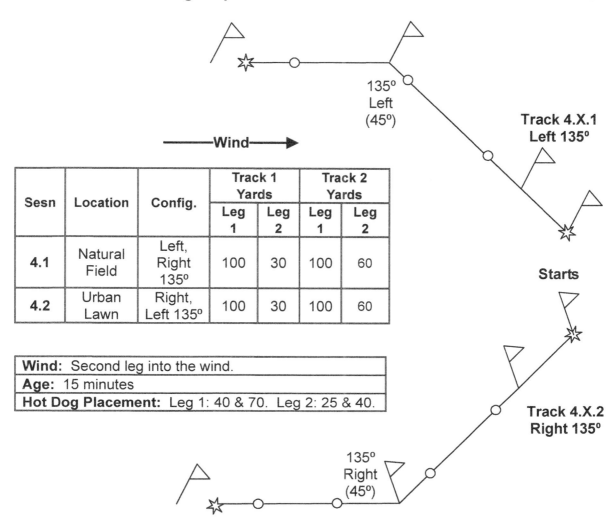

Sesn	Location	Config.	Track 1 Yards		Track 2 Yards	
			Leg 1	Leg 2	Leg 1	Leg 2
4.1	Natural Field	Left, Right 135°	100	30	100	60
4.2	Urban Lawn	Right, Left 135°	100	30	100	60

Wind: Second leg into the wind.
Age: 15 minutes
Hot Dog Placement: Leg 1: 40 & 70. Leg 2: 25 & 40.

Purpose:
- Introduce Open 135° Corners to show the dog that tracks can turn.

Tracklayer:
- For these sessions, use areas with no contamination or only light contamination and do not add intentional contamination.
- Lay the second leg into the wind.
- To make a 135° corner, you will turn 45°. At the corner, extend one arm to the side and one arm in front, then bisect to see a landmark at 45°.
- Use four flags per track so the handler will know exactly where the track is laid.
- Lay the second leg with short hard steps for the first 20 yards, then use normal steps.
- Lay both these tracks and then run them in sequence.
- For high-energy dogs and handlers, it is OK to lay a third track per session.

Phase 4. Introducing Corners

Handler:
- Keep 15' behind your dog as you approach the corner.
- Stop yourself before the corner.
- Encourage your dog to search and find the new leg.
- Face down the direction of the first leg until your dog circles or needs help.
- Keep up the party at each article. Have fun with your dog!

Evaluation:
- In your journal and summary log (page 69) note how your dog works the corners. Also, note how he maintains his attitude on each leg.
- Most dogs should advance on to the full 90° corners regardless of how they do on these open corners — they do not need to be perfect to advance. If your dog is unable or unwilling to find any of these four second-legs, try to figure out what might have been bothering him and then repeat these two sessions.

Reminder — Keep Treats Away from Corners

- Treats are most meaningful for the dog as a reward for doing the right thing or for solving a problem.
- Using them right on the corner will stop the dog at the corner, but the dog isn't learning to stop at corners because the scent changes there.
- Using them near the corner on the new-outgoing leg may lure the dog onto the new leg, but should be unnecessary. Withdrawing lures like this will take great care and repetitions for the dog to properly learn to find the new leg without the lures.
- My general rule is place the treat at least 25-30 yards from the corner, both on the incoming leg and the outgoing leg. That way, the dog solves the corner-problem and gets rewarded. This promotes learning and enthusiasm.
- For legs shorter than 60 yards, I do bring the treat into 20-25 yards to avoid not being able to use a treat at all.

Sessions 4.X Single 90° Corner Tracks in Natural Fields and Urban Lawns.

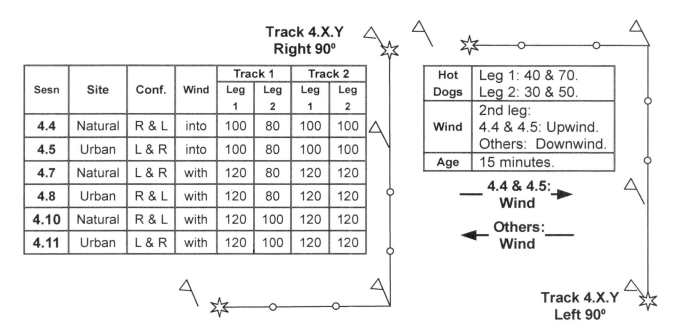

Sesn	Site	Conf.	Wind	Track 1 Leg 1	Track 1 Leg 2	Track 2 Leg 1	Track 2 Leg 2
4.4	Natural	R & L	into	100	80	100	100
4.5	Urban	L & R	into	100	80	100	100
4.7	Natural	L & R	with	120	80	120	120
4.8	Urban	R & L	with	120	80	120	120
4.10	Natural	R & L	with	120	100	120	120
4.11	Urban	L & R	with	120	100	120	120

Hot Dogs	Leg 1: 40 & 70. Leg 2: 30 & 50.
Wind	2nd leg: 4.4 & 4.5: Upwind. Others: Downwind.
Age	15 minutes.

Purpose:
- Introduce 90° Corners.

Tracklayer:
- For these sessions, use areas with little contamination and do not add to it.
- Lay the second leg into the wind for the first two sessions and downwind for the remaining sessions.
- Lay the second leg with short hard steps for the first 20 yards, then use normal steps.
- Extend your arms at the corners to sight landmarks at 90°.
- Use four flags per track so the handler will know exactly where the track is laid.
- Lay the tracks one after the other keeping them about 50 yards apart.
- For high-energy dogs and handlers, it is OK to lay a third track per session.

Handler:
- Keep 15' behind your dog as you approach the corner.
- Stop yourself before the corner.
- Encourage your dog to search and find the new leg.
- Face in the direction of the first leg until your dog commits to the next leg or needs help.

Evaluation:
- In your journal and summary log (page 69) note how your dog works the corners. Also, note how he maintains his attitude on each leg.
- If your dog is confused on most corners after 4 or more of these 90° sessions, skip to Phase 4GT Gradual Turns on page 70.

Sessions 4.x Curbed-Island Serpentines with Curbed Corners

Sesn	Site	Configuration	Wind	Track 1 Yards		Track 2 Yards	
				Leg 1	Leg 2	Leg 1	Leg 2
4.3	Parking Lot	Right, Left Curbs	into	60	20	60	40
4.6	Parking Lot	Right, Left Curbs	with	80	45	80	75
4.9	Parking Lot	Right, Left Curbs	with	100	60	100	90

Parking Lot
15 minutes

Start

Purpose:
- Introduce 90° corners on hard surfaces. Corners should be supported by curbs if possible.

Tracklayer:
- It is useful to use sidewalk chalk to mark the direction of the track crossing each gap.
- At the end of each island, the tracklayer randomly decides to go to the left or right side of the next island, makes a mark on the asphalt with colored chalk, and then proceeds halfway across where she drops a hot dog. She then proceeds in the same direction to the island, marks the curb with chalk, and drops an article a short way down that curb.
- Walk behind the handler on the track.

Handler:
- The handler's job is to patiently let your dog investigate the gaps so he can discover the footprints lead to hot dogs and also to the correct side of the next island.
- Don't rush your dog at the gaps.
- Stay on the end of the previous island until your dog is fully committed to the track in the gap or has reached the far side on the correct side of the island.
- If your dog wants to go down the next island on the wrong side, let him go a ways, but then gently restrain him so he continues to investigate and finds the hot dogs on the correct side.
- At every article, have a fun party with your dog.

Evaluation:
- In your journal and summary log (page 69) note how your dog tracks, indicates the article, how he investigates and sorts out the gaps and the next island, and his level of enthusiasm for the tracks.

Field-Only Sessions 4.1f–4.6f

- These tracks are done in natural fields or on uncontaminated sports fields.
- Session 4.1f see session instructions on page 63. Place hot dogs at 40 & 70 on the first leg, and 35 and 50 on the second leg.
- Sessions 4.2f–4.6f, see session instructions on page 65. Place hot dogs at 40 & 70 on the first leg and 35 & 70 on the second leg.

Session (Info)	Turns	Wind	Track 1 Yards		Track 2 Yards	
			Leg 1	Leg 2	Leg 1	Leg 2
4.0f	Practice Linework — See page 62.					
4.1f (4.1)	Left, Right 135°	into	100	30	100	45
4.2f (4.4)	Right, Left	into	100	30	100	60
4.3f (4.5)	Left, Right	into	100	50	100	100
4.4f (4.7)	Right, Left	with	120	50	120	120
4.5f (4.8)	Left, Right	with	120	80	120	120
4.6f (4.10)	Right, Left	with	120	100	120	120
4.7f	Review and Evaluation — See 4.12 on page 68.					

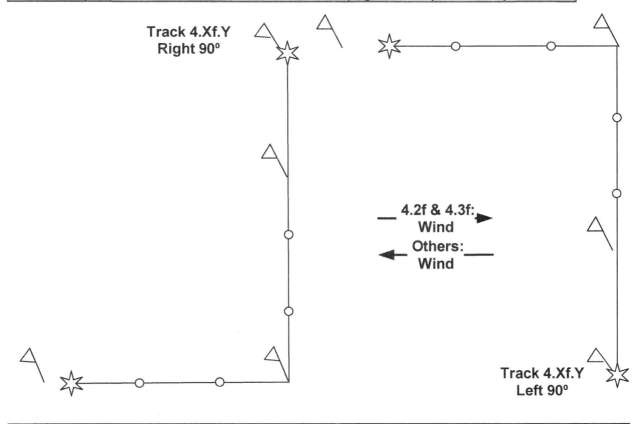

Phase 4. Introducing Corners

Session 4.12 Review and Evaluation.

Session 4.12 is to review how you and your dog are doing on corners. If your dog has the general idea and is fairly successful, just move forward to Phase 5. This is true even if your dog is not perfect as there will be a lot more corner practice in Phase 5.

Remedial work is in order if, after completing all of Phase 4, your dog continues to act lost on many corners, does not seem to adopt any search tactics, and gives up or looks to you for help. Remedial work is also needed if he happens to come upon the next leg (say by chance or after some encouragement), or if he does track it but acts just as confused the next time he comes to a corner.

Dogs who lack self-confidence, some puppies, and dogs who have little spatial awareness are susceptible to confusion on corners. I once tracked three litter sisters who each exhibited this symptom and developed the gradual-turn schedule to help them learn. They all went on to be competent trackers and earn their TDs.

If your dog indicates loss of scent at the corner and then quickly gives up, or if he fails to stop at the corner and just keeps going, you and your dog should do the GT.1–GT.6 progression that uses open angles, and then gradually close up towards 90°.

Sample Journal Log Entry — Phase 4

Session: __4.4__
Dog: __Haute__
Date: __7/2/2015__
Layer: __Sil__
Location: __Fir Island Silage__
Weather: __Warm 78, Sunny__
Wind: __Nil__
Length: __100/80, 100/100__
Age: __15__
XT Age: _____

Evaluation:

Excellent first 90 Corner Session
Tall dense silage grass over her head. Lots of porpoising thru tall grass.

Good search on first track.
She got hot searching on second, helped.

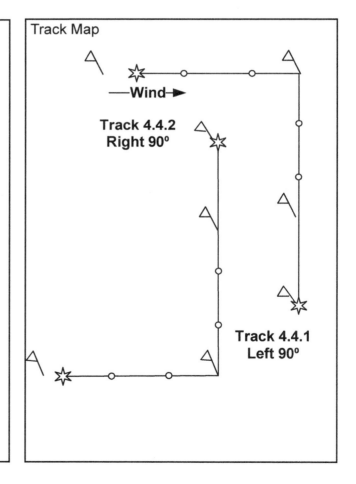

Track Map

Track 4.4.2 Right 90°

Track 4.4.1 Left 90°

Phase 4 Summary Log

Session	Location	Track Config.	Date	Evaluation
4.1	Natural Field	Left, Right 135º		
4.2	Urban Lawn	Right, Left 135º		
4.3	Parking Lot	Right, Left Curbs		
4.4	Natural Field	Right, Left		
4.5	Urban Lawn	Left, Right		
4.6	Parking Lot	Right, Left Curbs		
4.7	Natural Field	Left, Right		
4.8	Urban Lawn	Right, Left		
4.9	Parking Lot	Right, Left Curbs		
4.10	Natural Field	Right, Left		
4.11	Urban Lawn	Left, Right		

Phase 4. Introducing Corners

Phase 4GT.X — Gradual Corners (Optional Remediation)

Gradual corners are a good way to remedially teach dogs who are confused on corners. Over a set of six sessions, introduce slight bends in the track and gradually make them sharper until the dog is handling 90° corners. The turns should be "randomly" to the left and right; however, the second leg must always be exactly upwind. This means you must plan the direction of the first leg so that a turn of the correct angle will be directly upwind.

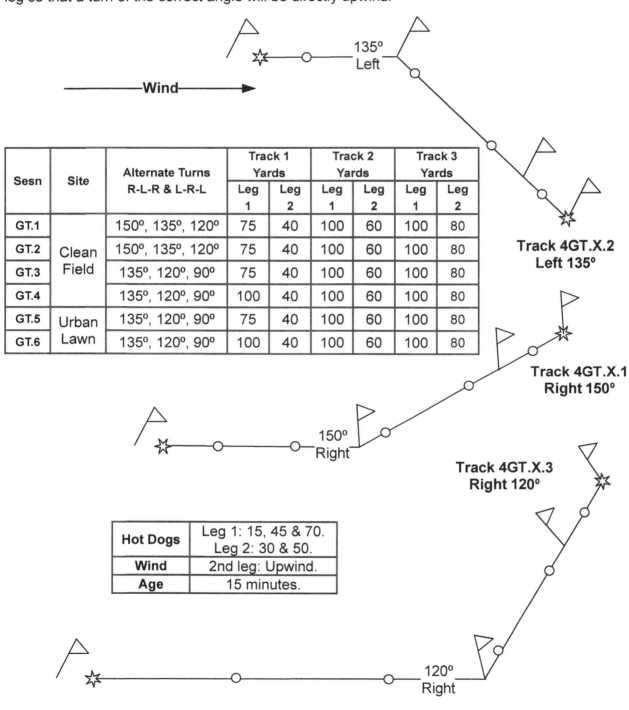

Sesn	Site	Alternate Turns R-L-R & L-R-L	Track 1 Yards		Track 2 Yards		Track 3 Yards	
			Leg 1	Leg 2	Leg 1	Leg 2	Leg 1	Leg 2
GT.1	Clean Field	150°, 135°, 120°	75	40	100	60	100	80
GT.2		150°, 135°, 120°	75	40	100	60	100	80
GT.3		135°, 120°, 90°	75	40	100	60	100	80
GT.4		135°, 120°, 90°	100	40	100	60	100	80
GT.5	Urban Lawn	135°, 120°, 90°	75	40	100	60	100	80
GT.6		135°, 120°, 90°	100	40	100	60	100	80

Hot Dogs	Leg 1: 15, 45 & 70. Leg 2: 30 & 50.
Wind	2nd leg: Upwind.
Age	15 minutes.

Purpose:
- Optional remediation for dogs who remain confused at corners.

Tracklayer:
- The first four gradual-turn tracks are in clean fields (little contamination in last 12 hours).
- The tracklayer must pay attention to the wind, which is tricky because it is the second leg that must be aligned into the wind.
- If there really is no breeze at all, use the prevailing wind direction.
- In order to lay the second leg exactly into the wind, aim the first leg to allow the specified turn angle to bring you directly upwind. See the figure on the next page for a useful compass rose.
- Alternate right and left turns throughout.
- Use four flags per track so the handler will know exactly where the track is laid.
- Use different color flags for each track so the handler does not get confused by flags on the next track.
- Lay both tracks in sequence keeping them 50 or more yards apart. Then run them.

Handler:
- Keep 15' behind dog as you approach the corner.
- Stop yourself before the corner.
- Encourage your dog to search and find the new leg.
- Face down the direction of the first leg until your dog circles or needs help.
- Have a party at every article.

Evaluation:
- In your journal and a blank summary log note how your dog works the corners. Also, note how he maintains his attitude on each leg.
- If your dog continues to act confused during this set of sessions, repeat several sessions with the second leg downwind. You want to see your dog act with confidence before proceeding to the next phase of training.
- After GT.6, return to 4.7 and repeat through 4.12.

Session	Location	Alternate Turns R-L-R and L-R-L	Track 1 Yards		Track 2 Yards		Track 3 Yards	
			Leg 1	Leg 2	Leg 1	Leg 2	Leg 1	Leg 2
GT.1	Clean Field	150°, 135°, 120°	75	40	100	60	100	80
GT.2	Clean Field	150°, 135°, 120°	75	40	100	60	100	80
GT.3	Clean Field	135°, 120°, 90°	75	40	100	60	100	80
GT.4	Clean Field	120°, 90°, 90°	100	40	100	60	100	80
GT.5	Urban Lawn	135°, 120°, 90°	75	40	100	60	100	80
GT.6	Urban Lawn	120°, 90°, 90°	100	40	100	60	100	80
GT.7	Now Repeat 4.7–4.11							

Useful Corner Angles
(Tracklayer Turn Angle)

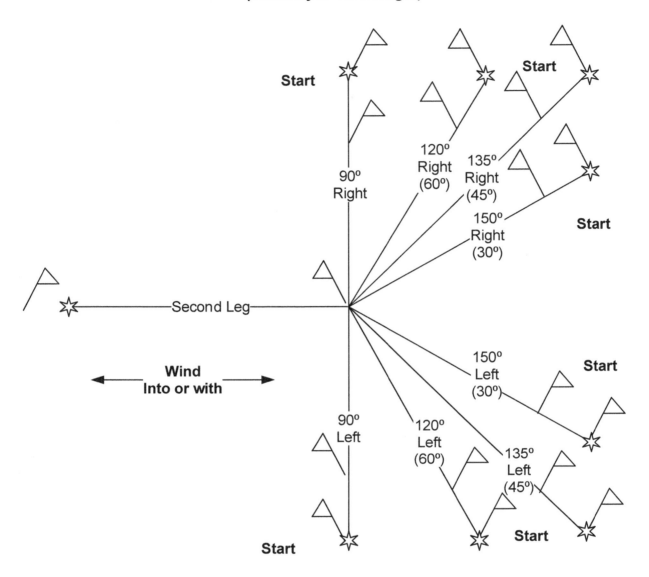

In this diagram, all the tracks start on the right-hand side and end on the left. If you wish to do the opposite when you are in the field, turn the page upside down.

Phase 5. Multiple Corners

Purpose:
- Practice right and left turns on the same track.
- Practice tracking in all wind directions.
- Learn to read the dog.

Strategy:
- Keep the dog on the track.
- Allow the dog to notice the change of scent at a corner, then investigate and search the corner area for the new leg.
- Encourage the dog to take the new leg quickly.
- Watch the dog's posture and the way he scents when he is on and off the track.

How to use this chapter:
- Look through the table below, which summarizes the training structure of this phase, and read the discussion section that follows.
- Practice corner communications on corners with a friend acting like your dog; see page 81.
- Do the 12 sessions that rotate between natural fields and urban lawns.
  - For the alternative field-only training schedule, see page 84.
  - For urban-only training, do natural-field sessions on urban lawns.
- It is OK to also do more parking-lot curbed-island serpentines if you think your dog will benefit.
- Keep a detailed log of each session using a format like the one shown on page 31 and keep a summary log like the one shown on page 86.
- Finally, do the review session on page 85 to evaluate your dog's progress and your own handling skill development.

Phase 5 Session Schedule:

Session	Location	No. Trks	Age Min	Track 1 (yards)			Track 2 (yards)		
				Leg 1	Leg 2	Leg 3	Leg 1	Leg 2	Leg 3
5.0	Practice — see 5.0 on page 81.								
5.1	Natural Field	2	15	100	75	25	100	100	50
5.2	Natural Field	2	15	100	75	25	100	100	50
5.3	Urban Lawn	1	15	100	75	25			
5.4	Urban Lawn	1	15	100	75	50			
5.5	Natural Field	2	15	100	100	75	125	125	100
5.6	Natural Field	2	15	100	100	75	125	125	100
5.7	Urban Lawn	1	15	120	90	45			
5.8	Urban Lawn	1	15	120	90	60			
5.9	Natural Field	2	15	100	100	75	125	125	100
5.10	Natural Field	2	15	100	100	75	125	125	100
5.11	Urban Lawn	1	15	150	120	60			
5.12	Urban Lawn	1	15	150	120	90			
5.13	Review								

Discussion:

These sessions introduce the dog to tracks with multiple corners and give the dog and handler practice with corners under a variety of conditions. The tracks are called zigzag tracks since they make sharp turns (typically 90°) to one side and then to the other. Also, the wind direction is disregarded, and the first track is aged 15 minutes.

Ideally, follow the schedule's pattern of two sessions on natural fields followed by two sessions on urban lawns. The urban lawns can have paths or narrow road crossings. The first session-pair is focused on developing the dog's skill for the field TD and the second session-pair is for developing those same skills in the more complex urban environments of contaminated lawns and hard-surface crossings.

Within a session-pair, the first track first turns left one session and first turns right the other session. Feel free to switch these sessions within pairs if it makes it easier to lay out the two tracks in your fields. In some fields, you can start the second track a short distance from the end of the first. Keep the parallel legs at least 50 yards apart.

If you have fallen behind on your parking-lot curb-work or do not feel your dog has the idea of tracking across small flat gaps, it would be helpful to intersperse some parking-lot tracks within this phase's schedule.

After numerous tracks with a single corner, a few dogs are confused by the second corner. You've changed the rules of the game again. However, they quickly learn this new, more complex game and become comfortable with tracks with multiple corners.

Review the discussion about corners from Phase 4 (page 57) before proceeding. If you are seeing consistent signs of overshooting corners by more than forty feet, playing at the corners, or quitting, reassess your handling and training techniques and consider the gradual-turn sessions discussed in Phase 4 (pages starting on 70).

Optional, Focusing on your Immediate Goals

This is one logical place for a handler to assess if she wants to continue to train for the TD and TDU in parallel or if she wishes to focus on one or the other for a while.

The handler/trainer who wants to focus on the TD at this point could proceed by following the Field-Only schedule in this and all remaining Part I phases. The TDU focused handler could proceed by following the Urban-Only instructions in this and all remaining Part I phases.

The patient handler with less urgent titling goals will proceed to interweave all the sessions in the balanced way indicated by this main schedule.

Reading Your Dog. In this phase, your dog will get to practice lots of corners, and you will improve your own line handling on corners. Most importantly, you will improve your skill in reading your dog because in the next phase the tracks will not be marked by stakes and flags.

You need to notice how your dog acts when he is right on the track, a little bit off the track, and when he has lost the scent. How he holds and moves his head and nose, the arch of his back, the position of his tail, and how he pulls into the harness are all signals that can be read by the handler. Some dogs hold their head low to the ground and move their nose from footprint to footprint, creating a side-to-side swing of the head. Other dogs hold their head much higher, sniffing the scent as it rises off the ground. Some dogs hold their tail up when on the track, some hold it straight back, and others hold it down between their legs.

It is important for you to learn your dog's posture and actions:
- when he is tracking,
- when he is off the track,
- when he runs out of scent at a corner,
- when he investigates contamination,
- and when he finds and commits to the next leg.

Each day, note in your journal what behavioral signs you noticed your dog exhibit on the track.

Videoing your track is an effective way to learn to read your dog. Use an action camera like one of the GoPro models or similar cameras by Sony, Kodak, Nikon, and others. They are available at a wide variety of price points with just as wide a variety of features. High definition and 60 FPS operation are great, but even standard definition will help you. Alternatively, have your tracklayer video you using your smartphone or tablet. This view will show both you and the dog and can point out handling errors as well as dog behavior.

Reading the Landscape. You will also find it useful to learn to read the landscape so you have a better idea of where you are in the field. The first step in reading the landscape is to note a landmark in line with the leg you are on. Then when the dog loses scent at the next corner, you can stay oriented in the field as the dog searches for the next leg.

Practice the first step in reading the landscape by looking over your dog after he has committed to a new leg and note the landmark ahead of the dog. Probably, the tracklayer used this same landmark. You can confirm this landmark by also noting whether the next corner flag is in line with the dog and landscape as well.

Communication on the Corner. It is essential that you develop a consistent means of communication with your dog on corners. We have discussed one aspect of communication: reading your dog. There is another equally important aspect that will help you out of many difficult situations — by establishing a system of two-way corner communication, you can double-check that your dog is taking the correct track after a corner.

On a blind corner where you cannot see where the corner is or where the new leg goes, it is natural to be a little uncertain whether the dog is correct. Since you will be facing blind corners in the next phase, it is time to start developing your corner communication while you still have flags to reassure yourself that all is well.

A system of communication that works very well consists of this sequence of steps:
- Your dog clearly indicates loss of track within a few yards of the actual corner.
- You read your dog's behavior, recognize the loss of track, and stop.
- Your dog purposefully searches for the new leg while you maintain a light-comfortable tension.
- Your dog notices the new leg as he searches and follows it several feet as you let the line out while maintaining light-comfortable tension.
- You increase the tension slightly and verbally ask your dog "Is this the good track?"
- Your dog leans into the harness (His way of saying "Yes!").
- You immediately resume your normal light-comfortable tension, step out behind your dog, and praise your dog quietly.
- You climb back up the line so you are following at 15–20'.
- Your dog receives a reward a short distance down the new leg.

Communication is a two-way process. Both you and your dog have important things to communicate to the other. Your dog tells you about the track scent by his actions. You communicate your questions and confidence through slight adjustments in line tension.

This system of corner communication works so well because the skilled dog will invariably veer off a false track he is investigating when questioned about the good track. Therefore, if your dog does not veer off the line he is taking, you have great confidence he is on the original good track. You communicate your confidence to your dog quickly, which strengthens his self-confidence. Now, if your dog is distracted even a few yards farther along the track, say by a deer crossing or another scenting difficulty, you are both ready to handle this new situation. Without this type of communication, you will be uncertain about the new track direction when the subsequent distraction confounds the situation.

Work on this process of corner communication while the flags are still up and there is always a food drop 30–40 yards past the corner to reward your dog for pulling into the harness when you question him. Avoid jerking the line when you increase the tension and ask the question. Some dogs may be initially put off by even a gentle increase in tension, but when you happily encourage your dog to continue on the new leg; he will learn it is just something that you do on corners. He will quickly come to understand the communication and appreciate your clarity.

Trust vs Disbelief

There is a saying in the tracking community to be the "dope on the end of the rope." I have never felt that was good advice although there are times when it might be appropriate.

If you follow a well-structured training program, your dog will be clear, confident, and committed on the track and you will be able to trust him and follow him to the end of the track.

On the other hand, if your dog lacks confidence following realistic test-like tracks, you will distrust your dog in a test and end up either messing him up or following him in the wrong direction, either to the whistle. It is only in this case that you might luckily succeed by being a dope and following your dog wherever.

Build skill and confidence in your dog, build skill and confidence in yourself, and you can enjoy the pleasure of trusting your confident dog on a blind track.

Wind Direction. Typical tracking behavior of a dog tracking in several different wind directions is illustrated in the figure below. The wind is blowing from the top of the page to the bottom for all the four tracks shown. A particular dog's path is shown by the curving-dashed lines.

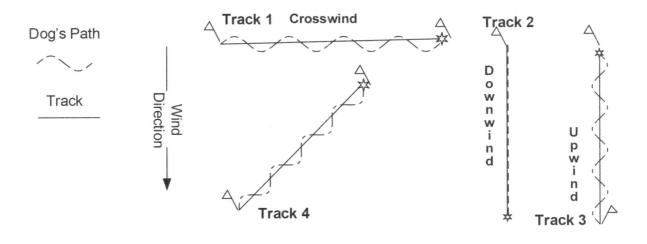

Track 1 is laid in a 90° crosswind. The dog tends to be blown downwind of the track. He may naturally come back to the track and track there awhile before being blown downwind again. In some conditions, he may even track upwind of the track.

Track 2 is laid directly downwind. Most dogs who have been trained to stay close to the track will be quite good about staying right on top of a downwind leg.

Track 3 is laid directly upwind. Many dogs will cast from side to side while tracking upwind as shown by the wavy lines. They may follow the swirling scent coming downwind from the track ahead, or they may attempt to detect differences in scent strength.

Track 4 is laid at a 45° angle upwind. Dogs tend to show a combination of the tracking behavior on upwind and crosswind tracks on such angled tracks.

It is important to understand these wind-influenced tracking behaviors so you can recognize them in the field and train your dog to stay very close to the footsteps. You train by raising your arm and increasing the tension when the dog is off the track. The height of your arm and the amount of tension are proportional to the distance the dog is off the track. You want to make it easy for the dog to track right on the track, somewhat difficult for the dog to track three feet off the track, and nearly impossible for the dog to track six to ten feet off the track. This line tension contrast in combination with the frequent food rewards that occur right on the track will tend to make the dog track close to the footsteps. This is also the most reliable place to track.

If you allow the dog the freedom to track ten to twenty feet off the track, your dog will learn it can follow the track out there by detecting subtle differences in scent strength along the fringe of the scent coming from the track. However, such fringe followers do not make reliable trackers, because the swirling eddies make the fringe a very complex and difficult place to track. In addition, it is much easier to read a dog that is tracking in a straight line than it is to read one tracking an irregular fringe. So it is best to teach the dog that no matter how good a fringe follower he

---

Phase 5. Multiple Corners

might be, he will be a better tracker and have the easiest time by staying right over the footsteps. Moreover, you will be able to read his tracking behavior much more easily when the flags come down. Since you will not know where the track goes, you will have to read your dog to know when he is on the track and when he is having difficulty finding it. If your dog is primarily using the fringe to follow the scent, consider the remedial training on page 406.

Scent Phenomena. Although people cannot smell nearly as well as a dog can smell, observant handlers can learn a lot by watching their dog's behavior in different conditions. I will point out some phenomena to look for, the dog behavior commonly associated with it, and a training behavior you should adopt when it happens with your dog.

1. Scent tends to pool in low areas. Dogs may be drawn off a track into depressions of various sizes. These pools probably smell similar to the track, so it is hardly a mistake for the dog to check it out. Allow your dog to briefly check out the pool, then happily encourage him to continue on the good track even if you have to point it out to him.
2. Scent rises as the sun warms a sloping meadow. You will often see a dog track upslope of the track on a windless sunny morning. Treat it like a crosswind — make it fun to stay right on the track.
3. Scent falls downhill. Without the sun warming the air and causing it to rise, one tends to see a dog tracking downslope of a track traversing a hillside. Again, treat it like a crosswind — make it fun to stay right on the track.
4. Scent hangs along fences and brush lines. When a track goes near a fence or brush line, you may see the dog go over to the fence or brush and act like he is tracking over there. As with scent pooling in low areas, allow your dog to check it out, but then happily encourage him to continue right on the track. Your dog is likely to become unreliable if he is allowed to follow the irregular fringe line of the scent.
5. The track ages faster in hot, dry weather than in cool, damp weather. Dogs act like the scent is fainter or harder to find in hot, dry weather unless they are already accustomed to it. Be extra careful to run your tracks at the specified time in hot, dry weather. If it is unusually hot and dry, run the track a little younger than specified in the schedule.
6. Different vegetation affects how the tracks smell. Dogs tracking in one type of vegetation, like grass, break off the track at a transition to a different type of vegetation, like weeds. They notice the difference in scent and search around for the original track. This is good. They have to learn that the track in the weeds is the same as the one in the grass. Teach this by first always placing an extra food drop 10–20 yards past a change in vegetation. Then, allow him to search by himself for a short while. If the dog does not commit to the leg in the new vegetation, happily help and encourage him to do so.
7. Scent is swept away from the top of hills. Dogs tracking over the crest of a ridge line or knoll of a hill tend to lose the track there and need to search for it again. Perhaps the microclimate of the knoll causes the vegetation to be sparser than the surrounding hillside and the soil to be more compact. Perhaps the geometry of the knoll allows the wind to sweep much of the scent away. With enough practice, dogs do learn to track over a knoll, but it is clearly more difficult for them than flat areas. Train for knolls and ridge lines, just like changes in vegetation.
8. Scent is pushed away from tree lines. If a track parallels a tree line close to the trees, dogs will sometimes track well away from the trees and the track. As a first approximation, the turbulence caused by the tree line causes the scent to swirl as far out into the field as the trees are tall. Therefore, the dogs that track away from the tree line may be really tracking the scent that has swirled away from the track. In training, treat this just like a crosswind and keep your dog close to the track. See the diagram on page 306 for a visualization of this type of turbulence.

Watch for these and other behaviors in your dog while he is tracking. Being familiar with them can help you to read your dog better on a blind track. For example, on a blind track, if my dog tracked down a hill and then lost the track, I must be willing to back farther up the hill to find a corner than if it was a perfectly level area. Understanding these phenomena also helps with training. For example, knowing it is "normal" for a partially trained dog to track poorly on an over-aged track on a hot day, you can help the dog quickly and freely in this unfortunate situation. You also know the next track should be younger than normal and easier than normal to maintain the dog's motivation to track.

Urban Scent Phenomena are often viewed as special or different than those found in natural fields. In fact, each effect in the urban environment parallels those in a more natural environment. But the sharper definition of urban features can make the effects very strong and so much more noticeable. We have already seen our dogs tell us that scent pools along curbs, and as we expand our tracking into a wider variety of urban settings, we will see solid hedges, fencing and buildings acting much like fences, brush line, and tree lines in natural fields. The man-made urban structures more strongly affect the air flow that moves scent around than their natural counterparts.

Corner Communications

Corner communication is the most important handler skill you can learn and is a prerequisite for following a dog on a blind track. Become the handler your dog deserves by learning how to handle on a corner so you stay in sync with your dog and he stays in sync with you.

See Session 5.0 Practice Corner Communication on page 81.

TD Tracking in the Suburbs

As you proceed through your dog's training, there may be times when you cannot get out to natural fields to do your training. As mentioned on page 8 and again on page 165, you can do a lot of "field" tracking on sports fields or parks. Lawn grass apparently smells a little different than field grass to your dog and there will be more human and dog natural contamination than you find in most rural fields, but the dog can find the track and learn his skills while you learn your skills as well. I tend to choose the least contaminated locations and times of day when this is necessary.

Handling Tips — Starting and Corner Rituals. It is good to develop a consistent ritual for starts as well as corners. So your dog will be familiar with your ritual behavior and you will both be ready for blind tracks in the next phase. Your particular ritual may vary from mine; use what works best for your dog.

Here is some of my own ritual:
- Put the harness on either in the car or about 10' from the start flag.
- I walk the dog up to the start flag while the 40' line is still attached to the collar.
- Once at the start flag, I hold the dog there while switching the line to his harness.
- It is OK for your dog to stand, sit or down; whichever he prefers.
- Once the line is attached to the harness, I continue to hold the dog with his nose right over the start article or scent pad for a slow count of 10 or 20.
- Then I stand up saying "Find it" and leaving the article on the ground for the moment.
- I treat the start as a corner that I have not tracked into, so my handling at the start is just like at a corner. I am lucky since the directional flag indicates where the track goes, but that is a bonus. I use the same corner communication I will use at each corner.
- Once the dog is committed on the good track, I ask him "Is this the good track?" and he answers "yes", then I pick up the article and put it in my pocket, so both hands are free to handle the line smoothly.

Along each leg, I look over my dog and notice a landmark. It may or may not be the same landmark the tracklayer used, but it is useful to have a general reference. If the dog bends away from my first landmark and is clearly tracking, I find a better landmark.

When the dog indicates loss of track or otherwise has a change in behavior, I say "Yippee! We are at a corner that might go straight." Of course, in this phase with all the flags, you will know if it is a corner or not, but it is good to practice your corner ritual just as it is good to practice your starting ritual. So I stop and let the dog search or even verbally encourage him to search if needed.

By establishing consistent start and corner procedures, you will become a good handler while there are still flags to keep you from going too far astray, and your dog will become used to your procedures and comfortable with them. You will practice the corner procedure in this phase.

Tracklaying Tips. Intentional contamination is useful for the urban tracks in this phase. We stopped adding intentional contamination over the top of your urban-lawn tracks in Phase 4; now is a good time to add them in again. Ask the contamination layer(s) to avoid crossing within 20 yards of the start or a corner but once or twice per leg would be helpful.

When asked to lay a U-shaped track and the field is too narrow to allow a full-length second leg, instead lay a zigzag that is easier for tracks with short second legs. Or when asked to lay a zigzag and the field is not long enough for both full-length first and third legs, lay a U-shaped track instead.

There is an extensive section in the next phase on finding landmarks and other tracklaying skills, starting on page 92.

Session 5.0 Practice Corner Communications

Just as you practiced line handling at the beginning of Phase 2 and your corner line handling at the beginning of Phase 4, this time you are going to practice the full corner-communications line handling with a friend acting like your dog. Your friend can give you verbal feedback about what your line handling feels like. The exercise is very valuable experience for both handler and the person playing the dog.

Get together with a friend and have them play the part of your dog. For example, if your dog is playful, your friend should be playful. You should run through several corners and practice trying to increase the tension just a little after your dog starts to line out on the track. Your "dog" should give you verbal feedback about whether your line handling was well-timed and smooth. A common mistake handlers make is to move away from their initial pivot point too soon. Stay in place, use the full length of your line and let your dog be responsible for searching for, finding and committing to the new leg.

Dog Actor:
- Give the handler feedback when the line tension is too light or too strong, or when you feel jerking checks.
- For the first 2–3 practice corners, be a good dog and search and find the new leg quickly.
- For the next corner track, try to keep going in a straight line past the corner.
- For the next practice corner, search only on the side away from the new leg until the handler faces in the new direction or encourages you gently to go search over there.

Handler:
- Keep 15' behind the "dog" as you approach the corner.
- Stop yourself before the corner, perhaps 5–10' before.
- Practice the whole sequence of corner communications:
  - Your dog's change of behavior indicates loss of track within a few yards of the actual corner.
  - You read your dog's behavior, recognize the loss of track and stop.
  - Your dog purposefully searches for the new leg while you maintain light-comfortable tension.
  - Your dog notices the new leg as he searches and follows it several feet as you let the line out, all the while maintaining light-comfortable tension.
  - You increase the tension slightly and verbally ask the dog "Is this the good track?"
  - Your dog leans into the harness (His way of saying "Yes!").
  - You immediately resume your normal light-comfortable tension, step out behind the dog and praise him quietly.
  - You climb back up the line so you are following at 15–20'.
  - Your dog receives a reward a short distance down the new leg — say "Attagirl" to your dog actor.
- If "dog" does not find new leg quickly, face down the direction of the first leg until the "dog" commits to the next leg, or you have to help him (see page 59).

Sessions 5.X Natural-Field Zigzags.

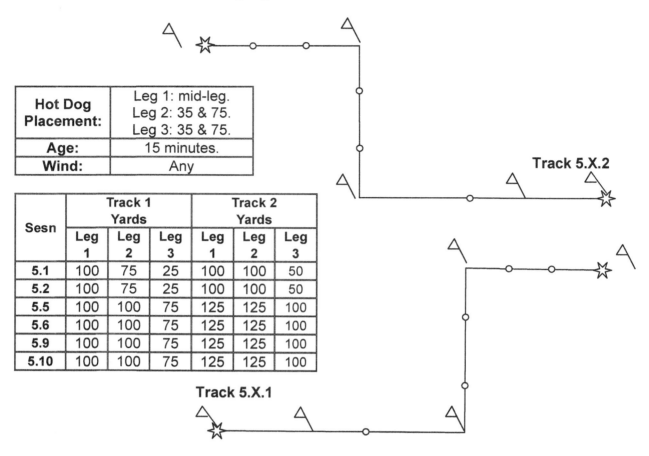

Hot Dog Placement:	Leg 1: mid-leg. Leg 2: 35 & 75. Leg 3: 35 & 75.
Age:	15 minutes.
Wind:	Any

Sesn	Track 1 Yards			Track 2 Yards		
	Leg 1	Leg 2	Leg 3	Leg 1	Leg 2	Leg 3
5.1	100	75	25	100	100	50
5.2	100	75	25	100	100	50
5.5	100	100	75	125	125	100
5.6	100	100	75	125	125	100
5.9	100	100	75	125	125	100
5.10	100	100	75	125	125	100

Purpose:
- Introduce two-turn tracks and practice tracking in all wind directions.

Tracklayer:
- Make a map of these tracks as you lay them and include landmarks.
- Lay the first 20 yards of the second and third legs with short hard steps.
- Extend your arms at the corners to sight landmarks at 90 degrees.
- Use five flags per track so the handler will know exactly where the track is laid.

Handler:
- Develop a consistent start ritual as discussed on page 80.
- Stop before the corner. Maintain good line-tension at the corner.
- Practice Corner Communication.
- Make sure you are using line tension to keep your dog close to the legs in all wind conditions.

Evaluation:
- Note in your journal and your summary log (page 86) how your dog works the corners and how he maintains his attitude on each leg.
- Note how you are reading your dog — what signs indicate he is on or off the track.

Sessions 5.X Urban-Lawn Zigzags.

Sesn	Track Yards		
	Leg 1	Leg 2	Leg 3
5.3	100	75	25
5.4	100	75	50
5.7	120	90	45
5.8	120	90	60
5.11	150	120	60
5.12	150	120	90

Simultaneous Contamination

Track 5.X.1

Hot Dog & Article Placement:	Leg 1: mid-leg. Leg 2 & 3: Small Article.
Age:	15 minutes.
Wind:	Any

Purpose:
- Introduce two-turn tracks and practice tracking in all wind directions.

Tracklayer:
- Make a map of these tracks as you lay them and include landmarks.
- Lay the first 20 yards of the second and third legs with short hard steps.
- Use five flags per track so the handler will know exactly where the track is laid.
- It is OK to do two of these zigzags per session if the dog and handler want more work.

Contamination Tracklayer:
- Lay contamination right after tracklayer lays each leg. Stay 20 yards from start and corners.

Handler:
- Let your dog investigate each contamination track to the full-line length, then restrain, reel-in and re-scent.
- Stop before the corner. Maintain good line tension at the corner.
- Practice Corner Communication.
- If needed, encourage your dog to search and find the new leg.
- Have a fun party at every article. Don't rush to restart your dog even if he wants to get back to the track quickly.

Evaluation:
- Note in your journal and your summary log (page 86) how your dog works the corners, how he maintains his attitude on each leg, and whether he is making the right contamination choices.
- Note how you are reading your dog — what signs indicate he is on or off the track.

Field-Only Sessions 5.1f–5.7f

- These tracks are done in natural fields or on uncontaminated sports fields.
- Session 5.0f, practice corner communications with a friend playing the dog (page 81).
- Sessions 5.1f–5.6f, see detailed session instructions on page 82.
- Each track has two corners in a zigzag (one to the right and one to the left).

| Session | Track 1 (yards) | | | Track 2 (yards) | | |
(Info)	Leg 1	Leg 2	Leg 3	Leg 1	Leg 2	Leg 3
5.0f	Practice Corner Communications on page 81.					
5.1f (5.1)	100	75	25	100	100	50
5.2f (5.2)	100	75	25	100	100	50
5.3f (5.5)	100	100	75	125	125	100
5.4f (5.6)	100	100	75	125	125	100
5.5f (5,9)	100	100	75	125	125	100
5.6f (5.10)	100	100	75	125	125	100
5.7f	Review and Evaluation — see page 85.					

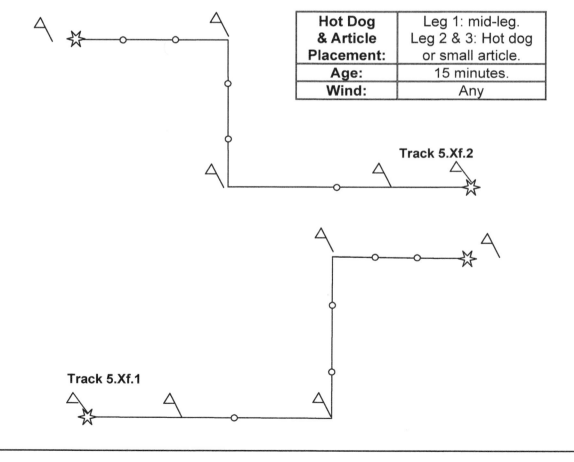

Hot Dog & Article Placement:	Leg 1: mid-leg. Leg 2 & 3: Hot dog or small article.
Age:	15 minutes.
Wind:	Any

Track 5.Xf.2

Track 5.Xf.1

Session 5.13 — Review

Purpose:
- Review your dog's progress and summarize his accomplishments.

Evaluation:
- You should be starting to feel comfortable with your line handling at the corners.
- Your dog should be enthusiastically tracking the legs and taking most corners with little problem. Ideally, your dog diligently searches at each corner and quickly becomes Clear-Confident-Committed to each leg.
- Write a summary of how your dog takes corners, how you handle him at the corners, and how to read him when he is past a corner and when he has taken the second leg.
- Write a review of his enthusiasm to start, his enthusiasm during the track, his enthusiasm on the corners, how close to the track he stays, how he reacts to the corners, and how he indicates the articles.
- Write down what you can do to encourage him to improve his needed skills.

Progress Decision:

The flags are going to disappear in Phase 6, and many people find that scary. Don't worry; it is part of the learning process where you will get to practice actually reading your dog while your tracklayer acts as a safety net and keeps you from getting too far afield.

To me, Phase 6 is the most fun phase because neither my dog nor I have to be perfect. My dog gets to learn to stay with the track in spite of his handler being a little or even a lot uncertain. And I get to learn that I can trust him because we have trained many times, and I have shaped his tracking behavior so I can read him and believe him.

The question of whether you move forward to Phase 6 or do some remediation first does not come down to how you feel about it. It comes down to how your dog is doing. Look back at your log book for this phase and estimate whether he did at least 70% of the corners on his own. By on his own, I mean without restraining him from overshooting or taking the wrong direction, or his needing other forms of help (page 59).

Only look at the corners themselves, not at the intentional or natural contamination. If he exceeds this 70% threshold, move forward because he has an excellent understanding of his job and you need to put yourself into blind track situations to fully learn your job in your tracking partnership.

If your dog is still making a lot of errors, see if the errors are mostly confined to just the natural fields or mostly to the urban lawns. If mainly one or the other, focus some remedial sessions on that environment. Also, solicit feedback from your more experienced tracking friends. Take a video of you and your dog tracking to see if you are doing anything to confuse your dog on these corners.

Phase 5 Summary Log

Session	Location	Date	Actual Age	Evaluation
5.1	Natural Field			
5.2	Natural Field			
5.3	Urban Lawn			
5.4	Urban Lawn			
5.5	Natural Field			
5.6	Natural Field			
5.7	Urban Lawn			
5.8	Urban Lawn			
5.9	Natural Field			
5.10	Natural Field			
5.11	Urban Lawn			
5.12	Urban Lawn			

Phase 6. Reading Your Dog

Purpose:
- Teach the handler to read the dog without flags and to organize the search at corners.
- Teach the dog to circle 360° at the corners.
- Continue practicing tracks on contaminated urban lawns while adding more transitions.

Strategy:
- Remove all but the first two flags on the natural-field tracks.
- Some tracks include an acute angle to induce the dog to overshoot the corner and circle 360°.
- Urban-lawn tracks add more path and narrow road crossings while retaining flagged corners.

How to use this chapter:
- Study the table on the next page, which summarizes the training structure of this phase, and read the discussion section that starts below.
- Do the 12 sessions that rotate between natural fields and urban lawns (see pages 101+).
  - For the alternative field-only training schedule, see page 104.
  - For alternative urban-only training, use minimally-contaminated urban lawns for the natural-field sessions in the main schedule on page 88.
- Continue to keep a detailed log of each session using a format like the one shown on page 31 and keep a summary log like the one shown on page 106.
- Finally, do the review session on page 105 to evaluate the team's progress.

Discussion:

As a handler and trainer, it is a wonderful feeling to have developed your dog's skills and now get to focus on your own handling skills, particularly your ability to read your dog and trust him. Congratulations on your accomplishment; expect the fun to continue.

The natural-field tracks in this phase will be your first blind tracks. Three of the sessions feature tracks with acute turns that will be especially fun and exciting tracks for both you and your dog. These exercises help you to understand how to read your dog and show you how to organize his search for a lost track.

If you have been laying most of your dog's tracks yourself, go to extra effort to get tracklayers for several of the natural-field tracks, including the ones with acute corners so you have the opportunity to experience blind tracks. If there is no one in your area who can lay tracks for you, lay them yourself. Remember to handle neutrally, perhaps squinting with your hat brim pulled low over your eyes so you only look at your dog and not the landmarks.

Those who know that AKC rules prohibit acute-angle turns in test tracks may feel that this is an unfair test for an inexperienced dog and handler. As you will see in the discussion below, the point is to teach the handler and dog how to handle difficult corners, not to trick the dog or the handler. Fair or unfair, the acute turn track is a great learning experience for the dogs and handlers regardless of whether they easily succeed, they have to work at it, and even for those who need help from the tracklayer — every team benefits. What is really important to your future success as a tracking team is to learn from the exercise!

Phase 6 Session Schedule:

Sesn	Location	Config.	Age	Leg 1	Turn °	Leg 2	Turn °	Leg 3	Turn °	Leg 4
6.1	Natural Field	3-Corner All 90°	15	100	90	75	90	100	90	50
6.2	Natural Field	Downhill Downwind Acute	15	100	90	100	135	75	45	125
6.3	Urban Lawn w/ Paths	3-Corner Urban Lawn	15	60	90–120	40	90–120	40	90–120	40
6.4	Urban Lawn w/ Paths	3-Corner Urban Lawn	15	100	90–120	50	90–120	50	90–120	30
6.5	Natural Field	3-Corner All 90°	20	100	90	100	90	125	90	75
6.6	Natural Field	Downhill Downwind Acute	20	100	90	100	45	100	135	150
6.7	Urban Lawn w/ Paths	3-Corner Urban Lawn	20	75	90–120	60	90–120	60	90–120	40
6.8	Urban Lawn w/ Paths	3-Corner Urban Lawn	20	100	90–120	75	90–120	60	90–120	40
6.9	Natural Field	3-Corner All 90°	25	125	90	125	90	125	90	125
6.10	Natural Field	Downhill Downwind Acute	25	100	135	150	90	100	45	150
6.11	Urban Lawn w/ Paths	3-Corner Urban Lawn	25	90	90–120	75	90–120	60	90–120	40
6.12	Urban Lawn w/ Paths	3-Corner Urban Lawn	25	120	90–120	90	90–120	75	90–120	60
6.13		Review								

The tracks of the previous two phases were designed to teach the dog to notice the corner immediately and to take the new leg quickly and efficiently. By this stage, most dogs are noticing most corners within a few feet of the corner and are picking up the new leg with little delay. In addition, many dogs are marching around at least some of the corners without hesitation. This is great! It is exactly what we want our dogs to do. On a blind track, like a certification or test track, the dog might have difficulty with a corner because of unfamiliar or unusual tracking conditions. Because he might get some distance from a track, we must teach him how to find a new leg if he gets well past a corner or off a leg. The downwind-downhill acute tracks are an effective way to set up the situation where your dog gets well past the corner and needs to search behind you.

Downwind-downhill acute-angle corners are used to induce the dog and handler to go past the corner. The wind blows the scent of the track past the corner giving the dog something to smell there. On a downhill leg, most dogs speed up, so they will naturally tend to overshoot the corner due to speed and momentum. Also, scent often drifts downhill, helping the wind carry the scent past the corner.

If the track design works as planned, the dog will take the handler (who is 15–20' behind the dog) well past the corner. The tracklayer should stop the handler when the handler is about 10' past the corner. So when she stops, the dog will have to circle behind the handler at least 10' to find the new leg.

Handling at a Blind Corner. The handler typically passes the acute corner and does not know where the next leg goes. The handler is going to feel quite lost. Nevertheless, it is important that the handler executes her job with care and confidence. Her job, of course, is to organize the search, and makes sure the dog investigates all directions at several different distances from the handler. The following discussion explains in detail how the handler can help her dog search the full 360° while maintaining her own orientation in the field.

As you follow your dog on each new leg, notice a landmark over your dog as he tracks in a straight line. This is the handler's reference direction that is useful when the dog breaks off at the next corner. When the dog's change in behavior indicates he is at or past a corner, you should stop. From there, the track may go in any direction except straight back the way you came. In addition to your incoming leg landmark reference direction, you may also notice a ground marker at the stopping point that will help you stay in place while pivoting.

The dog should circle the handler at various distances until he detects and takes the new leg. However, some dogs have learned in the last two phases of training that the corner is always between him and the handler. Therefore, the dog has had no reason to go behind the handler. These dogs will circle and search in front of the handler, but they are reluctant to circle behind the handler. Such dogs will respond well to the pivoting described below.

The handler stops, continues to face the reference direction and expects the dog to search in front. If the dog circles in one direction or the other to about 60°, the handler should quietly pivot in that direction by 90°. The handler's reference direction should now be over one shoulder, and the inward leg (and tracklayer) should be over the other shoulder. With luck, the dog will continue to search in that direction. When the dog again gets to 60° relative to the handler's new direction, again quietly pivot 90° to face directly back toward the inward leg and the tracklayer. If the dog turns around and heads back toward the reference direction, the handler should quite happily wait until the dog gets to 60° relative to the handler's direction and then pivot in that direction by 90°. The Golden Search Rule is: "Whenever the dog gets within 30° of a shoulder, pivot toward that shoulder".

At some point in this search, the dog will find the new leg, and you will be off again. You will need to recognize his on-track behavior and be willing to go with the dog when he indicates the new leg. Before this commitment happens, the handler needs to stay aware of where the dog has searched and where he has not yet searched so she will be able to support the dog throughout the corner experience.

Phase 6. Reading Your Dog

The handler may control how far from the handler the dog circles. You want to get the dog to do two or three complete circles, each at a difference distance. If the dog circles only at one distance, the handler should reel-in some line or let some line out to encourage the dog to look more places. The exact distances depend on the handler and the dog, but ideally, the first would be between 6' and 10', the second should be between 10' and 20', and the third would be between 20' and 40'. For an energetic dog, a third circle at 30' and a fourth circle at 40' is safer than a single third circle somewhere between 20' and 40'.

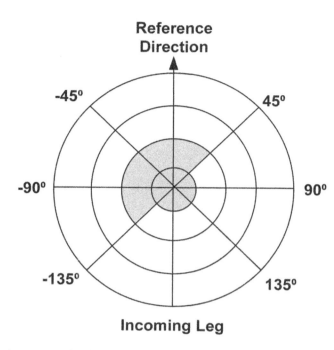

As your dog circles, you are noting and remembering exactly where he has searched and where he has not searched. One way to remember where he has searched is to keep a mental picture of a circle in mind and fill in the sections of the circle as your dog searches. The figure on the left shows a typical mental picture when the dog has completed one complete circle at 10' and has circled part of the next circle at 20'. If your dog has not committed to a new leg and there is an area he has not searched, you should pivot toward that direction until your dog searches it.

Once the dog has circled three or four times from this pivot point, the handler must be willing to back up about 15' toward the inward leg and try circling again. In a real test, the handler must be willing to back up several times. In this training exercise, once should be enough. Induce the dog to circle again at two or three distances. The dog will cross the new leg at several different places and at several different angles, so he is likely to recognize it and commit to it on one of these crossings.

In all this circling, the dog will cross the incoming leg several times. He may try to backtrack it. If he does, only let him go a few feet before increasing the tension and saying something like "Isn't that where we came from? Find the good track. That's right. You can find it." Steadily increase the tension until you have stopped the dog within 10' of where he started to backtrack or until he has diverged from the inward leg. Since we never double or triple lay any legs, he will quickly learn there is nothing to be gained by backtracking.

If your dog comes to your feet and looks at you plaintively, he may be saying "I'm confused, help me." The first time he does this, encourage him to get back to tracking in a happy voice. If he does it repeatedly on a particular corner, or if he cannot be induced to search again, it is time for you to move. Take a few steps back towards the inward leg. Happily, enthusiastically, excitedly, tell him something like: "Find it. Go ahead, you can find it. Yes, you can do it. That's good, find it!" Keep chatting to your dog and keep taking steps backward until you are at the corner (the tracklayer can tell you when you are at the corner). If your dog still won't search, take a few steps down the new leg and happily encourage your dog to "Find it!" Keep walking down the new leg with your dog on a short line encouraging him to find it until he starts tracking again.

It is not a serious problem for your dog to quit on a complex new situation like this acute corner. By happily getting him past it, we teach him that there is more to find and that it is fun to find it. Your dog may feel it is unfair to be faced with something new and difficult, but we know that such situations are a necessary part of training. It is important for your dog to learn that even if he loses the track, he can find it again by searching diligently.

A dog that quits every time he is faced with a new situation or that repeatedly quits when faced with difficulty needs confidence building and tracking drive building. See Phase 8 on problem solving for some ideas, pages 133+. However, dogs that are taught using positive methods (like this one) are unlikely to develop serious quitting problems.

To recapitulate the corner handling procedure:
- Stay 20' behind your dog as you approach the corner.
- Note a distant landmark in front of your dog.
- Allow your dog to take you past the corner but no more than 10' past the corner.
- Note a landmark on the ground at your feet where you stop.
- Encourage your dog to circle.
- Turn 90° whenever your dog gets within 30° of either shoulder.
- Turn even earlier if your dog is stuck in one area and has not searched other areas.
- Control the distance your dog circles and have him circle at several distances.
- Back up to the corner if the dog has circled three or four times or if he wants to quit.
- Encourage your dog down the new leg if he won't take it.
- Stay calm and happy no matter how flustered you really want to be.

This CORNERS mnemonic was created by Carla Baker at a seminar and may help you remember the procedure.

C	Change of behavior is noticed.
O	Own your spot — stop right there.
R	Reconnoiter — notice where you are.
N	Note your dog's intent and where he lines out.
E	Enquire "Is this the good track?"
R	Response from the dog confirms.
S	Say "I believe You", then climb up the line.

Since half of Phase 6 tracks are blind, it is helpful to have some self-talk that will go a long way towards letting your dog solve the corner problem and find the new leg, rather than guessing which way it goes and possibly encouraging your dog to go in the wrong direction.

I call this important handling technique for blind tracks **At a Corner That Might Go Straight**. The technique complements the basic corner handling procedure with a handler mental approach to keep the handler neutral and avoid having the handler make subtle or even obvious suggestions on which way to go.

- Whenever your dog signals a loss or change in scent, you stop as you have learned to do for marked corners. Now smile and say to yourself "Yippee! We are at a corner that might go straight. This is the best place to be. Life is good." And then follow all the pivoting rules, line-tension rules and corner-communications rules described in the bulleted list above or the CORNERS mnemonic.

You will be surprised how effective this self-talk is to keep you calm and help you avoid rushing your dog into a quick decision. Essentially it breaks the blind track down into a start and 4–6 simple straight legs. The start is a corner that you have not tracked into and almost certainly goes straight in TD and TDU. The dog lines out on each leg, you do your corner communications and you step off following your dog, confident that this is a good track. So a TD or TDU test is not a very complicated thing, just a series of 4–6 straight legs separated by corners that might go straight. You have trained your dog and trained yourself, so you will both do great.

In addition to providing a simple handling procedure that is widely applicable to all tracking situations, it also shifts the responsibility to the dog for making the good-track decision.

Tracklayer's Instructions. This phase primarily uses three-corner and four-corner tracks so only one track is laid per session.

The tracklayer should realize it is important to know the exact location of each corner and the exact direction of each new leg. While laying the track, the tracklayer should leave clippies at all corners except the acute. A "**clippie**" is a clothes pin with a piece of surveyors tape, or a piece of surveyors tape tied to some grass or a weed, or even something that looks like a tiny haystack made by twisting the grass into a tight stack and wrapping it with a band of grass. At the acute, note a distinctive ground marker near the corner so you can find it later. Supplement your ground marker by triangulating your position using two distant landmarks in a line to the side. Don't use a haystack or clippie at the acute since that is likely to slow the dog down and make him notice the corner before overshooting it.

The tracklayer must make a map of the track as she lays it. The map will help her remember where the corners are and should be given to the handler after the track is run for the handler's journal.

For each leg, the tracklayer should note one or two distant landmarks in the direction of the new leg. It is much easier to walk in a straight line if you walk toward two distant landmarks in a line. Show these landmarks on your map. Also note a nearby ground marker at each corner (haystack, tape, clothespin, rock, stick, or flower). See page 94 for an example demonstrating how landmarks-in-a-row make it easy to walk in a straight line.

You will be an even more successful tracklayer if you triangulate each corner. Say you are going to turn right. First look to the left and find two distant landmarks that line up with each other. The direction does not have to be exactly opposite the direction of the next leg, just generally in the opposite quadrant. So you will have the line of the incoming leg, the triangulation line, and the line of the outgoing leg. With all three, you will have a much better chance of finding the exact location of the corner, if the dog and handler need help getting back on the track.

The photographs above show the landscapes from a single field to the East (top), South, West, and North (bottom). At first glance, there is not much available to the East since the train is moving. But in the center just above the train is a tall bare snag; there is also a dark bush under the train on the right-hand side and distinctive treetops on the skyline. To the South, one can see

Phase 6. Reading Your Dog

distinctive shapes of trees, utility poles, buildings, and a silo. It can be hard to find two distant landmarks in a line that are themselves well separated, although you can often find distinctive clumps in the grass at a middle distance. To the West, the mountains are very distant, and the houses and trees are quite close so there are many opportunities to find two well-separated landmarks in a line. The North is also good where the staggered ridge-lines offer some in-line landmarks as well as the puddle in the field with the trees and buildings behind.

You can verify two landmarks in a line are usefully distant from each other by leaning to the left and then leaning to the right. If they change separation, they will make good in-line landmarks that can keep your legs straight. They also make excellent landmarks for triangulating your corners.

The three landscapes shown on the previous page exemplify the value of two landmarks in a row. Look to the left of the copse of trees for a small barn. The top view is from a step to the left of the corner (left side of barn lines up with the fence post), the middle view is from the corner (right side of the barn lines up with the left most tree), and the bottom view is from a step to the right of the corner (barn is half obscured by tree). Of course, avoid stomping around the corner and just lean side to side rather than taking full steps. For perspective, the copse is 350 yards, and the barn is 1,600 yards from the viewer.

Of course, not all field tracking is done on huge flat farmed fields, so if you are lucky, you can find many distinctive landmarks at varying distances. Whether it is nearby open woods or undulating landscapes, as shown below, the available landmarks are plentiful.

Making 90° corners consistently requires some practice that you have had since Phase 4. To improve your 90° corners, avoid looking in the general direction of the next leg until you have independently determined where 90° is relative to the incoming leg. If you look first and see a prominent landmark, you will be unconsciously prejudiced towards believing that is 90°. Once you are good at turning 90°, turning 135° to make a 45° acute turn is not hard. First turn 90°, then split the angle between that direction and the direction you came from.

A typical **field map** looks something like the figure below. It may not be quite as neat since most of us draw out maps on paper by hand. What is important about a map is it shows the track shape and documents the landmarks for each leg and each corner. As a result, you can exactly pinpoint the footsteps anywhere along the track where the dog gets in trouble. Map-making skills take practice, but they are skills that will greatly enhance your own, your dog's, and your companion's dog's success in tracking.

How you lay the acute-angle corner is important. At most corners, you stop at the corner while making a haystack, deciding what direction to go, and updating your map with landmarks. At the acute, do not make the haystack. Decide the next direction to go and update your map. Take extra care to triangulate this corner since there is no clippie to mark it. Note the triangulated landmarks on your map, as well as any ground markers near the acute corner.

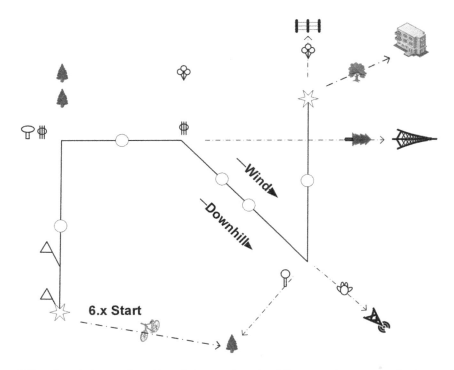

The location of the food drops leading into and out of the acute corner is important. We have two drops on the inward leg to speed the dog up. The second drop cannot be close to the acute corner, since a dog who stops at the drop may not pick up enough momentum to be carried past the corner. The drop coming out of the acute is an important reward for accomplishing a complex task. However, it cannot be close to the corner or it will attract (lure) the dog onto the new leg before he has a chance to overshoot the corner. Therefore, the drops should be at least 40–50 yards from the acute corner.

While the track is being run, the tracklayer should:
- follow along behind the handler but stop at least 30' before the corner.
- tell the handler to stop if she gets 10' past the corner.
- if the dog quits, tell the handler where the corner is located and where the new leg goes.
- if the tracklayer is lost, admit it to the handler. The handler can decide whether to search for the track or just throw out a spare glove and play with the dog. The second course of action is usually the wisest.

Reading Your Dog. Up until now, the handler has enjoyed well-marked tracks because the primary training purpose was to teach her dog tracking skills. In the previous phase, you started to notice how your dog looked when he was tracking, how he looked when he veered off the track, how he looked when he overshot a corner, how he looked when he was searching for the new leg, how he committed to the new leg, and how he indicated the article. I hope you paid careful attention because the blind tracks in this phase will be your quiz — this quiz is designed to help you learn, not to be judgmental.

Your skill in reading your dog was not perfected in the past phases' tracks and will not be perfected in this phase. Your reading skills will continue to improve as you practice in varied conditions. You will continue to perfect your ability to read your dog as long as you track him. You must always strive to improve and refine these reading skills:

What is your dog's:	Where is your dog:	Under various conditions:
body posture	on the track	wind direction
head carriage	slightly off the track	track age
nose activity	somewhat off the track	humidity
consistency of direction	well off the track	time of day
speed	approaching a corner	weather
	on a corner	individual tracklayer
	past a corner	tracklayer's footwear
	way past a corner	tracklayer's familiarity to the dog
	approaching a food drop	
	near a food drop	contamination
	on an animal track	distractions
	near ground animals	
	approaching an article	
	near an article	
	indicating an article	

As you learn to read your dog in various situations and under various conditions, you will become more than a big bump at the end of the tracking line. You can know when to help your dog during training, and you can supervise his tracking activity at a test.

At both your certification test and your TD test, you cannot help or guide your dog. However, if you can read your dog, you can avoid following him when he is obviously making a mistake. As an extreme example, you might be happily tracking along when your dog notices a couple picnicking off to the side of the track. Say your dog turns toward the picnickers. Is he dashing over to them to beg for food or is he taking a corner? You should be able to read your dog well enough to know the difference. Most judges will accept your stopping your dog from going to the picnickers if they think you can tell whether the dog is tracking or not. Luckily, most judges are experienced at reading dogs so they can read the same things as you read.

If you have access to a sports camera like a GoPro that mounts on your head or your chest, take advantage of it. Or, if you can get someone following you on the track with a cell phone or better camera, video these tracks and review them to see if you are seeing all the behavioral messages your dog is expressing as he nears the corner, searches, and commits to the new leg.

Withdrawing Mid-leg Treats. Some trainers speculate that they should withdraw the mid-leg food drops now that the tracks have several corners and their dogs are tracking well. Unlike competitive dog sports like obedience, rally, or agility, you will only be tested in tracking a very few times. Once you pass, you will have few opportunities to enter that level of test again. So we have the luxury of maintaining a fairly high level of primary rewards in our training. Of course, we will reduce the frequency of rewards in training tracks, but we do not have to reduce them to zero. It is important to maintain rewards along the track throughout our dog's training to maintain the high level of enthusiasm we require of him.

We will teach the dog to track on food-less tracks starting in Phase 7 (see page 111 for the procedure, but it is unnecessary to do so now). I recommend keeping the rewards available once or twice per leg so the dog is rewarded after any difficult corner or scenting difficulty he experiences on the track.

Urban-lawn Tracks. The urban-lawn tracks in this phase are a natural extension of the previous work doing two zigzags with contamination. These urban track sessions are a single track that has three turns with contamination in the middle of each leg.

Another new feature of these urban-lawn tracks is that they are intentionally laid to cross paths and narrow roadways. These features can occur anywhere along a leg, but the tracklayer must avoid turning on them. If the dog is doing well with these types of tracks, the tracklayer can turn five yards before or shortly after a hard-surface crossing, but not right on the hard surface itself.

The contamination layers can cross the track right before or right after these transitions if they are in the middle of legs, but they should stay more than 20 yards from the start or corners.

Helping — Reviewing the Delicate Balance. On a blind track, most failures are caused by the handler being impatient and unconsciously suggesting to the dog where the track must go. Quite frankly, handlers are seldom good at guessing where the track goes.

Balancing letting the dog solve the problem with helping the dog when necessary can be tricky. Helping is needed throughout training to show the dog what is desired. Letting the dog sort the scent out and find the track on his own is necessary for the team to successfully navigate a blind track. The hierarchy of help shown below formalizes the balance by allowing the handler to be patient and then use the minimum amount of help that the dog requires.

You will inevitably need to help your dog on blind tracks, but you don't know where it goes. Your tracklayer will be able to step up and tell you exactly where the track is and what direction it is going. Anytime the dog is truly unable to find the track, you and your tracklayer shift from working a blind track to working a training track. So it is important to review the hierarchy of helping steps to keep them in mind.

Helping your dog offers him the opportunity to learn what is correct in this scenting situation and to develop his skills so he can behave in a way that you can read and follow on blind tracks.

The steps of the helping hierarchy are so important that I repeat them here even though they were introduced on page 59 in Phase 4. When your dog encounters a scenting problem, first let him try to solve it himself. Be patient and don't rush him. Before he gets frustrated and starts to think about quitting, you should help him. Always try to help as little and as gently as possible.

The *"Be Patient"* part is very important to avoid some common training problems. Handler impatience leads to:
- Training your dog to grab whatever contamination track is near his nose.
- Training your dog to give up responsibility and just go wherever you want to go.

Here is a hierarchy of help levels from least to most:
1. **Face in the Correct Direction** — dogs are very aware of our body posture and turning your body to face the new leg suggests to your dog what is correct.
2. **Restraint** — restrain your dog when he is at the end of his line and wanting to search farther in the wrong direction or commit to a contamination track out there.
3. **Reel-in and Re-Scent** — by bringing your dog back to you, there is the opportunity to re-scent him and get him focused on what you want him to follow.
4. **Make it Easy** for your dog to take the good track by reducing line tension and taking a few steps in the correct direction.
5. **Reel-in and Point** to the correct track and direction.
6. **Reel-in and Love the Track** on your knees, move forward slowly, talk lovingly to the footsteps until your dog moves forward in front of you focused on this interesting thing. Aka "You are Juliet, the track is Romeo, and we ignore the audience (your dog)".

When loving the track, the words you say don't matter, but how you say them does — emotionally love the track itself and forget about your dog — he will get interested in what you find so interesting. If you need a script, see the text box on page 60.

Acclimation helps a dog become familiar with the environment around him so he is able to focus on working for his treats and for you.

Most dogs become comfortable in the kinds of fields used for TD tracking quite quickly and there is little need to consider acclimation in any formal way in their training. TDU areas can be much more distracting, with people and dogs moving about and playing nearby. While some dogs are naturally able to focus in complex environments, most dogs find it very difficult concentrating on their task (tracking) in the complex environments in which they sometimes find themselves.

For examples of problematic distractions, see the section on urban distractions on page 260.

Regardless of the location, make sure you get your dog out of the car and able to sniff around the edge of his tracking site well before it is time to begin. Be positive with him without becoming a codependent with your dog regarding the scary things that he may be focusing on or imagining what may pop out of the weeds nearby. Take more time to do this with sensitive dogs.

For many dogs, acclimating to urban TDU environments is much more difficult than acclimating in fields, but the reverse can certainly become a concern as well. Your dog may worry about the bull bellowing behind the fence or the dogs barking and running in the neighbor's yard. Regardless of the urban versus field environments, help your dog become comfortable in the environment before asking him to track in an environment that he perceives as scary or provocative.

The basic technique to help your dog acclimate is to walk him on lead near areas of distraction and gradually approach the distraction. Use lots of cookies starting well before he notices the distraction. Ideally, give the cookies only when he is comfortable enough to look to you for cookies. If your dog is only able to look at the distraction, move farther away until he is comfortable enough to ask for cookies. Very gradually work your way closer to the distraction.

Sometimes distractions suddenly appear very close to us with little chance to escape quickly to a comfortable distance. Shorten your lead so you are basically holding onto your dog at the collar and quietly and confidently reassure your dog that he will be OK. Feed your dog treats if he is willing to take them. Slowly find a way to extract yourself from this close encounter until your dog is able to be comfortable again.

For help working through difficult acclimation issues, see http://denisefenzi.com/, search for acclimation, and see the kinds of exercises she uses to acclimate an obedience dog to its environment. Those same exercises will work well when adapted for tracking dogs. See also the section on urban distractions starting on page 260.

Sessions 6.X Natural-Field Minimal TD

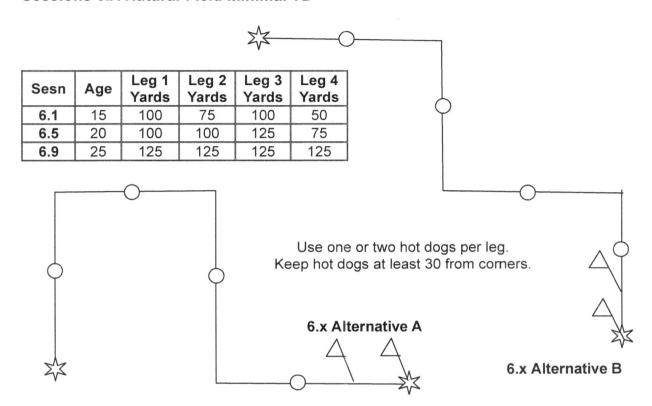

Sesn	Age	Leg 1 Yards	Leg 2 Yards	Leg 3 Yards	Leg 4 Yards
6.1	15	100	75	100	50
6.5	20	100	100	125	75
6.9	25	125	125	125	125

Use one or two hot dogs per leg.
Keep hot dogs at least 30 from corners.

6.x Alternative A

6.x Alternative B

Purpose:
- Introduce three-turn tracks, increase age, and practice reading the dog.

Tracklayer:
- Choose one of the two shapes above or make up your own three-turn track.
- Make a map of this track as you lay it. Include landmarks.
- Extend your arms at the corners to sight landmarks at 90 degrees and note them.
- Use only two flags at the start and at 30 yards. Use clippies or haystacks at the corners.

Handler:
- If someone else (reliable) can lay the track, don't watch the track being laid.
- Learn to read your dog — on track, off track, at a corner, and committing to a new leg.
- Note the landmarks for each leg.
- Have a fun party at each article, if you are using extra articles in lieu of some hot dog drops. Don't rush to restart your dog even if he wants to get back to the track quickly.

Evaluation:
- Note in your journal and your summary log (page 106) how your dog works the corners and how he maintains his attitude on each leg.
- Note how you are reading your dog — what signs indicate he is on or off the track — and how you are handling the uncertainty of having corners marked only with clippies.

Phase 6. Reading Your Dog

Sessions 6.X Natural-Field Downwind-Downhill Acute

6.2, 6.6 & 6.10
Natural Field with 45° Corners

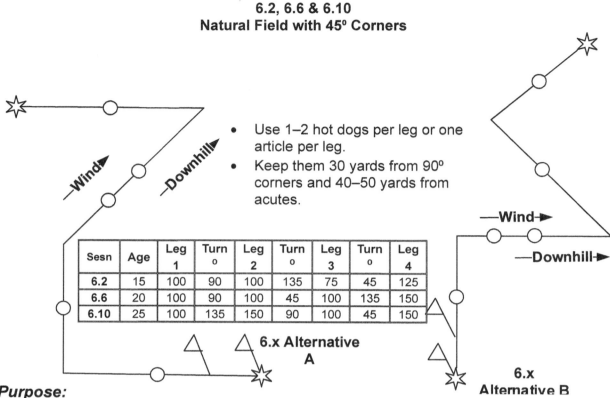

- Use 1–2 hot dogs per leg or one article per leg.
- Keep them 30 yards from 90° corners and 40–50 yards from acutes.

Sesn	Age	Leg 1	Turn °	Leg 2	Turn °	Leg 3	Turn °	Leg 4
6.2	15	100	90	100	135	75	45	125
6.6	20	100	90	100	45	100	135	150
6.10	25	100	135	150	90	100	45	150

Purpose:
- Teach the dog to circle behind handler.
- Teach the handler to help the dog to circle 360°.

Tracklayer:
- Choose one of the two shapes above or make up your own three-turn track with a downhill-downwind acute. If there is no wind, just use a downhill leg or vice versa.
- Make a map of this track as you lay it. Include good landmarks.
- Extend your arms at the corners to sight landmarks at 90 degrees and note them.
- Corner angles are between the two legs — the tracklayer turns 135° to make a 45° corner.
- Use only two flags at the start and at 30 yards. Use ground markers and triangulate corners.
- Follow and provide support to the handler as needed (see page 96).

Handler:
- Learn to read your dog: on and off the track, loss of scent at a corner, searching for the new leg, and committing onto a new leg.
- When your dog cannot find it, encourage him to circle 360° several times before backing up.
- Have a fun party at the glove and at intermediate articles, if used.

Evaluation:
- Note in your journal and your summary log (page 106) how your dog works the corners, particularly the acute turn. See sample logs at the end of Phase 8, page 147.
- Note how you are reading your dog — what signs indicate he is on or off the track.
- Note if he circles behind you on his own or you need to encourage him to do so.

Sessions 6.X Urban-Lawn Tracks with Contamination.

**6.3, 6.4, 6.7, 6.8, 6.11, 6.12
Urban Lawns with Path Crossings
and Contamination**

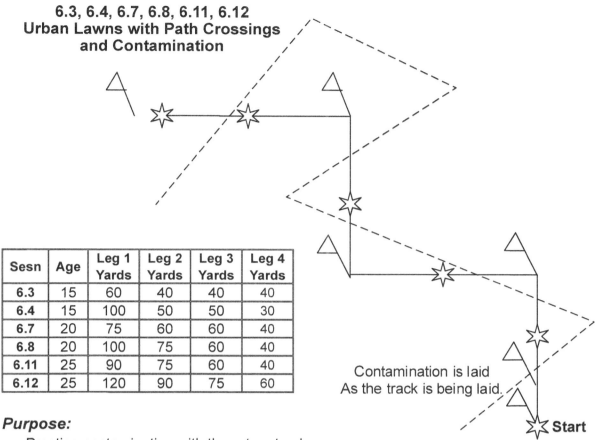

Contamination is laid
As the track is being laid.

Start

Sesn	Age	Leg 1 Yards	Leg 2 Yards	Leg 3 Yards	Leg 4 Yards
6.3	15	60	40	40	40
6.4	15	100	50	50	30
6.7	20	75	60	60	40
6.8	20	100	75	60	40
6.11	25	90	75	60	40
6.12	25	120	90	75	60

Purpose:
- Practice contamination with three-turn tracks.

Tracklayer:
- Use urban lawns with sidewalks and narrow driveways you can cross.
- Just cross the sidewalks or driveways, no turns on them. OK to mark transitions with chalk.
- Use either left-right-left or right-left-right configuration if possible.
- Use six flags per track so the handler and contamination layer knows exactly where the track is laid.

Contamination Tracklayer:
- The contamination layer should cross the track right after the tracklayer completes a leg.
- OK to contaminate right before or right after a path crossing but avoid contaminating within 20 yards of the start or a corner.

Handler:
- Restrain your dog if he commits more than 30' on intentional or natural contamination.
- Help your dog happily if he does not sort it out on his own.
- Have a party at every article.

Evaluation:
- Note in your journal and your summary log (page 106) how your dog looks when investigating contamination compared with searching on a corner or new leg.

Phase 6. Reading Your Dog

Field-Only Sessions 6.1f-6.7f

- These tracks are done in natural fields or on uncontaminated sports fields.
- A single track per session.
- Vary shape of tracks each session.
- For detailed instructions for 3-corner 90° sessions, see page 101.
- For detailed instructions for the downwind-downhill acute sessions, see page 102.

Session (Info)	Configuration	Age	Leg 1	Corner Angle	Leg 2	Corner Angle	Leg 3	Corner Angle	Leg 4
6.1f (6.1)	3-corners All 90°	15	100	90	75	90	100	90	50
6.2f (6.2)	Downhill Downwind Acute	15	100	90	100	135	75	45	125
6.3f (6.5)	3-corners All 90°	20	100	90	100	90	125	90	75
6.4f (6.6)	Downhill Downwind Acute	20	100	90	100	45	100	135	150
6.5f (6.9)	3-corners All 90°	25	125	90	125	90	125	90	125
6.6f (6.10)	Downhill Downwind Acute	25	100	135	150	90	100	45	150
6.7f	Review								

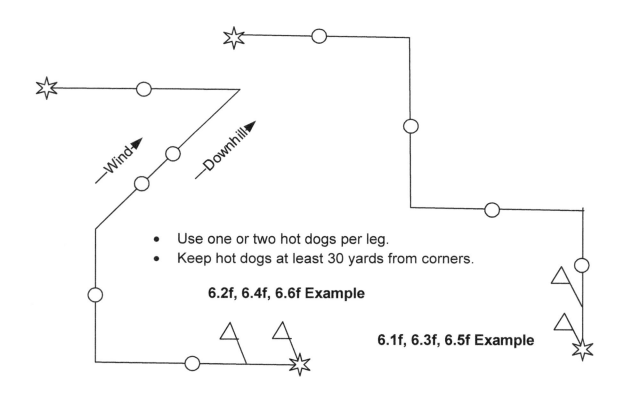

- Use one or two hot dogs per leg.
- Keep hot dogs at least 30 yards from corners.

6.2f, 6.4f, 6.6f Example

6.1f, 6.3f, 6.5f Example

Sessions 6.13 Review and Evaluation.

Most handlers and dogs are ready to proceed directly to Phase 7 after they complete these twelve sessions. Ideally, your dog diligently searches at each corner and quickly becomes Clear-Confident-Committed to each leg. Plus you are now able to tell when his behavior changes at a corner, when he is searching, and when you should follow him after he commits to the next leg.

If you have not been able to get a good downhill-downwind acute, do repeat 6.2, 6.6, or 6.10 making a special effort to get a good downhill leg with the wind at your back.

If you think the downhill-downwind acutes have been well-laid, but your dog never overshoots the corner and has never had to circle behind you to find the next leg, you have a problem but a good problem. It is a "good problem" because your dog is really doing a great job on corners. It is still a problem because your dog does not have experience circling behind you and committing at a weird angle. For dogs who have never overshot the acute, use the technique described in the box "Extending the Acute." Only do this with dogs who have never had to circle behind you.

Extending the Acute

The one dog I trained with this "good problem" was Mr. Q, an excellent footstep tracker, who never overshot corners by even a body length. What I did as a tracklayer was lay the incoming leg 6–10' too long, then continuing to face in the same direction, backed up the 6–10' to where I wanted the corner and made the acute there. As the handler, I stayed about 10' behind him on the line as I approached the acute so it was likely he had to circle behind me. He did, but he found committing to that new leg different and was a little tentative the first time. However, a couple of those extended acutes was all it took to convince him that sometimes the track does weird things and he may have to circle behind Pops.

Phase 6 Summary Log

Sesn	Site	Config.	Date	Actual Age	Evaluation
6.1	Natural Field	3-Corner All 90°			
6.2	Natural Field	Downhill Downwind Acute			
6.3	Urban Lawn w/ Paths	3-Corner Urban Lawn			
6.4	Urban Lawn w/ Paths	3-Corner Urban Lawn			
6.5	Natural Field	3-Corner All 90°			
6.6	Natural Field	Downhill Downwind Acute			
6.7	Urban Lawn w/ Paths	3-Corner Urban Lawn			
6.8	Urban Lawn w/ Paths	3-Corner Urban Lawn			
6.9	Natural Field	3-Corner All 90°			
6.10	Natural Field	Downhill Downwind Acute			
6.11	Urban Lawn w/ Paths	3-Corner Urban Lawn			
6.12	Urban Lawn w/ Paths	3-Corner Urban Lawn			

Phase 7. Track Age

Purpose:
- Teach the dog to happily track 30–75 minute-old tracks.
- Make the dog thoroughly familiar and happy with TD- and TDU-complexity tracks.
- Practice reading the dog on the blind tracks.

Strategy:
- Half the tracks are in the field and alternate between track age and practicing blind tracks.
- Half the tracks are on urban lawns and alternate between intentional contamination near corners and practicing blind urban tracks.
- Track-age sessions use two tracks, a younger one and an older one.
- Carefully observe your dog's enthusiasm to track as the tracks get older.
- Some handlers and dogs need only complete through 7.12 to move on to Phase 8.

How to use this chapter:
- Study the table on the next page, which summarizes the training structure of this phase, and read the discussion section.
- Do the first 12 sessions rotating between natural fields and urban lawns (pages 118+).
  - For the alternative field-only training schedule, see page 122.
  - For the alternative urban-only training schedule, see page 124.
- Keep a detailed log of each session using a format like the one shown on page 31 and keep a summary log like the one shown on page 126.
- Do the 7.13 review session on page 125 to evaluate the team's progress. Choose to go on immediately to Phase 8 or continue on with 7.14 through 7.21.
- If you do 7.14 through 7.21, do the 7.22 review session on page 125.

Discussion:

Until now, your dog has followed tracks up to 25 minutes old. We want him to happily follow tracks up to 75 minutes old. A TD test track is 30 minutes to 2 hours old, but the vast majority of them are 30–60 minutes old. Therefore, we want to concentrate on getting the dog to be a happy tracker in this time range. Some trainers who choose to get ready for their TD or TDU test as quickly as possible move to Phase 8 after 7.12. Other trainers choose to complete 7.13 through 7.21 so their dog has experience with tracks over an hour old.

We add age slowly so the dog learns this older scent is just as rewarding as the younger scent he has been following for quite a while. Even if you have occasionally been late to a track in the past, go through this progression as it will build your dog's confidence tracking scents in the normal age range of TD and TDU tracks.

Phase 7 Session Schedule:

Sesn	Site	Config.	Mark	Track 1				Track 2			
				Age	Legs	Turns	Yards	Age	Legs	Turns	Yards
7.1	Natural Field	2 U-Tracks, 2nd first.	Flags	20	3	Right	250	35	3	Left	250
7.2	Natural Field	Full TD Complexity	Blind	30	4–5	R & L	400–500				
7.3	Urban Lawn	Contamination	Flags	20	3–4	R & L	300				
7.4	Urban Lawn	Simple TDU Track	Blind	25	3–4	R & L	300–350				
7.5	Natural Field	2 U-Tracks, 2nd first.	Flags	30	3	Left	250	45	3	Right	250
7.6	Natural Field	Full TD Complexity	Blind	40	4–5	R & L	400–500				
7.7	Urban Lawn	Contamination	Flags	30	3–4	R & L	325				
7.8	Urban Lawn	Simple TDU Track	Blind	35	3–4	R & L	325–375				
7.9	Natural Field	2 U-Tracks, 2nd first.	Flags	40	3	Right	300	55	3	Left	300
7.10	Natural Field	Full TD Complexity	Blind	50	4–5	R & L	400–500				
7.11	Urban Lawn	Contamination	Flags	40	3–4	R & L	350				
7.12	Urban Lawn	Simple TDU Track	Blind	45	3–4	R & L	350–400				
7.13		Review									
7.14	Natural Field	2 U-Tracks, 2nd first.	Flags	50	3	Left	300	65	3	Right	300
7.15	Natural Field	Full TD Complexity	Blind	60	4–5	R & L	400–500				
7.16	Urban Lawn	Contamination	Flags	50	3–4	R & L	375				
7.17	Urban Lawn	Simple TDU Track	Blind	55	3–4	R & L	375–425				
7.18	Natural Field	2 U-Tracks, 2nd first.	Flags	60	3	Right	300	75	3	Left	300
7.19	Natural Field	Full TD Complexity	Blind	70	4–5	R & L	400–500				
7.20	Urban Lawn	Contamination	Flags	60	3–4	R & L	400				
7.21	Urban Lawn	Simple TDU Track	Blind	65	3–4	R & L	400–450				
7.22		Review									

This phase is composed of four types of sessions:

1. The first type is on natural grass fields with minimal contamination. Each session adds ten minutes to the track age. You lay two simple U-shaped tracks with flags on all the corners and run the second-laid track first and the first-laid track second. Often the first-laid track gets older than intended, particularly if you have a slow dog or a dog who has problems with the first-run track. That is OK, but the intent is to run the first-laid (second-run) track about 15 minutes older than the second-laid (first-run) track.

2. The second type is a TD complexity track on natural grass fields with no flags other than the start and directional flags. The tracklayer can use haystacks (twisted grass) or clippies (clothespins with a short length of surveyors tape) to indicate the corner locations, but the markers should be subtle enough not to be obvious to the handler so the dog-handler team can practice blind tracks.

3. The third type is a 3–4 turn zigzag on urban lawns with intentional contamination at the start and near the corners. If no intentional-contamination layer is available, choose a heavily used lawn with lots of natural contamination.

4. The fourth type is a 3–4 turn TDU-like track with a variety of transitions from lawn to narrow hard surface and back again to lawn. Do not have corners on a hard surface. Try to keep the total hard surface to 40–100 yards per track. If possible, avoid using flags at the corners or chalk at the transitions. If the handler is not confident that the tracklayer can find the exact location of the track, use flags and chalk to mark these tracks.

Adding Age. We don't initially try to get dogs to do 1–2 hour-old tracks because many dogs will face motivational problems if introduced to older tracks too quickly and because dogs who can track 2-hour-old tracks typically also notice 24-hour-old tracks. So, there is some proofing required to teach a dog to stay with the 2-hour-old track rather than be attracted off on the 24-hour-old track. Due to the way test tracks are laid out the day before the test, 24-hour-old conflicting tracks are fairly common at a test. Unless you have trouble getting into a test and have lots of time to train, your best odds for passing a TD test are to train an enthusiastic dog on 30-60-minute old tracks, rather than confuse your dog with age-related issues to solve.

We introduce age in a carefully controlled fashion because dogs initially lose the track somewhere in the aging progression and struggle to re-find it. With careful practice, they become comfortable with tracks in this age range and become reliable trackers.

Glen Johnson called this phenomenon the "hump" and attributed the issue to the changing characteristics of the scents. Your dog has been following some combination of person scent and ground scent — both have been in generous supply and have been easy for your dog to follow. As you remember from the introductory chapter, the personal scent is from the particles that have fallen off the tracklayer, and the ground scent is from the vegetation crushed and dirt disturbed by the tracklayer's footsteps. As we age the tracks, the components of the various available scents evaporate at different rates so their relative concentrations change. At some point, the scent changes sufficiently to affect your dog's notion of what he is following. When this happens, many dogs show loss of track and act as if they cannot smell any track. The timing when the "hump" occurs varies primarily with temperature and humidity; it is also influenced by all the other factors that affect scenting: wind, weather, sunlight, rain, ground cover, dirt compactness, tracklayer, and your dog.

When the dog faces the "hump" and quits, we want to be in a situation where we can help the dog. We will gently and positively lead the dog through the track until he picks it up. Through this process, the dog will learn the scent characteristics can change with age, but it remains the same track.

The technique is to lay well-marked simple U-shaped tracks so we know where the track goes if the dog quits. We lay two of these tracks per session and run the fresher track first to motivate the dog on the first fresh track. That's right, lay the two tracks in one order and run them in the opposite order. You will need to lay the tracks quickly and efficiently and be ready to run the dog as soon as the second-laid track ages sufficiently.

For these U-shaped field tracks used for aging, we maintain one to two treats in the middle of each leg (at least 30 yards away from the corners).

If you are doing the urban TDU first, you can do these tracks on a relatively uncontaminated sports field rather than a natural grass field or meadow.

TD-like Tracks: We train TD complexity tracks to give the dog experience with these types of tracks and to give the handler additional practice in reading their dog in a variety of conditions. If you have chosen to focus only on urban tracking, you can skip these TD-like sessions for now.

One important reason we alternate the age sessions and the 4–5 leg sessions is to avoid burnout while aging the tracks. Some handlers get bored laying five straight sessions of two U-shaped tracks when they are sure their dog is ready for TD complexity tracks and that they need more practice reading their dog. In fact, many of the U-shaped tracks are uneventful. Nevertheless, they should be fun for the dog, and it is up to the handler to ensure that fun. On the other hand, dogs that are forced to learn age too quickly may be able to do a few older tracks OK but soon lose enthusiasm. So the alternating schedule is designed to allow the dog to learn age without losing motivation while giving the dog and handler additional practice to improve skills taught in previous phases.

Since this phase requires tracklayers to design and lay TD test-like tracks, it is useful to know what the TD test track is like. The table below lists the primary track design parameters for an AKC and CKC TD track.

Comparison of AKC and CKC TD test Tracks

	AKC	CKC
Age:	30–120 minutes.	30–120 minutes.
Length:	440–500 yards.	400–450 meters.
Start:	Start flag with article, 30 yard directional.	Start flag with scent pad, 30 meter directional.
Articles:	Cloth article at start and glove or wallet at the end.	Glove or wallet at the end.
Corners:	3–5, Rights & Lefts, at least 3 90°, no acutes.	3–5, Rights & Lefts, at least 2 90°, no acutes.
Crosstracks:	None.	None.
Obstacles:	None.	None.
Line:	20–40', Handler may work as close as 20'.	16–49', Handler may work as close as 10'.

Learning to Plot Test-like Tracks. Excellent tracklayers learn to plot test-like TD and TDU tracks so the dog learns to track realistic track complexity and the handler learns to follow her dog and read her dog in these test-like situations. By test-like, I mean appropriate complexity that fully complies with each of the TD design parameters sown on the previous page or with each of the TDU design parameters shown on the next page. Not too complex, not too simple, but just right.

One thing that can be tricky at some tracking sites is getting at least one 90° left turn, at least one 90° right turn and another 90° or two in the space available. One or two of the turns should be well out in the open so the handler cannot guess which way it goes. The shapes shown on page 116 are all valid TD shapes. If the first two corners are 90° going in opposite directions, you can open up the third or fourth turns and they remain valid track shapes.

Other things that sometimes make a simple shape difficult to design are changes of cover close to corners, ground animals, contamination by people or animals, or visual distractions.

Take your next opportunity to help at a tracking test by volunteering to be a tracklayer. That way you will see firsthand the considerations the judges make when designing the track.

Of course, in addition to designing and laying an excellent test-like track, you need to be able to locate each corner and leg precisely in case the dog runs into trouble and needs help getting restarted in the right place. Make a map, note your landmarks for each leg, and triangulate each and every corner.

Mid-leg Hot Dog Withdrawal. Some dogs have grown so accustomed to the regular hot dog per leg treat that they lose enthusiasm when faced with a test track without treats. To prepare the dog and maintain his enthusiasm for the track even if the hot dogs are missing, we start to withdraw the hot dogs on the TD-like tracks 7.2, 7.6, 7.10... by omitting them on the first leg(s) and jack-potting on the subsequent leg.

In the table below, I show the training pattern where the dog will learn that if hot dogs are missing at the start of a track, if he keeps going he will hit a jackpot. For the legs with multiple hot dogs, I place them 5 yards apart starting 30 yards after the corner. This sequence of multiple hot dogs seems to impress most dogs.

	Leg 1 Hot dogs	Leg 2 Hot dogs	Leg 3 Hot dogs	Leg 4 Hot dogs	Leg 5 Hot dogs
7.2	None	2	1	1	1
7.6	None	None	3	1	1
7.10	1	1	1	1	1
7.15	None	None	None	4	1
7.19	None	None	None	None	5

If you use articles as reward points on field tracks for any reason, 2–3 articles spaced 10 yards apart should impress the dog as will upping the level of the party at each of the articles.

You can use the table above anywhere in your training. Note that once you have completed this hot dog reward schedule, you go right back to using a hot dog drop or an article on each leg as reward points — they are crucial for times when the dog struggles at a corner or scent transition so don't go naked for whole tracks.

Intentional contamination is a good idea for half of your urban tracks. If the dog is doing well and is confident tracking on lawns, add intentional contamination at the start and near the corners. If the dog lacks confidence on urban lawns, add intentional contamination but keep it away from the start and the corners.

The diagram below shows how to slice and bisect a corner — avoid doing both to the same corner. The bisect contamination crosses exactly over the corner. The slice contamination is done 1–3 yards to the inside of the corner. Use flags on the corners for these contaminated tracks so the contamination layer and handler knows where the corners and legs are.

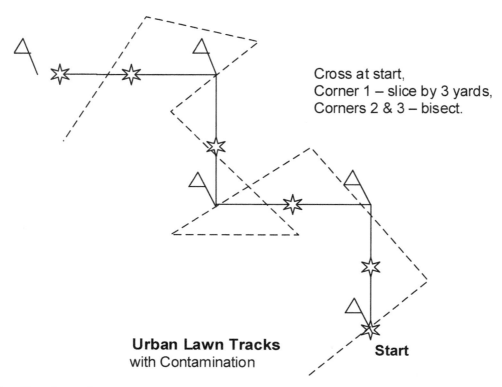

Cross at start,
Corner 1 – slice by 3 yards,
Corners 2 & 3 – bisect.

Urban Lawn Tracks
with Contamination

Start

TDU-like Tracks. These tracks provide TDU practice right along with our aging and TD-like tracks. If you have chosen to focus on the TD-only or TD-first, you can skip these sessions.

Comparison of AKC TDU and CKC UTD Test Tracks

Essential Parameters	AKC TDU	CKC UTD
Length	400–500 yards	300–400 meters
Age (minutes)	30–120	60–120
Corners	3–5	3–5
Hard-Surface Corners	None	1 or more
Ratio Non-Veg to Total	10–30%	About 33%
Non-Veg Surface Types	At least 1	At least 1
Start Article	Leather or Cloth	Scent pad only
Start Surface	30+ yards veg	25+ meters veg
Other Articles	Leather or Cloth.	Cloth, wood, plastic, or leather

The CKC UTD is similar to the AKC TDU except it also has a hard-surface turn, a minimum age of 60 minutes, and requires a CKC TD before it may be entered. While these extra UTD skills are not part of the TDU-focused curriculum, all the TDU skills will be required for CKC UTD. So the CKC-only trainer should follow this plan so she is ready to jump ahead to the UTD skill development in the first VST Phase.

For this phase, the urban-lawn tracks have an article in the middle of each leg that serves as a reward point. Consider omitting the article on the first leg and then having two on the second leg about 10 yards apart as a jackpot similar to the hot dog withdrawal described for field tracks above.

Three realistic TDU tracks are shown. The first shows a three-turn test track that uses sand on a baseball infield and a play area for much of the non-vegetated surfaces and ends in an asphalt parking lot.

2. Image © 2016 Google

Phase 7. Track Age

The second winds a four-corner track through residential housing. It uses the available asphalt driveways and concrete sidewalks for the non-vegetated surfaces and has many more transitions than the track on the previous page.

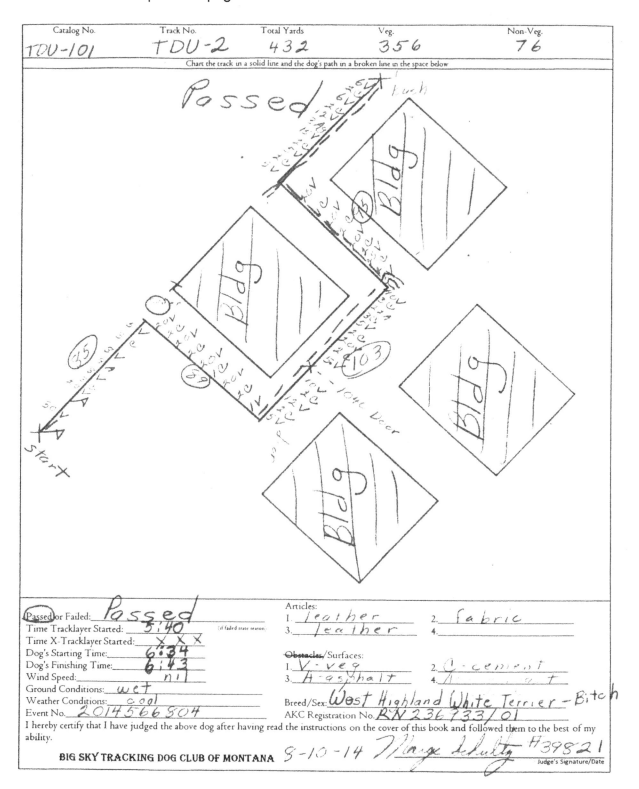

The third is less typical than the first two and shows extensive use of bends on and off sidewalks to avoid making a real turn on a hard surface. This creative bending was necessary to plot a test track in an available area of the campus.

3. Image © 2016 Google

Controlling Complexity. It is fine for the tracklayer to design her own track shape, but ask her to be careful to constrain the complexity of the track to the desired level. Length, number of corners, corners near barriers or transitions, road crossing, and contamination all increase the complexity and difficulty of the track. It is easy to be inventive and increase too many of these at the same time. If you find your dog struggles too much on these tracks, reduce complexity for a few tracks before picking it up again. It is never wrong to do a simple two-corner zigzag in a nice field and run it at 20 minutes to restore and improve your dog's confidence and enthusiasm.

TD and TDU Track Shapes. In this phase, your tracklayer is asked to lay "Full TD Complexity" blind tracks and "Simple TDU" blind tracks. If the dog is doing well on urban tracks, the TDU tracks can also be full complexity. Otherwise, the urban tracks should be simple meaning 3–4 corners rather than 4–5, and closer to 40 yards of hard surface rather than nearly 120 yards.

It is useful to have examples for the less experienced tracklayers. Considerable variation is possible with leg lengths so long as the total comes close to the desired 440–500 for TD and 400–500 for TDU. Any of the four-turn tracks can be reduced to three-turns by having longer legs and stopping where the final corner is shown. Each of the corners can be flipped right for left and left for right creating the same shape seen in a mirror. All of the tracks could be laid either in the direction shown or from the end back to what is shown as the start. One of the corners could be altered to be more than 90° like is shown in the upper left. The tracklayer should avoid short legs less than 50 yards. Some of these shapes have unofficial names that you can use to help communicate with your tracklayer what you desire.

TD and TDU Track Shapes.

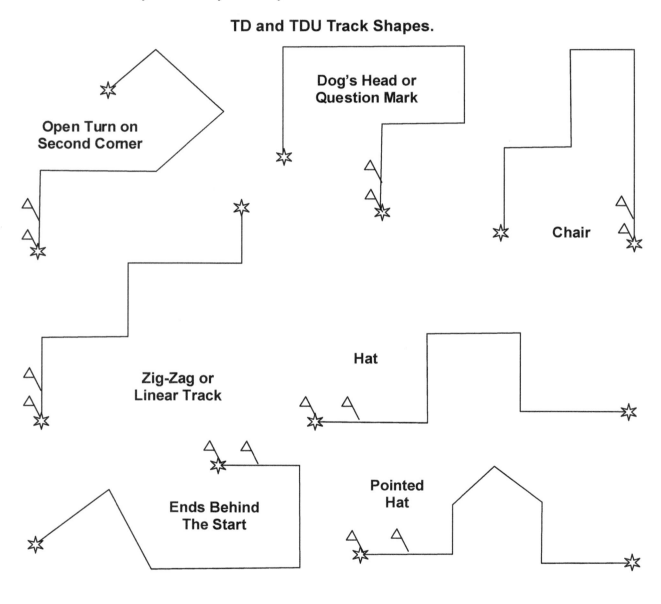

Handling Surface Transitions. At each surface transition, expect your dog to go back and forth several times before committing to the new surface. Sometimes he will find it easy, but expect him to go back and forth and be patient to let him work out the change in scent at each surface transition.

Ready to be Certified. Before you can enter an AKC test, a tracking judge or suitable evaluator needs to certify your dog's readiness. The judge or evaluator does so by giving you a test-like track at a suitable location. You should read the AKC Tracking Regulations before trying a certification. A suitable evaluator is someone who has earned an AKC TDX or VST in the last 10 years, knows the rules, and can lay a fair test-like blind track.

After session 7.12, you and your dog should be ready to be certified to enter TD or TDU tests. You may actually be ready to be certified earlier in the phase if your dog is doing well and is confident. Building the dog's confidence on older tracks and also building the handler's skill and confidence to read and follow her dog on blind tracks are critical skills for the team to be successful.

To get your dog certified, look up AKC tracking judges in your state from the AKC web site and contact nearby ones by phone or email. If no judge lives near you, find an experienced tracking person in your community or a nearby community. Arrange a date and time that is convenient for both of you. They will designate the location.

For CKC tests, you do not need to be certified, but it is a good idea to have a blind TD-like track put in by someone with the experience to make sure it complies with CKC requirements. Passing that track is an informal self-certification that will give you confidence you are ready to enter a test.

Some dogs may need more practice with different tracking conditions, additional work to clarify issues, or more fun to raise their level of enthusiasm. Some handlers may need more work reading their dog. More work in this phase, and in particular the customizations in the next phase, will help you work through those issues.

Stormy weather is used by some people as an excuse to skip training. If you find yourself saying it is too wet, too cold, or too windy today to go tracking, I can only hope you are talking about a hurricane or blizzard. Unless there is an obvious safety issue, your certification test and your titling test will not be rescheduled because of stormy weather. Both you and your dog need to be accustomed to tracking in the elements before your test, so you can be successful in any weather. It requires good foul weather gear to be comfortable (or at least tolerably uncomfortable) in driving rain at 40°. Most dogs don't mind it once they know they get to track and earn treats.

Tests in many areas of the country are scheduled in the spring and fall because the weather is typically more temperate. That means the test day may be warmer than usual or colder than usual or stormier than usual. So take the opportunities to train in stormy weather all through your training.

Session 7.x Adding Age with Two U-Shaped Tracks

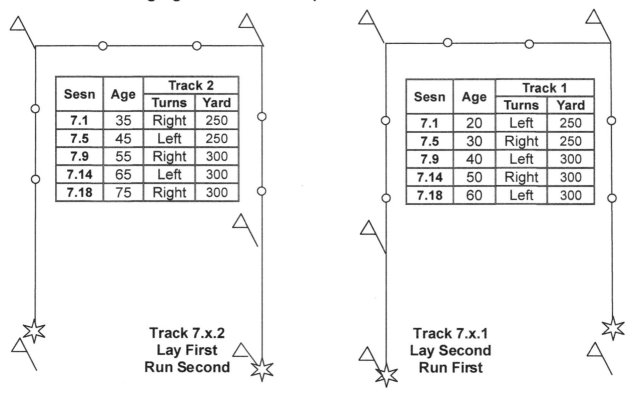

Sesn	Age	Track 2 Turns	Track 2 Yard
7.1	35	Right	250
7.5	45	Left	250
7.9	55	Right	300
7.14	65	Left	300
7.18	75	Right	300

Sesn	Age	Track 1 Turns	Track 1 Yard
7.1	20	Left	250
7.5	30	Right	250
7.9	40	Left	300
7.14	50	Right	300
7.18	60	Left	300

Track 7.x.2 Lay First Run Second

Track 7.x.1 Lay Second Run First

Purpose:
- Age tracks and get over the "hump".

Tracklayer:
- Use different color flags for each track.
- Use flags at the start, 30 yards, on all the corners, and after the article.
- The handler must know where the track is so the dog can be helped if needed.

Handler:
- These are good tracks to lay yourself.
- If your dog quits, happily help him by leading him through the rest of the track. As you point out the track, express your adoration for this wonderful track. When he starts to track again, let out the line and follow him.

Evaluation:
- Note in your journal and your summary log (page 126) how your dog works the tracks as they get older.
- If your dog stops working or acts like there is nothing to find, note the age of the track at that point in time. Reduce age on the next similar session and subsequently increment age slowly.

Session 7.x Full TD Blind Tracks

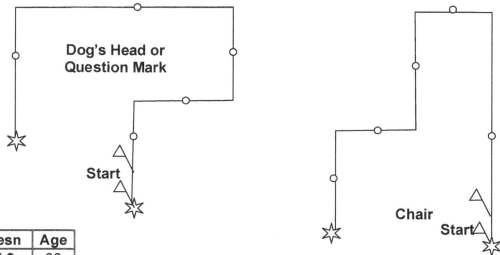

Sesn	Age
7.2	30
7.6	40
7.10	50
7.15	60
7.19	70

- Unmarked – do not mark the corners or legs.
- 4–5 turns, both right & left.
- 400–500 yards.

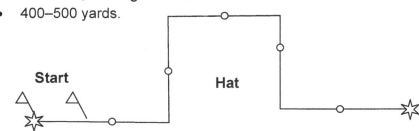

Purpose:
- Practice reading your dog.
- Build perseverance without food by moving drops toward the middle or the end of track.

Tracklayer:
- Choose one of the track designs above or see page 116 for additional examples.
- It is OK to swap rights and lefts or to design your own.
- Mark all corners and after the article with an inconspicuous clippie, haystack or ground marker.
- Place hot dogs as directed by the handler.
- You must know where the track is so you can help the handler if the dog gets lost.

Handler:
- If you lay these yourself, keep your eyes on your dog until he commits to a new leg, then look up and confirm he is going in the correct direction.
- Work on your corner handling and communication.

Evaluation:
- Note in your journal and your summary log (page 126) how your dog works the tracks as they get older. Continue to observe and record his level of enthusiasm. See sample logs on page 147.
- The tracklayer should note whether she was able to find all the corners from her map.

Phase 7. Track Age

Session 7.x Urban-Lawn Tracks with Corner Contamination

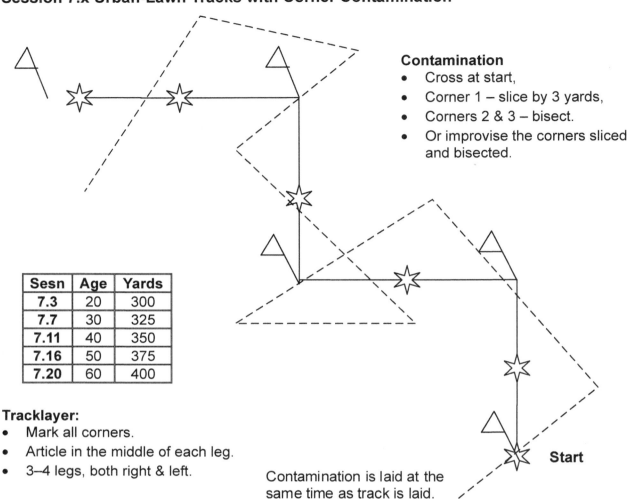

Contamination
- Cross at start,
- Corner 1 – slice by 3 yards,
- Corners 2 & 3 – bisect.
- Or improvise the corners sliced and bisected.

Sesn	Age	Yards
7.3	20	300
7.7	30	325
7.11	40	350
7.16	50	375
7.20	60	400

Tracklayer:
- Mark all corners.
- Article in the middle of each leg.
- 3–4 legs, both right & left.

Contamination is laid at the same time as track is laid.

Purpose:
- Practice dog with intentional contamination at the start and the corners.

Tracklayer and Contamination Layer:
- OK to swap rights and lefts.
- Mark all corners and the end so the contamination layer and the handler know the track location.
- Contamination layer randomly slices or bisects each corner and crosses legs in the middle.
- Don't get inventive with the contamination unless the dog is doing very well on simple contamination.

Handler:
- Restrain your dog if he commits more than 30' on intentional or natural contamination.
- Help your dog happily if he does not sort it out on his own.

Evaluation:
- Note in your journal and your summary log (page 126) how your dog works the contamination versus the track itself.

Session 7.x Urban-Lawn TDU-like Tracks with Narrow Hard-Surface Transitions

Tracklayer:
- Mark the start & 30 yards.
- Corners and end unmarked.
- 3–5 turns, both right & left.

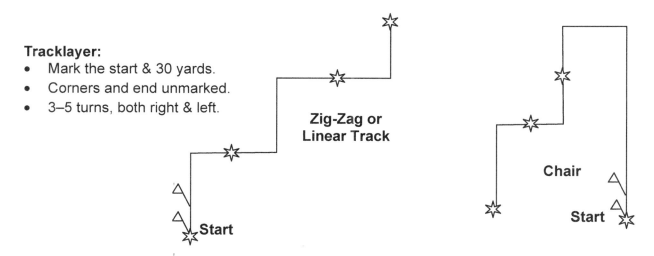

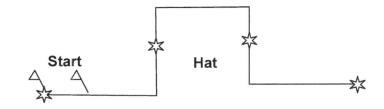

Sesn	Age	Yards
7.4	25	300–350
7.8	35	325–375
7.12	45	350–400
7.17	55	375–425
7.21	65	400–450

Purpose:
- Practice reading your dog on blind urban tracks.

Tracklayer:
- Choose one of the above track designs. It is OK to swap rights and lefts, or design your own.
- Only flag the start and at 30 yards. Triangulate each and every corner as well as the end.
- See pages 113–115 for example TDU test tracks and a description of the difference between simple and full-complexity.
- Drop treats as directed by handler.
- While none of the corners should be directly on hard surface, ideally, about one per session should be shortly before a hard-surface transition or shortly after the track returns to lawn. By shortly before and after, I mean by about 5 yards. This makes the dog have to solve the corner within a short distance or else he will need to find the track on the hard surface.
- You must know where the track is so you can help the handler if the dog gets lost.

Handler:
- If you lay these yourself, keep your eyes lowered on your dog until he commits to a new leg, then look up and confirm he is going in the correct direction.
- Work on your corner handling and communication.

Evaluation:
- Note in your journal and your summary log (page 126) how your dog works the tracks as they get older, and which handler skills are excellent and which need improvement.

Phase 7. Track Age

Field-Only Sessions 7.1f-7.12f

- These tracks are done in natural fields or on uncontaminated sports fields.
- Alternate two U-shaped marked tracks with single blind TD-like tracks following the schedule shown below.
- The 2 U-Track sessions are summarized on the next page with detailed tracklayer, handler and evaluation instructions on page 118.
- The Full TD Complexity sessions are summarized on the next page with detailed tracklayer, handler and evaluation instructions on page 119.

Sesn (Info)	Config/	Marked	Track 1				Track 2			
			Age	Legs	Turns	Yards	Age	Legs	Turns	Yards
7.1f (7.1)	2 U-Tracks, Lay 2nd first.	Flags	20	3	Right	250	35	3	Left	250
7.2f (7.2)	Full TD Complexity	Blind	30	4–5	R & L	400–500				
7.3f (7.5)	2 U-Tracks, Lay 2nd first.	Flags	30	3	Left	250	45	3	Right	250
7.4f (7.6)	Full TD Complexity	Blind	40	4–5	R & L	400–500				
7.5f (7.9)	2 U-Tracks, Lay 2nd first.	Flags	40	3	Right	300	55	3	Left	300
7.6f (7.10)	2 U-Tracks, Lay 2nd first.	Blind	50	4–5	R & L	400–500				
7.7f	Review									
7.8f (7.14)	2 U-Tracks, Lay 2nd first.	Flags	50	3	Left	300	65	3	Right	300
7.9f (7.15)	Full TD Complexity	Blind	60	4–5	R & L	400–500				
7.10f (7.18)	2 U-Tracks, Lay 2nd first.	Flags	60	3	Right	300	75	3	Left	300
7.11f (7.19)	Full TD Complexity	Blind	70	4–5	R & L	400–500				
7.12f	Review									

2 U-Track Sessions. See page 118 for detailed tracklayer, handler and evaluation instructions.

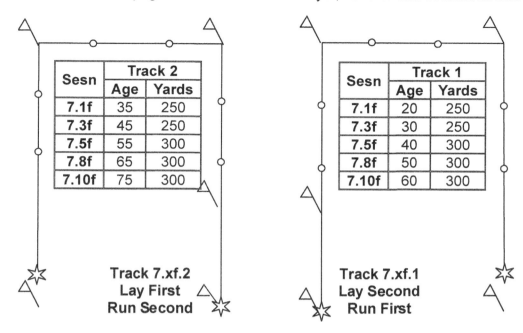

Sesn	Track 2	
	Age	Yards
7.1f	35	250
7.3f	45	250
7.5f	55	300
7.8f	65	300
7.10f	75	300

Track 7.xf.2
Lay First
Run Second

Sesn	Track 1	
	Age	Yards
7.1f	20	250
7.3f	30	250
7.5f	40	300
7.8f	50	300
7.10f	60	300

Track 7.xf.1
Lay Second
Run First

Full-Complexity TD. See page 119 for detailed tracklayer, handler and evaluation instructions.

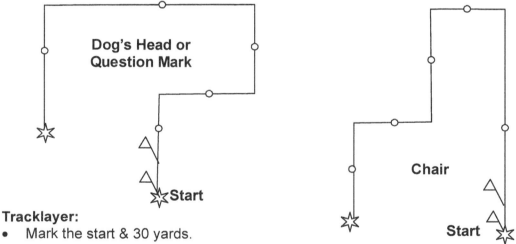

Tracklayer:
- Mark the start & 30 yards.
- Leave corners unmarked.
- 3–4 turns, both right & left.
- 400–500 yards.

Sesn	Age
7.2f	30
7.4f	40
7.6f	50
7.9f	60
7.11f	70

Phase 7. Track Age

Urban-Only Sessions 7.Xu

Use the following schedule along with the track descriptions from Phase 7 starting on page 107.
- The U-shaped track sessions should be on minimally-contaminated urban lawns, following the detailed tracklayer, handler and evaluation instructions on page 118.
- The intentionally-contaminated tracks should be on urban lawns with path and road crossings, following the detailed tracklayer, handler and evaluation instructions on page 120.
- The TDU-like track sessions should be on campus-like environments near buildings, pathways and lightly traveled roads, following the instructions on page 121.

Sesn	Configuration	Marked	Track 1				Track 2			
			Age	Legs	Turns	Yards	Age	Legs	Turn	Yard
7.1u (7.1)	2 U-Tracks, Lay 2nd first.	Flags	20	3	Right	250	35	3	Left	250
7.2u (7.3)	Contamination	Flags	20	3–4	R & L	300				
7.3u (7.4)	Simple TDU	Blind	30	4–5	R & L	400–500				
7.4u (7.5)	2 U-Tracks, Lay 2nd first.	Flags	30	3	Left	250	45	3	Right	250
7.5u (7.7)	Contamination	Flags	30	3–4	R & L	325				
7.6u (7.8)	Simple TDU	Blind	40	4–5	R & L	400–500				
7.7u (7.9)	2 U-Tracks, Lay 2nd first.	Flags	40	3	Right	300	55	3	Left	300
7.8u (7.11)	Contamination	Flags	40	3–4	R & L	350				
7.9u (7.12)	Simple TDU	Blind	45	3–4	R & L	350–400				
7.10u	Review and Evaluate									
7.11u (7.14)	2 U-Tracks, Lay 2nd first.	Flags	50	3	Left	300	65	3	Right	300
7.12u (7.16)	Contamination	Flags	50	3–4	R & L	375				
7.13u (7.17)	Full TDU	Blind	55	4–5	R & L	400–500				
7.14u (7.18)	2 U-Tracks, Lay 2nd first.	Flags	60	3	Right	300	75	3	Left	300
7.15u (7.20)	Contamination	Flags	60	3–4	R & L	400				
7.16u (7.21)	Full TDU	Blind	65	4–5	R & L	400–500				
7.17u	Review and Evaluate									

Session 7.13 & 7.22 Review and Evaluation

Now is an excellent time to review your dog's tracking performance and your handling skills. In the next chapter, you will use this evaluation to individualize your training program to the needs of you and your dog. Your future tracking success will be enhanced by objectively evaluating you and your dog, so spend a few minutes now to think about these questions. Consider also the observations of a trusted tracking friend, but you are responsible for the evaluation.

These questions should be answered based on your dog's performance in his last 3–5 TD-like tracks (if you have followed the schedule exactly, that is sessions 7.2, 7.6, 7.10, and optionally 7.17, and 7.19). Separately, answer the questions for your last 3–5 TDU-like blind tracks (7.4, 7.8, 7.12, and optionally 7.17, and 7.21). If this is your 7.13 review also consider your last unmarked track or two in Phase 6. If an unusual event occurred on one of these sessions (say a soccer team started to play right in the middle of your track), drop that session from consideration and add the next most recent unmarked track in Phase 6.

1. When you arrive at the tracking field or approach his track, is your dog obviously excited to be there and impatient for his track?
2. In the last five TD-like (or separately TDU-like) tracks, did you help him find the track more than once or twice?
3. On the best 80% of his opportunities to work a corner, does he find and commit to the new leg quickly and enthusiastically?
4. On the best 80% of your opportunities to read your dog on a corner (without flags), do you read his tracking behavior and believe your dog quickly and confidently?

These questions may require a little amplification, so I will discuss what I look for in more detail.

1. For question 1, different dogs show excitement in many ways from obvious to subtle. I am interested in whether he anticipates the fun he is going to have as soon as he gets to the tracking field or approaches the track.
2. For question 2, be objective about what it means to help a dog, and the count is over all five tracks, not per track. Don't count any normal training-handling techniques like increasing the tension or raising your arm if your dog gets a little off the track. Do count places where you have to point out the track to him or keep him from committing to a false direction. The only exception to counting these places is if your dog was committing to an obvious distraction, and he went back to tracking promptly when you asked him to "Find the good track" without actually facing down the new leg or pointing it out to him.
3. For question 3, look for your dog's behavior to be purposeful and easy to read the vast majority of the time. While 100% would be ideal, 80% is fine; your dog will have additional practice before getting in a test.
4. For question 4, look for your ability to read your dog the vast majority of the time. Experienced handlers should have 95% plus ratings, but it takes time to accumulate the experience needed to consistently read your dog and the confidence to consistently believe him.

For your 7.13 review, if you answered all four questions "yes", then move right on to Phase 8. Otherwise, finish the remaining sessions of Phase 7.

For your 7.22 review, move right on to Phase 8 where we'll diagnose the issues more deeply and formulate a specialized training plan for you and your dog.

Phase 7. Track Age

Phase 7 Summary Log

Sesn	Site	Config.	Date	Actual Ages	Evaluation
7.1	Natural Field	2 U-Tracks, 2nd first.			
7.2	Natural Field	Full TD Complexity			
7.3	Urban Lawn	Contamination			
7.4	Urban Lawn	Simple TDU Track			
7.5	Natural Field	2 U-Tracks, 2nd first.			
7.6	Natural Field	Full TD Complexity			
7.7	Urban Lawn	Contamination			
7.8	Urban Lawn	Simple TDU Track			
7.9	Natural Field	2 U-Tracks, 2nd first.			
7.10	Natural Field	Full TD Complexity			

Sesn	Site	Config.	Date	Actual Ages	Evaluation
7.11	Urban Lawn	Contamination			
7.12	Urban Lawn	Simple TDU Track			
7.14	Natural Field	2 U-Tracks, 2nd first.			
7.15	Natural Field	Full TD Complexity			
7.16	Urban Lawn	Contamination			
7.17	Urban Lawn	Simple TDU Track			
7.18	Natural Field	2 U-Tracks, 2nd first.			
7.19	Natural Field	Full TD Complexity			
7.20	Urban Lawn	Contamination			
7.21	Urban Lawn	Simple TDU Track			

Phase 8. Perfecting Skills

Purpose:
- Improve motivation, skill, commitment, and communication.
- Make the dog thoroughly familiar and happy with TD- and/or TDU-complexity tracks.

Strategy:
- Customize the tracks to address individual aspects of training needing improvement.
- Maintain and build enthusiasm.

How to use this chapter:
- To choose the right next steps for your dog's tracking training, do the evaluation exercise in the discussion session that will direct you to choose the Plan A, B or C session schedule.
- Before you skip there, read the remainder of the discussion on problem solving (page 132) that will help you with specific issues.
- Then do the Plan 8A, 8B or 8C sessions appropriate for your dog.
- Specialized Training:
  - The field-only trainer will do all sessions in natural fields or lightly-contaminated sports fields.
  - The urban-only trainer will do all sessions in urban campus-like environments among buildings with a mix of lawns and hard surface.
- Remember to keep up your detailed log of each track, as well as your summary log.

Discussion:

If you have not yet done session 7.13 or 7.22 (review and evaluation) in the previous chapter, please do that now before proceeding. You will use the results of that evaluation to customize your training plan.

Following this process to evaluate your dog and prescribe a customized tracking plan tailored to your dog does take a little effort. It is worth the effort since it is almost like having a private lesson with an expert. It requires such care in following detailed directions that some people may want to skip the whole thing. Since the full customization method will more accurately and finely describe a plan suited to your and your dog's training needs, I strongly encourage you to try to use the full method. There is a short-cut method shown on page 130 for those who have too much difficulty completing this more detailed process.

This may be a good time to focus on one test or the other. For many, you will find more TD tests in your area than the newer TDU so the TD might be your first choice. But for some, the TDU test may be easier to find.

The CKC UTD is similar to the AKC TDU but also has a hard-surface turn, a minimum age of 60 minutes, and requires a CKC TD before it may be entered. While these extra UTD skills are not part of the TDU-focused curriculum, all the TDU skills will be required for CKC UTD. So the CKC-only trainer should follow this plan so she is ready to jump ahead to the UTD skill development in the first VST Phase.

In setting up the custom-tracking plan, each question from 7.13 or 7.22 is first considered individually, then a chart is used to select one of four training plans. The chosen training plan is further customized to match your and your dog's particular situation.

1. **When you arrive at the tracking field or approach his track, is your dog obviously excited to be there and impatient for his track?**

Ideally, your dog is having so much fun so consistently that he jumps around and barks excitedly as you drive up to your favorite tracking field or is excited when he approaches his track. However, it is quite reasonable to answer "Yes" to this question for any form of excitement your dog shows in this situation. The essential point is your dog anticipates what is coming up as soon as he has a clue that he will soon get to track. If you answered Yes to this question, continue your current level of motivational rewards for your dog.

If your dog is excited and happy when he is actually tracking but fails to anticipate the fun when you arrive at the tracking site or approach his track, you may question how extensively you need to increase his motivational drive to track. You probably don't have to increase your level of motivation a lot, but it will help if you increased it some. A dog that cannot be bothered to be excited in anticipation of the track will be a better tracking dog if his motivation level increases.

If your dog is not showing excitement on the track, you need to substantially increase the positive motivational rewards he gets for working for you. You have to discover what really motivates him. Some dogs demand a higher wage than others, so be willing to increase your pay scale. What motivates him may be food, or special food, or toys, or special toys, or a tennis ball, or getting to go for a big run, or a wild wrestling match with you, or something else. It does not matter what it is; it only matters you provide it for your dog at the end of the track in a way that your dog values highly.

If a dog has regular access to a reward, he will value it less than if it is special. If your dog is even a tiny bit overweight, consider putting him on a diet. And don't feed him for at least 12 hours before tracking unless he has a medical condition that requires more frequent feeding. Whether or not he is overweight, move most of his regular pre-track meal to the end of the track. If your dog has free access to toys at home, pick them up and only give him toys as a reward for tracking. By washing the toys after each use, you remove the old saliva and make the toy fresh and special again. Toys survive machine washing and drying many times.

Remember to enjoy yourself and show your pride in your dog's accomplishment. It is a whole lot easier for your dog to be happy about tracking if you are happy about where you are, what you are doing, and what your dog is doing. Find the good in any situation and say something aloud to your dog about it. If you are a reserved person, get rambunctious and loud. If you are a talkative person, praise your dog softly. Your dog is doing something very special with you, show him your appreciation in a special way.

At this point, you have established your current evaluation of your dog into one of three categories:
> **Anticipates:** when you arrive at the tracking site or approach the track, he anticipates the fun he will have tracking,
> **On-track:** has lots of fun on the track itself, but does not get excited until on the track,
> **Unexcited:** does not get enthusiastic or excited on the track.

> ### Shortcut Plan.
>
> Some readers may find this customization process too detailed and complicated. Although it is a valuable process to go through, those of you who really wish to wing it may want to take a shortcut here. The shortcut method requires you make a three-way choice as follows:
>
> - If your dog needs additional motivation or is slow to solve corners, do Plan C (page 142), and then go on to Phase 9.
> - If you or your dog just needs a little more work, do Plan B (page 139), and then go on to Phase 9.
> - Otherwise, do Plan A (page 136), and then go on to Phase 9.
>
> I do recommend you go through the full customization plan. It will more finely tune your training to your dog's actual needs. Nevertheless, the shortcut method will work for many of you and is a better alternative than giving up on tracking or just entering a test to see what happens.

2. In the last five TD-like (or separately TDU-like) tracks, did you help him find the track more than once or twice?

As the discussion in session 7.13 and 7.22 emphasized, you need to be very objective when evaluating what it means to help your dog. In training, we freely help your dog whenever he needs help (once we give him ample opportunity to solve the situation himself). In a test, you are not going to know where the track goes, so you are not going to be able to help your dog. Therefore, it is important to monitor how many times you need to help and use that information to fine-tune the level of difficulty of the tracks.

If your dog needs help too often, say once or more per track, he is likely to either get discouraged or expect help from you whenever he loses the track. So you need to back off on the difficulty of the tracks until he gains confidence and skill in the problems he must solve.

On the other hand, if he almost never needs any help, we must evaluate if he is facing difficult enough challenges. If the two of you are working blind TD test-like tracks in new locations, then you need not increase the difficulty. If not, gradually increase the difficulty of the tracks until they more closely match the requirements of the test.

The third situation is where you need to help him less than once per track but more than once in the last five tracks. You are probably progressing nicely. So long as you see no signs of loss of motivation, you can keep up the same level of difficulty.

Therefore, you have now evaluated your dog into one of three categories:
- **0–2:** two or fewer times helped in last five TD-like tracks.
- **3–4:** three-to-four times helped in the last five TD-like tracks.
- **5 or more:** five-or-more times helped in the last five TD-like tracks.

3. **On the best 80% of his opportunities to work a corner, does he find and commit to the new leg quickly and enthusiastically?**

Whether or not your dog needs help, he may be easy or hard to read. A dog that is easy to read is a joy to track. It is well worth the effort to structure your training to maximize the ease with which he can be read. Review the discussion on corners in phases 4–6.

To be easy to read, your dog needs:
- to follow the straight legs close to the track,
- show loss of track distinctively,
- search for the new leg purposefully,
- and commit to the new leg quickly and irresistibly.

We will work on improving his corner skills using simple-marked zigzags with lots of rewards along the track.

Therefore, you have now evaluated your dog in four aspects of being easy or hard to read and your evaluation should match one or more of these five alternatives:

    Easy to read. Quick, clear commitment.
    Not close to straight legs. Tracks away from the straight legs or weaves widely.
    Tracks straight past corners. Does not clearly indicate loss of track at a corner.
    Weak searching at corners. Does not search with a purpose.
    Weak commitment to new legs. Does not commit to new leg quickly and irresistibly.

The first is easy to read (congratulations) and the remaining four are not so easy to read, which means there are opportunities to improve your dogs tracking skills so he will become easy to read.

While a dog may be classified with multiple symptoms, focus first on the highest one on the list.

4. **On the best 80% of your opportunities to read your dog on a corner (without flags), do you read his tracking behavior and believe your dog quickly and confidently?**

This question pertains to the handler's ability to read the dog. It requires a great deal of experience to read a dog in any tracking situation. Don't expect to be perfect right away or even with your first dog. Nevertheless, you can become very good if you try. Reread the discussion in Phase 6 on page 97 on reading your dog.

Therefore, you have now evaluated your own ability to read your dog:
    Yes. I read my dog 80–100% of the time and believe him quickly and confidently.
    No. I read my dog confidently less than 80% of the time on blind corners.

Match your set of answers to one of the rows in the table below:

Excitement Level	Helped	Quick Clear Commit	Handler Believes Dog	Summary of Plan	Plan / Page
Anticipates or on-track	0–2	Easy to read.	Yes	4 TD-like or TDU-like tracks in different locations.	8A-Short (A7-10) Page 136
Anticipates or on-track	0–2	Easy to read.	No	10 TD-like or TDU-like "blind" tracks in different locations, some with 2 flags mid-leg.	8A-Full (A1-10) Page 136
Little excitement	0–2	Easy to read.	Yes/No	10 TD-like or TDU-like "blind" tracks in different locations with flags mid-leg.	8B Page 139
Any	3–4	Easy to read.	Yes/No	10 TD-like or TDU-like "blind" tracks in different locations with flags mid-leg.	8B Page 139
Any	Any	No	Yes/No	10–14 sessions, 2 tracks/session, 2-corner zigzag tracks with 2 flags mid-leg. Increase motivation, improve tracking skills.	8C Page 142

In the table above, look down the rows to find the first row where the four left columns agree with your four answers. A short summary of the prescribed plan is in the next column and the left column names the plan and gives you a page pointer to the full description of the plan and the schedule of sessions to follow.

Problem-Solving Philosophy. This is a good place to point out a bit of valuable training philosophy according to Glen Johnson (1977):

> If a dog is not performing in the manner I expect him to perform then I am doing something that has to be wrong. In scent work the dog is the one that knows what he is doing and is always right while the handler, unable to determine just what or how he is doing it, can only set up the situation and hope that it will be conducive to the dogs learning if designed and implemented correctly.

This is very useful training advice because it reminds us of who is responsible for what, and it also points out the importance of structuring the situation to facilitate learning. This training philosophy should serve as the basis for all problem-solving strategies. The strategy should be designed to encourage the dog to learn the desired behavior. If the dog fails to perform as desired, the problem-solving strategy or our implementation of it is at fault, not the dog.

This training philosophy is very powerful and should be "top of mind" when sorting out what to do about any training issue. If you find yourself getting frustrated with your dog, recall this bit of philosophy and see if you cannot find a better way to teach the desired behavior.

Specific Problem-Solving Techniques. These techniques are for particular issues as part of plan A, B or C (described in the remainder of this chapter). Or use them with other simple track designs.

- **Not easy to read on corners.** We will work on improving his corner skills using simple-marked zigzags with lots of rewards along the track. Each of the four aspects of being easy to read (close to the legs, shows loss of track, searches purposefully, commits quickly) can be improved within the context of the marked zigzags. You may want to work on all these aspects at the same time or focus on each of these aspects in turn, but focus on the first one that has weakness.
    - For a dog that is not following over the top of the footsteps, use longer legs on your zigzags, put markers or flags every 50 yards, and move up the line so you are only 10' behind your dog. Use line tension and use raising and lowering your arm to keep your dog close to the track. Narrow your definition of being close to the track. Use lots of food on the track to reward him for being close to the track.
    - For the dog that does not show a distinctive loss of track, use markers 5 yards (15') before each corner and work 15' behind your dog. When you come alongside the flag, your dog is on the corner. Slow him up and stop him within five to ten feet of the corner.
    - For the dog that does not search with purpose, use food on the track at 30, 35, 40, 45, and 50 yards beyond every corner. Keep this up until your dog shows he clearly anticipates the food sequence and works the corner with a clear purpose. Then start to spread the food out. Finally, slowly and randomly reduce the food so there is typically only one piece about 30–45 yards past a corner.
    - For a dog that does not commit to a new leg as soon as he finds it, or is tentative in his commitment, use the same 5-drop food sequence described above. It is important to improve your own clarity of communication and quickness of commitment with these dogs. When your dog begins to anticipate the food sequence ahead, adopt a clear communication sequence between you and your dog as he commits to a new leg. When he has moved along the new leg 6'–30', increase the tension slightly above normal (don't pull back as that would be a correction) and verbally ask your dog if this is the good track. Your dog should lean into the harness and pull you along the track. The very instant he starts to lean into the harness, you must reduce the tension to normal, step off after your dog, and quietly praise him for being so clever.

- **Poor starts (but the rest of the track is good):** Lay a 50–75 yard straight starter track after laying every track, but run the starter before the main track. Place a food drop 15–45 yards after each start on all tracks.

- **Weak or no article indication:** Repeat the Article Oval exercise on page 53. For other tracks, place a marker 20' before the article, don't let the dog pass the article, give lots of heart-felt praise and reward for stopping or being stopped. Don't rush to restart the dog after an intermediate article. Play the "glove game" after every track and play it on non-tracking days. Your dog needs to value each and every article even though he also loves to follow the track.

- **Overshooting corners.** Some dogs tend to track a considerable distance past the corner. The Phase 8 Plan C zigzag tracks are designed to extinguish overshooting by motivating the dog to abandon the line quickly once past the corner, to search efficiently for the new leg, and commit to it quickly to get to the treats. See page 142. On regular tracks put a clippie 15' (5 yards) before the corner so the handler will know the corner is coming up and can encourage the dog to stop and search.

- **Takes animal tracks:** Identify the dog's most favorite reward and make sure he only gets it at the end of the track. Lay marked tracks in areas where you think animals may cross your track. Mark the track with a couple of flags on each leg, not necessarily at the corners. If you can predict where animals cross your track, place a food drop 15–30 yards past the area. Place two food drops on every other leg. When the dog tries to take an animal track, let him investigate it 10' to 40', then move forward down the good track happily calling to your dog something like "Look over here. Is this the good track? Let's find the good track!" and help him down the track a few yards. Be happy and excited and he should start forward along the good track. Help him the rest of the track if need be. If you are tempted to think your dog is lying to you when he commits to something other than the good track, see the text box on page 234.

- **Distracted by ground animals, birds, or animal dung:** Identify the dog's most favorite reward and restrict access to it except at the end of the track. Lay tracks that cross areas with ground animals or birds or animal dung. Lead up to this area with easy tracking and exit the area with easy tracking. Use food drops 20, 25, 30, 35, and 40 yards past the area and end the track after another 30–50 yards. Let the dog investigate the area briefly, then ask him to return to the main track. Help him happily, if you need to help. Use the most favorite reward at the track end. Repeat for many sessions, but limit distraction area to once per track. If your dog refuses to leave the distraction, tell him "Yuck!", then happily help him down the track (see "Loving the Track" on page 60).

- **Uninterested in tracking anymore:** If the dog loses his former motivation, the most likely cause is too much complexity too soon. The added complexity may be due to progressing in the training too fast for the dog, aging the tracks too quickly, recent hot, dry weather, or difficult cover changes or unpleasant cover. Any of these issues should be fine if it happens in one session and does not repeat too soon. But when faced with a series of these difficulties, the dog may well get discouraged. Compounding the dog's discouragement is a handler attitude that diminishes right along with the dog's and the two of them spiral to further disinterest. Back up in your training using simpler track designs, at a younger age, and in better conditions, so your dog and you can have fun. Then proceed slowly, keeping a sharp eye out for any sessions that inadvertently become too difficult. Be careful to follow that too-difficult session with a motivational session. Also consider the re-motivational plan in Appendix A, ATE 4, on page 408.

- **Corners near transitions:** On an urban track, a transition right after a corner requires the dog to search for and commit to the new leg in the first few yards or on the hard surface itself. Either is much more difficult than a corner well out on a lawn. Use this sequence, where you repeat each step several times until the dog's confidence solving the puzzle improves:
1. Start out laying a track with one or more corners about 10 yards before a hard surface transition and place 5 tiny treats evenly spaced across the hard surface.
2. Then lay the track just 5 yards from the transition.
3. Then with the corner 5 yards before the corner, reduce the number of tiny treats to 3.
4. Then reduce the number of tiny treats to a single one in the middle.

- **Shortcuts to upwind articles:** While your dog may have excellent air-scenting capabilities and search skills, taking 50-yard shortcuts to an upwind article is a problem in tests. For most dogs, the work done in the first four phases made it clear to the dog that staying close to the track was the best choice.

If the dog wanders on the fringe most of the time, consider the fringing remediation on page 406.

If the dog stays close to the track on crosswind legs even when there is another leg 50 yards upwind with an article and the shortcuts only happen while the dog is searching on a corner, then we will use the track shape shown below. It utilizes the reward structure of five hot dogs per leg or two articles per leg. It also uses two flags mid-leg, so the handler can verify the new-leg direction at each corner. It uses a three-corner track where the first leg and third legs are upwind, and the second and third corners turn in the same direction as shown in the diagram below.

There should be an article at about 30 yards down the fourth leg and another directly upwind of the first corner. Articles on the second and third legs are optional. The handler should focus on increasing and decreasing the tension on the straight legs to encourage the dog to remember that staying close to the track is the best place to be. The handler should be willing to allow the dog to overshoot the first corner up to 40', but restrain him if he tries to take a shortcut to the final article. Ditto if he tries to go upwind to the first article on the fourth leg from anywhere on the second leg. In either case, after restraining the dog at 40', encourage him back to the track, gesture down the new leg or, if necessary, love the track. He will soon be rewarded by the five hot dog sequence.

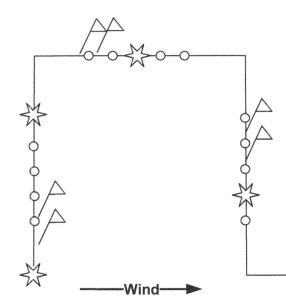

—Wind—➔

Phase 8 Plan for Shortcuts
1. 1st, 2nd & 4th legs from 75 to 100 yards,
2. 2nd & 4th must be the same length.
3. 1st & 3rd legs upwind.
4. 3rd leg 100 yards decreasing to 40 yards over several sessions and with an article mid-leg and hot dogs as space allows.
5. Five hot dogs per leg at 30, 35, 40, 45 & 50 yards.
6. Article at 35 yards on 2nd leg & 30 yards on 4th fourth leg.
7. Two flags mid-leg about 4 paces apart.

Plan 8A Schedule — Polishing Skills in New Fields or at New Sites:

This plan calls for different locations each session. Try several new locations or locations you have not used in a long time. Find sites that are similar to those used to hold tests. You may not be able to find all brand-new tracking sites, but you should find a few or different ways to use old ones, so the dog becomes accustomed to variety. Apply this plan to the TD and the TDU separately.

If your dog is handling corners well, make the corners blind (no flag, no clippie, no haystack), but put a flag fifty yards down each leg. Don't look for the flag until you have committed to following your dog. For example, use a wide brimmed hat down over your eyes so you can see no farther in front of you than your dog. Once he commits to a new leg, you increase the tension slightly, he pulls into the harness, you reduce the tension and step out, and then you raise your head and verify that the flag is right ahead of you. (If so, pop a small piece of candy in your mouth! If not, back up to the corner and smile). Keep this up for many sessions until your confidence in your dog increases so that you remain confident when you remove the flags.

If your dog is not handling corners well, he may be confused or uncertain by your lack of confidence. Help the dog become easy to read, then shift into the sequence described above to improve your own confidence.

Easy-to-read dogs who are believed by their handler should start at session 8A.7. Other handlers who need more practice reading their dogs should start at 8A.1.

Sesn	Location	Turns	Yards	Markers	Suggested Design	Age
8A.1	New field	3–5	400–500	2 flags mid-leg	Choose from Phase 6	30
8A.2					Choose from Phase 7	40
8A.3					Hat.	50
8A.4					Chair.	35
8A.5					Zigzag.	45
8A.6					Dog's Head.	55
8A.7				Haystacks	Chair with an open last turn.	30
8A.8					Hat with an open last turn.	45
8A.9					Dog's Head with an open turn.	30
8A.10					Zigzag with an open turn.	55
8A.11					Evaluate as in 7.13, 7.22	

Phase 8 Plan A Sessions 1–10.
1. Each leg 50–125.
2. One or two hot dogs per leg.
3. Mark track as shown in table.
4. Age as shown in table.

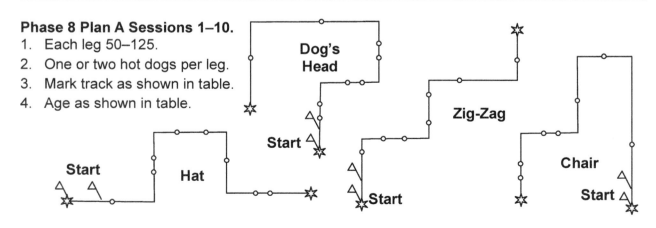

If you have laid all your dog's tracks, find someone else to lay a couple of tracks in this phase. Have them follow 30–50 yards behind you talking quietly as if they were judges following you on a track. Your dog needs to be accustomed to people following you on the track.

Tracklayer:
- Design TD-like or TDU-like tracks that have three-to-five turns and that are 400–500 yards long. Be creative in your design but avoid anything very complex.
- For the first 6 sessions, use two flags about mid-leg and about 4 paces apart so the handler can see the direction of the new leg to confirm the dog is correct.
- For unmarked tracks, use subtle markers on corners like clippies, haystacks, ground markers, or nothing at all. Triangulate all corners, especially unmarked ones. Make good maps. Be able to find the track and help the dog if he needs help.
- Use 1–2 hot dog treats per leg unless the handler prefers using an article in the middle of every leg.
- For TDU tracks, have an intermediate article on one or two of the legs in place of or in addition to the hot dogs.

Handler:
- Work on your corner communication.
- Use extra treats 30 yards after corners if his commitment begins to falter.
- Watch your dog's motivation level. If it drops two sessions in a row, back off the difficulty of the tracks. Reduce difficulty by decreasing age, length, number of corners, roughness of terrain, or increase the familiarity of the fields.
- If you have a particularly bad day, add a fun session with a simple-marked track on a familiar field.

Evaluation and Possible Adaptations:
- Keep track of your progress in both your detailed tracking log and the summary log on the next page. See sample logs on page 147.
- For 8A.11, evaluate your dog as you did in session 7.13 or 7.22.
- If you continue to have top evaluations, or even if it has dropped a bit, move on to Phase 9.
- Only stop to do some remedial work if your dog has become difficult to read. Otherwise, press on to the next phase while taking note of what continues to need work.
- If your dog develops corner problems and is no longer easy to read, consider remedial work with Plan C. If the problem is minor, a few sessions may clean it up. Finish off with two or more sessions like those described above and move on to the next phase.

Plan 8A Summary Log

Sesn	Site	Config.	Date	Actual Ages	Evaluation
8A.1					
8A.2					
8A.3					
8A.4					
8A.5					
8A.6					
8A.7					
8A.8					
8A.9					
8A.10					

Plan 8B Schedule — Building Confidence:

This plan calls for different locations each session. Try several new locations or locations you have not used in a long time. Find sites that are similar to those used to hold tests. You may not be able to find all brand-new tracking sites, but you find a few new sites or different ways to use your regular sites. Your dog needs to become accustomed to a wide variety of sites.

Apply this plan to the TD and the TDU separately.

Sesn	Location	Turns	Yards	Markers	Suggested Design	Age
8B.1	New field	3–5	400–500	2 flags mid-leg	Choose from Phase 6	30
8B.2					Choose from Phase 7	35
8B.3					Hat.	40
8B.4					Chair.	45
8B.5					Zigzag.	50
8B.6					Dog's Head.	55
8B.7				Haystacks	Chair with an open last turn.	30
8B.8					Hat with an open last turn.	45
8B.9					Dog's Head with an open turn.	55
8B.10					Zigzag with an open turn.	30
8B.11					Evaluate as in 7.13, 7.22	

Phase 8 Plan B Sessions 1–10.
1. Each leg 50–125.
2. Three hot dogs per leg.
3. Mark as shown in the table.
4. Age as shown in the table.

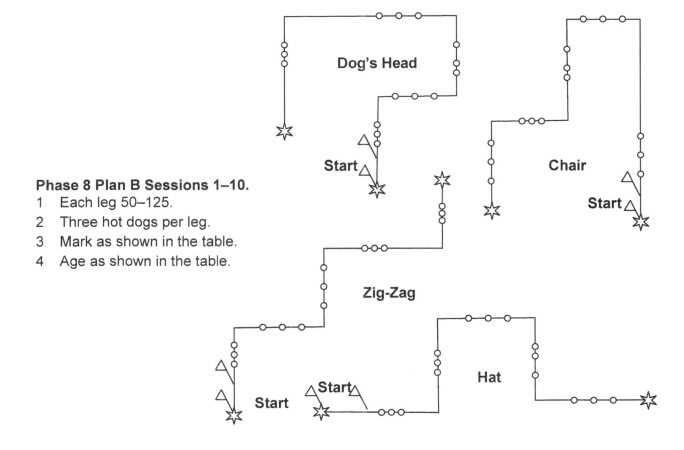

Phase 8. Perfecting Skills

If you have laid all your dog's tracks, find someone else to lay a couple of tracks in this phase. Have them follow 30–50 yards behind you talking quietly as if they were judges following you on a track. Your dog needs to be accustomed to people following you on the track.

Tracklayer:
- These tracks are motivational. Use 2–3 hot dogs per leg or an article in the middle of every leg. For TDU tracks, have an intermediate article on one or two of the legs in place of or in addition to the hot dogs.
- Design TD-like or TDU-like tracks with three-to-five turns that are 400–500 yards long. Be creative in your design, but avoid anything very complex.
- For the first 6 sessions, use two flags about mid-leg and about 4-6 paces apart so the handler can see the direction of the new leg to confirm the dog is correct.
- For unmarked tracks, use subtle markers on corners like haystacks, clippies, ground markers, or nothing at all. Triangulate all corners, especially unmarked ones. Make good maps. Be able to find the track and help the dog if he needs help.

Handler:
- Work on your corner communication.
- On the first six marked tracks, focus on minor issues like being wide on crosswind legs, over-shooting some corners, or committing to the next leg without confidence.
- Use extra treats 30 yards after corners if his commitment begins to falter.
- Watch your dog's motivation level. If it drops two sessions in a row, back off track difficulty. Reduce difficulty by decreasing age, length, number of corners, hilliness of terrain, or increase the familiarity of the fields.
- If you have a particularly bad day, add a fun session with a simple-marked track on a familiar field.

Evaluation:
- For session 8B.11, evaluate your dog as you did in session 7.13 or 7.22.
- If your evaluation improved, move on to Phase 9.
- Only stop to do some more remedial work if your dog has become difficult to read. Otherwise, press on to the next phase while taking note of what continues to need work.
- If your dog develops corner problems and is no longer easy to read, consider additional remedial training from Plan C. If the problem is minor, a few sessions may clean it up. Finish off with two or more sessions like those described above and move on to the next phase.

Plan 8B Summary Log

Sesn	Site	Config.	Date	Actual Ages	Evaluation
8B.1					
8B.2					
8B.3					
8B.4					
8B.5					
8B.6					
8B.7					
8B.8					
8B.9					
8B.10					

Phase 8. Perfecting Skills

Plan 8C Schedule — Skill Development:

This is a motivational remedial sequence to improve the dog's skills while enhancing his enthusiasm for the track. You enhance motivation by using a sequence of 5 hot dogs on each leg including the first leg, spaced at 30, 35, 40, 45, and 50. Dogs find this very motivating much like a jackpot. If you are unable to use food on the track, use two articles 10 yards apart in the middle of each leg and have a big party with your dog with lots of treats and play. Don't rush to restart your dog after these intermediate articles, play with him some more.

Apply this plan to the TD and the TDU separately.

Unlike plans 8A and 8B, this plan does not expect you to find new tracking fields each day. If things are going well, make some of these sessions on new tracking fields. Find sites that are similar to those used to hold tests. You may not be able to find brand-new tracking sites, but you should be able to find different ways to use them, so the dog becomes accustomed to variety.

Session	Tracks	Turns	Yards	Markers	Design	Age
8C.1	2 zigzags	2x2	400–500	2 flags mid-leg	2 Zigzags with 5 treats	30
8C.2						45
8C.3						30
8C.4						50
8C.5						30
8C.6						40
	Evaluate: if corners are now good, proceed; if not, repeat 8C.1–8C.6.					
8C.7	TD-like	3–5	400–500	2 flags mid-leg	Hat.	30
8C.8					Chair.	40
8C.9					Zigzag.	50
8C.10					Dog's Head.	60
8C.11				Haystacks	Chair with an open last turn.	30
8C.12					Hat with an open last turn.	40
8C.13					Dog's Head with an open turn.	50
8C.14					Zigzag with an open turn.	30
8C.15	Evaluate as in 7.13, 7.22					

Work on improving his corner skills using simple-marked zigzags with lots of rewards along the track. Each of the four aspects of being easy to read (close to the legs, shows loss of track, searches purposefully, and commits quickly) can be improved within the context of the marked zigzags. If you need to focus on more than one aspect, focus on the first one listed with a weakness.

- For a dog that is not following close to the footsteps, use longer legs on your zigzags, put markers or flags every 50 yards, and move up the line so you are only 10' behind the dog. Use line tension, raising and lowering your arm to keep the dog close to the track. Narrow your definition of being close to the track. Use lots of food on the track to reward the dog for being close to the actual footsteps.
- For the dog that does not show a distinctive loss of track, use corner markers 5 yards (15') before each corner and work 15' behind your dog. When you come alongside the flag, the dog is on the corner. Slow and stop him within 5–10' of the corner.

- For the dog that does not search with purpose, use food on the track at 30, 35, 40, 45, and 50 yards beyond every corner. Keep this up until the dog shows that he clearly anticipates the food sequence and works the corner with a clear purpose. Then start to spread the food out. Finally, slowly and randomly reduce the food so there is typically only one piece about 30–45 yards past a corner.
- For a dog that does not commit to a new leg as soon as he finds it, or is tentative in his commitment, use the same 5-drop food sequence described above. It is important to improve your own clarity of communication and quickness of commitment with these dogs. When the dog begins to anticipate the food sequence ahead, adopt a clear communication sequence between you and the dog. When he has moved along the new leg 6–30', increase the tension slightly above normal (don't pull back as that would be a correction) and verbally ask your dog if this is the good track. The dog should lean into the harness and pull you along the track. The very instant he starts to lean into the harness, you must reduce the tension to normal, step off after your dog, and quietly praise him for being so clever.

If you have laid most of your dog's tracks, find someone else to lay a couple of tracks in this phase. Have them follow 30–50 yards behind you talking quietly as if they were judges following you on a track.

A zigzag track is a two-corner track like those seen in Phase 5. A sample is shown below, that can be used for the first six sessions by adjusting the lengths of the leg. If your tracking field has trouble accommodating two zigzags, make one of them a U-shaped track (both corners in the same direction like the tracks in 7.1, 7.5...). Use two flags mid-leg past every corner.

Phase 8 Plan C Sessions 1–6.
1. Each leg 80 to 100 yards.
2. Average 250 yards per track, 500 total.
3. Five hot dogs per leg at 30, 35, 40, 45, & 50.
4. Two flags mid-leg about 4 paces apart.
5. Age as shown in the adjacent table.

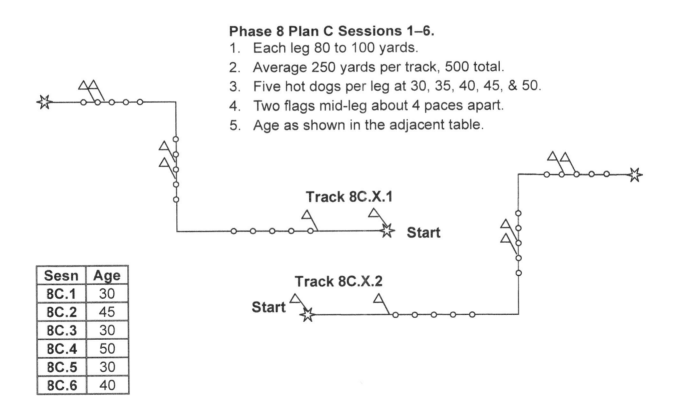

Sesn	Age
8C.1	30
8C.2	45
8C.3	30
8C.4	50
8C.5	30
8C.6	40

Phase 8. Perfecting Skills

For the last eight sessions, design TD-like or TDU-like tracks with three-to-five turns and that are 400–500 yards long. Use subtle markers on corners, like haystacks, ground markers, or nothing at all. Triangulate all corners, especially unmarked ones. Make good maps. Be able to find the track and help the dog if he needs help.

Sesn	Flag	Design	Age
8C.7	2 flags mid-leg	Hat.	30
8C.8		Chair.	40
8C.9		Zigzag.	50
8C.10		Dog's Head.	60
8C.11	Hay-stacks	Chair with an open last turn.	30
8C.12		Hat with an open last turn.	40
8C.13		Dog's Head with an open turn.	50
8C.14		Zigzag with an open turn.	30

Phase 8 Plan C Sessions 7–14.
1. Each leg 80+.
2. Five hot dogs per leg at 30, 35, 40, 45, & 50.
3. Mark as shown in the table.
4. Age as shown in the table.

Tracklayer:

- These tracks are motivational; avoid complications like difficult changes of cover or being near distractions in the field.
- For TD tracks, use 5 hot dogs per leg as shown, or hot dog then article then hot dog about 5 steps apart, or two articles spaced in the middle of each leg.
- For TDU tracks, have an intermediate article on one or two of the legs, in place of, or in addition to the hot dogs or tiny treats.
- Keep treats at least 30 yards from each corner.
- Once the dog searches for the new leg purposefully and commits to it with confidence, start to spread out the 5 hot dog sequence and then gradually reduce the number of hot dogs per leg.
- For the first 6 sessions, lay two 2-turn zigzag tracks per session.
- For the remaining sessions, design TD-like or TDU-like tracks with 3–5 turns that are 400–500 yards long. Be creative in your design, but avoid anything very complex.
- For the first 10 sessions, use two flags mid-leg and about 4 paces apart, so the handler can see the direction of the new leg to confirm the dog is correct.
- For unmarked tracks, use subtle markers on corners like haystacks, ground markers, or nothing at all. Triangulate all corners, especially unmarked ones. Make good maps. Be able to find the track and help the dog if he needs help.

Handler:

- Work on your corner communication.
- Watch your dog's motivation level. If it drops two sessions in a row, back off track difficulty. Reduce difficulty by deceasing age, length, number of corners, hilliness of terrain, or increase the familiarity of the fields.
- If you have a particularly bad day, add a fun session with a simple-marked track on a familiar field.
- Work on the skill areas identified as weak by your dog's evaluation:
  1. If he is not close to the straight leg, raise the line and increase tension somewhat. When he returns closer to the track, lower your hand and return gradually to light-comfortable tension. When he realizes that there is a jackpot on each leg, he should be willing to stay close to the track to get to it faster.
  2. If he goes straight past corners with no indication you can see, have the tracklayer put a small marker 15' before the corner. When he has passed the pre-corner marker by 30', he is 15' past the corner so increase the tension to stop him. Encourage him to search and circle around you. When he realizes that there is a jackpot waiting on the next leg, he should be more obvious in his loss of track indication.
  3. If he does not search at corners and wanders aimlessly or tries to quit, encourage him to circle and make it easy for him to find the next leg. When he realizes that there is a jackpot waiting on the next leg, he should become more purposeful.
  4. If he notices the new leg but does not commit to it, or only follows it weakly with no enthusiasm, make it easy for him to follow the leg. When he realizes that there is a jackpot waiting on the next leg, he should become more purposeful.

Evaluation and Possible Adaptations:

- For session 8C.15, evaluate your dog as you did in the discussion section of this phase (page 128).
- If your evaluation improved, move on to Phase 9.
- Only stop to do additional remedial work if your dog has become difficult to read. Otherwise, press on to the next phase while taking note of what continues to need work.
- Throughout your training, it is never wrong to redo a session or two of zigzags with five hot dogs on every leg, either as a motivational session or to allow you to work on your corner handling.

Plan 8C Summary Log

Sesn	Site	Config.	Date	Actual Ages	Evaluation
8C.1					
8C.2					
8C.3					
8C.4					
8C.5					
8C.6					
8C.7					
8C.8					
8C.9					
8C.10					
8C.11					
8C.12					
8C.13					
8C.14					

Sample Journal Log Entry — Phase 7

Session: 7.10
Dog: Twizzle
Date: 9/1/12
Layer: Sil
Location: Brown Ave
Weather: Warm, Partly Cloudy
Wind: 0-1
Length: 450
Age: 45

Evaluation: Very Good

Twizzle in season day 5.
Slow start but committed on own.
Wary of nearby hay stacks, but able to track past.
Excellent commitment into tall cover.
Slow to commit upwind.

Track Map

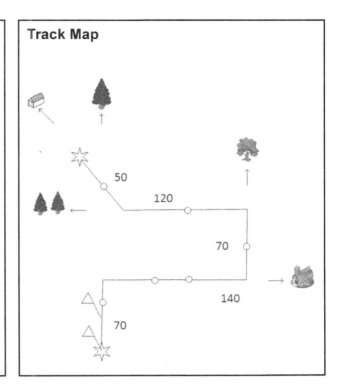

Sample Journal Log Entry — Phase 8

Session: 8A.8
Dog: Twizzle
Date: 9/17/12
Layer: Orci Urna
Location: Campbell Valley
Weather: Sunny Warm
Wind: Nil
Length: 470
Age: 50

Evaluation: Excellent

Dew damp ankle-high grass

Frequently distracted by tracklayer & spectators who were close behind, but she was willing to go back to work.

Track Map

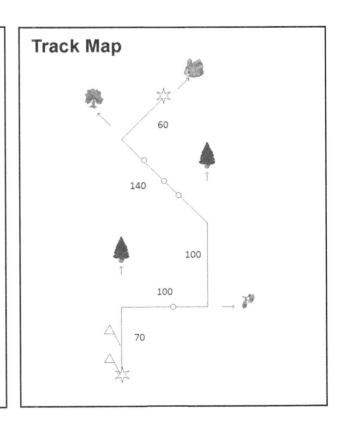

Phase 8. Perfecting Skills

Phase 9. Preparing for the TD or TDU Test

Purpose:
- Prepare you and your dog for the Tracking Dog and/or the Tracking Dog Urban test.

Strategy:
- Familiarize you and your dog with test-like terrain and tracking conditions.
- Teach your dog to ignore some common handler errors.
- Peak your dog's performance for the test.
- (Optional) Teach your dog to track 2-hour-old tracks while ignoring 24-hour-old tracks.

How to use this chapter:
- This phase includes two training progression schedules to utilize depending on how much time it takes to get into a test.
- Read the discussion section completely that describes how tracking tests are organized, the importance of gaining site and test familiarity, how to proof your dog for handling errors, optionally aging tracks to the full two hours, how to peak your dog's performance for test day, and how to be successful on test day.
- Specialized Training:
  - The field-only trainer will do all sessions in natural fields or lightly-contaminated sports field.
  - The urban-only trainer will do all sessions in urban campus-like environments among buildings with a mix of lawns and hard surface.
- Remember to keep up your detailed log of each track as well as your summary log.

The CKC-focused handler who already has their TD and wants to jump ahead to the UTD work should be patient and follow the aging schedule in 9A that is part of this phase as well as the proofing-handler-error sessions that are part of 9P. The additional UTD skills related to hard-surface turns are developed in the V1S UTD Supplement but these aging and handler-proofing skills are required as well.

Discussion:

Tracking tests are different than most other dog events because of the limited number of dogs who can be tested at any one event. It typically takes two judges and five to fifteen helpers two full days to put on a single TD or TDU test for twelve dogs. That is a lot of volunteers to help your dog get his title. In AKC tests, you need a certification that your dog is ready in order to enter a test. While not required for a CKC TD test, doing a fully blind test-like track successfully without any help is recommended.

Some tests have many more entrants than tracks. For an AKC test, all entrants are randomly drawn after the closing date to determine who gets in. Recently CKC adopted a similar draw-for-entry system.

I hope that you get into the test you enter. However, if you become an alternate, attend the test anyway. If one of the regular dogs fails to show up or gets sick at the last minute, the alternates are offered the track in the order they were drawn at the closing. Even if you do not get into the test, you will get to see some of the dogs run and become more familiar with the way tests are run. Be sure to verify that the test-like tracks you have been plotting for your dog in training match the complexity of the tracks you see at the test. Also consider the terrain, cover, wind, weather, presence of animals or people working nearby, and the presence of ground animals, wildlife, people and loose dogs on the tracking fields themselves.

In fact, it is a good idea to watch a tracking test before you enter just so you will be familiar with the way things happen at a test. Feel free to lay tracks for a test before you are ready to enter one. If you have a suitable vehicle, offer to provide transportation for the tracklayers and handlers between the tracking fields.

You will find a description of what to do on the day of your test on page 154. In the next few pages, you will find the training program to follow to be prepared for your test day.

Preparation Processes. Now that you have a well-prepared and skillful tracking dog, and now that you are a well-prepared and skillful handler, there are only a few more details to consider as you approach your dog's TD or TDU test. We will consider each of the pre-test issues and then you will plan your training accordingly.

Certification was mentioned in Chapters 6, 7 and 8. If you are preparing for an AKC TD or TDU test, you will need to be certified by an AKC judge or evaluator as a prerequisite to entering a test. This is done by having a judge put you through a TD or TDU test-like track. So, if you are not already certified, go ahead and get it done. For dogs who already have their CKC TD, their passing that test may qualify them for an AKC certification if the design of their CKC passing track happens to comply with the requirements for an AKC TD. Most, but not all, CKC TD tracks comply with AKC TD requirements; so you will need to send your judge's map to AKC for your certification.

Look ahead at the calendar for the next few tracking tests and decide which you will enter. That decision generates your time-line and allows you to plan the number of training sessions that can be worked between now and the test.

Site Familiarity. It is my experience that dogs and handlers who are familiar with a tracking test site are more likely to pass than those who are unfamiliar with the site. The dirt and vegetation at each site probably smell a little different to the dog. In addition, it is quite common for a site to harbor some unusual conditions that may distract the dog when he tracks there for the first time. So when you enter a test, try to find out as much as you can about the test site.

Can you track there before the test? While many tests are held at public parks that allow you to track, many other tests are held at private or restricted sites that allow tests but do not allow public access. Avoid using the actual site the week before the test even if it is available for public use. If you cannot use the actual site, find a similar site — one that is likely to have the same sort of microecology as the actual test site. In addition to being familiar with the terrain and cover at the test sites, being familiar with the weather conditions at the site may be useful as well. Some areas are prone to wind while others are less windy. If you regularly train in one of the less windy areas, find out if the tests you may enter are windy. If so, you need to find a way to train in the wind in spite of the convenience of training in your regular tracking haunts.

I personally try to track at a test site (or a similar substitute) two to four times before a test. If my dog and I are comfortable after two sessions, we leave it at that. Nevertheless, it is good to allow time for up to four sessions in case there are problems the first time or two at the site. I once tracked at a test site a few weeks before a test and discovered that my dog was totally distracted by what the geese left behind as they foraged there. This site was several hours from my home, so it took considerable effort to get back there several more times to get him completely comfortable with the site. Since I was willing to drive several hours to the test, I had to be willing to drive several hours to prepare for it. He ended up drawing the hill that the geese favored and passing the test (see page 212). You will not know what you are unprepared for until you actually track at the site, so go to the extra effort to become familiar.

Peaking Performance for the Test. You can do a few things in the last couple of weeks before a test to make sure that the dog's skill and enthusiasm for tracking is at its peak. The general idea is to work the dog quite hard two to three weeks before a test, then back off to motivational tracks the first half of the pre-test week, followed by a layoff for 3–4 days before the test. You want your dog to be highly enthusiastic for tracking when you take him out of your car on test day, which means he has to be under-worked for several days before. As well as avoiding tracking training for 3–4 days, I avoid other types of training for 2–3 days. See Schedule 9P on page 152.

Proofing Handler Errors. Almost all handlers make handling mistakes in tests. The handler gets nervous and does something that they would not ordinarily do. It is so likely to happen in a test that I like to expose my dog to the experience of handler error so that he learns to continue on the track in spite of it. The proofing sessions are set up to allow you to act weird on a couple of corners and be assured that the dog will be highly rewarded as soon as he overcomes your stupidity. These proofing sessions are included in the test preparation schedule on page 152 and described in more detail on page 153.

Aging to Two Hours Old (Optional but Recommended). Up until now, we have avoided teaching the dog to track past about 75 minutes because they tend to become quite interested in 24-hour-old tracks once they learn to track 90–120-minute-old tracks. Unfortunately, the way tracks are plotted the day before a test makes it likely that your dog will have to distinguish his test track from a false track made on plotting day. Once you teach a dog to follow a 2-hour-old track, you also must teach him to correctly distinguish the original track from 24-hour-old tracks. This is not hard to do but it does take a little extra time and effort.

The idea is to increase the age of the tracks in 10-minute increments from 60 minutes to 120 minutes. Use TD-like tracks and intersperse the aged track sessions with an occasional 30-minute-old motivational track. Use enough 30-minute-old fun tracks to keep your dog's enthusiasm up even if he has a little difficulty learning to follow the older tracks.

Once this first step is done and your dog seems comfortable tracking 2-hour-old tracks, you set up pairs of days that you can track in the same place. The first day, you lay a TD or TDU track in the field and run it just as usual. You make a very good map and become thoroughly familiar with the landmarks in the field. You may even leave a few clippies or pieces of surveyor's tape in strategic locations along the track overnight. The next day, you lay a different TD-like or TDU-like track that crisscrosses the first track in known places. Be sure to leave a couple of nice food drops 10–30 yards past the places the two tracks cross. If your dog notices yesterday's track, allow him to investigate it. If the dog tries to commit to the wrong track for more than 20–40', move up the correct track past where they cross and happily call your dog to find the good track. Point at the good track, be very happy, be very excited about this good track, and your dog will quickly get the idea and get the food drops you left. Get down and love the track, if necessary.

Remember to pick up the clippies the day before.

You may need to repeat this double day process three to six times to allow your dog to fully understand the concept and learn to stay with the original track.

Track Age Schedule (Optional but Recommended). This plan is for dog-handler teams with enough time before their test to complete the whole track-age schedule as well as the test preparation schedule. While a TD or TDU track will be 30–120 minutes old, most are 30–60 minutes old. Sometimes they get older than an hour because a dog or two before you in the test order takes a long time, so this schedule is useful to follow if you have time to do so. If you do not have time to do both, skip this track-age schedule and go on to the test preparation schedule. This twenty-one session schedule takes two to three months to complete assuming you track two to three times a week.

Design TD-like (or TDU-like as appropriate) tracks that have three to five turns and that are 400–500 yards long. Be creative in your design but avoid anything very complex.

Session	Location	Markers	Design	Age
9A.1	Anyplace	Clippies	TD-like	1:00
9A.2				1:10
9A.3				1:20
9A.4				:30
9A.5				1:30
9A.6				1:40
9A.7				1:50
9A.8				:45
9A.9				2:00
9A.10	Site A	Clippies +	Fun TD-like	1:30
9A.11	Site A — Next Day	Clippies	TD crosses 9A.10	1:00
9A.12	Fun familiar site	Clippies	TD-like	:30
9A.13	Site B	Clippies +	TD-like	1:45
9A.14	Site B — Next Day	Clippies	TD crosses 9A.13	1:15
9A.15	Fun familiar site	Clippies	Fun TD-like	:45
9A.16	Site C	Clippies +	TD-like	2:00
9A.17	Site C — Next Day	Clippies	TD crosses 9A.16	1:30
9A.18	Fun familiar site	Clippies	Fun TD-like	:30
9A.19	Site D	Clippies +	TD-like	2:15
9A.20	Site D — Next Day	Clippies	TD Crosses 9A.19	1:45
9A.21	Fun familiar site	Clippies	Fun TD-like	:45

Use subtle markers on corners like clippies, haystacks, ground markers, or nothing at all. Triangulate each corner, especially the unmarked ones. Make good maps. Be able to find the track and help the dog if he needs help. If you had to help your dog more than once in the past five TD-like tracks, add a small flag or marker mid-leg to give you confidence that you know exactly where the track is located. For the first day of the two-day session pairs (9A.10, 9A.13, 9A.16, 9A.19), leave some clippies or surveyors tape on the track to help you be sure of the landmarks and where tomorrow's track can cross today's. Leaving the markers overnight is indicated by "Clippies +" in the table above. Be sure to pick them up after tracking there the second day.

Phase 9. Preparing for the TD or TDU Test

Remember to keep detailed logs of each track as well as a summary log as shown on page 157. Continue to work on your corner communication and keeping your dog close to the straight legs. Use extra treats 30 yards after corners if his commitment begins to falter.[1]

Watch your dog's motivation level. If it drops two sessions in a row, back off track difficulty. Reduce difficulty by decreasing length, number of corners, hilliness of terrain, or increase the familiarity of the fields. If you have even one particularly bad day, add a fun session with a simple-marked track on a familiar field.

For the second day of the two-day paired sessions (9A.11, 9A.14, 9A.17 or 9A.20), if your dog notices yesterday's track, allow him to investigate it. If your dog tries to commit to the wrong track for more than 20–40', move up the correct track past where they cross and happily call your dog to find the good track. Point at the good track, be very happy, be very excited about this good track, and your dog will quickly get the idea, and then he gets the food drops you left.

If your dog is still committing to yesterday's tracks by the end of this schedule, add a few more sessions in the three-session pattern of 9A.10 through 9A.21. However, I expect your dog is beginning to get the idea about staying on the track that he started on.

Test Preparation Schedule. This plan is for dog-handler teams who are preparing for a test. Feel free to adjust this to fit your and your dog's particular needs. As the test approaches, do the last three sessions on the days indicated and avoid tracking or other strenuous activity for your dog on the four days before the test. Even if you have been training TD and TDU in parallel, you want to do the 9P schedule independently for each test.

Session	Location	Turns	Yards	Markers	Design	Age
9P.1	Fun familiar site	5–6	400–500	Flags mid-leg	Proof Handler Errors	30
9P.2	Test-like site	3–5	400–500	Flags mid-leg	TD-like	20
9P.3	Fun familiar site	5–6	400–500	Flags mid-leg	Proof Handler Errors	45
9P.4	Test-like site	3–5	400–500	Haystacks	TD-like	30
9P.5	Fun familiar site	5–6	400–500	Flags mid-leg	Proof Handler Errors	60
9P.6	Test-like site	3–5	400–500	Haystacks	TD-like	45
9P.7	Anyplace 8 days before test	4–6	500–600	Haystacks	TD-like Long but fun	50
9P.8	Anyplace 7 days before test	4–6	500–600	Haystacks	TD-like Long but fun	45
9P.9	Fun familiar site 5 days before test	3–5	250	Haystacks	Short Easy Fun	30

For sessions one through six, design TD-like tracks that have three-to-six turns and that are 400–500 yards long. Be creative in your design but avoid anything very complex. Use subtle markers on corners like haystacks, ground markers, or nothing at all. Make good maps. Be able to find the track and help the dog if he needs help.

Remember to keep detailed logs of each track as well as a summary, shown on page 158.

Proofing Handler Errors Sessions. For the sessions where you proof handler errors (9P.1, 9P.3, 9P.5), look at the track and select two or three easy corners to do the proofing. Make sure there are two food drops 30 and 35 yards past these corners. Common handler errors are:
- Unusually high tension when the dog commits to the new leg.
- The line goes slack while the dog is searching.
- Follow the dog in an uncertain/disbelieving manner with a slack line or a very tight line.
- Inadvertently stand on the line as the dog commits to the new leg.
- Stand your ground and refuse to follow the dog on the new leg the first time he tries to commit.

Each session, select one or more of these common handler errors and act it out on those corners. Be as much of a ham as you need to be to put your dog off a little bit. Once your dog reacts to your acting, stop acting and return to your normal handling.

If your dog quits searching, happily help him with the correct track. Be very happy and upbeat about showing him the track and encouraging him to find it. If your dog continues to search but fails to take the new leg the next time he crosses it, help him as described above. If your dog continues to search but avoids returning to the area of the new leg in a few minutes, help him as needed.

As your dog tracks the next leg, watch his attitude. Wait to proof another handler error until his enthusiastic attitude returns to normal. It may take another corner or two for him to regain confidence in his teammate who seems to be having a very off day.

Watch your dog's motivation level. If it drops two sessions in a row, back off track difficulty. Reduce difficulty by decreasing age, length, number of corners, hilliness of terrain, or increase the familiarity of the fields. If you have even one particularly bad day, add a fun session with a simple-marked track on a familiar field.

Distant Test Sites. If you are traveling a long distance out of your area to a test, you should make every effort to be there well before the test. But in some cases, you may be unable to arrive at the test area until just a few days before the test. The earlier you can arrive, the better; but few of us can arrive at a national specialty tracking test two to three weeks before the event in order to follow the 9P schedule on the previous page.

Talk to the test secretary or someone local to the test site who is familiar with the site and get a good description of the site. Find some place near your home that approximates the site and track there. When you get to the test area, walk your dog around in another area similar to the test site, and then give your dog the following sequence of tracks: A 50-yard straight track 15 minutes old, a 70x50 yard single-corner "L" track 25 minutes old, and a 75x75x50 zigzag track 35 minutes old. If you think your dog might take more than 10 minutes to run a track, lay them one at a time. Don't use the test site for these last minute tracks unless you are there more than a week before the test.

Phase 9. Preparing for the TD or TDU Test

On the Day of the Test arrive early for the draw where the dogs' running order is determined. The time and location of the draw are indicated on the premium list and judging schedule for the test.

If I am unfamiliar with the test site, I may drive by the site the night before the test to make sure I can find it. I typically arrive about a half-hour before the draw, so I have plenty of time to get lost, put on my boots, and exercise my dog before the draw. Typically, the dog that runs first will be at his start about fifteen to twenty minutes after the draw, so you should be prepared. On the other hand, the dog who runs twelfth in a twelve-dog test may have to wait four hours after the draw before getting to start his track.

When it is your turn, you may be able to walk to your track, you may be able to drive some place near it, or you may have to ride in a stranger's truck to get to your track. However you get there, you will meet two judges who, despite their perhaps imposing demeanor, are rooting for you to pass just as much as you are hoping to pass. They will tell you where the track starts and when you can start it.

By the time you get to the test, you and your dog are very well prepared to pass. Unless some very unusual distraction occurs, or unless you completely forget all your handling and communication skills, you and your dog will pass. You probably cannot do anything about very unusual distractions, but your training up to now has prepared you for most usual distractions and many unusual ones. You can remind yourself that you need only to read your dog, trust him, communicate to him your confidence in his skill and follow him. You know how to do all these things, so relax and just do them.

Do use your corner-communication sequence on every corner in the test. If your dog gets into trouble on the track, organize his search. Recall the circling methods taught in Phase 6. Get him to circle at several different distances from you. If he cannot find it, back up toward the last place he was definitely tracking (which is probably near the corner). If he still cannot find it there, and particularly, if there is some unusual scent condition in the area, circle your dog in ever-larger circles until he can reach past the unusual scent condition. Let your dog lead; move in general harmony with your dog when is moving in his search for the good track. If your dog is about to quit, do what you need to do to get him started again. Even if the judges fail you for guiding, you will be no worse off than if they fail you for quitting. I believe it is no worse to be failed for guiding than it is to be failed for quitting.

Remember to be patient and let your dog thoroughly search the area where he first indicated a change in scenting behavior. Once you do decide to move, whether backing up or expanding the dog's search area, avoid leading your dog since that may be interpreted as guiding. Stepping backward or side stepping as your dog is moving will allow the team to get where it might be good to search, without the handler walking some place with intent. See page 163 for additional discussion of the differences between training, handling, and guiding as well as page 76 for a discussion of trust.

Tracking is a wonderful sport. If you have had a great time training for your TD and TDU, you may want to go on to train for the TDX and VST tests. The TDX test is much more difficult than the TD, but your TD training has laid the solid foundation upon which your advanced training will be laid. The VST test is much more difficult than the TDU test, but your TDU training has built a firm foundation for going on to the VST. A good deal of training is required for each advanced test.

Wizard's TD and Cow-Herding Test, 1991

After Mr. Q earned his TDX in February (see his story on page 212), his older sister Wizard and I were faced with a dilemma — all the remaining TD tests we could enter this tracking season in Northern California were on heavily-grazed cow pastures. She had been recently certified but had never trained on horse or cow pastures. Either we could wait until next year, or we could learn to track on cow pastures.

The first test was in only a week (I had not known the site had horses when I entered it), and the other test with cows was in only four weeks. So I tried to figure out how to introduce her to horses and cows without completely confusing her. As it turned out, we failed the first test because the deep horse footprints created scent pools she was not used to and because of the heavy rain rather than because of horses on the track.

To train a dog on cows, I decided I needed to control the age of the track, and how recently cows had been over the area of the track. So I started her with 15-minute-old tracks in a corner of a pasture where the cows were not actively grazing. I increased the age to 30 minutes over the next several sessions while keeping to inactive areas of the pasture. I dropped back to 20 minutes when I laid the first track through cows actively grazing. Again, I increased the age over several sessions until she was doing tracks older than 30 minutes in areas where cows had grazed during and after I laid the track. Only once did we happen to have a cow right on the track when she ran it, but it moved away well before Wizard got to that place on the track.

During this training process, I noticed Wizard started to lose some enthusiasm when she was confused by cow tracks. While I normally train with about one piece of hot dog per leg, I decided to try putting three to five pieces of hot dog in quick succession on each leg. I went 40–50 yards down the first leg and placed a hot dog on each of the next three to five steps. On each succeeding leg, I started the hot dogs about half way down the leg and increased the number of paces between pieces. So by the fifth leg, I placed the hot dogs at five-pace intervals. Her attitude and speed really picked up when she came to the hot dog area. These extra rewards helped me keep her motivation high while training her more intensely than I ordinarily train a Westie temperament.

After a month of training, she was nearly reliable on cows. We drew the first track and drove right up to our track. She started out quickly and made it to the third corner without much difficulty. As she started out on the fourth leg, she was heading toward a herd of about thirty cows on the hillside above us. She did not notice them, but the cows and I were watching each other intently. As she approached them, she finally looked up at them. Some ran away, so she tracked another 10 yards. Then several started to run towards her, she looked up and barked, and they ran away. She kept on tracking until she got to the area they had just been grazing. She started to cow track so I gave her a little line so she might get past the area they had messed up. In another ten yards, she circled back like she was at a corner. Well behind me, her nose went down and she started moving in a straight line. By the time she had traveled the long fifth leg, she had been blown some yards off the track. But she came back to the glove and earned her TD.

According to the tracklayer, the cows were milling about the end of the track when she laid it. After she had placed the glove, two of them started to play tug of war with it. Luckily, they dropped it close enough to the track and Wizard was able to find it.

Twizzle's TDU Test, August 2014

At the 5:45 am draw on what will turn into a hot summer day in Missoula, Montana, I draw TDU track 2 for Twizzle. See page 114 for a map of her track that weaved through married student residential housing at the University of Montana.

Twizzle is happy when I start to get her tracking gear on, but not as excited as normal. Perhaps she senses some nervousness in me, but I do not feel particularly nervous. So I walk her over to the waiting starting flag. As we approach the start, she puts her nose down and really focuses on several spots (footsteps or pee spots?) I hold her at the start to breathe in the scent of the sock for a count of ten. She is focused on the track as I release her, and she immediately adopts her tracking posture as she lines out.

In 20 yards she turns back and stares at the judges. In a light tone, I tell her that "they can be there" and "back to the track." She looks incredulously at me then returns to the track and ignores the judges for the rest of the track.

She notices several contamination crosstracks and a piece of obvious trash, but she quickly rejects them and returns to the main track. When she comes to an asphalt driveway, she quickly commits across it and finds the track on the other side. She indicates change of scent, quickly checks left, then nails the right turn along the front of the housing. She tracks past a building and almost up to the next when she loses the scent. She first searches to the right, finds some contamination and investigates it briefly. Then she circles around to the left, finds the next leg — "Is this the good track?", "Yes!" as she accelerates, "I believe you" as I follow with a happy smile. About halfway between the combined lengths of the buildings she finds a nice heavy leather square. "Yippee!" I praise her and rub her playfully telling her how clever she is. She is ready to start up when no treats are forthcoming. She takes off happily and pauses only momentarily before committing across a two-row parking area to the grass on the other side.

Before she gets between the next set of buildings, she loses scent and starts to search. It is obvious that there is a lot of contamination in this area and she is having trouble finding the next leg. After several circles she finds the track to the left with conviction, and we are off. As she passes the last building before the street she indicates loss of scent but wants to search ahead closer to the street. I have to move with her since light poles, utility poles and mailboxes are in the way of the line. She seems drawn to the left back over the parking-lot entrance but does not commit and circles back to the initial loss of scent point. Just beyond it, she finds the track, commits to it, and we take the last leg to her cloth glove and TDU.

Twizzle did a wonderful job of taking responsibility to search for and stay with the original good track. I am very proud of her for ignoring the distracting contamination of dogs, people, and squirrels who messed up the simplicity of the track.

Phase 9A Summary Log

Sesn	Site	Config.	Date	Actual Ages	Evaluation
9A.1		TD-like		1:00	
9A.2		TD-like		1:10	
9A.3		TD-like		1:20	
9A.4		TD-like		:30	
9A.5		TD-like		1:30	
9A.6		TD-like		1:40	
9A.7		TD-like		1:50	
9A.8		TD-like		:45	
9A.9		TD-like		2:00	
9A.10		Fun TD		1:30	
9A.11		TD cross		1:00	
9A.12		TD-like		:30	
9A.13		TD-like		1:45	
9A.14		TD cross		1:15	
9A.15		Fun TD		:45	
9A.16		TD-like		2:00	
9A.17		TD cross		1:30	
9A.18		Fun TD		:30	
9A.19		TD-like		2:15	
9A.20		TD Cross		1:45	
9A.21		Fun TD		:45	

Phase 9P Summary Log

Sesn	Site	Config.	Date	Actual Ages	Evaluation
9P.1					
9P.2					
9P.3					
9P.4					
9P.5					
9P.6					
9P.__					
9P.__					
9P.__					
9P.__					
9P.__					
9P.7		Long Fun TD	Test – 8 days before		
9P.8		Long Fun TD	Test – 7 days before		
9P.9		Short Easy Fun	Test – 5 days before		

Part II — Advanced Tracking towards the TDX

TDX is a complex, strenuous team sport. There are a number of advanced skills that a dog and handler should master in preparation for a TDX test. This training plan combined with your thoughtful application of it, plus some perseverance and hard work will prepare you and your dog for one of the most challenging and rewarding tests in dogdom. It is a most enjoyable and rewarding journey, so enjoy every step along the way.

The nature of training for an advanced test like TDX requires more adaptation on the part of the trainer to build the required skills in both the dog and the handler. Phases X1–X3 are explicit schedules you can follow as closely as you followed the TD/TDU sessions in Part I. They do include checklists of tracking situations to include in your tracks, some of which require some thoughtful consideration on your part. Phase X4 also provides training structure but requires even more initiative from the trainer to tune the track designs to the specific skill needed by the handler and dog. Phase X5 provides the finishing touches for the great tracking team. Given the foundation developed in Part I of this book (and it is wise to review that foundation from time to time), you can be confident that your thoughtful adaptation of this TDX plan will be successful.

Now a natural question is whether to intermix urban tracking with your TDX training. The answer is it is up to you. While there are some synergies, you are likely to find your dog and yourself making progress at different rates in each style. While I typically focus strongly on the TDX when I am training it, I often find myself far from a TDX field and choose to work contamination exercises and hard-surface exercises in nearby sites. It does not hurt either venue's skill development. While it is natural to expect synergy between crosstracks and contamination, neither seems to reinforce the other very much. Plan to build the dog's understanding of staying on the good track separately for tracks in natural fields and those on urban lawns.

Training Philosophy:

In a TDX test, the dog faces a variety of complex tracking problems. If we practiced and proofed them all, the dog will lose motivation to track and probably die of old age before being ready to enter a test. Rather than proof all possible TDX tracking problems, we expose the dog and handler to a representative sample of TDX problems, and by doing so, we teach the dog to solve complex tracking problems. Furthermore, we maintain such a high level of motivation that the dog is willing and anxious to solve them.

Not every TD dog-handler team will be successful in advanced tracking. Most excellent and very good TD teams can succeed with the TDX, but those teams that just squeaked by their TD may find the TDX more difficult than they care to attempt. If you are in doubt, start and see how you and your dog respond to the necessary training. Somewhere in the first few phases of training, you will either find yourself totally committed, or you will realize that there are more important things to do with this particular dog.

TDX Test Overview:

A TDX test track conforms to the following guidelines:

	AKC	CKC
Age:	3–5 hours.	3–5 hours.
Length:	800–1000 yards.	900–1000 meters.
Start:	Single flag, article.	Single flag, scent pad.
Articles:	Four dissimilar, one at start, two intermediate, plus the final glove.	Three leather articles, typically gloves, dog must find final article and one other.
Corners:	5–7, acute discouraged.	5–8, acute OK.
Crosstracks:	2 people cross in two places about 90 minutes after the main track.	1 person crosses in 2 places about 60 minutes after the main track.
Obstacles:	at least 2 obstacles, often difficult.	None required; changes of cover and some obstacles OK.
Line:	20–40'.	10–49', handler should typically work well back on line.

Advanced Skills Required:

TDX is an advanced test of field tracking and is much more difficult than the TD. Key additional skills needed by the aspiring TDX dog:
- Blind start without a directional flag requires the dog's clear commitment right at the start.
- 3–5 hour age requires considerable focus and stamina over the 800–1000 yard length.
- Crosstracks require deep understanding by the dog so he resists taking attractive fresher tracks.
- Variations in cover require matching the track scent as it varies with cover changes.
- Variation in terrain including steep segments up and down requires stamina of the dog and handler alike.
- Compound physical and scenting obstacles require problem solving to find a lost track in complex scenting situations.
- Noticing and indicating articles to the side of the dog's tracking path requires skill.
- Perseverance, confidence, and commitment are required to convince the often uncertain handler to follow along.

TDX is a team sport that requires considerable handler and trainer skill as well as dog skill:
- Maintaining the dog's motivation by avoiding too many difficult issues per track, or too little reward while the dog masters the many skills required of him.
- Dog reading skills to understand what your dog is doing in complex scenting situations.
- Staying connected with your dog so you remain a team even in difficult conditions.
- Shifting responsibility for "Staying with the Good Track" to your dog.
- Recovering from being off track. Specifically, helping your dog search a large area without taking responsibility away from the dog.
- Landscape reading skills so you stay oriented in the field when your dog needs help.
- Staying positive and happy through training periods where things go wrong.
- Trusting your dog because you have trained him to love to stay on the good track.

TDX Training Overview:

- First, gradually age the track to three hours while introducing the dog to single flag starts, multiple articles, and simple obstacles.
- Second, return to fresh tracks but with crosstracks at half the age of the track, and gradually age the track to five hours. Also, introduce some compound obstacles while continuing to build your dog's skills and your own handling skills.
- Third, another fresh-to-old track sequence while continuing your crosstrack, obstacle, and handling training.
- Fourth, vary age and complexity so many of your tracks are TDX test complexity and handled without markers. You are building your dog's skill, your own skill, and your joint teamwork. Some of these TDX-complexity tracks should be laid by a trusted tracklayer so you don't know where the track goes.
- Once you and your dog can pass about one-third of your blind TDX test-like tracks in Phase X4, promote yourselves to Phase X5 and start to enter tests while continuing to work on improving weaker skill areas.

Handlers who recently trained for the TD or TDU test will have emphasized reading and following their dog on blind tracks. For their TDX training they should initially put blind tracks on the back burner and focus on training their dog to understand the complexities of TDX tracks so he works them in a way that his handler can read him and trust him. So, you will shift to marked tracks for Phases X1, X2, and X3 while you build your dog's skill with age, complexity and crosstracks. During these phases, you will often need to guide or help your dog so he learns what is correct and rewarding. Avoid treating these tracks as tests of how good your dog is; treat them as training opportunities. In Phases X4 and X5 you will shift back to blind tracks after your dog's skills are solid. Then you will be able to read and follow your dog in the more complex situations found on TDX tracks.

Most Important — Maintain Motivation:

Throughout TDX training, frequently intersperse the main training sessions with motivational tracks — tracks that are much younger and much easier than the main training tracks. The phase schedules include some motivational tracks but do them more frequently if your dog's enthusiasm starts to drop even a little.

Throughout TDX training, condition yourself and your dog by long walks or jogs in hilly backcountry. This will keep you both in shape so fatigue does not interfere with your judgment as a handler or both team members' enjoyment of the training tracks.

Always keep a training journal so you can look back and discover what types of conditions you have missed in your recent training and so you can detect how drops in motivation or new problem behaviors began.

If your dog becomes deeply demotivated at any time in your TDX training, consider the re-motivation plan in Appendix A (ATE 4) on page 408.

Basics Skills Revisited

Maintain the fundamental principles presented in Part I:
- Motivation, motivation, motivation.
- The dog should track very close to the track.
- The dog is responsible for leading you down the track.
- You must maintain a light-firm tension on the line at all times; stay in contact with your dog.
- Corner communications!!!
- Read your dog.
- Read the landscape — maintain your orientation in the field.
- Organize your dog's search when he has trouble.
- When your dog needs help, do so happily! It is an opportunity to teach.

As the track gets older and older, many dogs that stayed close to TD-aged tracks start to act as though the scent near the footsteps is "too faint", "too strong", or "bad smelling", preferring to track several feet downwind of the track. Don't let them hoodwink you; they can track close to older tracks if you show them that is the best, most rewarding way to track. So when a dog starts to track wide of the track, use line tension and raising your hand to make it easiest for the dog to stay right on the track. Make sure you have frequent reward points along the legs to increase the value of the track. With a dog that stays close to the track, you will have a much easier job reading your dog once you progress to blind tracks again.

Corner communication takes on added importance in TDX work and takes on the added dimension of obstacle communication as well. Your dog will face situations in this work where there is a sequence of closely spaced obstacles. If your dog can clearly communicate to you that he is on the track in only a short distance and if you can quickly communicate to him your confidence that he is right, you will both be fully prepared for the next obstacle. If there is doubt in your mind when he reaches that next obstacle, both of you will have difficulty overcoming the second obstacle.

Advanced Basics

When a track has multiple articles, the intermediate articles are great places to reward your dog and to give him water. Your dog should become so enthusiastic about the track that unless you make finding articles very special, your dog may overrun articles without bothering to point them out to you. So you will need to build both a very strong tracking drive as well as a very strong article indication. Great treats or toys for the articles, fun play at each article, and genuine enthusiasm on your part, combined with never allowing him to miss an article, will build that strong article indication. Play the glove game at the end of the track and even on non-tracking days.

Dogs may be taught to indicate articles in a variety of ways. Some people suggest having the dog retrieve the article, but I advocate having them stop at the article and optionally stand, sit or down. The reason I do this is because it makes for more reliable restarts. If you and your dog are tracking several feet downwind of the track and the dog curves into the article and retrieves it, you and your dog will end up a few feet off the track when you restart. You might be restarting him on a deer track for all you know. On the other hand, if your dog stops at the article and you walk up to the dog, then when you restart him, you will be restarting him right on the track. How fortuitous!

TDX Equipment. The figure on the right shows some typical articles and equipment for TDX training: clockwise from the upper left is a flag, a leather glove, two eyeglass cases, a scarf, a sock, two clippies, and a roll of surveyor's tape. Other typical articles include cloth hats, other types of cases, and belts. All are about the size of a hand. The same harness and line used for TD are suitable for the TDX and all your dog's tracking.

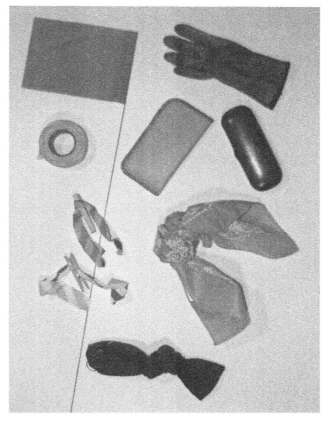

Note that a dozen or more clippies (clothes pins) may be used when laying a full TDX track. Clothes pins are convenient because they are easy to grab as you pass them later when running the track. See 92 and 168 or more information on clippies.

To **restart** your dog after playing with him at the intermediate article, just stand up and give your tracking command. Most dogs will quickly realize that there is more tracking to do and go right back to work.

Any time a dog has trouble restarting, let him try to work it out then happily help him find the track. If that does not work, place a treat or a second article about 30 yards past the first for several sessions.

Active Handling.

Handling needs to be active at all stages of training and testing. While training your dog, you will be developing your active handling skills which will be useful during testing. But you will need additional handling skills to develop and teach your dog his needed skills.

Guiding versus Active Handling. Many handlers focus on the test prohibition of guiding and fail to handle or even train their dog during their practice tracks. All during your dog's TDX training, and particularly during the first three phases of it, completely ignore the idea that guiding is bad and focus on training your dog, as well as learning to handle.

As each training track starts, it is fine to try to handle without helping your dog as this shifts the responsibility to the dog to make the decisions. Still, be quick to help your dog as soon as he needs it, so you end up helping as little as possible while encouraging your dog to learn to be successful. As his learning solidifies, he will become a better, more reliable, tracking dog who will understand how to follow the complex track.

You also will need to learn to handle your dog to promote his learning as well as to allow him to sort out the track complexities and follow the good track, even when complex obstacles and crosstracks make that a tricky thing to do. Recommendations of how to handle to teach your dog skills are described in each of the exercise types.

> ### *Don't Mail-In the Praise*
>
> Many handlers go through the motions of praising their dog at the articles and fail to emotionally engage him when doing so. It is not surprising their dog doesn't respond very much. It is much like what one sees at a stuffy dinner party where the guest stiffly says "Thank you very much" and the host formally replies "You are most welcome, my dear."
>
> High-quality praise and play at every article are essential to build value for the articles. Otherwise, your dog is going to glance at the article as he goes along the track and you won't notice it.
>
> He needs to feel your love and appreciation of him and his work every time you play and praise him. Roughhouse with him, tug with him, pet him, feed him treats, and enjoy him, whatever he likes a lot. When he feels your love, he will respond and work hard to earn that kind of praise again.

TDX dogs should be able to determine **track direction**. Throughout your training, you have avoided letting your dog backtrack tracks. Whenever the opportunity arises during circling or searching, keep him from backtracking a track more than about 6–15'. Most dogs will learn to determine track direction within 2–5 footsteps and many can determine the direction within a single footprint. I speculate that the 2–5 footstep dogs learn to distinguish very subtle scent strength differences while the single-footprint dogs learn to distinguish the smell of the heavy heel compression from the relatively lighter toe push-off or that the heel somehow smells different than the toe. While I prefer the single-footstep dog, some dogs don't learn the trick and require another few footsteps to confirm. A simple technique for teaching track direction is to approach the start flag from an acute angle, but don't try it until the dog is doing reliable angled starts. For a set of exercises that will help your dog understand track direction, see the recommended exercises in Appendix A (ATE 1) on page 402.

The primary technique used to **shift the responsibility** to the dog is the basic corner handling procedure of pivoting in one place, letting the line out when the dog wants to investigate a scent radially, using corner communications (Is this the good track?), following your dog once he has committed, and immediately climbing back up the line to 15–20' where you follow him normally (20' in an AKC test). If you stop or check your dog quickly when he investigates a false scent trail or follow him too quickly when he tentatively investigates a possible scent trail that happens to be correct, he will learn to depend on you to confirm his choices and be uncertain on a blind track when you cannot. Phases X1–X3 are all about training your dog's skills, but while you are doing that, you should also avoid helping him inadvertently, so he learns to take responsibility for where the track goes.

Once a track gets to be an hour and a half old, **food drops** tend to get dry, covered with ants, or stolen by birds. So I tend to use frequent articles along the track that give me the opportunity to reward my dog with food. I also use "cupcakes" that are a small piece of food frozen within a cupcake paper full of water. Placed upside-down on the track, by the time the dog gets to the cupcake, the ice has melted, and the food is still fresh. You may also use jackpots that are food in small margarine or yogurt tubs and that are left on the track sealed. You may have to open the lid for the dog once he finds it. Clicker-trained dogs can be signaled when they reach the reward point with a click while you come forward to help the dog access his reward but timing of the click is critical. Verbal praise is also good if used judiciously and sparingly along the track. A quiet "Good Boy" may be appropriate right after he makes the right choice and commits to the next section of the track. "Good Boy" before he has fully committed is a form of hinting or helping.

Another treat that can be used on older tracks in some TDX training environments is freeze-dried lamb-lung. When training in the rough terrain of most TDX environments, it can be cut into ½" pieces. When training in more urban environments like park lawns and sports fields, the smaller ⅛" to ¼" tiny treat size can be used. For a nice jackpot type reward, try a treat-article-treat sequence where each is about 5–10 yards apart.

Regardless of the size and type of the treat, if your dog misses some of them along the way, it is OK. If he misses most of them, then the pieces are too small, or the dog does not value them highly enough to act as primary reinforcers. Try something he values more.

TDX training takes quite a while. It is normal to **take a break** one or more times during this training because the weather is too hot, the snow too deep, or for some other reason. Resuming training correctly can quickly bring you and your dog back to the skill level where you stopped while restoring even more enthusiasm in the dog. Resuming training incorrectly can solidify your problem areas and seriously damage motivation.

Short breaks of a couple of weeks can be ignored while breaks of two months or more may cause a significant drop in proficiency and must be handled carefully. Depending on your dog, breaks of 3 to 7 weeks may be more or less significant.

Resume training by starting with a 45-minute-old track and adding 30 minutes to each track until you get back to the oldest track you had done before. If you have done several crosstrack patterns previously, have crosstracks on at least two of these tracks. Resume your training two sessions before the last one completed before the break. If you try to speed up your training progress by skipping this resuming-after-a-break sequence, you will actually slow it down by later requiring many additional problem-solving and motivation-building sessions.

Here is a typical resuming-after-a-break sequence for a dog whose last track before the break was session X2.11 (a 3-hour-old TDX track about 650 yards long). First do sessions R.1 to R.6 and then return to session X2.15 and continue from there.

Session	Track Age	Crosstrack Delay	Crosstrack Flags	Track Length	Number Corners	Number Obstacles
R.1	:45	none		400–500	4–5	0
R.2	1:15	none		500–600	4–5	1
R.3	1:45	:50	On track	600–700	4–5	1
R.4	:45	none		400	4–5	0
R.5	2:15	1:00	5 yds off	500–600	4–5	0
R.6	2:45	None		600–700	4–5	1

If the field tracking season is less than the whole year in your area, consider using sports fields and parks to extend your TDX training. There is a lot of aging and crosstrack work you can do in them. And near them, you can find nice TDX obstacles like hedges with gaps, tree lines, and paved roads and paths. Of course, do as much work in natural fields as possible (See pages 7-8).

Phase X1. Aging the Track to Three Hours

Purpose:
- Introduce the dog to older track scent by gradually aging the track to 3 hours.

Strategy:
- Gradually age the track to three hours old.
- Introduce the dog to single-flag starts.
- Introduce the dog to simple obstacles.
- Practice intermediate articles and the subsequent restart.

How to use this chapter:
- Look through the table below, which summarizes the training structure of this phase, and read the discussion section that follows.
- Do the 18 sessions listed following the age, length, and number of corners as closely as possible as described starting on page 172. Use natural fields whenever available, but much work can be done on urban lawns as well.
- Keep a detailed log of each session using a format like the one shown on page 31 and keep a summary log like the one shown on page 178.
- Do the X1.19 review session on page 174 to evaluate the team's progress.

Phase X1 Session Schedule:

Session	Track Age	Track Yards-	Start Angle	Number Corners	Number Obstacles	Articles
X1.1	1:00	400–500	0°	3–4	0	1 per leg
X1.2	1:10	500–600	15° L	4–5	1	1 per leg
X1.3	1:20	500–600	15° R	4–5	1	1 per leg
X1.4	1:30	500–600	15° R or L	4–5	1	1 per leg
X1.5	0:45	400	30° L	2–4	0	1 per leg
X1.6	1:40	600–700	30° R	4–5	0	1 per leg
X1.7	1:50	600–700	30° R or L	5–6	1	1 per leg
X1.8	2:00	600–700	45° L	5–6	1	1 per leg
X1.9	0:30	500	45° R	2–4	0	1 per leg
X1.10	2:10	600–700	45° R or L	4–5	1	1 per leg
X1.11	2:20	700–800	60° L	5–7	1	1 per leg
X1.12	2:30	700–800	60° R	5–7	1	1 per leg
X1.13	0:45	400	75° L	2–4	0	1 per leg
X1.14	2:45	600–800	75° R	5–7	1	1 per leg
X1.15	3:00	600–800	90° L	5–7	1	1 per leg
X1.16	3:15	600–800	90° R	5–7	1	1 per leg
X1.17	0:45	400	any	2–4	0	1 per leg
X1.18	1:30	1000	any	6–8	0	1 per leg
X1.19	Review					

Discussion:

Slowly stepping up the age of tracks does the best job of teaching the dog scenting skills so he is confident following three to five hour-old tracks. If during your TD work you exposed your dog to many 90–120-minute-old tracks and your dog is very confident on them, it is OK to start at session X1.6 and proceed per the schedule above.

Sadly, I find numerous intermediate TDX hopefuls whose dogs are not comfortable and confident with tracks in the 3–5-hour range because they skipped blocks of sessions in this phase and the next two phases. The typical explanation is they were late getting back to a track intended to be 90 minutes old, and the dog did fine on it even though it was 2:30 old. So they continued on from there. If it were only so easy to build a dog's confidence. Success on one track does not indicate mastery. When I am late for a track, I run it happily, but then I go back to the correct age in the next session and step up in age as the schedule indicates.

Another version of this same sort of thing happens in places with temperate winters. Say the Phase X1 training starts in the fall and the dog only learns to follow older tracks in cool, damp conditions. As soon as it gets warm in the spring, the dog starts to struggle right at the start of his tracks. This is because scent ages faster in warm, dry conditions, and so the real scent age of the spring tracks is much older than the tracks being done in the middle of the winter.

When this happens to my dog, I immediately reduce the age of the tracks within the context of the tracks the dog is otherwise doing, to find the track age the dog is comfortable and confident tracking. Then I step up in age in a manner similar to what is shown in Phases X1–X3 but doing the kinds of tracks he would otherwise be doing.

Article Indication and Restarts. Probably your dog has already had multiple intermediate articles on his TDU tracks and probably on some of his practice TD-like tracks; regardless, it is a good time to practice the restart from intermediate articles. Do make sure your dog stops and indicates each article. To do that, you need to make sure you have a nice party for your dog at every article on every track. Some handlers rush their dog to restart because they are afraid their dog will get distracted by the play and may not restart well. Don't worry, be happy. Your dog will quickly learn to restart after an article that was topped-off by a good play. That is what training is all about. If you let your dog glance at an article and move back to the track in training, he'll do that in tests, and you will miss the glance walk over the article, and hear the dread whistle. Make the article high value to your dog, as high a value as your dog values the track. This requires that you add value to each and every intermediate article along each and every training track.

If your dog has not been introduced to article restarts or is reluctant to get back to tracking, add a grab-and-go reward like a food-drop about 30 yards past each intermediate article. When you restart him, use a pleasant, encouraging voice saying something like "Back to the track. Yes, you can do it. Good dog."

All tracks should have a **single flag start** with an article at the flag for AKC or a scent pad at the start for CKC. Approach the flag at the angle indicated in the schedule. Hold your dog right at the article — do not let him start up without spending 10–20 seconds at the start. Let him play with the article if you can keep his nose right over the start. For CKC trainers, hold your dog with his nose over the scent square just as AKC handlers hold their dog over the article.

As a handler, think of the start as a corner that you have not tracked into. Use full corner communications and be sure to tell yourself "Yippee! We're at a corner that might go straight." This will be particularly important for blind tracks since you will not know the direction of the first leg. It will be very helpful to get your dog accustomed to you treating the start in this way.

Each track in your TDX training should have at least **one reward per leg** and more on particularly long legs. For tracks under 90 minutes old, you may be able to use food drops as you did in TD training, which is good because they are grab-and-goes that reward the dog without interrupting his tracking. For older tracks and for other situations where leaving food on the track is undesirable, use an article as a reward point.

Use a glove or wallet at the end. Use scarves, socks, plastic eyeglass cases, belts, hats, combs, and other personal articles for the other locations. When you introduce a new article, particularly one that has hard, smooth surfaces, mark it with a clippie so you can happily help your dog indicate it. If he ignores it, restrain him and make a big fuss about how much fun it is to find this article just as though he did it himself.

Clippies. You will find it convenient to mark important areas of the track in subtler ways than a big old stake. Many people use clothes pins with surveyor's tape, or orange clothes pins clipped on nearby branches, or they use brightly colored yarn or surveyor's tape. Placing them high keeps most of them from being noticed by the dog. Placing them low will also work fine. If your dog notices them, just say "Thank you. Back to your track." See page 92 for additional information on clippies and other ways to mark your track.

Be **ready to help** all during this phase as described in the TDX introduction about training and handling on page 163. Your dog is likely to have difficulty with track age once or more during this phase and on some new obstacles. He may quit, act like the track is very difficult to find, or track very slowly with little commitment. This is normal. You must be prepared to help your dog through a track until he gains confidence in handling these more difficult scenting conditions. You may want to put two flags midway down each leg so you can keep your bearings when you need to help your dog. Clippies on the corners are most useful.

Whenever your dog really loses the track, you first remind him what he is following by having him sniff the start article. Once your dog has had practice doing this, it will be a valuable technique to use in a test should your dog lose the track or get confused. So, whenever you need to help your dog, first show him the start article and have him get a good sniff of it. Then ask him to track again.

If he still has trouble, you will start to actively help him. Remember to put on a dynamic outward display of enthusiasm whenever you help him. Show your dog how much fun it is and how much confidence you have in him. Pull your dog back to the track right beside you, hold the line right above the harness, lean down and express your love of the track. You are Juliet, and the footsteps in the grass are Romeo. Express yourself to the grass, not the dog. Keep doing that while slowly moving along the track until your dog takes off in front of you and starts tracking again. Be sure you are having fun so your dog knows it! See page 60 for more on loving the track.

I lay almost all my own TDX training tracks because I always want to know exactly where the track is located in case I have to help my dog. Once I have the dog trained, I introduce other tracklayers so the dog is familiar with other footsteps, and I become familiar with handling this dog on blind tracks. If this is your first time training for a TDX, you will need to work quite a few blind tracks in phase X4 and X5 to become proficient handling a dog through blind tracks.

If you have already trained your dog on 2-hour-old tracks during Part I, you may wonder if you can skip right to session X1.10. Unless you incorporated single flag angle starts, multiple articles, and obstacles in your previous training, you should start no later than X1.6. Even so, start at the beginning if you took a break for more than 2 months or if the dog is not highly motivated as discussed in Phase 8.

Keep in mind the discussion on Basic Skills Revisited on page 162 and Advanced Basics on page 162 throughout your training.

A sample track taken from Mr. Q's tracking journal (session X1.8) is shown below. It shows the type of information I kept in his tracking log. I used index cards and wrote the notes on the back of the card. Many people use larger sheets but I find index cards convenient because they fit in my pocket.

You may note that the track has two obstacles rather than the single one specified by X1.8. Good catch. You will find that you run into more obstacles than you plan to when you start laying your track. It's OK; you can help your dog if he needs it. Just try to have an article soon after each obstacle — another thing I was unable to do on the pictured track.

Note also the wind and weather shown in the log. Mr. Q was happily tracking in the major storm with 50 mph winds and heavy rain. Tracking in stormy weather is important training since your test will not be canceled for a storm unless there is a real safety issue.

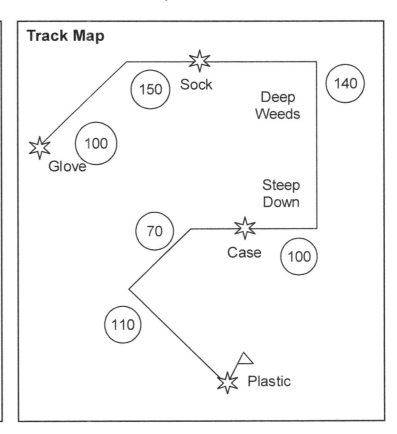

Dog: *Mr. Q*
Layer: *Sil*
Age: *2:00*
Length: *660*
Location: *Gatehouse & Vale*
Date: *Winter, 1990*
Weather: *Stormy, Heavy Rain*
Wind: *Gusty to 50 MPH*

Report: *Excellent.*

Good start & Article recognition.

Not bothered by wind.

Some tiring at 450 — remained willing and determined.

Phase X1. Aging the Track to Three Hours

Track Complexity, Obstacles, and Ground Covers.

By **track complexity,** I mean how difficult a particular track is for your dog. The complexity of a track is influenced by the age, length, and number of corners of the track. It is also affected by the number and type of crosstracks, the variety of ground covers, the number of cover changes, any terrain extremes traversed, and the number, type, and characteristics of obstacles. And finally, the weather — including the temperature, wind speed and amount of solar radiation — influences the actual complexity for the dog.

By consciously trying to control track complexity, we can train our dogs on tracks of gradually increasing complexity so they can sort out the particular novel difficulties along the track, be as successful as possible, and learn the fastest. Of course, we do not have the sensitive noses of our dogs, so our understanding of track complexity will always be imperfect. It is useful to have a general sense of what makes a track difficult for your dog so you can train him in a way that improves his skill and he becomes confident and committed on high-complexity tracks.

From the *AKC Tracking Regulations*, Chapter 4, Section 5 we see the purpose and definition of an **obstacle:**
> The purpose of an obstacle is to test one or more of the following:
> 1. The dog's ability to adapt to changing scent conditions;
> 2. The dog's ability to continue scenting while overcoming physical obstacles; and
> 3. The dog's ability to continue scenting under difficult and varied handling conditions.
>
> Various types of terrain and cover, including gullies, plowed land, woods, and vegetation may be used. Natural obstacles, like streams, or man-made obstacles, like fences, bridges, or lightly traveled roads may be used.

For training purposes, I find it useful to identify "simple obstacles" and "compound obstacles."
- A **simple obstacle** is one that is fairly isolated from corners or other obstacles that is crossed directly without a change in direction. A road crossing may be a simple obstacle if it is crossed with a considerable stretch of grass track approaching it and leaving it.
- A **compound obstacle** is an obstacle combined with a corner right before, or in, or right after, so the dog must adapt to the varied scenting conditions while searching for the next leg.
- Or a **compound obstacle** is a combination of multiple obstacles in close proximity so the dog must adapt to multiple scent conditions without having an easy stretch of grass track in between to regain confidence. See page 180 for further description of compound obstacles.

Typical simple obstacles are:
- Significant changes in cover like entering tall weeds from short cover, or entering and exiting woods.
- Crossing a simple dirt road, a narrow paved road, a brush line, a fence, or a small stream.
- Crossing standing water, an irrigation ditch, some rocks, or a stone wall.
- Traversing areas with ground animals, horses, cows or birds.
- Steep terrain, up or down.

Only use **simple obstacles** in this phase. Be sure you know where the track goes through the obstacle and be ready to happily help the dog. Use dirt road crossings, fences, changes-in-cover, trees, streams, and gullies. Cross straight through the obstacle, if possible. Avoid multiple obstacles close together or sharp turns right before, in, or right after the obstacle. Keep individual obstacles some distance apart. Road crossings can be introduced even though many are really compound obstacles since they tend to have ditches on one or both sides, or fences, or changes of cover. Keep them as simple as possible in Phase X1 and avoid turning close to them. Use your observation of your dog behavior to decide whether your dog finds them difficult or fairly simple.

CKC-only trackers need to handle road crossings and entering and exiting wooded areas. But their TDX test track will generally have fewer and easier obstacles than many AKC TDX tests, so CKC-only trackers need not focus on quite as much variety and complexity of obstacles as AKC trainers need to do.

When introducing a new type of ground cover or a new type of obstacle, try to do so in a controlled fashion. This is particularly true of difficult covers and obstacles. Try to design the track so there is some easy tracking right before the difficult area, some easy tracking right after the difficult area, and an article 20–40 yards past the difficult area where you can reward your dog for a job well done.

Trainers should be familiar with the types of ground covers and obstacles their dog may face in a test and gradually expose their dog to these challenges during their TDX training. You should be familiar with common obstacles used in tests in your area as well as a representative sample of others. In Phase X4, I include a big table of obstacles, ground covers, and other track design parameters to help you analyze his exposure so you can focus on giving him the additional ones he needs to be successful — see pages 217 through 220. For the first three TDX phases, note the obstacles and ground covers in your logs as you give your dog a wide variety of suitable experiences. In all his TDX training, there is no need to make your dog experience every type of obstacle as there are really too many to experience in his training lifetime. Just give your dog a wide variety of obstacles. When he has trouble with a particular obstacle, note the issue and repeat that obstacle again in later sessions.

In this phase, you should avoid obstacles that are physically difficult for the dog. In later phases, such physically-challenging obstacles should be a normal part of your tracks. If your dog has difficulty with the physical size of an obstacle, you can always help him across. It is best to give the dog the chance to sort the scent out, decide himself to cross the obstacle, find his own way across, and re-find the track on the other side. If the stream is too wide for him to jump across, the strands of the fence too narrow for him to slip through, or the obstacle too high for him to climb over, you can physically assist him. This is true even in a test. Of course, on a blind track, you will not know whether it actually goes across the obstacle. It might turn right at the obstacle. You may get the dog across and he cannot find anything on the other side. So, you have to be ready to help him get back, and let him search more on the incoming side.

Your review at the end of each TDX phase should include a summary of the types of obstacles your dog has been exposed to and some sense of how confidently he is able to negotiate them.

Tracklaying. TDX Tracklaying is more complex that TD tracklaying. The tracks are longer, with more corners, with obstacles and crosstracks. Tracklayers should review the basic tracklaying and map making techniques on pages 92-96. They should also carefully study the discussion of track complexity and obstacles in this section as well as each TDX phase's discussion.

Sessions X1.x Building Age using Basic TDX Tracks

Purpose:
- Gradually increase track age and length.
- Introduce blind starts and simple obstacles.
- Maintain motivation.

Example Basic TDX Track Shapes.
- Mid-leg flags.
- Always use clippies near corners.

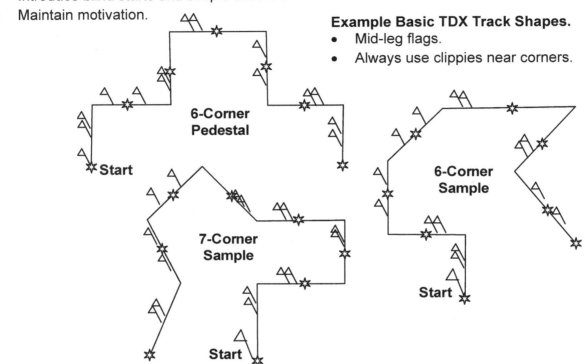

Sesn	Track Age	Track Yards	Start Angle	Number Corners	Number Obstacles	Articles	
X1.1	1:00	400–500	0°	3–4	0	1 per leg	
X1.2	1:10	500–600	15° L	4–5	1	1 per leg	
X1.3	1:20	500–600	15° R	4–5	1	1 per leg	
X1.4	1:30	500–600	15° R or L	4–5	1	1 per leg	
X1.5	0:45	400	30° L	2–4	0	1 per leg	Motivational
X1.6	1:40	600–700	30° R	4–5	0	1 per leg	
X1.7	1:50	600–700	30° R or L	5–6	1	1 per leg	
X1.8	2:00	600–700	45° L	5–6	1	1 per leg	
X1.9	0:30	500	45° R	2–4	0	1 per leg	Motivational
X1.10	2:10	600–700	45° R or L	4–5	1	1 per leg	
X1.11	2:20	700–800	60° L	5–7	1	1 per leg	
X1.12	2:30	700–800	60° R	5–7	1	1 per leg	
X1.13	0:45	400	75° L	2–4	0	1 per leg	Motivational
X1.14	2:45	600–800	75° R	5–7	1	1 per leg	
X1.15	3:00	600–800	90° L	5–7	1	1 per leg	
X1.16	3:15	600–800	90° R	5–7	1	1 per leg	
X1.17	0:45	400	any	2–4	0	1 per leg	Motivational
X1.18	1:30	1000	any	6–8	0	1 per leg	

Tracklayer:
- Get the basic design parameters from the handler including length, number of corners, age, flagging, article frequency, mid-leg rewards, and the nature of any desired obstacles.
- Using a single article per leg may work well to maintain enthusiasm. Other patterns like two articles about 30 yards apart, or even a treat at 30, an article at 45, and a treat at 60 may help motivate some dogs. Keep rewards at least 30 yards from corners or obstacles if possible.
- Actual track design requires considering the available terrain, cover changes, and potential obstacles. The sample shapes shown on the previous page are just a few examples.
    - Shorter tracks having 3–5 corners can use basic shapes similar to TD shapes (see page 116).
    - Longer tracks with 6–8 corners may have more complex shapes.
- Use the land you have and design a track that fits what is available. Make it simpler than requested rather than more difficult.
- Note session X1.18 is 1000 yards long and has no obstacles. The track should be simple and fun so the dog is happy on long tracks.
- The track labeled "6-Corner Sample" above has an acute fifth corner that is typical in CKC and unusual in AKC. Doing acutes can be good training, even though they are not a significant part of the AKC test.

Handler:
- Give the tracklayer basic design parameters including length, number of corners, age, flagging, article frequency, any mid-leg rewards, and number and nature of obstacles.
- Approach the start at the designated angle. The start is a corner you have not tracked into.
- Hold your dog at the start 10–20 seconds, so he can memorize the scent.
- Use your whole line to allow your dog to make his choices before you move forward at the start, corners, and other scent disturbances.
- Use corner communications, then walk up the line to 15–20' right after he and you commit to the new direction, see page 91.
- Notice landmarks even when there are markers ahead.
- If your dog struggles, first encourage him verbally saying he can do it, then help happily as much as needed, rather than have him get frustrated.
- Give lots of treats and praise at each article.

Evaluation:
- Note in your journal and summary log (page 178) details of the track and your evaluation. Note also the kinds of obstacles used and how the dog worked them.
- You may see him struggle on older tracks particularly on warm sunny days. This is why we mark these tracks — so you know where the track is and you are able to help your dog when needed.
- Maintaining motivation is a key goal of this phase. Keep if fun and reduce complexity if your dog's motivation drops. See page 223 regarding controlling complexity if the dog seems overwhelmed by the tracks.
- If your dog struggles on several successive days, re-evaluate by doing a review (see page 174) before going on with this phase.

Sessions X1.19 Review

Review and evaluate how your dog's tracking, your handling, and your tracklaying have improved in this phase.

- Review your journal and summary log looking for
    - Skills that have improved since the start of the phase.
    - Recurrent issues that might need improvement.
- While optional in this phase, it is good practice to summarize the types of obstacles and ground covers your dog has experienced. Review your logs and fill in a copy of the charts on pages 217 to 220, so you will be encouraged to add a few more during the next phase.
- For most dogs, these 18 sessions are effective in allowing the dog to learn to focus on the older scent while adapting to longer tracks with occasional obstacles.
- Consider if some of the obstacles were too difficult for your dog and note how you should make them simpler when you next have the opportunity to do something similar. See also page 223 for more on controlling track complexity.
- While few dogs will be fully confident with 3-hour-old tracks, they should show some competency even if they struggle in a couple of places per track.
    - If so, you can go right on to Phase X2 once you have completed all these sessions.
- If your dog is struggling more than that and you have to help him on most legs, you may have added complexity too quickly for this dog. This often happens if the weather has turned warmer or drier during this phase, or if the tracklayer added complexity in the track design by including too many obstacles, too difficult obstacles, or tracked through difficult terrain and cover.
    - If so, step back to a place in the phase where your dog was tracking confidently.
    - Then step through the sessions, possibly using the remedial variations below as appropriate, before going on to Phase X2.

TDX Problem Solving and Remediation:

If your dog loses motivation for several sessions, step back to where he was having fun and add a starter track before the main track, keep the main track shorter, and have a more over-the-top exciting party at each article. A starter track is a fifty-yard straight track laid after the main track and run before the main track.

If your dog struggles to search for, find and commit to new legs at corners, do three or more sessions of Phase 8 Plan C zigzags at track ages with which your dog is comfortable, until your dog's corner performance improves (see page 142). Then step back a few sessions in this Phase X1 schedule and continue while monitoring his clear-confident-commitment throughout his tracks. Remember, it is never wrong to do a few Plan 8C zigzags to rebuild corner skills and motivation.

If you identify other specific issues you want to deal with now, look ahead at the specific problem-solving techniques described in Phase X4 Problem-Solving Sessions on page 236 and apply them now within the context of your Phase X1 or X2 track design constraints.

For a completely demotivated dog, consider the re-motivation plan in Appendix A on page 408.

Important Reminder

These issues are repeated here because they are so important to successful advanced training.

- **Motivational Tracks** (page 161): Frequently intersperse the main training sessions with motivational tracks — tracks that are much younger and much easier than the main training tracks.

- **Conditioning** (page 161): condition yourself and your dog by long walks or jogs in hilly backcountry.

- **Corner Communication** (pages 91-92):
    - Your dog clearly indicates loss of track within a few yards of the actual corner.
    - You read your dog's behavior, recognize the loss of track, and stop.
    - You say "*Yippee! I'm at a corner that might go straight. Cool!*"
    - Your dog purposefully searches for the new leg while you maintain a light-comfortable tension with no slack.
    - Your dog notices the new leg as he searches and follows it in a straight line 10–20'.
    - You increase the tension slightly and verbally ask your dog "Is this the good track?"
    - Your dog leans into the harness.
    - You immediately decrease the tension back to your normal light-comfortable tension, step out behind your dog, and praise your dog quietly.
    - Your dog receives a reward a short distance down the new leg

- **Journal** (page 7): Always keep a training journal so you can look back and discover what types of conditions you have missed in your recent training and so you can detect how and when a problem behavior began.

- **Close to the Track** (page 162): Your dog should track very close to the track; right over the footprints is ideal, a few feet off is OK. On marked tracks use increased tension to make it slightly harder for your dog to track a few feet to the side and stop him if he tries to track more than 6' to 10' away from the track.

- **Active Handling** (page 163): On blind tracks, read your dog, read the landscape, organize his search, and trust your dog. You are an important member of this tracking team and should contribute so long as you avoid taking the lead and making decisions for your dog.

- **Helping** (pages 99 & 163): When your dog needs help in training, do so happily! It is an opportunity to teach.

- **Shifting Responsibility** (page 164): On marked tracks when your dog is doing well, make sure you avoid confirming that your dog is correct immediately — let some line out before you follow him then climb back up the line once you start following.
    - Your goal is to be able to let the line out to 35–40' on every corner or obstacle as the dog commits and then immediately climb up the line to 15–20'. Only do this when your dog is confident, support him by following more quickly to build his confidence.

Clever, Cute & Cool — Twizzle's TDX Test

In late October 2013 at the Spokane Dog Training Club test, I drew track 5 for my almost two-year-old Twizzle. Her start was in an area that I had not been in for over a decade so it was essentially unfamiliar to me. On the way to the start we passed a badger den, but she did not pay any attention to it (whew).

As I held her at the start for my normal count of 20, her nose was working, and she had figured out the direction — but when I released her, she was less confident, and she searched around briefly before committing nicely to the first leg. So I followed, seeing a distinct small bush that might be the landmark. After what turns out to be 75 yards, she indicated loss of scent and circled to the right before coming around to the left and found a track in the bare rocky sand — I looked over her as she was lining out and saw a badger hole at the base of some weeds ahead. She did a nice job staying right on the track through that area.

After 115 yards, we came up to a fence line with some taller weeds and a cow path alongside it. She first went down the cow path to the right for a short distance, then up to the wire fence, then down the cow path to the left 20', then back to the right just up against the fence. When she got perhaps 25' out to the right along the fence, she looked through the fence like perhaps it had gone through there but then came back to the cow path and started to the right when she came on the most interesting badger hole of the day. Her head was fully down the hole when I walked up toward her saying "Yuck, no mouses today." She looked at me briefly, then stuck her head and upper torso even deeper in the hole. Soon enough she extricated herself, headed out along the cow path and took my 40' line to the end committing weakly to the cow path to the right. I followed. She got more confident and committed the farther along the path she went until she held to the line of the track as the path bent off to the right. Soon she came to the first intermediate article, stopped and shook (Yippee).

She went another thirty yards up to a corner on a bare rocky wind-swept hillside, where she quickly found and committed to the next leg to the right. Over the top of her as we traversed these rough sandy-rocky-holey undulations I could see a green freeway sign in the distance. She was moving out, and I was following as fast as I could, huffing and puffing behind her. After 155 yards, she came to the base of a rocky outcrop and seamlessly turned again to the right (it felt open but the judges maps shows a 90º turn). She traversed up this hillside, over the top of the outcropping, bent to the left, and plunged down the precipice on the other side, where I had to slow her to make my own way down. Out into the flat another 30 yards to the second intermediate article (Yippee, Yippee).

I paused to give her water and then she set out again 125 yards to crosstracks that she noticed but got beyond. In 40 yards, we were approaching the dirt road that we had driven over on the way to the start — my car was to the right some distance and the spectator cars were to the left some distance. On the previous 4 tracks, the judges seemed to avoid crossing this primary access road, so my mind was working furiously that we turn soon, but I avoided letting Twizzle know my concerns.

She searched to the left and right of the near side of the road, crossed the road somewhat to the left of the track and searched until she came to the leg on the other side and nicely committed ahead. Another badger hole near another corner, "*what's new? Just another badger hole*". She committed to the right and seemed to find two tracks about 10 yards apart, one that seemed to be the tracklayer and one that seemed to be a distraction, perhaps animal tracks. It turns out there were crosstracks on the last leg, so perhaps they were what confused me but not her. We kept on another 50 yards when she circled to the right then to the left and came up to the glove (Yippee, Yippee, & Yippee).

Twizzle was impressive earning her TDX that day, dealing especially with the badger holes and the sparse, dry vegetation, because over the past year we had tracked there six sessions over three separate occasions.

Phase X1. Aging the Track to Three Hours

Phase X1 Summary Log

Sesn	Site	Date	Config. & Obs.	Track Age	Evaluation
X1.1				1:00	
X1.2				1:10	
X1.3				1:20	
X1.4				1:30	
X1.5				0:45	
X1.6				1:40	
X1.7				1:50	
X1.8				2:00	
X1.9				0:30	
X1.10				2:10	
X1.11				2:20	
X1.12				2:30	
X1.13				0:45	
X1.14				2:45	
X1.15				3:00	
X1.16				3:15	
X1.17				0:45	
X1.18				1:30	

Phase X2. Age Again and Crosstracks

Purpose:
- Gradually age the track from 1-5 hours while introducing crosstracks and more obstacles.

Strategy:
- Repeat gradually aging the main track, this time from one hour to five hours old.
- Introduce the dog to crosstracks.
- Introduce more simple obstacles and some compound obstacles as well.
- Maintain motivation.

How to use this chapter:
- Look through the table below, which summarizes the training structure of this phase, and read the discussion section that follows.
- Do the 21 sessions listed following the age, length, and number of corners as closely as possible. Use natural fields whenever available, but much work can be done in urban parks as well.
- Keep a detailed log of each session using a format like the one shown on page 31 and keep a summary log like the one shown on page 192.
- Do the X2.22 review session to evaluate the team's progress on page 190.

Phase X2 Session Schedule:

Sesn	Track Age	Track Yards	XT Delay	Track/XT Pattern	XT Flagging	Num. Turns	Num. Simple Obs.	Num. of Compound Obs.
X2.1	1:00	400–500				4–5	1–2	0
X2.2	1:20	500–600				4–5	2–3	1
X2.3	1:00	400	0:30	U Over U	On Track	2	0	0
X2.4	1:40	600–700				4–5	3–4	0
X2.5	0:45	400				3–5	0	0
X2.6	2:00	600–700				4–5	1–2	0
X2.7	2:20	500–600				5–6	2–3	1
X2.8	1:30	400	0:45	X Over U	On Track	2	0	0
X2.9	2:40	500–600				5–6	3–4	0
X2.10	0:30	500				3–5	0	0
X2.11	3:00	600–700				5–7	1–2	0
X2.12	3:20	500–600				5–7	2–3	1
X2.13	2:00	400	1:00	U Over U	5 yds off	2	0	0
X2.14	3:40	500–600				5–7	3–4	0
X2.15	0:45	400				3–5	0	0
X2.16	4:00	600–800				5–7	1–2	0
X2.17	4:20	600–700				5–7	2–3	1
X2.18	2:30	400	1:15	X Over U	5 yds off	2	0	0
X2.19	4:40	500–600				5–7	3–4	0
X2.20	2:00	1000				6–8	0	0
X2.21	0:45	400				2–4	0	0
X2.22	Review							

Discussion:

Aging the tracks a second time in a progressive sequence will improve your dog's confidence in tracking older tracks. Dogs do not gain mastery by following 3-hour-old scent a few times in Phase X1; it was just introduced to them there. The best way to build mastery and confidence is to repeat the progression of aging the track from an hour up to five hours in 20-minute increments. Throughout these progressively aged tracks we take the opportunity to introduce the dogs to new obstacles, including some compound obstacles.

All tracks should have a single-flag start with an article (for AKC training) or a scent pad (for CKC training). Approach the flag with the dog at various angles so your dog learns to find the direction of the first leg, and not to simply run out in front of you. Remember to hold your dog right at the article or scent pad; do not let him start up without spending 10–20 seconds at the start. Let him play with the article if you can keep his nose right over the start. The start is just a corner that you have not tracked into — use normal corner communications. If your dog is not committing to the track quickly at the start, precede each main track with a 50-yard starter track laid right after the main track is laid, and run it right before the main track is run.

These tracks should all have four or more articles; most should have an article on every leg. I use articles wherever I want to reward my dog. He gets lots to goodies when he finds an article, so he is rewarded for "overcoming" the tracking problems and for finding the article. This tends to make him article-sure and keeps him motivated. Every once in a while, "forget" to give him treats after an article so he is accustomed to restarting without a reward. See page 162 for more ideas for rewarding your dog on the track.

Obstacles are highly varied in their nature as described in Phase X1 on page 170. In addition, the same or a similar obstacle can present different issues for your dog to solve each time he confronts it. This is because varying track age, terrain, and weather can combine with the obstacle to present different problems to be solved by the dog and handler. Thus, multiple exposures can provide enrichment that builds the tracking team's experience and ability to solve similar complex problems in the future.

Consider making copies of the Ground Cover, Obstacles, and Design Parameters tables on pages 217–220 for this phase of your TDX training. This will allow you to track the dog's recent experience with obstacles and perhaps suggest other obstacles to try as you progress through this phase.

Compound Obstacles are two obstacles in close proximity, or a corner right before, in the middle of, or right after an obstacle. Although AKC has minimum distances between crosstracks, articles, and obstacles, there is no minimum distance between a corner and an obstacle or between two obstacles. The simpler the rest of your test, the more likely it is that the judges will use compound obstacles or a corner before, in or after an obstacle. You must be prepared for compound obstacles.

Once a dog is comfortable handling most typical obstacles found in tests in your area, start to introduce him to compound obstacles and corners in, before or after obstacles. Keep these compound obstacles well separated from other problem areas, and place an article 30–50 yards past the area so the dog can be rewarded for completing the compound obstacle. Help the dog if you need to. This is another step in your dog's learning, and it is an important step.

Typical compound obstacles are:
- corners in heavy weeds, under trees, on dirt, or in unusual cover;
- corners on or before or after a road, tree line, fallen tree, foot bridge, ditch, stream, footpath;
- complexes of obstacles like the junction of a stream and a footpath or of two roads;
- sequences of obstacles in close proximity like fence-ditch-road-ditch-fence obstacles.

If the dog can solve one obstacle and then separately solve the second, it is just two simple obstacles. When the two are close together or combined with a corner, the problem-solving difficulty is compounded and much harder than the sum of its separate parts.

You may notice your dog quitting at difficult compound obstacles — it is as if he is saying, "This is too difficult." First just encourage him verbally to go back to work. If he persists, use it as an opportunity to help your dog to go on. Be happy and show your enthusiasm for the track and how much fun it is to be on the track with him. Expect your dog to learn that difficult obstacles are a part of the activity, and that if he keeps searching, he will find it, and then the track will become easy again, and he will have a lot of fun. As you are working difficult obstacles, pay particular attention to monitoring and limiting the overall difficulty of the tracks as described below.

Handling at Obstacles and Compound Obstacles is really the same as handling at corners (page 80). Stop when your dog's behavior changes and use your line to allow your dog to thoroughly search the area; when he starts to commit, let the line out and allow him to follow the track until you are almost out of line; "Is this the good track?" and then follow him with confidence.

However, obstacles can sometimes present tricky situations for the handler where she must move away from her pivot point to keep the line untangled or to allow the dog room to search around a large physical obstruction. When doing so, I like to sidestep rather than follow full face-on — side-stepping keeps the dog from considering my movement a suggestion that what he is investigating right this instant is a good thing to follow. Side-step by turning your chest and feet a quarter-turn to the side but keep your eyes on your dog and where you are going while you follow your dog.

Some difficult physical obstacles may be hard for the dog or handler to negotiate. A handler may help her dog so long as she doesn't indicate the location or direction of the track. For example, a handler of a small dog might need to carry him across a stream, or a handler of a large dog might need to hold a wire fence up so he can crawl underneath. The handler may need her dog to stop on the other side while she finds a way to surmount the obstacle herself.

Crosstracks are very important in TDX because they are the only type of "scenting obstacle" you know will be on every test track. Even if you have worked extensively in fields with natural foot traffic contamination, explicitly teaching crosstracks is both necessary and important.

Since few people have extra crosstrack layers available for every practice session, and since some dogs lose motivation when faced with intensive crosstrack training every session, we spread out the crosstrack training sessions and intermix them with aging and general obstacle training sessions, as well as occasional motivational sessions.

Some people speculate that their dog already understands crosstracks because of all the natural and intentional contamination he has handled on urban tracks. It is a very reasonable speculation, but sadly it does not turn out to be correct. Even VST dogs are seen to take TDX crosstracks in tests and often their handlers admit they did not explicitly train TDX crosstracks because of the dog's experience with contamination. So please don't skip these crosstrack sessions in Phase X2 or X3 or you will very likely regret it.

Before you start crosstracks, you must decide whether you will allow the tracklayer to cross her own track. We did this for many years because the dogs could learn to distinguish track age and stay with the same age track on which they started. It is very convenient to lay your own crosstracks since you never have to worry about getting another person or two to lay them at just the right time. However, it may be a big disadvantage for dogs who will do urban tracking, since the TDU and VST require a dog to follow the tracklayer scent rather than the complex of tracklayer, crushed vegetation, and disturbed dirt scents — all at a particular track age. By teaching a dog to attend to track age and not tracklayer identity on TDX crosstracks, you are teaching him the wrong lesson for VST. Therefore, I now recommend you always use crosstrack layers who are different from your tracklayer. If you are sure you do not want this dog to do TDU or VST, go ahead and cross your own track. It works very well as a TDX-only training technique. When you first do it, you can change your boots and add a weighted backpack while laying the crosstracks.

In AKC tests, crosstracks are made by two people walking side-by-side about 4' apart. In CKC, crosstracks are made by a single person. It is common to be unable to have access to crosstrack layers every time you can track. On those days that a crosstrack layer is available, lay the next track with crosstracks from this phase. Serviceable AKC-style double crosstracks can be made by a single person walking the crosstrack twice, either up-and-back putting down two side-by-side crosstracks that go in different directions, or twice in the same direction. I prefer the twice in the same direction method, but use the up-and-back method when that is all I can get the crosstrack layer to do. On tracking days when no crosstrack layer is available, lay the next session from this phase that does not specify crosstracks.

As the tracklayer lays the track, she places tall, visible flags each place the crosstrackers should cross the track. Put just one crosstrack flag on the track or put two, one to each side of the track, which makes it easier for the crosstrack layers to see their angle of approach. Make sure the crosstrack flags look different than other flags you use to mark the track. Note on the tracklayer map the crosstrack landmark in the direction the crosstrack layers will be walking. It is very important to be extra-extra careful with your instructions because crosstrack layers have been known to go astray when given inadequate directions.

Crosstracks in tests should always cross the main track at 90°. In training, 30–50% of the crosstracks should be at angles down to 45°. Getting experience with angled crosstracks solidifies the dog's understanding of crosstracks.

Crosstrack age or crosstrack delay refers to the time between when the tracklayer starts to lay the track and when the crosstrack layers begin laying the crosstracks. Crosstrack layers should always stay away from the area of the start. Keeping at least 75 yards from the start is a good practice.

After the first few crosstrack sessions, the crosstrack layers move the crosstrack flags a few yards off the track. Once this happens, the handler will have to remember that the flags are no longer directly on the main track. Moving the flags keeps the dog from becoming dependent on the crosstrack flags as a signal that these are crosstracks. The distance to move them depends on the dog's tendency to notice flags, but they should remain in the general area to remind the handler that this is a crosstrack and not a corner.

Note that the main tracks are quite simple and short when teaching crosstracks. The first shape is a "U over a U" is illustrated on page 186 and creates four 90° crosstracks. The second shape is an "X over a U" is illustrated on page 188 and creates four 45° crosstracks. These 45° crosstracks are easier for the fast dog to notice and more enticing to the dog, so they are likely to provide good training opportunities.

Keep the crosstrack layers 75 yards from the start and 50 yards from other parts of the main track so the dog is not smelling their lingering scent as he starts the track.

Handling on the crosstrack is important. Until the dog learns the concept of distinguishing the crosstracks from the main track, he is likely to take the fresher crosstracks any time he notices them. Therefore, your job is to teach him that the articles, fun, and goodies are found on the main track, not on the crosstracks. You do this by allowing your dog to investigate the crosstracks anytime he notices them; let him follow the crosstracks 20–40' while you stay on the track yourself and use somewhat higher than normal tension. If he does not break off the crosstrack on his own, move forward on the main track until you are a few yards past the crosstracks while calling happily to your dog about how exciting and cool the track is over here! You must be happy and enthusiastic. You are teaching, not correcting. Lean down and tickle the grass right on the track as you reel in your dog, show him the track and help him down the main track until he takes off in front of you. If tickling does not do the trick, lean down and love the track yourself while ignoring your dog. It is a good lesson anytime you are able to show your dog and remind him the fun is always on the good track.

The key to having your dog really understand crosstracks is for him to notice the crosstracks and then choose to return to the good track on his own. You will notice your dog bypasses many crosstracks, which is fine. We go to all the effort to lay a crosstrack pattern so the dog has learning opportunities and does learn to choose the good track. So when your dog notices the crosstrack, let him investigate it even to the end of your 40' line. Avoid checking him as he investigates and is making his decision. Checking is suddenly increasing the tension on the line or any other mild forms of restraint.

If your dog circles back looking for the main track, great. If he wants to commit farther out the crosstrack, stop him, pull or call him back to be re-scented, and tell him "Find the good track" in a positive tone. If he repeatedly tries to commit to the crosstracks, you will need to pull him in, put him at your side firmly but neutrally, and lean down and love the track yourself while you slowly move along the main track until he gets interested and moves forward.

Even after your dog is very experienced with crosstracks, occasionally he will be fooled by a particular set of tantalizing crosstrack conditions. Maintain a happy and enthusiastic attitude! It is an opportunity to remind the dog to stay on the main track.

Crosstrack Variations

Several of my recent dogs have not understood crosstracks using just the main schedule's plan even though many student's dogs seem to get the idea quite quickly. I have utilized the additional techniques outlined at the bottom of page 187 and eventually my dogs figure out their job. Be patient and ready to adapt your training to your own dog's needs.

Sessions X2.x Simple Sub-TDX Tracks with Controlled Complexity

Purpose:
- Allow the dog to gain experience solving scenting and physical obstacles.
- Assure the dog there is always fun and rewards once the obstacle is solved.
- Allow the dog to gain experience following older tracks with their fainter and variable odor.
- Begin transitioning the handler to semi-blind tracks by marking the track with only clippies.

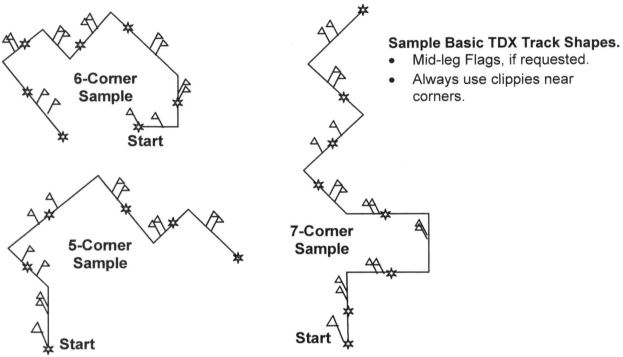

Sample Basic TDX Track Shapes.
- Mid-leg Flags, if requested.
- Always use clippies near corners.

Session	Track Age	Track Yards	Num. Corners	Num. Simple Obstacles	Num. Compound Obstacles
X2.1	1:00	400–500	4–5	1–2	0
X2.2	1:20	500–600	4–5	2–3	1
X2.4	1:40	600–700	4–5	3–4	0
X2.5	0:45	400	3–5	0	0
X2.6	2:00	600–700	4–5	1–2	0
X2.7	2:20	500–600	5–6	2–3	1
X2.9	2:40	500–600	5–6	3–4	0
X2.10	0:30	500	3–5	0	0
X2.11	3:00	600–700	5–7	1–2	0
X2.12	3:20	500–600	5–7	2–3	1
X2.14	3:40	500–600	5–7	3–4	0
X2.15	0:45	400	3–5	0	0
X2.16	4:00	600–800	5–7	1–2	0
X2.17	4:20	600–700	5–7	2–3	1
X2.19	4:40	500–600	5–7	3–4	0
X2.20	2:00	1000	6–8	0	0
X2.21	0:45	400	2–4	0	0

Tracklayer:
- Get the basic design parameters from the handler including length, number of corners, age, clippies, article frequency, on-track food rewards, and the nature of any obstacles.
- Actual track design requires considering the available terrain, cover changes, and potential obstacles.
  - Shorter tracks having 3–5 corners can use basic shapes similar to TD shapes (see page 116).
  - Longer tracks with 6–8 corners may have more complex shapes. There are some examples on the previous page and in Phase X1 on page 172, but there are many more possibilities.
- Use the land you have and design a track that fits what is available. Make it simpler than requested, rather than more difficult.
- Placing an article 30 yards past any obstacle and after most corners rewards the dog's successful choices.
- Walk behind the handler and help if she is unsure where the track is located or it is going.

Handler:
- Give the tracklayer basic design parameters including the length, number of corners, age, clippies, article frequency, any food rewards, and number and nature of obstacles.
  - The motivational sessions should be fun for the dog and for you. Don't skip them.
- Approach the start, varying angles each session. The start is a corner you have not tracked into.
- Hold your dog at the start 10–20 seconds so he can memorize the scent.
- Use your whole line to allow your dog to make choices before you move forward at the start, corners, and other scent disturbances.
- Use corner communications, then walk up the line to 15–20' right after he and you commit to the new direction.
- Notice landmarks while trying to ignore the flags and clippies.
- If your dog struggles, first encourage verbally that he can do it. If he still can't solve the puzzle, help happily as much as needed rather than have him get frustrated.
- Give lots of treats and praise at each article.

Evaluation:
- Note in your journal and summary log (page 192) the details of the track design including the obstacles and your evaluation of the dog ability to follow it on his own and your ability to read him.
- You may see him struggle on older tracks particularly on warmer sunny days. That is why we mark these tracks — so you know where the track is and can help your dog when needed.
- If your dog struggles on several successive days, re-evaluate by doing an early review (see page 190) before going on with this phase.

Sessions X2.x U-over-U Crosstracks.

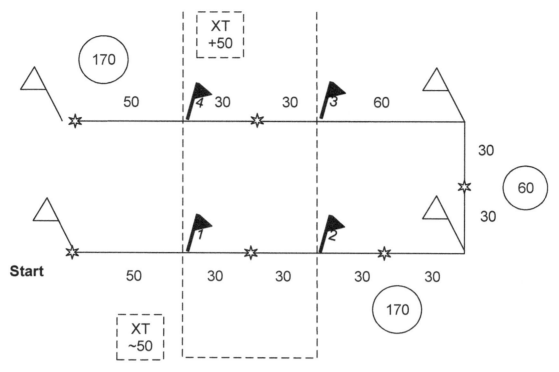

Session	Track Age	Track Yards	XT Delay	Track/XT Pattern	XT Flagging
X2.3	1:00	400	0:30	U Over U	On Track
X2.13	2:00	400	1:00	U Over U	5 yards off
X3.3	3:00	400	1:30	U Over U	10 yards off

Purpose:
- Teach the dog that the good track should be followed even when there is a fresher track that would be fun to track as well.
- Assure the dog there is always fun and rewards once the crosstrack is solved.
- Allow the dog to gain experience following older tracks with their fainter and variable odor.

Tracklayer:
- Use a field measuring at least 250 yards by 160 yards that will allow the track design shown above to be laid with the distances indicated.
- Avoid changes of cover or obstacles near the crosstrack to avoid affecting how the dog sorts out the two tracks.
- Use tall main-track flags at the start, both corners, and the end so they will be visible at a distance.
- Place crosstrack flags as shown on the track. They must be tall enough to be visible at a distance and a different color than the main-track flags.
- For inexperienced crosstrack layers, place two crosstrack flags at each crossing, angled in the direction the crosstrack layers will be going when they cross.

Crosstrack Layer:
- Start laying the crosstracks from the side of the field, starting at least 50 yards to the side of the track, at the "XT Delay" period after the tracklayer laid the main track.
  - Start on either side of the "U" as field access dictates.
  - Continue at least 50 yards past the second crossing before turning and paralleling the main track.
- If the handler asks for the crosstrack flags to be moved, do so as you walk along.
- If there is a second crosstrack layer, she should walk 4' to your side.

Handler:
- Approach the start, varying the approach angle each session. The start is a corner you have not tracked into.
- Look down the first leg and make sure you understand which flag is the corner flag and which flags are the crosstrack flags; the latter may be to the side of the actual track.
- Hold your dog at the start 10–20 seconds so he can memorize the scent.
- Use your whole line to allow your dog to make his choices before you move forward at the start, corners, and crosstracks.
- Use corner communications, then walk up the line to 15–20' right after he and you commit to the new direction (page 80).
- When your dog notices a crosstrack, let him investigate it at least to 20' to the side. If he wants to commit farther, stop him, pull or call him back to be re-scented, and tell him "Find the good track."
  - Once he gets the basic idea, let him investigate a crosstrack all the way to 40'
- If your dog repeatedly tries to commit to the crosstracks, you will need to pull him in, put him at your side firmly but neutrally, and get down and love the track yourself until he gets interested and moves forward (see pages 183 for crosstrack handling and 60 for loving the track).
- Give lots of treats and praise at each article.

Evaluation:
- Your dog may not notice all the crosstracks, which is normal. This is why we put many crosstracks on the same track so he will notice a few and have opportunities for learning.
- Your dog does not need to be perfect at solving crosstracks at the end of Phase X2 or even Phase X3. It is OK to repeat a few of these sessions now or later in your training.

Variations

There are several variations of this exercise which can help individual dogs understand crosstracks before moving on to the more complex crosstrack exercises like the X-over-U or the M-over-U.

- A single straight long leg with 4-8 crosstracks. More walking for the crosstrack layers, but some dogs learn better without mixing regular corners and crosstracks.
- Reduce the distance between crosstracks from 60 yards to 40 yards with the reward article at 20.
- Add an extra leg at the beginning to allow the dog to get comfortable with the track.

Sessions X2.x X-over-U Crosstracks.

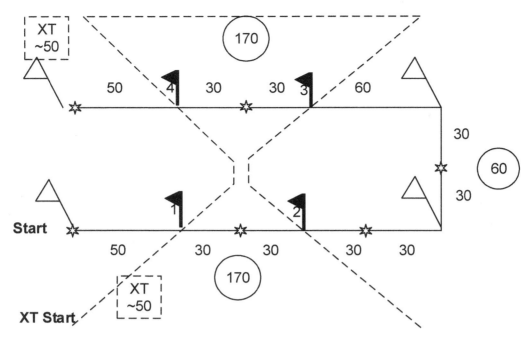

Session	Track Age	Track Yards	XT Delay	Track/XT Pattern	XT Flagging
X2.8	1:30	400	0:45	X Over U	On Track
X2.18	2:30	400	1:15	X Over U	5 yards off
X3.7	3:30	400	1:45	X Over U	10 yards off

Purpose:
- Teach your dog that the good track should be followed even when there is a fresher track that would be fun to track as well.
- Make crosstracks noticeable and enticing by angling 45° to the main track.
- Assure the dog there is always fun and rewards once the crosstrack is solved.
- Allow the dog to gain experience following older tracks with their fainter and variable odor.

Tracklayer:
- Use a field measuring at least 250 yards by 160 yards that will allow the track design shown above to be laid with the distances indicated.
- Avoid changes of cover or obstacles near the crosstrack to avoid affecting how the dog sorts out the two tracks.
- Use tall main-track flags at the start, both corners, and the end so they will be visible at a distance.
- Place crosstrack flags as shown on the track. They must be tall enough to be visible at a distance and a different color than the main-track flags.
- For inexperienced crosstrack layers, place two crosstrack flags at each crossing, angled in the direction the crosstrack layers will be going when they cross.

Crosstrack Layer:
- You are trying to angle the crosstracks so they cross about 45° to the main track.
- Start laying the crosstracks from the side of the field at least 50 yards to the side of the track by lining up the first and third crosstrack flags.
  - Crosstrack flags are numbered as the dog will encounter them.
  - If the crosstrack flags will be completely removed, place a flag here at the start to use to align the third crosstrack angle.
- Start laying at the "XT Delay" period after the tracklayer laid the main track and walk past the first crosstrack flag and halfway to the third one.
- Turn left 90° toward the fourth crosstrack flag and proceed to cross the track there and go another 70 yards.
- Turn right and parallel the third main-track leg until the third and first crosstrack flags align.
- Cross the track at the third crosstrack flag and proceed about halfway towards the first flag.
- Turn left 90° toward the second crosstrack flag, cross the track there, and go another 70 yards before exiting the field.
- If the handler asks for the crosstrack flags to be moved, do so as you walk along.
- If there is a second crosstrack layer, she should walk 4' to your side.

Handler:
- Approach the start varying the angle each session. The start is a corner you have not tracked into.
- Look down the first leg and make sure you understand which flag is the corner flag and which flags are crosstrack flags, which may be to the side of the actual track.
- Hold your dog at the start 10–20 seconds so he can memorize the scent.
- Use your whole line to allow your dog to make choices before you move forward at the start, corners, and crosstracks.
- Use corner communications, then walk up the line to 15–20' right after he and you commit to the new direction (page 80).
- When your dog notices a crosstrack, let him investigate it even to the end of your 40' line. If he wants to commit farther, stop him, pull or call him back to be re-scented, and tell him "Find the good track." The second time, re-scent and gesture down the track taking a few steps with him to make it easy for him to commit to the good track.
- If your dog repeatedly tries to commit to a crosstrack, you will need to pull him in, hold him at your side firmly but neutrally, and lean down and love the track yourself until he gets interested and moves forward (page 99).
- Give lots of treats and praise at each article.

Evaluation:
- Your dog may not notice all the crosstracks, which is normal. That is why we put many crosstracks on the same track so he will notice a few and we have opportunities for learning.
- Your dog does not need to be perfect at solving crosstracks at the end of Phase X2 or even Phase X3. It is OK to repeat a few of these sessions now or later in your training.

Sessions X2.22 Review

Review and evaluate how your dog's tracking, your handling, and your tracklaying have improved in this phase.

- Review your journal and summary log looking for
  - Skills that have improved since the start of the phase.
  - Recurrent issues that might need improvement.
- While optional in this phase, it is good practice to summarize the types of obstacles and ground covers your dog has experienced. Review your logs and fill in a copy of the charts on pages 217 to 220, so you will be encouraged to add a few more types during the next phase.
- For most dogs, these 21 sessions are effective in allowing him to learn to focus on the older scent while adapting to longer tracks with occasional compound obstacles.
- While few dogs will be fully confident with 3-hour-old tracks, they should show some competency even if they may struggle in a couple of places per track.
  - If so, you can go right on to Phase X3 once you have completed all these sessions.
- If your dog is struggling more than that and you have to help him on most legs, you may have added complexity too quickly for this dog. This often happens if the weather has turned warmer or dryer during this phase, or the tracklayer added complexity in the track design by including too many obstacles, too difficult obstacles, or tracked through difficult terrain and cover.
  - If so, step back to a place in this phase where your dog was tracking confidently.
  - Then step through the sessions, possibly using the remedial variations below as appropriate, before going on to Phase X3.

TDX Remediation:

If your dog loses motivation for several sessions, step back to where he was having fun and add a starter track before the main track, keep the main track shorter, and have a more over-the-top exciting party at each article. A starter track is a fifty-yard straight track laid after the main track and run before the main track.

If your dog struggles to search for, find and commit to new legs at corners, do three or more sessions of Phase 8 Plan C zigzags (see page 142), at track ages with which your dog is comfortable until his corner performance improves. Then step back a few sessions in this Phase X2 schedule and continue while monitoring his clear-confident-commitment throughout. Remember, it is never wrong to do a few Plan 8C zigzags to rebuild corner skills and motivation (see page 142).

If you identify other specific issues you want to deal with now, look ahead at the specific problem-solving techniques described in Phase X4 Problem-Solving Sessions on page 236 and apply them now within the context of your Phase X2 or X3 tracking training constraints.

For a fully demotivated dog, consider the re-motivation plan in Appendix A on page 408.

Sample Journal Log Entry — TDX Phase 2

Session: __X2.6__
Dog: __Twizzle__
Date: __11/22/12__
Layer: __Sil__
Location: __South Pasture__
Weather: __Cloudy, Cool__
Wind: __5-10__
Length: __575__
Age: __2 hours__
Obstacles: __tree turn, mud, steep down.__

Evaluation: __Excellent!__

__Full search on 90°-start, but good commitment.__
__360 search on 1st corner, good commitment__
__Cut corner under trees.__
__Search mud but no recognition, tried to fringe, restrained & showed her.__
__Overshot turn 4, needed restraint.__
__Good on turn 5.__
__Excellent article recognition.__

Track Map

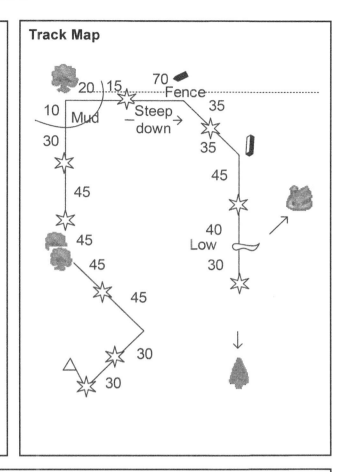

Article Parties

We often get routine in how we praise our dog at articles. Since many dogs are self-rewarded by following the track, we have to work hard to make the articles just as important as the track itself. We need to have a party with the dog at every article along a track. A party should last 20 to 60 seconds at intermediate articles and close to 5 minutes at the end.

What do we expect from a good party — fun, food, and music:
- For fun, you have to do something with your dog that he loves whether it is petting, touching, tricks, tugging, or wrestling.
- For food, it must be special, high-value food that your dog gets only on the track. Food presentation is also important. Emphatically counting out "1-penny, 2-penny, 3-penny, 4-penny, 5-penny", offering a huge jackpot, or letting him help himself from your treat bag, are all good ways to make the food exciting.
- For music, genuine, heartfelt praise and appreciation are music to your dog's ears and heart. Tell him how amazing he is and how proud you are of him.

See also "Don't Mail in the Praise" on page 164.

Adapted from Carla Baker, private communication.

Phase X2 Summary Log

Sesn	Site	Date	Config. & Obs.	Track Age	Evaluation
X2.1				1:00	
X2.2				1:20	
X2.3			XT	1:00	
X2.4				1:40	
X2.5				0:45	
X2.6				2:00	
X2.7				2:20	
X2.8			XT	1:30	
X2.9				2:40	
X2.10				0:30	
X2.11				3:00	

Sesn	Site	Date	Config. & Obs.	Track Age	Evaluation
X2.12				3:20	
X2.13			XT	2:00	
X2.14				3:40	
X2.15				0:45	
X2.16				4:00	
X2.17				4:20	
X2.18			XT	2:30	
X2.19				4:40	
X2.20				2:00	
X2.21				0:45	

Phase X2. Age Again and Crosstracks

Alicia's TDX Track, a Detailed Description (1984)

The following is from an article I wrote for the monthly training newspaper Front & Finish. F&F is now an online publication www.frontandfinish.com. Note that Alicia was my first tracking dog and the article describes a number of handling techniques that I no longer recommend.

At the 9:00 draw, we luckily get the first track; wonderful! We drive up to the knoll that will serve as the command post for the day, get our equipment together (a harness, two 40-foot lines in case one gets hopelessly tangled, and two water bottles). Then into the jeep with the judges, Mid Rothrock and Connie Alber, and we head back into the hills about eight miles.

As we bump and bounce over the rutted road, I think to myself: Today will be the day that will culminate four years of practice and seven months of intensive conditioning and training. We have practiced all tracking conditions, every type of obstacle, and all the situations we might encounter. Today will be our day! If I can just keep telling myself that, maybe I'll believe it and not be so nervous.

"If you walk back toward that fallen tree, you'll be able to see the starting flag; you may start at any time," says one of the judges as we get out of the jeep. Alicia follows me with a wag in her tail toward the fallen tree. The terrain is hilly open oak and pine forest with 2' tall grass.

We approach to within 20 feet of the starting flag, and I kneel down to put on the harness. I wet down her white coat with one quart of water, put on her harness, attach her line, and pause one last moment to collect myself. As I kneel there, I can smell a strange odor. Oh no! There must be wild ginger around here, and we have never practiced in ginger before. I wonder if it will bother her. Why didn't we walk back here last week so she could have practiced in ginger? It's only eight miles to walk. Don't be foolish, calm down, she can do it!

At the starting stake, I down her, pick up the plastic checkbook cover that is lying there and hold it to her nose. She struggles to get up as she is anxious to start, but I keep her down for 30 seconds to fix the scent in her nose as I survey the scene. There are some light tracks in the grass to the right and a heavier track to the left. Alicia breaks free so I say "Find it" and she has started. She moves forward 10 feet and circles to her right. She notices the light tracks that I think is where the tracklayer came in, follows them about five feet, rejects them as going in the wrong direction, and circles back to the left. I keep the tension up, so she stays in a 10' circle. That way, if she does not notice the track on one crossing, I can give her more line, and she may notice it at a different distance. As she crosses the heavy track in the grass, her head goes down, but her momentum causes her to cross the track a couple of feet before she swings back to the right. I give her more line, so she intersects the track a few feet farther and follows the track in the grass. The 20' knot goes by when I start my standard spiel "Have you found it? Are you sure?" all the while increasing the tension so she must really commit herself. She is sure, and I start to follow at the 30' knot and walk up the line to the 20' knot.

She has good tension on the line during the first leg and is in her characteristic tracking position of head down and tail almost straight back as we come up a small rise. She breaks off, circles a little to the right then back to the left where I can see a track through the grass going up a hill. She notices it and heads straight along the second leg of the track. In about 30 yards, she stops and shakes, which is how she indicates articles, but then goes straight on. I stop where she indicates and look down as the line slips through my hand. Nothing here; the tracklayer must have stopped to pull up a stake or something. I start to catch up with her as I notice a track going to the right down into a vale. She does not notice it but keeps going into a bare spot under a tree. "Did she miss the corner?" I wonder. But she is quite certain, so I follow her under the tree where she has already made a right-hand corner (onto the third leg) and is quite sure of herself. Soon, she stops and shakes again and stays where she is. I walk forward on the line to see a pale sock under her body.

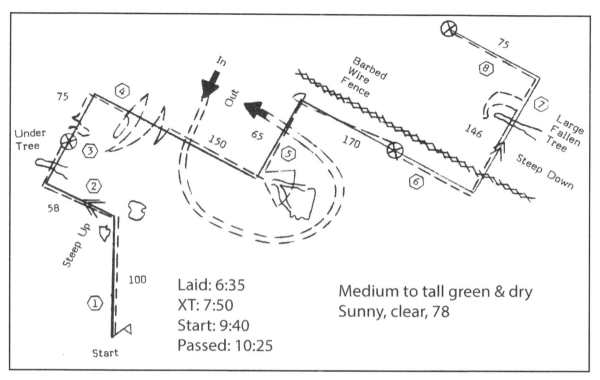

I praise her, play with her, give her more water that she does not want and play with her some more. I stand up and repeat "Find it!" She fiddles around the spot a little hoping I'll remember the hot dogs but soon heads off to the right of the track down toward the vale that we have been paralleling on this leg. I increase the tension so she breaks off and circles back up to the track that she crosses without noticing and goes uphill a little ways. She circles back and picks up the track and is off again. She soon breaks off to the right again, and as I reach the place I can again see a track in the grass crossing the vale and heading up the other side.

She is very sure of herself as she heads down into the vale on the fourth leg, putting lots of tension on the line. As we get to the bottom, I notice many light tracks crossing every which way. The area is typical habitat for deer and judging by the number of tracks crossing all over, they must have had a convention here last night! Alicia is almost past this area without noticing when she breaks off to the right with her head and tail up. I let her go a short distance but increase the tension as she does. She breaks off and heads straight back toward me. She passes me and heads up the vale in the opposite direction. She circles over to a couple of oak trees with poison oak below where she does a little mousing. "No mouses today, Alicia!" She breaks off and heads back to the right-hand side of the track. She really commits herself to one of the tracks in the grass that is heading straight back toward our second leg. This can't be correct. There is no way they could have a leg along here heading so close to the second leg. They would box themselves in. And I'd seen a track going straight across the vale before she broke off this leg. I increase tension until I stop her with me about 20 feet off the track. She circles back to my left and I follow, so that she may hit the track above this area of confusion. There is a tree between us as we circle, so I move farther away from the track to get around the obstacle and resume my circling toward the track. First I cross the track, then she does but without noticing it. I hope I wasn't wrong about that track she just committed herself to. She circles beyond me and sticks her head and shoulders full in a hole. "No mouses today, Alicia," I intone once more. She circles back toward the track, straddles it with her body and hunches her back to defecate. Is she defying me for not giving her the hot dogs, or for pulling her off the other track? In her due time, she moves forward away from the track. I start to back up as she circles back, crosses the track once more with a little head bob, angles back to it and heads up the hill along the track. She is putting no pressure on the line at all, and I am afraid to put tension on it as I follow her.

She stays on the fourth leg of the track for some distance — neither of us noticing the first set of crosstracks on this leg. Soon, she is directly approaching a tree trunk. As she comes up to it, she veers to the right and goes out with her head up for about 20 feet. When she swings a little from side to side with her head up, I know she is not tracking, so I increase tension until she circles around to the left. The grass is too deep to see her directly, just the line being pulled in a circle. All of a sudden, she stops and starts rubbing her head on the ground from side to side. I quickly walk up the line to get a view of her. Her face hair is plastered with some green sticky weed, and she can't see. I kneel down and clean off her face. A quick check underneath to remove a few stickers from her front legs and belly. She is panting very heavily but seems okay. I stand up, say "Find it!" once more, and start to ease back to where I was when she ran into the weeds. She pauses a moment, then follows me back and sits at my feet, panting, looking up at me as if to say "Haven't I done enough today?". I kneel down again, give her some water that she drinks this time, pet her lightly and tell her how important it is to go on. When her panting is a little less severe, I stand up and say "Find it!" again. At first, she does not move, then she moves past me, circles about 5 feet, indicates a track and is off again. A left-hand corner must have been in front of the tree as she is heading in a new direction now.

She has a little more tension on the fifth leg, but she is still panting very hard. Again, neither of us notices the crosstracks on this leg. In a short distance, she is approaching a barbed-wire fence but veers off to the left about ten feet in front of it. Her head is up as she circles about ninety degrees, then she heads straight back to cross her track just in front of me. As she lines out, I realize she is in the right-hand rut of a very overgrown dirt road. She is quite sure of herself so I follow on the sixth leg. She stays in the rut, with occasional side steps into the deep grass. Slowly, she drifts off to the left-hand rut and a little beyond toward the barbed-wire fence. Quickly, she veers back to the right and as I look ahead of her, there is something red in the grass. She stops on top of it, shakes and turns back to watch me approach her and her new red bandanna.

We have been out in the direct sunlight this whole leg, and she is very hot. I praise her, play with her, wet her down once more, and play with her again telling her how wonderful she is. I feel rushed, probably due to nervousness, so I don't take the time to let her cool down as much as I should. Too quickly, I am up, saying "Find it!" She just sits there, panting, not even looking at me. I look back at the judges and ask if it is OK to rest her a few minutes. Mid says, "Don't take too long". Oh no, I think as I kneel back down to shade Alicia, they think we are taking too long but if I don't let her cool off Alicia will never finish. I hold myself there a full minute until I sense a little easing of Alicia's panting. Then I can't stand it anymore and stand up and say "Find it, Alicia. Just a little more to go." She sits in the rut another ten seconds before she finally moves into the deep grass to the right of the rut. She heads at a forty-five degrees angle to the track, so I increase tension and she swings back into the rut.

This is a very long leg, 170 yards in all. As I walk along behind Alicia, I try to calculate how far we have gone. It feels like we have been at least three thousand yards by now, but that was just the second article. As I am miscalculating, Alicia veers off a few feet to the right, then quickly circles back to the left and heads straight under the barbed-wire fence we have been paralleling so long. It is no barrier to her, and as I approach it, I can see a single track in the deep grass going down the hill, crossing an enormous log and going on beyond. But my immediate concern is the barbed-wire fence that now lies between me and Alicia, who is picking up speed as she heads downhill into the shade. The bottom strand seems high enough for me to get under quickly. Due to all the problems we have already had, I don't want to stop Alicia as I clamber through the fence. So I dive under the fence on my back and come up on the other side walking back up the line. Luckily, there was no barbed wire on the ground under the fence, as there so often is under old fences, and we are safely on the seventh leg.

The arch of the branches high overhead form a natural cathedral through which Alicia and I track. This is what tracking is all about! I think as Alicia, sure of herself, pulls me down the track. The sights and sounds of spring in a pristine forest delight me as the scents of the track delight my dog. Even when she comes out of the shade into the drying sunshine, she pauses only momentarily to check that this is still the correct track before continuing on toward our goal.

Looking over Alicia as we continue down the slope I see a huge fallen tree. She reaches the fallen tree. She pauses only a split second before she disappears under it. I walk the rest of the way up the line and peer over the 4' high log to see her through a vee. It is really a double-trunked tree that has fallen, and she is lying there peering out under the second trunk. Immediately, she disappears under it and is off down the track on the other side. I drop the line and scramble over the trunks. She looks back at all the noise I make but goes on without losing pace.

As I stand there letting the line pull out through my hands, I look down and see a track coming down along this side of the trunk from the left. They might have walked around the tree, instead of going over it, and left the last article up at the end of the tree? Just then, the 20' knot goes through my hand; I step forward; Alicia goes from shade out into the sun and doubles back toward me. She comes straight back and marches in a most determined fashion up the side track I had noticed just moments before. I follow her up to the exposed roots, which she marches around and down the other side. As soon as she reaches the place she had crawled under, she turns around and marches back up to the roots where I stand. She starts to go down into the depression made by the uplifted root to do a little mousing, so I repeat "No mouses today, Alicia. Find it!" She heads out parallel to the track from the roots of the tree, under the shade of a line of trees. Finally, she swings down and picks up the track again.

She is under the shade of a convenient tree when she circles quickly to the right but zips back to the left where she picks up a track. "Is this the original track? Is this the good track?" I ask as the line plays out through my hand under increasing pressure. She is sure of herself and I follow on the eighth leg. In about 30 paces, she stops and shakes as though there was an article but quickly moves on. I stop at the place and as the line moves through my hands kick the leaves to see if there is anything hiding. Nothing here but we must be getting close to the end. In another few paces, she stops again, shakes once and then moves on. More leaves get kicked when I reach the spot, but nothing is there. She takes me up a little hill. As she gets to the top, she stops, shakes real hard, turns half way back toward me and nuzzles a leather wallet up into view.

I fall down with her, praising her and telling her how good she is. There will be a long walk back to the truck and a long ride back to base camp — she will eat well for this fantastic accomplishment.

To succeed in this test, we both had to be at our peaks as trackers. Also, Alicia had to be in peak physical condition and we had to work smoothly together as a team. In two of the three tests we failed the year before, there were other tracks on which we would have done much better than the track we happened to draw. I suspect that Alicia would have failed the track she passed if she had to run it a few hours later in the day as temperatures continued to rise.

There were times as we approached her previous three unsuccessful tests when I pushed Alicia to her limit as an eight-year-old Westie. The first winter we trained after her TD, I was in a panic for the two of us to experience everything. Three days a week I threw obstacle after obstacle at her. We were "lucky" enough to get into three tests that winter, and for each I subjected her to a barrage of tracks, trying to practice every condition she might encounter. By her last test, she was worn out and the summer break was a welcome vacation.

As summer ended, I could see the string of six winter and spring TDX tests lying before us. With great enthusiasm, I broke out the tracking harness and put in our first track of the season. Unfortunately, the enthusiasm was mine. She remembered the long grueling tracks of the previous spring and was not sure this was going to be fun. I should be explicit that any casual observer would have thought her quite enthusiastic. What she lacked was that extra enthusiasm she'd need to keep working on a difficult track when an obstacle made her lose the scent and have to search a wide area to find it.

She and I would have to take a different tack; find a way to get the training we needed without turning her off. As fall turned into winter and two tests went by that we didn't get into, I could be more and more relaxed about our practice schedule. To maintain enthusiasm, I limited practice tracks to small pieces of a TDX track. But it became clear that the piecemeal TDX tracking technique did not leave Alicia in good enough physical condition to negotiate an 800–1000 yard track. So we started a jogging program twice a week to complement our twice a week tracking schedule. By April, we had built up to three miles through the hills. Actually, we would jog up the hills and walk down them, as this was easier on my knees and gave her a chance to catch her breath. She didn't like to jog (well, neither do I) but at least her enthusiasm for tracking was unbounded.

Phase X3. More Crosstracks, and Age Progression Once Again

Purpose:
- Build confidence on older tracks by gradually adding age while improving the dog's understanding of crosstracks.

Strategy:
- Repeat gradually aging the main track from one hour to five hours old.
- Continue progressively training crosstracks so the dog thoroughly understands them within the context of simple-marked tracks where you can help your dog if needed.
- Introduce more simple and compound obstacles as well.
- Maintain motivation.

How to use this chapter:
- Look through the table below, which summarizes the training structure of this phase, and read the discussion section that follows.
- Do the 17 sessions listed following the age, length, and number of corners as closely as possible. Use natural fields whenever available, but much work can be done on urban lawns as well.
- Keep a detailed log of each session using a format like the one shown on page 31 and keep a summary log like the one shown on page 209.
- Do the X3.18 review session on page 208 to evaluate the team's progress.

Phase X3 Session Schedule:

Sesn	Track Age	Track Yards	XT Delay	Track/XT Pattern	XT Flagging	Num. Turns	Num. Simple Obstacles	Num. of Compound Obstacles
X3.1	1:00	400–500				4–5	1–2	0
X3.2	1:30	500–600				4–5	2–3	1
X3.3	3:00	380	1:30	U Over U	10 yds off	2	0	0
X3.4	0:45	400				3–5	0	0
X3.5	2:00	600–700				4–5	1–2	0
X3.6	2:30	500–600				5–6	2–3	1
X3.7	3:30	380	1:45	X Over U	10 yds off	2	0	0
X3.8	0:30	500				3–5	0	0
X3.9	3:00	600–700				5–7	1–2	0
X3.10	3:30	500–600				5–7	2–3	1
X3.11	2:30	760	1:15	M Over U	20 yds off	2	0	0
X3.12	0:45	400				3–5	0	0
X3.13	4:00	600–800				5–7	1–2	0
X3.14	4:30	600–700				5–7	2–3	1
X3.15	3:30	760	1:30	M Over U	20 yds off	2	0	0
X3.16	2:30	1000				6–8	0	0
X3.17	0:45	400				2–4	0	0
X3.18	Review							

Discussion:

Stepping up in age a third time turns out to be good training and important for the development of your dog's confidence on older tracks. Just doing more older tracks is not as valuable as following this pattern of easy (young) to hard (old). So Phase X3 provides that third aging sequence while continuing the basic crosstrack training that was started in Phase X2.

Please don't skip this phase because you think your dog doesn't need this stuff, which seems to repeat material you have already done. This phase is critical in building the three C's of TDX — clear-confident-commitment by the dog.

All the X3 sessions without crosstracks are similar to the X2.x sub-TDX sessions on page 184. Control the age and complexity as indicated in the X3 session schedule on the previous page. Seek out new locations with obstacles that your dog has not handled before.

After one more U-over-U and one more X-over-U crosstrack session, you and your dog will be ready for the daunting M-over-U sessions. For some dogs, this will be enough focused crosstrack exercises and, along with some normal tracks with crosstracks, will leave your dog with a good understanding of how to work crosstracks. Some other dogs, for example my own Westies, will need more focused crosstrack sessions in Phase X4 and X5.

Consider making copies of the Ground Cover, Obstacles and Design Parameters tables (pages 217 to 220) for this phase of your TDX training. This will help you to track the dog's recent experience with obstacles and perhaps suggest other obstacles to try as you progress through this phase. If you kept track of the obstacles encountered in Phase X2, review that list. Do more of the obstacles where you needed to help your dog or where he showed less than clear-confident-commitment while navigating the obstacle. Add to the variety of obstacles, which may require visiting different tracking fields.

Your **training goals** for this phase are:
- Maintain a high level of motivation for your dog to stay with the track and indicate the articles along the way.
- Your dog shows clear-confident-commitment while he handles almost all aspects of each track.
- Practice reading your dog in all typical TDX situations so you will be able to follow him on fully blind tracks.
- Improve your handling techniques at the starts, corners, crosstracks, and obstacles.
- Shift the full responsibility of staying with the good track to your dog.

Maintaining a high level of motivation requires interspersing easy tracks every few sessions, having parties at each article, having a big party at the end of each track (even ones that do not go well), and showing your dog how impressed you are with his accomplishments.

When a dog tracks with clear-confident-commitment close to the track, you will have an easy time reading him and following him. That will make it much easier for you to do so in the difficult places along the track where your dog has to sort the scents out and figure out which is the good track.

As you practice reading your dog, review areas where you had doubts about following your dog. Consider if he needs to do some focused exercises to improve his clear-confident-commitment in these situations. Many handlers assume they should figure out how to read extremely subtle signals that the dog is on the good track, whereas they would become a better team if they focused on improving the dog's skill in these difficult situations.

In this phase, your preparation for blind tracks continues by starting to remove some of the corner flags when you have a trusted tracklayer. Tracks that are only marked with clippies at the corners are semi-blind since the handler cannot see them at a distance. Their presence at the corners reassures the handler compared to fully-blind tracks with no markings.

Review the recommended handling techniques at:
- Starts — a start is a corner you have not tracked into (page 80).
- Corners (page 80).
- Crosstracks (page 183).
- Obstacles (page 181).
- Really difficult obstacles (pages 181 and 237).

Have your tracklayer video you as you handle some tracks and review your own handling techniques to see where you could improve. Become the handler your dog deserves.

Most the tracks in this phase are TDX-like but with reduced length, complexity, and age. The image below shows an example sub-TDX track. The white track is about 800 yards long and includes a ditch-road-ditch crossing compound obstacle, into and out of the woods obstacles, and two crosstracks. The track could be made more difficult by turning in the woods or extending the third leg so the third corner is right against the pond. It could be made easier, for example, by omitting the crosstracks, or by shortening the first or last legs.

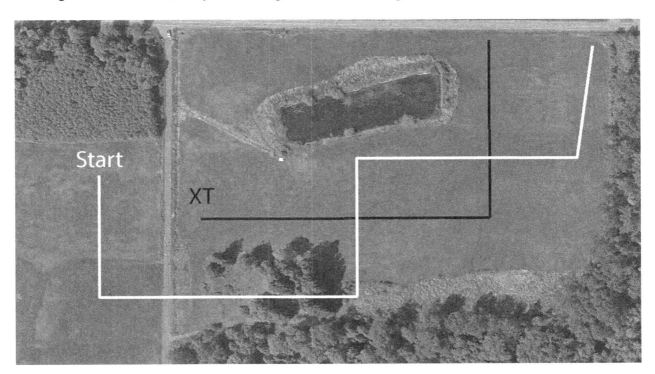

Sessions X3.x Simple Sub-TDX Tracks with Controlled Complexity

Purpose:
- Allow the dog to gain experience solving simple scenting and physical obstacles.
- Assure the dog there is always fun and rewards once the obstacle is solved.
- Allow the dog to gain experience following older tracks with their fainter and variable odor.
- Transition the handler to semi-blind tracks by only marking the track with clippies.

Sample Basic TDX Track Shapes.

Use clippies near some or all corners as requested.

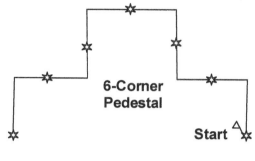
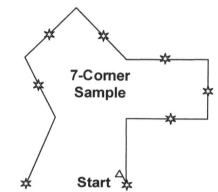
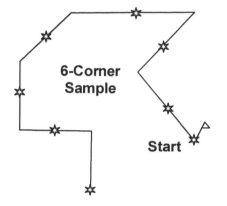

Session	Track Age	Track Yards	Number Corners	Number Simple Obstacles	Number of Compound Obstacles
X3.1	1:00	400–500	4–5	1–2	1
X3.2	1:30	500–600	4–5	2–3	1
X3.4	0:45	400	3–5	0	0
X3.5	2:00	600–700	4–5	1–2	1
X3.6	2:30	500–600	5–6	2–3	1
X3.8	0:30	500	3–5	0	0
X3.9	3:00	600–700	5–7	1–2	1
X3.10	3:30	500–600	5–7	2–3	1
X3.12	0:45	400	3–5	0	0
X3.13	4:00	600–800	5–7	1–2	1
X3.14	4:30	600–700	5–7	2–3	1
X3.16	2:30	1000	6–8	0	0
X3.17	0:45	400	2–4	0	0

Tracklayer:

- Get the basic design parameters from the handler including length, number of corners, age, clippies, article frequency, on-track food rewards, and the nature of any obstacles.
- Actual track design requires considering the available terrain, cover changes, and potential obstacles.
  - Shorter tracks having 3–5 corners can use basic shapes similar to TD shapes (see page 116).
  - Longer tracks with 6–8 corners may have more complex shapes. Some examples are shown on the previous page as well as pages 172 and 184.
- Use the land you have and create the track that fits what is available. Make it simpler than requested rather than more difficult.

Handler:

- Give the tracklayer basic design parameters including length, number of corners, age, clippies, article frequency, any food rewards, and the number and nature of obstacles.
- Approach the start, varying angles each session. The start is a corner you have not tracked into.
- Hold your dog at the start 10–20 seconds so he can memorize the scent.
- Use your whole line to allow him to make his choices before you move forward at the start, corners, and other scent disturbances.
- Use corner communications, then walk up the line to 15–20' right after he and you commit to the new direction.
- Notice landmarks while trying to ignore the clippies.
- If your dog struggles, first encourage verbally that he can do it, then help happily as much as needed rather than have him get frustrated.
- Give lots of treats and praise at each article.

Evaluation:

- Note in your journal and summary log (page 209) the details of the track and your evaluation.
- You may see him struggle on older tracks particularly on warmer sunny days. That is why we mark these tracks — so you will know where the track is and you will be able to help your dog when needed.
  - If your dog struggles a lot, consider using some of the remedial variations discussed on page 174.

TDX Tracking in the Suburbs

As you proceed through your dog's training, there may be times when you cannot get out to natural fields to do your training. As mentioned on page 8 and again on page 165, you can do a lot of "field" tracking on sports fields or parks. I tend to choose the least contaminated locations and times of day when this is necessary.

There are also great opportunities for obstacle training in most parks - hedges, tree lines, and paths, Look at your local parks as opportunities to train and gain skills. You will need to repeat some work in natural settings, but you will be way ahead and been having fun as well.

Session X3.3 is just like the U-over-U Crosstrack sessions described on page 186. Control the age and the distance. Have the crosstrack layer move the crosstrack flags to the side of the track as shown in the table below.

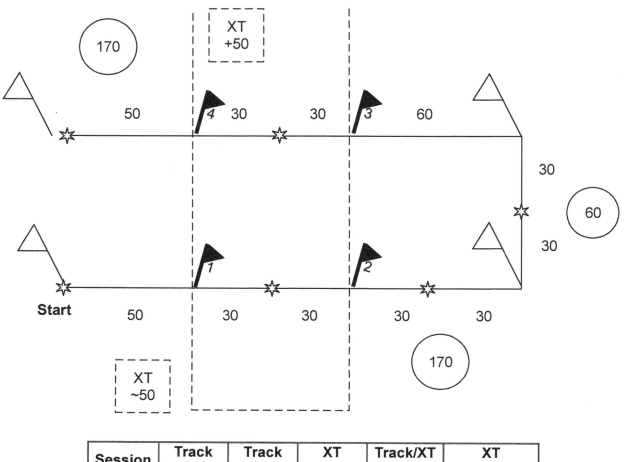

Session	Track Age	Track Yards	XT Delay	Track/XT Pattern	XT Flagging
X3.3	3:00	400	1:30	U Over U	10 yards off

Keep the Crosstrack Flags Visible

Some handlers notice that their visually acute dog is attracted to the crosstrack flags and so request they be removed. I recommend keeping the flags visible and off the track in spite of these tendencies. The point of this and similar exercises is to have your dog notice the crosstrack and reject it on his own. Having a flag help him notice the crosstrack is excellent, even if we end up having to help the dog return to the good track a few times. This is how the dog will learn. Also removing the flags typically leads to a handler who becomes confused along the track and handles her dog incorrectly. Having the handler know where the crosstracks are exactly will help the dog more quickly learn how to do the right thing.

Session X3.7 is just like the X-over-U Crosstrack sessions of Phase X2 described on page 188. Control the age and distance. Have the crosstrack layer move the crosstrack flags to the side of the main track as shown in the table below.

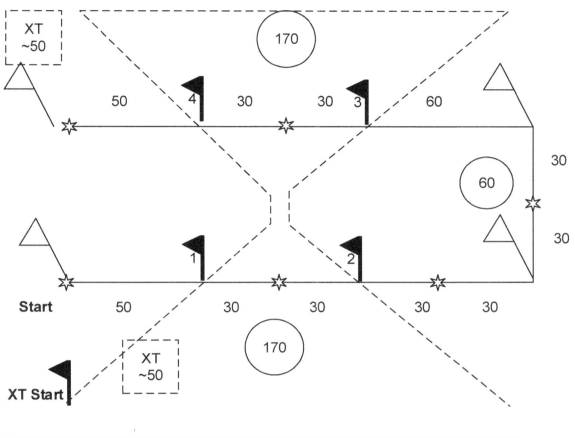

Session	Track Age	Track Yards	XT Delay	Track/XT Pattern	XT Flagging
X3.7	3:30	400	1:45	X Over U	10 yards off

Crosstrack layer:

- If you are requested to pick up all the crosstrack flags, put a flag where you begin lining up the first and third crosstrack flags. That way, when you are lining up on the opposite side to make the third crosstrack, you have something to align.

Crosstrack Training Goal

Your goal is to fully shift the responsibility for making the good-track choice at every crosstrack encountered. That means no checking or restraining your dog when he investigates a crosstrack until he goes 35–40' out on it. And it means staying at your pivot point until your dog commits 35–40' down the good track before you climb up the line to 15–20'. The M-Over-U pattern on the next page is an excellent exercise to achieve that goal, but the U-Over-U and X-Over-U patterns may continue to be used as well. Many of our dogs require using these exercises more than the minimum prescribed by the main schedule.

Phase X3. More Crosstracks, and Age Progression Once Again

Sessions X3.x M-over-U Crosstracks.

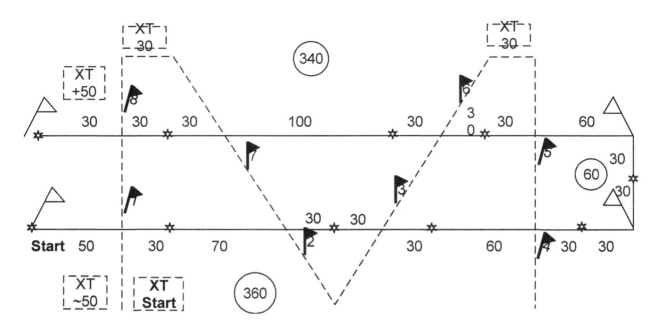

Session	Track Age	Track Yards	XT Delay	Track/XT Pattern	XT Flagging
X3.11	2:30	760	1:15	M Over U	20 yards off
X3.15	3:30	760	1:30	M Over U	20 yards off

Purpose:
- Teach the dog that the good track should be followed even when there is a fresher track that would be fun to track as well.
- Assure the dog there is always fun and rewards once the crosstrack is solved.
- Allow the dog to gain experience following older tracks with their fainter and variable odor.

Tracklayer:
- See tracklayer note on page 211 for hints to avoid problems laying this track.
- Use a field measuring 400x160 yards that allows the track design above to be laid with the distances indicated.
- Avoid changes of cover or obstacles that will affect the dog's handling of the crosstracks.
- Use tall main-track flags at the start, both corners, and the end so they are visible at a distance.
- Place crosstrack flags as shown on the track. They must be tall enough to be visible at a distance and a different color than the main-track flags. They will end up off the track because the crosstrack layer will be directed to move them 20 yards off the track (as shown above).
- For inexperienced crosstrack layers, place two crosstrack flags at each crossing angled in the direction the crosstrack layers will be going when they cross.

Crosstrack Layer:
- Start laying the crosstracks from the side of the field at least 50 yards to the side of the track at the "XT Delay" period after the tracklayer laid the main track.
- Line up the first and last (eighth) crosstrack flags, cross there and proceed at least 50 yards past the eighth flag. Crosstrack flags are numbered in the order the dog encounters them.
- Turn back and parallel the third main-track leg until the seventh and second crosstrack flags line up.
- Cross there and proceed until the third and sixth crosstrack flags line up. Turn and cross there and proceed at least 70 yards past the sixth flag.
- Turn and parallel the third leg until the fifth and fourth crosstrack flags line up. Cross there and proceed at least 50 yards past the fourth before exiting the field.
- Move the crosstrack flags about 20 yards off the track as you lay the crosstrack.
- If there is a second crosstrack layer, she should walk 4' to your side. If not, you can make two passes, moving the flags on the second pass.

Handler:
- See handler note on page 211 for hints to avoid tracklayer problems with this track.
- Approach the start, varying the angle each session. The start is a corner you have not tracked into.
- Look down the first leg and make sure you understand which flag is the corner flag and which flags are the crosstrack flags; the latter may be to the side of the actual track.
- Hold your dog at the start 10–20 seconds so he can memorize the scent.
- Use your whole line to allow your dog to make his choices before you move forward at the start, corners, and crosstracks.
- Use corner communications, then walk up the line to 15–20' right after he and you commit to the new direction (page 80).
- When your dog notices a crosstrack, let him investigate it even to the end of your 40' line. If he wants to commit farther, stop him, pull or call him back to be re-scented, and tell him "Find the good track." The second time, re-scent and gesture down the track, taking a few steps with him to make it easy for him to commit to the good track.
- If your dog repeatedly tries to commit to a crosstrack, you will need to pull him in, put him at your side firmly but neutrally, and get down to love the track yourself until he gets interested and moves forward (page 60).
- Give lots of treats and praise at each article.

Evaluation:
- Your dog may not notice all the crosstracks; this is normal. That is why we put many crosstracks on the same track so he will notice a few and we have the opportunity for learning.
- You may find your dog seems more likely to take a crosstrack after encountering several of them. If your dog is enticed by the repeated crosstracks, this exercise is worthwhile because it provides several valuable training opportunities.
- Your dog does not need to be perfect at solving crosstracks at the end of Phase X3. Twizzle, one of my recent TDX dogs, took many more sessions to really understand that she should reject those fun-smelling crosstracks all the time. Most dogs will get the idea by the end of Phase X3. But if they don't, you can insert some of these crosstrack patterns in your Phase X4 work.
- Note in your journal and summary log (page 209) the details of the track and your evaluation.

Sessions X3.18 Review

Review and evaluate how your dog's tracking, your handling, and your tracklaying have improved in this phase.

- Review your journal and summary log looking for
  - Skills that have improved since the start of the phase.
  - The extent your dog shows clear-confident-commitment to each leg of the track.
  - Recurrent issues that need improvement.
- While optional in this phase, it is good practice to summarize the types of obstacles and ground covers your dog has experienced. Review your logs and fill in a copy of the charts on pages 217 to 220 so you will be encouraged to add a few more types during the next phase.
- For most dogs, these 17 sessions are effective in allowing the dog to learn to focus on the older scent while adapting to longer tracks with simple and compound obstacles.
- While few dogs will be fully confident with 3-hour-old tracks, they should show some competency even if they may struggle in a couple of places per track.
- If so, you can go right on to Phase X4 once you have completed all these sessions.
- If your dog is struggling more than that and you have to help him on most legs, you may have added complexity too quickly for this dog. This often happens if the weather has turned warmer or drier during this phase or the tracklayer added complexity in the track design by including too many obstacles, too difficult obstacles, or tracked through difficult terrain and cover.
  - If so, step back to a place in the phase where your dog was tracking confidently.
  - Then step through the sessions possibly using the remedial variations below as appropriate before going on to Phase X4.

TDX Remediation:

If your dog loses motivation for several sessions, step back to where your dog was having fun and add a starter track before the main track, keep the main track shorter, and have a more over-the-top exciting party at each article. A starter track is a fifty-yard straight track laid after the main track and run before the main track.

If your dog struggles to search for, find and commit to new legs at corners, do three or more sessions of Phase 8 Plan C zigzags (see page 142), at track ages with which your dog is comfortable until your dog's corner performance improves. Then, step back a few sessions in this Phase X3 schedule and continue while monitoring his clear-confident-commitment throughout his tracks. Remember, it is never wrong to do a few Plan 8C zigzags to rebuild corner skills and motivation.

If you identify other specific issues you want to deal with now, look ahead at the specific problem-solving techniques described in Phase X4 Problem-Solving Sessions on page 236 and apply them now within the context of your Phase X3 tracking training constraints.

For a fully demotivated dog, consider the re-motivation plan in Appendix A on page 408.

Phase X3 Summary Log

Sesn	Site	Date	Config. & Obs.	Track Age	Evaluation
X3.1				1:00	
X3.2				1:30	
X3.3			XT	3:00	
X3.4				0:45	
X3.5				2:00	
X3.6				2:30	
X3.7			XT	3:30	
X3.8				0:30	
X3.9				3:00	

Phase X3. More Crosstracks, and Age Progression Once Again

Sesn	Site	Date	Config. & Obs.	Track Age	Evaluation
X3.10				3:30	
X3.11			XT	2:30	
X3.12				0:45	
X3.13				4:00	
X3.14				4:30	
X3.15			XT	3:30	
X3.16				2:30	
X3.17				0:45	

Sample Journal Log Entry — TDX Phase 3

Session: _X3.11_
Dog: _Twizzle_
Date: _6/16/13_
Layer: _Sil_
Location: _Brown St_
Weather: _Sunny, Warm_
Length: _760_
Age: _3:30_
XT layers: _Orci & Urna_
XT Age: _1:30_

Evaluation: _Excellent_

Start had been contaminated by a dozen dogs & she needed guidance to commit to the good track

She noticed most crosstracks & rejected them for the good track except perhaps for the 4th, where I hinted her too soon.

She liked cupcakes & treats at articles.

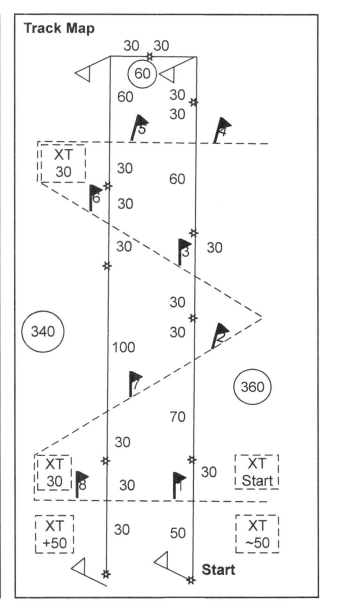

Tracklayer's Note: It is fairly common for a tracklayer to bend over to put in a flag or place an article and when she looks up, she sees another similar landmark. Try very hard to find two distinctive landmarks in a line for the first and third legs to save yourself the embarrassment of laying a sinuous track.

Handler's Note: It is fairly common for a tracklayer to bend over to put in a crosstrack flag or an article and stand up to see another similar landmark towards which she then heads. This creates an undulating main track that can look more like a banana than a "U". Relax handler, you and your dog will get through it. I am pretty careful to look at the field and flags before the crosstrack layers enter it and to walk out with the crosstrackers to help them figure out the crosstrack flags and how to navigate them.

Mr. Q's TDX (1991) — Sil reminisces after 25 years.

When Mr. Q earned his TDX in February of 1991, I apparently never wrote up the story of his track, or at least I cannot find it now after 25 years of moving from computer to computer. So unlike the other tracking stories in this book, the details were not recorded contemporaneously; but I am confident the essence and most details are accurate.

Mr. Q had loved to track from the first day he was introduced to it on short tracks. He even carried his glove all the way back to the car, which is most unusual for a Westie. He went on to progress in fine style and earned his TD his first season. I continued to train him for a couple of months until the spring foxtail grass seeds hardened into barbed needles, and so we stopped.

The following November, I was reluctant to start up again because it seemed likely that I would subject him to similar stress and burnout as Alicia (see story on page 194). So after a simple first track of the season, I sat down with him and tried to explain that it would be difficult for me to keep from pushing his training too hard. He assured me that he was a very tough dog and that he loved tracking, so we resumed with a 2–3 times per week training schedule mostly working alone. He made steady progress through the winter while I introduced age, obstacles of all sorts, and crosstracks laid by myself shortly after laying the main track (Since the advent of urban tracking, a tracklayer also laying the crosstracks is no longer recommended).

As I contemplated entering a late spring test, I had a friend lay a realistic TDX track and discovered I needed more practice handling him on blind tracks. Thus we did not enter any tests that year.

During August, I wanted to track, but that is too early to track in the fields of Northern California with their foxtail, star thistle, and rattlers. So I opted to track in business parks laying the track on Sunday mornings at about 5 and running them around 8. This gave me constant changes of cover, road crossings, and working through evergreen shrubs. I entered the one Northern California test in the fall but did not get in; then I got into three tests in a row in February.

The first test was at Skywalker Ranch north of San Francisco, and the next two were near Sacramento. At the first test, the track paralleled a dirt road and then crossed over it and through a barbed wire fence. Then came crosstracks, a 15' deep ravine crossing, under an oak tree, and then the second turn was on a dirt road. Talk about a lot of obstacles on a single leg. He handled everything up to the ravine with confidence, but when he came out of the ravine, he was to the side of the track and was unable to commit to the track in the prickly oak leaves or along the road.

The second track was in Brown's Ravine in Folsom. The cover was very short, but he followed it with confidence, turned and went under another oak tree where a camouflage sock was sitting in the oak leaves. He might have dipped his head over the sock, but I did not see it and plowed on, making a confident second turn, and we were off. I could hear some significant discussion behind me, but no whistle so we got the great experience of finishing that track without interruption even though we had failed (the AKC rules now instruct judges to inform exhibitors as soon as they fail). I thought it was a great experience, and he did finish the track with complete confidence.

We were in another test the next weekend in the same general area. I bought some camouflage articles at an army-navy store and headed up to the area on Tuesday to practice in those conditions with these invisible articles. Of course, as it turned out, he did not have any camouflage articles on his track the next weekend.

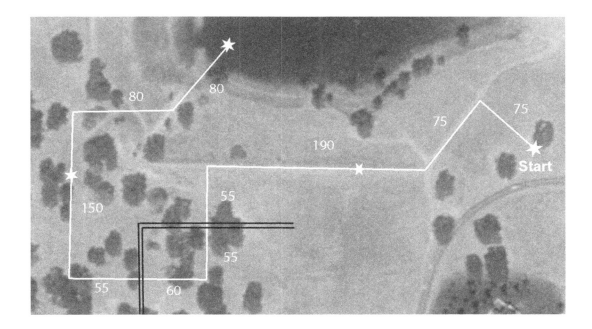

I drew track 1 and we walked to the starting flag from the nearby parking lot. The cover was tall woody star thistle plants from last year with dry grass underneath. 1991 was during a long California drought so the water in the reservoir was lower than pictured in the map above. He started confidently and then crossed a gravel road. But he could not find it on the other side. He finally committed to the road itself although not with the same confidence shown on the first leg. Shortly after we rounded a bend where the road crossed along the top of a rocky dike, there was an eyeglass case that gave me confidence he has his nose screwed on straight today.

Near the end of the dike, he turned to the left and easily handled the crosstrack on that leg and the next. Around another corner we found a scarf, and he went on quickly making the next right turn with confidence. At what turned out to be the last corner, he searched and went out to the right but without his normal confidence. At the end of the line, I followed him tentatively until he was 40 yards off before he turned around and brought me back to the corner. The judges later told me they had started out to the right before they realized they were getting too close to the dike and the third leg.

Finally, he found the good track to the left, which he followed with renewed confidence. As we entered a flat sandy glade that would normally be covered in water, he lifted his head at the smell of a glove and looked for it. But there was such a muddle of sticks and rocks he could not see it. So he carefully sniffed each and every piece of debris until he picked up the glove to show me his special prize.

Mr. Q became the second Westie to earn a TDX after my Alicia accomplished it 7 years earlier. I continued to train Mr. Q quite intensively for the TDX since there were no other tracking activities for us to enjoy at the time. He became better and better at handling difficult TDX-like and post-TDX tracks for the next few years. When VST was introduced in 1994, we worked at it and he loved it, but I was not able to teach him to be confident on the hard-surface corners in spite of lots of work. He taught me a lot about urban scent that positioned me better to train his son QT several years later.

Phase X4. Skill Improvement

Purpose:
- Refining your dog's skills and introduce the handler to blind TDX-like tracks.

Strategy:
- Build skill fluency in dog and handler as well as their teamwork.
- Introduce additional simple obstacles and more complex compound obstacles.
- Develop confidence on blind full-complexity TDX tracks.

How to use this chapter:
- Look through the table below, which summarizes the training structure of this phase, and read the discussion section that follows.
- Do the 13 sessions listed following the age, length, and number of corners as closely as possible. They are described starting on page 233.
- Keep a detailed log of each session using a format like the one shown on page 31 and keep a summary log like the one shown on page 244.
- Do the X4.14 review session on page 241 to evaluate the team's progress.

Phase X4 Session Schedule:

Sesn	Session Style	Training Focus	Track Age	XT Delay	Marked	Track Yards	No. Turns	No. Obs.
X4.1	TDX-like	Test-like Complexity	3:00	1:30	Blind	600–800	6–7	3–4
X4.2	Single Issue	Hard Obstacle	4:00	No XT	Clippies	500–600	4–5	1
X4.3	Problem-solving	Select One Issue	3:00	Optional	Clippies	300–1000	2–7	0–4
X4.4	Motivation	Fun	45–60	No XT	Optional	400–500	3–4	0–1
X4.5	TDX-like	New Obstacle	3:30	Optional	Blind	600–700	4–5	2–3
X4.6	Single Issue	New Obstacle	4:30	1:45	Clippies	500–700	4–5	2
X4.7	Problem-solving	Select One Issue	2–4:00	Optional	Clippies	300–700	2–7	0–4
X4.8	Motivation	Fun	45–60	Optional	Optional	300–400	2–3	0–1
X4.9	TDX-like	Age	5:00	1:15	Blind	600–800	5–6	1
X4.10	Single Issue	Hard Obstacle	3:30	No XT	Clippies	500–600	4–5	2
X4.11	Problem-solving	Select One Issue	2:30	Optional	Optional	300–1000	2–7	1–4
X4.12	Motivation	Fun	45–60	No XT	Optional	300–400	2–3	0–1
X4.13	TDX-like	Length	2–3:00	Optional	Blind	900–1100	6–7	0–1
X4.14	Review and Evaluate							
X4.15…	Do several Problem-Solving Sessions then return to X4.1 and redo all sessions.							

Discussion

Congratulations on developing all your dog's advanced TDX skills. As we start to introduce blind tracks, you can feel good that you and your dog have come this far in your TDX training. I imagine in previous sessions that segments, or whole tracks, may have turned out to be blind when a tracklayer forgot to mark it. You were able to read and trust your dog in your TD work, so you will be able to do so as well on these more complex tracks.

In the first three phases, you built up your dog's TDX skills and your own handling skills while avoiding fully blind tracks. In this phase, about one-quarter of your tracks will be blind while you continue to expose your dog to a wide variety of ground covers, obstacles, and test-like cross-tracks. Nearly half of the sessions will be focused on skill-building or problem-solving exercises. The remaining will be motivational tracks. The four blind test-like sessions will serve to evaluate your dog's skills and your own skills while giving you important practice with test-like TDX tracks.

The exact order and feature mix of the sessions are not important so long as the tracks vary in age from 2–5 hours old, and you continue to intersperse motivational tracks 0:45–1:00 hours old. The variety of the single-issue and problem-solving sessions is important, but the exact order of the sessions is not.

There is not a fixed number of sessions for this phase. You should train repeating this basic sequence of four types of sessions until you meet the criteria of passing several unmarked blind TDX-like tracks. Once you have done the first thirteen sessions, you evaluate your own and your dog's performance on your last four TDX-like blind tracks and decide if you are ready to move on to Phase X5 (TDX Test Preparation). If not, first do several problem-solving session (x4.15) and then redo the main sequence of thirteen sessions in different locations and using different obstacles or the same obstacles in different ways.

TDX tests are fundamentally difficult. Your quickest way to pass is to be fully prepared before focusing on entering tests. Even though you are very well prepared, your chance of passing is less than 50%. I start entering tests when I think my dog has a 33% chance of passing a test as demonstrated by his successfully passing all aspects of at least one out of three test-like blind tracks. At the very least, wait until you can pass all aspects of at least one test-like blind track, even if it takes you more than three tries to pass that one. For your reference, the AKC pass rate is about 15%.

Throughout your training keep in mind the discussion in the Training Overview, Basics Skills Revisited, and Advanced Basics on pages 161-162. In particular, incorporate the three indispensable training techniques: intersperse motivational tracks, condition yourself and the dog, and keep a detailed tracking log.

Session Style and Training Focus. About one-quarter of your tracking sessions should be TDX test-like blind tracks. Remember that a blind training track becomes a coached training session once the dog or handler makes mistakes requiring the tracklayer's help. This proportion of blind tracks with the tracklayer safety net provides a good balance by giving the handler valuable blind track handling experience, with the other sessions designed to build specific dog or handler skills or solve specific problems.

The **TDX-like tracks** should be basically compliant with the TDX test requirements with emphasis on the "training focus" and without necessarily including each and every TDX design requirement.

The **single-Issue tracks** are designed to include the training-focus element while keeping the rest of the track fairly short and easy. Single Issues are not necessarily problem issues for you and your dog, they are things like new or hard obstacles, age, and length that the dog and handler should experience regularly throughout their training. One single issue track I often include is to repeat a downwind-downhill acute session on page 102 at three hours to remind my dog to circle behind me.

The **problem-solving tracks** should be designed to include the particular issue once or twice along its length while keeping the rest of the track fairly easy. TDX problem-solving techniques will be addressed in detail on page 236 for sessions X4{.3, .9, .11, .15}. Many of the techniques can be incorporated into any of your tracks or in fact in any phase of your TDX training. As soon as you notice these issues, start to address them. If you notice more than one of these common problem areas, resolve the top-most first. Only work on one issue per problem-solving session.

- Weak general motivation.
- Poor starts.
- Fringe Tracking or Weak Corners.
- Weak or no article indication.
- Takes crosstracks.
- Distracted by ground animals or birds.
- Takes animal tracks.
- Unable to find and commit to the leg after searching off the track.
- Drop of enthusiasm on long tracks.
- Backtracking.
- Unusual Conditions.

For **physically isolated handlers** who never have a tracklayer other than themselves, consider some of your own laid tracks "blind" if you avoid looking at landmarks before your dog and you are fully committed to the next leg, and you remain disciplined handling your dog neutrally. In some locations, you can get natural crosstracks by having the track cross a common short-cut between paths on a nice day. Make every effort to include at least one or two tracks laid by someone else and weigh those results more heavily than your self-laid track results.

Acclimation. Familiarity with typical TDX fields and their associated environment is critical for TDX success. On page 100 the importance of acclimation was mentioned in the context of the TD and TDU. For the TDX, there will be widely varying environments that provide much more complexity to the sensitive dog. In addition to the basic acclimation exercises described there, you will need to spend time helping the dog become comfortable in the more difficult environments used for TDX.

Hunters nearby, dogs running behind fences or loose, invisible noises in the woods, unusual objects standing in the field, people walking around are just a few of the "scary" things that may distract your dog from successfully focusing on the TDX track. Helping your dog learn to acclimate to these typical TDX environments by taking long walks in them as well as training in them will allow him to acclimate faster to whatever environment is found at your test site.

Track Design Parameters including Obstacles and Ground Covers. By now your dog should be fairly familiar with many of the ground covers and obstacle types in the areas you use for training. Copy the tables on ground covers, obstacles and track parameters on page 217 through

220 so you can keep track of them during this phase. Make an effort to use novel ground covers, different obstacles, and novel terrain to help your dog generalize his skill at solving these important tracking problems.

The following tables list many types of covers and obstacles. The tables are in a form that you can monitor the number of times your dog has recently experienced these covers and obstacles and rate their recent performance in these covers and obstacles. Periodically fill in copies of these tables. By doing so, you will notice situations that need additional work.

You are not trying to handle all possible obstacles you might encounter in any test. That endeavor will wear out you and your dog. You are trying to expose your dog to a wide variety of ground covers, obstacles, and conditions so he has the experience to generalize to whatever you find at your actual TDX test.

In addition to differing ground covers and obstacles, many other track design parameters affect the overall difficulty of an individual track, as well as the dog's overall experience in solving problems in differing track situations. The tables on the next few pages show many of these design parameters and provide a convenient way for you to track the extent of your dog's recent experiences.

Obstacles, Ground Covers, and Track Design Parameters

Obstacles:	Cross or Thru *Simple*		Turn On or In *Compound*		Turn Into *Compound*		Zigzag Thru *Compound*	
	Num.	Rate	Num.	Rate	Num.	Rate	Num.	Rate
Dirt Road								
Paved Road								
Tree Line								
Brush Line								
Hedge								
Stump								
Fallen Tree								
Rocks								
Foot Bridge								
Derelict Car								
Ruin								
Irrigation Ditch								
Stream								
Dry Gulch								
Standing Water								

Obstacles:	Num.	Rate	Num.	Rate	Num.	Rate	Num.	Rate
Animals	Ground		Horses		Cows		Birds	
	Deer		Coyote		Dogs		Cats	
Fences	Barbed Wire		Climbing		Fallen Down		Turn At	
Corners	Acute		Curved		Sweeping		False	
Tall Changes in Elevation	Tree Line		Wall		Cliff Above		Cliff Below	
Footpaths	Cross		Follow		Turn on		Turn off	
Terrain	Swales		Bowls		Knolls/Ridges		Steep Slopes	
Curved Legs or Serpentine Legs	Sharp		Wide					

Ground Covers:	Num.	Rate	Num.	Rate	Num.	Rate	Num.	Rate
Grass	Tall		Medium		Short		Lawn	
Grass	Grazed		Swamp		Marsh		Manured	
Weeds	Thistle		Pampas		Nettles		Other	
Under Trees	Pine-Fir		Cypress-Cedar		Oak		Deciduous	
Dirt	Plowed		Hard Packed		Animal Pens		Furrowed	
Unusual	Gravel		Sand		Burnt		Freshly Mowed	
Crops	Corn-Tall		Corn Stubble		Vegetable		Other	
Other	Snow		Ice					

Track Design:

Track Age (Hours):	1–2	2–3	3–4	4–5	5+
No. of Tracks within last few months.					
Rate Recent Accuracy					
Rate Recent Enthusiasm					
Length (yards):	50–400	400–600	600–800	800–1000	1000+
No. of Tracks within last few months.					
Rate Recent Accuracy					
Rate Recent Enthusiasm					

Starts (Hours):	1–2	2–3	3–4	4–5	5+
Rate Recent Accuracy					
Rate Recent Enthusiasm					

Corners:	90°+ in Open	Acute	Near Obstacle	In Obstacle	Curved
No. of Tracks within last few months.					
Rate Recent Accuracy					
Rate Recent Enthusiasm					

Crosstracks (delay minutes):	Up to 60	60–75	75–90	90–105	105+
No. of Tracks within last few months.					
Rate Recent Accuracy					
Rate Recent Enthusiasm					

Articles:	Leather	Cloth	Sock	Belt	Paper
No. of Articles within last few months.					
Rate Recent Accuracy					
Rate Recent Enthusiasm					

Articles:	Soft Plastic	Hard Plastic	Metal	Heavily Scented	Lightly Scented
No. of Articles within last few months.					
Rate Recent Accuracy					
Rate Recent Enthusiasm					

Restarts After Articles:	Leather	Cloth	Other	With Reward	Without Reward
Rate Recent Enthusiasm when Restarting					

Weather Conditions	Num.	Rate	Num.	Rate	Num.	Rate	Num.	Rate
Wind Speed	Calm		5–10 mph		10–25 mph		25+ mph	
Temperature	Temperate		Cold		Warm		Hot	
Precipitation	Clear		Cloudy		Showers		Heavy Rain	
Humidity	Dry		Normal		Humid			

Crosstracks in Regular TDX Tracks. Some planning is required to plot good crosstracks in TDX-like tracks. Some examples are shown in the figures below. Note that on a practice track, there is nothing to prevent you from plotting three or four crosstracks rather than just two if that is the handler's tactical goal for this track or it allows the crosstrack layers easier access in and out of the fields. Try to allow at least 125 yards on the track before bringing in the first crosstrack so the dog has a chance to get comfortable with the track itself. Also, keep crosstracks at least 50 yards from all corners and at least 30 yards from an obstacle or an article.

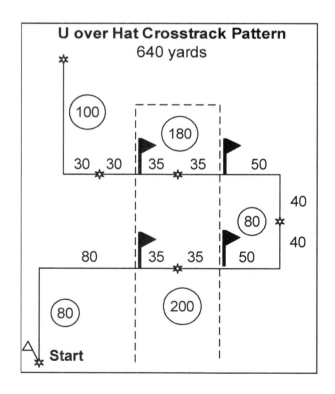

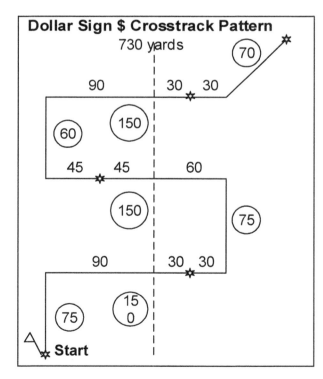

The diagram on the previous page labeled "U over Hat" has two crosstracks on leg 2 and two more on leg 4. Alternatively, it can be laid with just two crosstracks, one each on the second and fourth legs so long as the tracklayers can get off the field without crossing the track in other places.

On either of the two diagrams above, if you only have a single crosstrack layer, you can send her up-and-back 4' apart or ask her to loop around twice. For CKC, once is enough.

These simple shapes allow the crosstrack layers to align two flags and cross the track correctly. In other cases, have the tracklayer place two crosstrack flags at each crossing, one an arm's length to the left of the track and the other an arm's length to the right; this will allow the crosstrack layer to approach the crosstrack from the correct direction.

The track below is a reasonably good training track. Having all four crosstracks on the second leg makes them a concentrated challenge for the dog, which is fine, and finishing with some fun and doable simple obstacles is appropriate for this highly motivated dog. The use of the M-crosstrack on a single leg essentially uses the M-Over-U exercise (page 205) within the context of an otherwise TDX-like track design.

Dog: *Mr. 2*
Layer: *Sil*
Age: *2:00*
Length: *725*
XT: *1:00*
Location: *Lake Meadow & Vista*
Date: *Winter 1990*
Weather: *Clear, sunny.*
Wind: *0-5*

Report: *Noted XT by slowing down, head bob only.*
Took animal XT near bush 6 feet and then returned to track on his own.
Good on plastic belt but did not pick up.
Fast until last two legs, slow on last leg (he was tired).

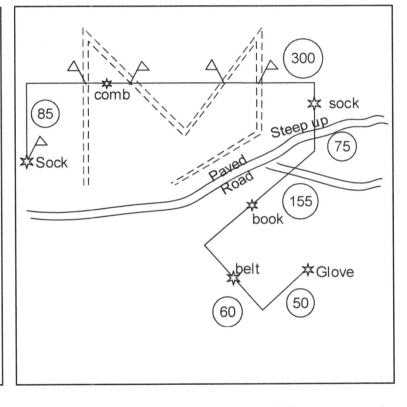

Note the track above lacks an article 30–35 yards past every crosstrack; articles as rewards should have been there. You always want to reward the dog for making the correct choice.

Phase X4. Skill Improvement

I call a crosstrack pattern "tight to the corner" or a "50–50" if the pattern is crosstrack, then 50 yards to the corner, then 50 yards to the second crosstrack. This pattern presents special scenting issues for the dog since the wind-driven fringe of the crosstracks may be overlapping the track for much of the 50 + 50 yard track between them. It is a pattern that should be practiced regularly, so your dog will be able to deal with it if it is used in his test. It is a common pattern many judges use because it is simple and conserves space.

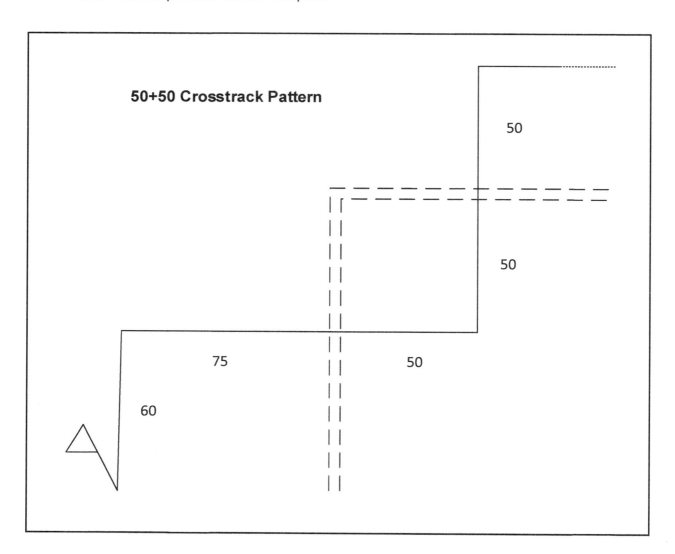

The sample TDX track shapes below show more typical test-like crosstrack patterns. The pattern where the crosstracks are on the second and fourth legs shown in the 7-Corner Sample is perhaps the most common pattern used in tests because it allows the judges to start in an open field, get the crosstracks in, and then find some obstacles. Crosstracks on the second and third legs are also a common pattern. The "6-Corner Sample" can be laid with a 90° fifth corner for an AKC track or the acute for a CKC track since the latter allows the use of acute corners.

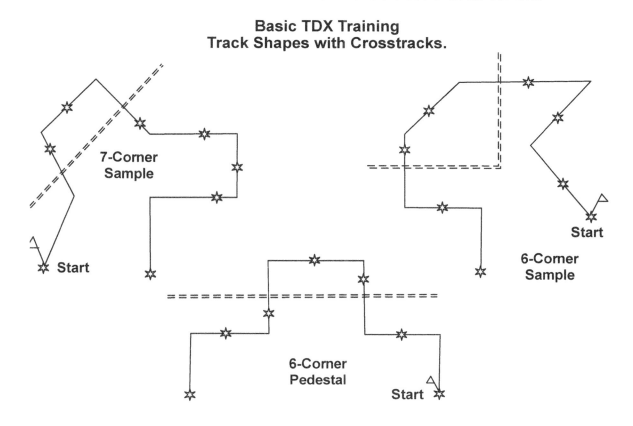

Monitoring and Controlling Track Difficulty

Monitoring and controlling track difficulty is the art and science of the successful tracking trainer. It is very important and needs to be done carefully and thoughtfully. Intuition helps as well. Use judicious complexity/difficulty adaptations when following this phase.

Long ago, I developed several mathematical schemes to calculate the difficulty of TDX tracks as well as to rate the success the dog is having on the track. None of the schemes were successful enough to repeat in detail here. The schemes tried to combine track age, length, number of corners, obstacles, crosstracks, and articles as measured against the experience level of the dog. The schemes all end up adding apple obstacles to orange obstacles and producing a lemon of a result.

In any case, to be a successful trainer, you need to control the overall difficulty of the tracks you lay or have others lay for your dog. A dog that faces too many consecutive tracks that are too difficult will lose motivation. The dog will learn to expect failure and can learn you will help him find the track. This does not make for a passing performance on a blind test track.

On the other hand, a dog that only faces simple tracks will not be well prepared for the test. So a trainer must use the best and only reliable gauge for track difficulty that she has available. That finely crafted precision instrument is, of course, your dog. At the end of every track, once you are done playing with your dog and are back at base camp, take a few minutes to recall your dog's performance and give it an overall rating. Consider everything, including his enthusiasm to start, his stamina at the end, and how many times you had to hint or help him. I use Excellent, Very Good, Good, Needs-Work, or Flawed as my **track rating** system. Use any scale you like. Try to be objective in your ratings; you are rating the overall performance of the track designer, the tracklayer, your dog and yourself, not just your dog. Talk it over with a tracking friend.

While following the schedule of tracks for Phase X4, base your specific tracking plans on the following general rules:

- If you have a long sequence of excellent ratings, you need to step up the difficulty of the tracks. Once you have raised it to test-like conditions, you are ready to move on to the next phase. I also look for several key indicators before trying the next phase such as a dog that is enthusiastic when tracking a four-hour-old track on a warm day, a dog that rejects crosstracks whenever he notices them, and a dog that can solve most new complex compound obstacles that he faces.
- Good training should have a mixture of excellent, very good, and good ratings with a very occasional needs-work or flawed rating. This type of training challenges your dog and gives him a fair opportunity to learn new skills and solidify old ones. The optimal mix depends on your dog's enjoyment of being challenged. Whatever you do, keep the rating mix high enough to maintain enthusiasm.
- When too many training sessions have low ratings, something is wrong and should be fixed. Perhaps you are challenging your dog too quickly. Perhaps you have too many obstacles on the track for the current skill of your dog. Perhaps your dog has lost motivation for some reason, and you need to rebuild his tracking drive. Perhaps you have mishandled your dog and created confusion for him. Don't blame your dog; don't blame yourself; these things happen and good trainers find a way out of them. Whatever the reason, it is up to you to find it and do whatever is necessary to remedy the problem.

Handlers and Tracklayers: Beware Complexity. Handlers, in particular, should monitor the "TDX-like" tracks their tracklayers are laying to make sure they are of appropriate complexity. Based on the recent performance of the dog, the handler may ask for an "easy" or "motivational" "TDX-like" track. If multiple tracks end up being super-difficult, the handler needs to help the tracklayer understand what is inappropriately difficult so the tracklayer can get better. Likewise, if the handler asks the tracklayer for challenging "TDX-like" tracks and several such tracks are all easy, the handler may need to explain to the tracklayer what she could have done to make the track challenging. When the handler is also the tracklayer, these conversations still need to occur even if they are with yourself.

If all the tracks you are doing are too easy, then you and your dog will not be prepared for your track when you get into a test. If all your tracks are too hard, your dog will get frustrated and lose motivation; a demotivated dog will not get you any closer to passing a test. Adjust the complexity up and down, so your dog is exposed to challenges while still maintaining a high level of motivation.

Handling Skills. In the first three phases of your TDX training, the emphasis has been on developing dog skills since the dog needs a high level of skill to successfully navigate a test-like TDX track. The handler also needs to focus on building her own skills, particularly in regards to handling near crosstracks and obstacles on unmarked blind tracks. You want to be the expert handler you know your dog deserves. So ask yourself these questions:

- Are you able to recognize your dog's change in behavior that indicates he is near a corner, crosstrack, change of cover, obstacle or article?
- Are you able to allow your dog the full length of your line while investigating a corner that might go straight before moving from your pivot point?
- Are you able to pivot and help your dog search the full 360°, before moving from the pivot point?
- Are you able to move quietly behind your dog while he searches for where the track emerges from a compound obstacle, without suggesting to your dog what you think is correct?
- Once your dog has exhausted the options within your line length, are you able to expand the search area by sidestepping, or moving backward, or spiraling out while your dog circles? See the exercise on page 405 to help develop this skill.

Reviewing videos of your dog tracking and your handling can help you improve these skills. Getting feedback from a tracking instructor, coach, mentor or peer can help as well. Always take a few minutes after you finish playing with your dog at the end of a track, to get feedback from your training spectators.

Realistic TDX Level Complexity. One of the things people new to the TDX training typically underestimate is the complexity of typical TDX test tracks. A TDX test-like track must have the following features (repeated from page 160).

	AKC	CKC
Age:	3–5 hours.	3–5 hours.
Length:	800–1000 yards.	900–1000 meters.
Start:	Single flag, article.	Single flag, scent pad.
Articles:	Four dissimilar, one at start, two intermediate, plus the final glove.	Three leather articles, typically gloves, dog must find final article and one other.
Corners:	5–7, acute discouraged.	5–8, acutes OK.
Crosstracks:	2 people cross in two places about 90 minutes after the main track.	1 person crosses twice about 60 minutes after the main track.
Obstacles:	At least 2 obstacles, typically difficult ones and more than 2.	None required; changes of cover and some obstacles OK.
Line:	20–40'.	10–49', handler should typically work well back on line.

To help you and your tracklayers understand typical TDX test complexity, on the following pages are maps of several AKC TDX test tracks and one CKC TDX test track along with explanations of some of the challenges. Since these are actual test tracks, the dog's path is shown as a dotted line. I have hidden the identity of the dog to avoid embarrassment. While your fields will not be identical, these examples may help you design appropriately challenging blind tracks. Other TDX tracks are shown on pages 176, 195, 213, 223, 243, and 250.

This first track started in a nice pasture with medium grass. While there were a number of obstacles in the area, they were mostly clustered in the upper right corner of the field. The track started out in a conventional way with the crosstracks on legs two and three. Shortly after the crosstracks, the dog had to handle crossing a single strand wire fence onto a mud road. It then proceeded to an area of many muddy cow paths alongside a circular ditch that surrounded a copse of tall trees. It turned alongside the ditch and followed beside the ditch for 50 yards where it came to a land bridge going right across the ditch and into the trees, but the track turned left out into the field and to an article. After that, there was a wide area of muddy cow paths sided with two wire fences. The rest of the track was out in the open pasture. So the dog had to sort out two corners at obstacles and two muddy crossings with single strand fences.

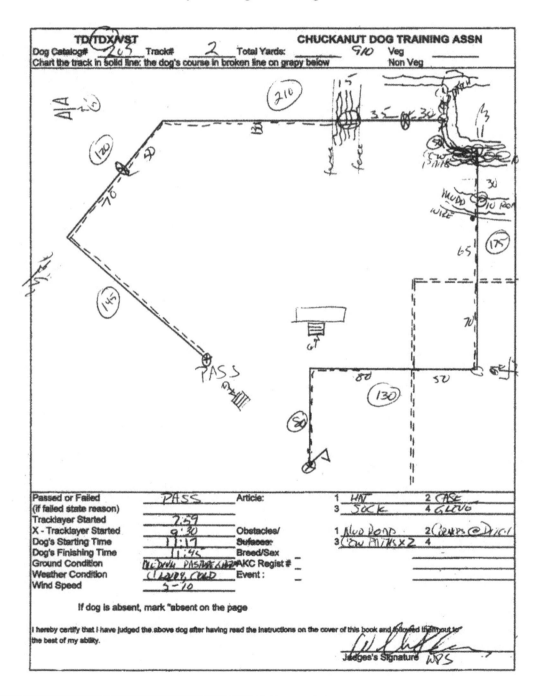

The next track shows an apparently similar pattern of crosstracks on the second and third legs followed by a series of obstacles. A big difference is the cover and terrain — ankle-high prairie grass sounds nice and is if your dog is accustomed to it. But it is actually thin, sparse cover on a sandy soil with a variety of weeds, rocks, and many inhabited critter holes. The official obstacles went up and down large rock outcroppings with a turn at the top of one of them both with swirling winds.

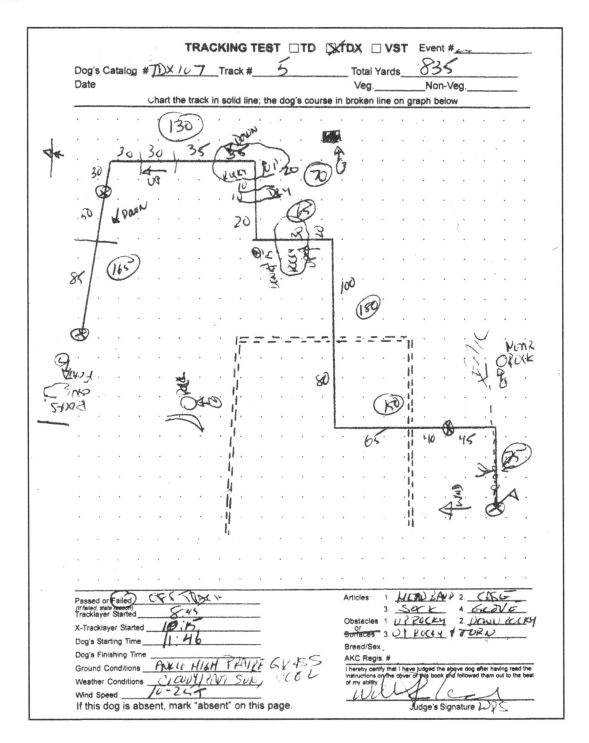

Phase X4. Skill Improvement

The next track was at the same site as the previous one and has the same kinds of cover and terrain. On this one, the crosstracks were in the middle of the track with an obstacle on the second leg and an interesting obstacle on the last corner and last leg. By coming up to the end of the rock outcropping, we offered the dog the opportunity to overshoot the corner. The varying height of the rock outcrop combined with swirling wind compounded the complexity.

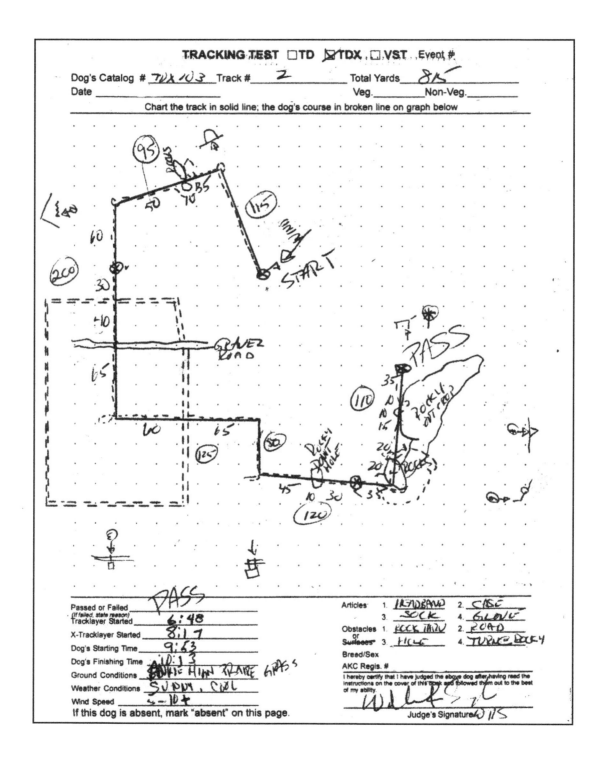

The next track shows the common "hat" pattern where the second and fourth legs hold the cross-tracks. This track was primarily on a flat area with lush calf-high green silage grass so the judges chose to use challenging obstacles to make the track worthy of the title. After the crosstracks, the track crossed a minor dirt road and passed by the end of a pond before crossing a 4' deep ditch, turning near a road and then returning to the dry ditch into which it turned. It followed the ditch for 60 yards before exiting to a short leg and the glove.

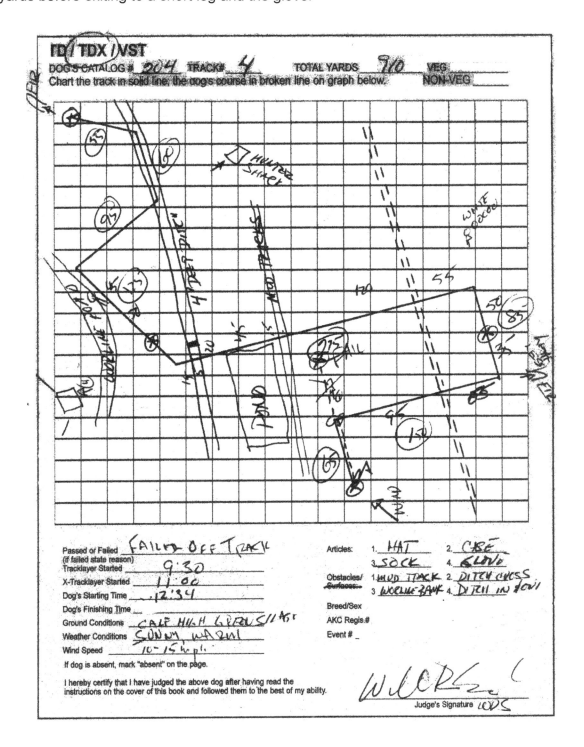

Phase X4. Skill Improvement

The last AKC track shows a passing TDX track, this one with six challenging obstacles. The second leg has a steep up, steep down, crosstracks, and ends at a barbed wire fence. The fourth leg has the second crosstracks, a rock outcropping, and a road crossing. The sixth corner is over a dirt dam at the edge of a pond and the head of a steep gully.

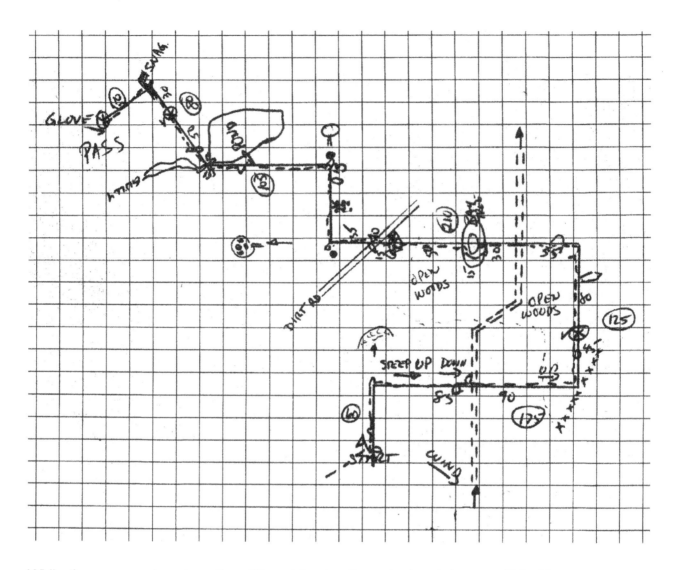

While these examples show five different tracks, the actual variety you will find in tests is much more highly varied as the design depends on the terrain and the judges.

One thing to notice is the tendency for the crosstracks to take up quite a large area of the track and the inevitable tendency for obstacles to cluster together. For a team that is not in shape, having the challenges near the end of the track will make them all the more difficult.

A sixth TDX track shows a passing CKC track, that was 905 meters (990 yards) long. It had a 75º acute on the fourth corner, crossing a culvert on the second leg, a corner at a tree line but no really difficult compound obstacles. What made this track particularly challenging was that several tracking people put in training tracks crossing this track after it was laid and before it was run. Luckily the dog was able to sort out the contamination and pass the test in spite of it.

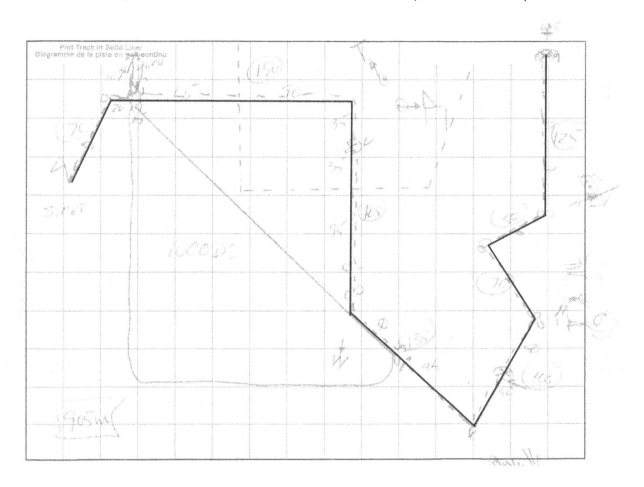

Unusual Conditions. Throughout your training, a variety of unusual conditions has probably cropped up along your track. Because of the complexity of TDX test tracks and the public nature of many of the test sites, "unusual" conditions occur with surprising frequency in real tests. So review the following list of "Unusual" Conditions and incorporate any of them intentionally in your normal TDX training.

"Unusual" Conditions Often Found at TDX Tests

Expose your dog on otherwise easy tracks to many of the following situations so if it happens to you in a test, you and your dog will be able to handle it. Although a few of these conditions might earn you an alternate track, you want to pass the first track you attempt because the alternate track is often the worst track of the day. In training, you will want to mark the track near these unusual conditions.

- Change of cover near the start or a footpath near the start.
- No article at the start — tracklayer did not leave it.
- An article at the start is blown off the track (e.g. toss it 6–10' to the side).
- An intermediate article is blown off the track.
- An intermediate article is a leather glove or a really cool toy.
- A corner at an article, right before, or right after an article.
- Crosstracks near an obstacle or near a change of cover.
- Contamination crosstracks over a corner.
- Crosstracks laid by a pregnant woman, by youngsters, or by someone with a limp.
- Crosstracks laid with short, heavy steps.
- Crosstracks laid by a car or truck crossing the track in grass.
- Crosstracks laid by a horse and rider.
- Crosstracks laid by an open vehicle like a golf cart.
- A group of bird-watchers crossed the track after it is laid or while the dog is tracking.
- Hikers crossed the track at about the same time it is laid.
- Hikers are standing on the track when it is run.
- Horses gallop across the track, or people on horses ride over the track, contaminating it.
- 4-wheel drive vehicles drive over the track.
- The tracklayer is a smoker or heavily perfumed — whatever the dog is not used to.
- The tracklayer is very nervous or stressed.
- The tracklayer suddenly becomes anxious, stressed or unsure somewhere in the middle of the track. Their scent will change.
- A flag is left along the track, or a flag has fallen over near the track.
- Loose dogs on track while it is being laid or while it is being run.
- Barking dogs the other side of a fence from the track.
- The track is near a busy road. (For safety, have a chain-link fence between the track and the road).
- The dog is taken out to the track in the back of a strange noisy, smelly vehicle.
- Stormy weather with lots of rain and high winds.
- Unusually warm day.

Some of these are hard to train for, but others are just a matter of finding the right location or going out when the weather is unusual.

Sessions X4{.1, .5, .9, .13} Test-like TDX Tracks

Purpose:
- Allow the dog and handler to gain experience on TDX-like tracks
- Handler transitions to blind tracks by mixing unmarked tracks with clippie-marked tracks.
- Test the dog and handler on some blind tracks to evaluate their next steps.

Sesn	Session Style	Training Focus	Track Age	XT Delay	Marked	Track Yards	No. Turns	No. Obs.
X4.1	TDX-like	Test-like Complexity	3:00	1:30	Blind	600–800	6–7	3–4
X4.5	TDX-like	New Obstacle	3:30	Optional	Blind	600–700	4–5	2–3
X4.9	TDX-like	Age	5:00	1:15	Blind	600–800	5–6	1
X4.13	TDX-like	Length	2–3:00	Optional	Blind	900–1100	6–7	0–1

Tracklayer:
- Get the basic design parameters from the handler including length, number of corners, age, crosstracks, clippies/unmarked, article frequency, and the nature of any obstacles.
- TDX track designs shown on pages 176, 195, 213, 223, 226–231, 243, and 250 can give you ideas.
- Actual track design requires considering the available terrain, cover changes, and potential obstacles.
- Use the land you have and make a track that fits what is available. Make it simpler than requested rather than more difficult.
- Follow the handler on the track. Wait to tell the handler she is wrong until she is 30–40' off the track committing in the wrong direction.

Handler:
- Based on how your dog has done on the past few tracks and the desired training focus, choose specific track design considerations and give the tracklayer the parameters including length, number of corners, crosstracks, age, clippies/unmarked, article frequency, and the number and nature of obstacles.
- Approach the start at varying angles each session.
- Hold your dog at the start 10–20 seconds so he can memorize the scent.
- Use your whole line to allow your dog to make his choices before you move forward at the start, corners, and other scent disturbances.
- Use corner communications, then walk up the line to 15–20' right after he and you commit to the new direction.
- Notice landmarks. Try to ignore the clippies if there, but these tracks should be blind if the tracklayer is trusted.

- If your dog struggles, first encourage verbally that he can do it, then help happily as much as needed, rather than allow him to get frustrated. Your tracklayer will help you so you can turn a blind track into a valuable training session.
- Give lots of treats and praise at each article.

Evaluation and Possible Adaptations:

- Note in your detailed tracking log and summary log (page 244) the details of the track including:
    - The track design or map.
    - The overall rating Excellent, Very Good, Good, Needs-Work, or Flawed.
    - Whether your dog was Clear-Confident-Committed on some or all of the track or not at all.
    - Any areas where you needed to help your dog.
    - Whether you needed to help your dog.
    - Whether you were confident reading and following your dog.
- Monitor your dog's clear-confident-commitment (see page 223) and consider whether you need to adjust the track difficulty for the next few sessions.
- The transition to blind full-complexity tracks can expose some dog and handler weaknesses. Evaluate and identify specific dog skills that can be improved as well as specific handler skills. Select specific exercises or design specific tracks that focus on each issue one at a time.
- If you see specific problems like those mentioned on page 236 occurring several times, make them your focus for the next problem-solving session or insert several sessions to work specifically on that problem.

Do Tracking Dogs Lie?

This question is here because you are starting to handle your dog on blind TDX-like tracks. You will find your dog makes mistakes, occasionally or pretty frequently, and you may be tempted to think that your dog is lying to you.

My simple answer is no, he may make mistakes, but when he commits to something that is not part of the track, he doesn't intend to deceive you.

Regardless of whether you agree or not, it is a training issue. As a trainer, you need both to develop your dog's skill to follow the original track and to build his motivation to choose to stay with the good track in all cases.

Sessions X4{.2, .6, .10} Single Issue Sessions

Purpose:
- Build specific skills in your dog and yourself.
- Single Issues are not necessarily problem issues for you and your dog, they are things like new or hard obstacles, age, and length that the team should experience regularly.

Sesn	Session Style	Training Focus	Track Age	XT Delay	Marked	Track Yards	No. Turns	No. Obs.
X4.2	Single Issue	Hard Obstacle	4:00	No XT	Clippies	500–600	4–5	1
X4.6	Single Issue	New Obstacle	4:30	1:45	Clippies	500–700	4–5	2
X4.10	Single Issue	Hard Obstacle	3:30	No XT	Clippies	500–600	4–5	2

Tracklayer:
- Get the basic design parameters from the handler including length, number of corners, age, crosstracks, clippies/unmarked, article frequency, and the nature of any obstacles.
- Actual track design requires considering the available terrain, cover changes, and obstacles.
- Use the land you have and make a track that fits what is available.
- Follow the handler on the track. Wait to tell the handler she is wrong until she is 30–40' off the track committing in the wrong direction.

Handler:
- Based on the particular training focus, choose specific track design considerations and give the tracklayer the parameters including length, number of corners, crosstracks, age, clippies/unmarked, article frequency, and the number and nature of obstacles.
- Hold your dog at the start 10–20 seconds so he can memorize the scent.
- Use your whole line to allow your dog to make his choices before you move forward at the start, corners, and other scent disturbances.
- Use corner communications, then walk up the line to 15–20' after commitment.
- Notice landmarks while trying to ignore any clippies.
- If your dog struggles, first encourage verbally that he can do it, then help happily as much as needed, rather than allow him to get frustrated. The tracklayer will help you so that you can turn a blind track into a valuable training session.
- Give lots of treats and praise at each article.

Evaluation and Possible Adaptations:
- Note in your detailed tracking log and summary log (page 244) the track design or map; the overall rating Excellent, Very Good, Good, Needs-Work, or Flawed; and whether your dog was Clear-Confident-Committed on the track; and any areas where you needed to help him.
- Monitor your dog's performance and clear-confident-commitment. Consider whether you need to adjust the track difficulty for the next few sessions (see page 223).
- If you see specific problems mentioned on page 236 occurring several times, make them your focus for the next several problem-solving sessions; You may insert several sessions to work specifically on these problems.

Sessions X4{.3, .7, .11, .15...} Problem-Solving Sessions

Purpose:
- Work on a specific troublesome issue by designing a track to primarily address that issue in a way that the dog and handler's skills improve.
- Like single-issue sessions, these tracks focus on a single problem — a dog or handler skill that needs improvement. These tracks tend to be shorter than test-like tracks unless the specific issue is the length of the tracks.

Session	Session Style	Training Focus	Track Age	XT Delay	Marked	Track Yards	No. Turns	No. Obs.
X4.3	Problem-solving	Select One Issue	3:00	Optional	Clippies	300–1000	2–7	0–4
X4.7	Problem-solving	Select One Issue	2–4	Optional	Clippies	300–700	2–7	0–4
X4.11	Problem-solving	Select One Issue	2:30	Optional	Optional	300–1000	2–7	1–4
X4.15...	Several Problem-Solving Sessions then return to X4.1 and redo all sessions.							

Discussion:

Review your dog's recent tracks and choose one dog skill or one handler skill you need to improve. Note that it is fairly common to need to do several sessions to remedially improve a specific skill. That is fine as it will be time and training well spent.

If you do multiple problem-solving sessions in a row like for X4.15..., do a motivational session every 3–5 sessions. If possible, design tracks that start with an easy motivating section of the track, then include a section for the issue at hand and finish with an easy motivating section of track.

If you notice more than one of the following common problem areas, resolve the top-most first.

- **Weak general motivation** is typically a result of overwork, aging too fast, warming weather, drying weather, lack of using treats that the dog values highly, or lack of handler enthusiasm. Look back in your log to where the dog was enthusiastic and repeat some similar session or try younger easier tracks for several sessions. Don't return to the Phase X4 sequence until the enthusiasm returns. If the root cause is:
  ◦ Overwork — then cut back the number of days per week you track.
  ◦ Age — find where the dog tracks confidently, then step up in 15–20-minute increments.
  ◦ Warming or drying weather — reduce age and step up in 15–30-minute increments.
  ◦ Low-value treats — find something your dog really loves.
  ◦ Very few handlers show their deep emotional appreciation for the dog's accomplishment at the intermediate and final articles. Spend 30–60 quality seconds at each intermediate article, even if your dog just wants to get back to the track, and spend 5 minutes playing with your dog at the end. Never think or say anything self-critical until well after the track.
  ◦ For a fully demotivated dog, consider the re-motivation plan on page 408.

- **Poor starts** but your dog gains enthusiasm once out on the track. Lay a 50–75-yard straight starter track after laying the main session track but run the starter before the main track. Place an article 50–100 yards after each main-track start. Ensure tons of fun at the end of every track, including the starter track and also have lots of fun at the intermediate articles.

- **Weak corners or fringe tracking.** If your dog prefers to track more than 10' to the side of the track or struggles to search for and commit to new legs at corners, do three or more sessions of Phase 8 Plan C zigzags (see page 142), at track ages with which your dog is comfortable, until your dog's corner performance improves. If that is younger than three hours old, do several sessions stepping up in age by 20–30 minutes until your dog shows you clear-confident-commitment on 3–4 hour-old tracks. See also the Not Easy to Read on Corners section, page 133, and the fringing remediation plan, page 406.

- **Weak or no article indication** is often due to the dog loving to track and the handler not making the articles equally valuable. Use a simple four-corner track with an article midway on each leg. Place a clippie or marker 20' before every article, don't let your dog pass the article, and give lots of heart-felt praise and valuable rewards for his stopping by himself or even if you had to stop him.

- **Takes crosstracks.** Repeat the M-Over-U crosstrack pattern (see page 206) or the X-Over-U crosstrack pattern (page 188). Pay particular attention to the way you communicate with your dog and restrain him from taking the crosstracks — let the dog sort out the crosstrack and choose to return to the main track, if at all possible. Avoid checking the dog with the line until he is more than 30' along the crosstrack or he will learn to depend on those line-checks. If needed, happily help the dog commit to the track.

- **Distracted by ground animals or birds.** Lay tracks that cross areas with ground animals or birds. Lead up to this area with easy tracking. Have an article 30 yards past the area. Let the dog investigate this area briefly, then ask him to return to the main track. Help him happily, if you need to help. Reward the dog with a jackpot (something the dog really wants) at the next article. Repeat for many sessions but limit distraction area to once per track. If the dog refuses to leave the distraction, tell him "Yuck!" while you tug him away, then happily encourage the dog to track; Love the track, if necessary.

- **Takes animal tracks.** Identify the dog's most favorite reward and restrict access to it except at the end of the track. Lay marked tracks in areas where you think animals may cross your track. Mark the track with a couple of flags on each leg, not necessarily at the corners. If you can predict where animals cross your track, place a food drop 15–30 yards past the area. Place two food drops on every other leg. When the dog tries to take an animal track, let him investigate it up to 40' before you restrain him, then move forward down the good track happily calling to your dog something like "Look over here. Is this the good track? Let's find the good track!", and help him down the track a few yards. Be happy and excited, and he should start forward along the good track. Help him with the rest of the track if need be. Hopefully, he will soon come to a delicious food drop and access to his most favorite reward.

- **Unable to re-find and commit to the leg when the dog gets off the track.** Compound obstacles and corners within obstacles often get the dog and handler off the track. It is important for the handler to organize the dog's search and give the dog a chance to find the track. Once the dog has exhaustively searched within the radius of the handler's current position, the handler should move some place to expand the search area. To design suitable track situations, use a "corner in an obstacle", ideally where the incoming leg is downwind. This situation makes it likely the dog will get off the track and have trouble finding the new leg. Review compound obstacles on page 180 for ideas that set up the situation within an otherwise simple track. See also the test-track examples in this phase and the next.

The handler should work on pivoting in one place until the dog searches 360° at several radii and then move slowly creating an outward spiral while continuing to circle her dog until the dog finds the track. If you think one way or another is more likely, start your outward spiral in that direction first but don't get too committed to your own ideas of where the track might go — your dog has the useful nose that is more reliable than your eyes and thoughts.

- **Backtracking.** If the dog backtracks when he finds the track after searching off the track for it, this exercise may help. Lay 3–5 straight 75–100 yard tracks with flags at each end and with only an end article. Approach each track from the side at 90° about 30 yards from the start. Let the dog backtrack a maximum of 15'. Reduce the maximum backtrack distance over multiple sessions. Then repeat the sequence by approaching the start from an acute angle. Also, see the more complete Track Direction training exercises in the Advanced Training Supplement on page 402.

- **Loses enthusiasm on longer tracks.** You will generally need to work on stamina for your dog and yourself off the tracking field. After the track is finished, I playfully jog back to our car, maintaining a spirit of fun. For long tracks, increase the rate of rewards or articles as you get farther along the track. For example, nothing on the first leg, one article on the second leg, an article and a grab-and-go treat on the third leg, a grab-and-go, an article and another grab-and-go on the fourth, etc. You can do a medium length track and then incrementally step up the length over subsequent sessions.

- **Shortcuts to upwind articles.** See page 135 for a detailed remedial plan. Follow the plan with TDX appropriate track age and terrain to make the exercise suit your current goals.

- **Fringing instead of tracking.** A full remediation plan is on page 406 and is recommended for any dog who consistently prefers to air scent rather than stay close to the track. For a dog with only an occasional fringing issue, a simple remediation plan is available: Start out using young tracks so the tiny treats are fresh. Once your dog is refocused on the track, add track age and TDX terrain types while continuing to use the marked serpentines with the tiny treats on footsteps 1, 3, 6, 10, 15, 21, (repeat) 22, 24, 27, 31, 36, 42, etc. If ants or insects make the treats less than a reward for the dog, keep to younger aged serpentines. When you return to normal tracks, have them well marked so you can continue to keep your dog close to the 2–4 hour-old tracks most of their length. See page 406 for a more extensive remedial plan.

- **Unusual conditions.** Choose something you and your dog have not experienced from the Unusual Conditions list on page 232, find a suitable location and incorporate it into your track. Try to have some relatively easy tracking before the unusual situation and some easy tracking after it, with several articles as reward points.

Tracklayer:
- Get the basic design parameters from the handler including length, number of corners, age, crosstracks, clippies/unmarked, article frequency, and the nature of any obstacles.
- The actual track design requires considering the available terrain, cover changes, and potential obstacles.
- Use the land you have and make a track that fits what is available. Make it simpler than requested rather than more difficult.
- If possible, design a track that starts with an easy motivating section, then include a section for the issue of the day and finish with an easy motivating section of track.
- Follow the handler on the track. Wait to tell the handler she is wrong until she is 30–40' off the track committing in a wrong direction.
- If the handler requests a video, record the dog and handler so the handler can see what the dog was doing, as well as what she did to influence the dog.

Handler:
- Choose a skill or problem to work on and specify the track design to tracklayer.
- Use your whole line to allow your dog to make his choices before you move forward at the start, corners, and other scent disturbances.
- Use corner communications, then walk up the line to 15–20' right after he and you commit to the new direction.
- Notice landmarks while trying to ignore the clippies.
- If your dog struggles, first encourage verbally that he can do it, then help happily as much as needed rather than have him get frustrated. The tracklayer will help you so you can turn a blind track into a valuable training session.
- Give lots of treats and praise at each article.

Evaluation and Possible Adaptations:
- Note in your detailed tracking log and summary log (page 244):
  - The track design or map.
  - The overall rating Excellent, Very Good, Good, Needs-Work, or Flawed.
  - Whether the dog was Clear-Confident-Committed on some or all of the track.
  - Areas where you needed to help your dog.
- Monitor your dog's performance and clear-confident-commitment. Consider whether you need to adjust the track difficulty for the next few sessions (see page 223).

Sessions X4{.4, .8, .12} Motivation

Purpose:
Have a fun session tracking to maintain the dog's motivation.

Session	Session Style	Training Focus	Track Age	XT	Marked	Track Yards	No. Turns	No. Obs.
X4.4	Motivation	Fun	45–60	No XT	Optional	400–500	3–4	0–1
X4.8	Motivation	Fun	45–60	Optional	Optional	300–400	2–3	0–1
X4.12	Motivation	Fun	45–60	No XT	Optional	300–400	2–3	0–1

Tracklayer:
- Get the basic design parameters from the handler including length, number of corners, age, crosstracks, clippies/unmarked, article frequency, and the nature of any obstacles.
- Actual track design requires considering the available terrain, cover changes, and obstacles.
- Shorter tracks having 2–5 corners can use basic shapes similar to TD shapes (see page 116).
- Use the land you have and make a track that fits what is available. Make it simpler than requested rather than more difficult.
- You follow the handler on the track and coach as appropriate.

Handler:
- Based on the session's motivational purpose, give the tracklayer very easy design parameters including length, number of corners, age, clippies/unmarked, article frequency, and the number and nature of obstacles. Keep the track simple.
- Run these tracks at 45–60 minutes. It is OK if they are older so long as they are well within your dog's very Clear-Confident-Committed track-age range.
- Approach the start, varying angles each session. The start is a corner you have not tracked into.
- Hold your dog at the start 10–20 seconds so he can memorize the scent.
- Use your whole line to allow your dog to make his choices before you move forward at the start, corners, and other scent disturbances.
- Use corner communications, then walk up the line to 15–20' right after commitment.
- Notice landmarks while trying to ignore the clippies.
- If your dog struggles, first encourage verbally that he can do it, then help happily as much as needed, rather than have him get frustrated. The tracklayer will help you turn a blind track into a valuable training session.
- Give lots of treats and praise at each article.

Evaluation and Possible Adaptations:
- Note in your detailed tracking log and summary log (page 244): the track design or map; the overall rating Excellent, Very Good, Good, Needs-Work, or Flawed; Whether the dog was Clear, Confident and Committed on some or all of the track; and areas where you needed to help.
  - We expect motivational tracks to have a rating of Excellent or Very Good. If not, consider simplifying the motivational tracks so they are fun for the dog and handler.
- Monitor your dog's Clear-confident-commitment (see page 223) and consider whether you need to adjust the track difficulty for the next few sessions.

Sessions X4.14 Review, Evaluate, and Next Steps.

Phase X4 is the heart of your TDX training. If you followed the schedule in the first three phases, you have done about fifty sessions building TDX skills plus another 13 in this phase. Most dogs and handlers need to loop through Phase X4 several times for the dog and handler to build their mutual skills and teamwork to a sufficient level to pass a real TDX test.

TDX tests are fundamentally difficult — review the five real TDX test tracks shown starting on page 226 as well as the story tracks on pages 176, 195, 213, 243, and 250. Your quickest way to pass a test is to be fully prepared to enter. Even once you are fully prepared, your chance of passing is less than 50%. The AKC pass rate is about 15%.

First, review and evaluate your own and your dog's performance on your last several TDX-like tracks before deciding on your next steps.
- Evaluate which of the recent TDX-like tracks X4{.1, .5, .9, .13} were actually blind for the handler. Laying it yourself, having the tracklayer leave clippies, or allowing the tracklayer to coach you from behind means the track becomes 'un-blind'.
- For isolated handlers who must lay all their own tracks and for the purposes of this evaluation, consider tracks blind that you laid but avoided looking at the landmarks as 'blind'.
- Note how often you had to help your dog by restraint, encouragement, or other methods listed on page 99. Don't count times when you needed to neutrally organize his search for a lost track unless you had to encourage or help him take the good track.
- Rate his overall clear-confident-commitment on each track.
- Rate your own confidence in reading and following him.

TDX-like	Date & Location	Blind (Yes/No)	Helped Dog (Yes/No)	Dog is Clear-Confident-Committed	Handler is Confident Reading Dog
T1					
T2					
T3					
T4					
T5					

Decide the next steps.
- If you passed without helping your dog on two or more fully test-like blind tracks that included crosstracks and obstacles, you are definitely ready to move on to Phase X5.
- If you passed without helping your dog on one test-like blind track that included crosstracks and obstacles, you can optionally move to Phase X5 or do some more X4 work.
- If you failed each complete track test but passed each except for one place, you are probably ready for Phase X5 but consider doing some more problem-solving X4.15 sessions first.
- You will make the most and fastest progress by doing several problem-solving sessions (X4.15) and then redoing all sessions in Phase X4.

Dessa's TDX Adventure

In 1998, Ch. Rime's Game Goddess TD and Sil entered the Westie National Tracking Test at Fair Hill in Northeastern Maryland. Fair Hill had been the DuPont hunting estate but is now a huge recreational area. Rolling hills, grassy meadows, and wooded areas are crisscrossed by horseback riding trails and gravel roads.

See the next page for the map of her track to help follow along with the description that follows.

The first leg of Dessa's track had been overrun by several off-lead dogs playing while their handlers hiked. Dessa had quite a time getting past the area of her first corner and onto her second leg. After searching for a long time and failing to commit to the track in this area three times, she finally did commit to the second leg and got past the disturbed area. After another corner, she found fresh pieces of a rabbit just off the track but responded to "No mouses today, back to the track!" She then found an article and her confidence and commitment to the track returned.

She took the next turn without pausing, passed the crosstracks without noticing them, crossed a dirt access road and indicated a corner toward a gap in the trees. Once past the woods, I reasoned (a dangerous thing for a handler to do) that since we had not had any crosstracks up to this point that this meadow was a perfect place to put them. So in 50 yards when she took a right turn and I could see two lines of footprints in the grass, I was worried. I asked her if this was the good track, and she leaned into her harness to tell me it was. I sheepishly followed her, knowing to trust my dog but really expecting the whistle. But we soon crossed the road again, past the real crosstracks, and found another article.

She was off in a jiffy and entered a narrow woods up against a 50 mph highway. She turned and merged onto a horse path that approached a bridge across the highway. She took a few steps onto the bridge, then turned back and picked up the track on another path leading away from the bridge. Once through another area of deep grass and brambles, we were heading straight for a flag. As we approached the flag, my heart was sinking thinking we must have overrun the glove or turned the wrong way. But Dessa was confident and soon found her glove and earned her TDX. She became the sixth Westie to earn a TDX, earning it on her first try.

Training Note

Our earlier training to leave ground animals and go back to the good track helped Dessa understand what needed to be done at the fresh rabbit parts. In one of these earlier training sessions, she came upon a mouse nest and became obsessed with them. I had to help her down the track more than 200 yards bent over tickling the grass before she would refocus on the track. Note that I had not yet discovered the power of Romeo and Juliet loving the grass in those days. I am sure she would have refocused sooner had I loved the track rather than just tickled it and encouraged (begged) her to track. Regardless, because we persevered in this training situation, she understood "No mouses today — back to the track!" and earned her TDX.

TRACKING TEST (TD/TDX/VST)

Dog's Catalog # __X3__ Track # __1__ Total Yards __835__
Date __9-80-98__ Veg. _____ Non-Veg. _____

Chart the track in solid line; the dog's course in broken line on graph below

[Hand-drawn track chart with annotations including: N arrow, TALLEST TREE, REF TREE, WOODS, BUSH, FLOWER, HOLLY, LEANING TREE, BALL TREE W VINES, CROSS TRACKS, SCENTING DB, START DROP NO. 1, DROP NO. 2 O'HAY, DROP NO. 3, DROP NO. 4, END. Yardage markers: 60, 75, 120, 180, 80, 50, 70, 40, 40, 80, 90, 10, 30, 30, 140, 120, 215, 85, 50.]

Passed or Failed	**PASSED**
(If failed, state reason)	
Tracklayer Started	7:00 AM
X-Tracklayer Started	8:15 AM
Dog's Starting Time	10:06 AM
Dog's Finishing Time	10:43 AM
Ground Conditions	3' to 6' GRASS
Weather Conditions	CLOUDY & DAMP
Wind Speed	NIL

If this dog is absent, mark "absent" on this page.

Articles:	1. HAT	2. SCARF
	3. SOCK	4. GLOVE
Obstacles or Surfaces	1. WOODS	2. WOODS
	3. SCENTING	4.

Breed/Sex __N.N.W. YER - BITCH__
AKC Regis. # __RM186752/02__

I hereby certify that I have judged the above dog after having read the instructions on the cover of this book and followed them out to the best of my ability.

Donna N. Thomas
Judge's Signature

Phase X4. Skill Improvement

Phase X4 Summary Log

Sesn	Site	Date	Config. & Obs.	Track Age	Evaluation
X4.1					
X4.2					
X4.3					
X4.4					
X4.5					
X4.6					
X4.7					
X4.8					
X4.9					
X4.10					
X4.11					
X4.12					
X4.13					

Phase X5. Preparing for the TDX Test

Purpose:
- Prepare you and your dog for the Tracking Dog Excellent test.

Strategy:
- Familiarize you and your dog with test-like terrain and tracking conditions.
- Teach your dog to ignore and overcome common handler errors.
- Peak your dog's performance for the test.

How to use this chapter:
- Look through the table below, which summarizes the training structure of this phase, and read the discussion section that follows.
- Do the sessions X5.1 to X5.8 roughly following the age, length, and number of corners. Use natural fields whenever available. Ideally, use TDX test sites or sites that are similar.
- Then review your and your dog's skills to choose 3–5 additional focused exercises from X4{.3, .7, .11} or other parts of Phase X4 to do as sessions X5.9.a, .b, ...
- 8 days before the test you are drawn into, switch to X5.10 and follow the schedule from there.
- If you enter and do not pass a TDX test, resume from X5.9a:X5.9x to work on your team's issues.
- Keep a detailed log of each session using a format like the one shown on page 31 and keep a summary log like the one shown on page 254.

Phase X5 Session Schedule:

Session	Location	Turns	Total Yards	Design	Age Hours
X5.1	Fun Familiar Site	4–6	600–800	Proof Handler Errors	2–5
X5.2	Test–like Site	5–7	700–1000	TDX–like	3–4
X5.3	Fun Familiar Site	4–6	600–800	Proof Handler Errors	3–5
X5.4	Fun Familiar Site	3–5	300–500	Motivational	1–3
X5.5	Test-like Site	5–7	600–1000	TDX-like	3–5
X5.6	Fun Familiar Site	5–7	400–500	Proof Handler Errors	2–5
X5.7	Test-like Site	3–5	700–1000	TDX-like	4–5
X5.8	Fun Familiar Site	3–5	300–500	Motivational	1–3
X5.9.a, .b, ...	Wherever	3–8	500–1000	X4{.3, .7, .11} or any other from X4	3–5
Repeat from X5.1, if not in a test yet.					
X5.10	Anyplace, 8 days before test	4–5	500–600	Short Easy TDX-like	3–5
X5.11	Anyplace, 7 days before test	4–5	500–600	Short Easy TDX-like	2–3
X5.12	Fun familiar site, 5 days before test	2–4	300–400	Very Short Easy Fun	2–3

Discussion:

Verify you and your dog have the requisite skills to be starting this fairly short and final TDX phase. See the evaluation on page 241 to make sure.

The basic process to prepare for a TD/TDU test was discussed in some detail in Phase 9 on page 148. This phase evolves that process to be appropriate for the TDX test. Proper preparation is even more important before a TDX test.

You need to do all of the following as a TDX test approaches:
- Expose your dog to the type of terrain he will face in a test, including visiting the site or a nearby site one or more times. Find out all you can about each test site that you might enter. Call the test secretary to find a contact who knows the site. Track at the site or a good substitute well before the test. Don't wait for the draw, go there weeks or months in advance.
- Prepare your dog to ignore and overcome common handler errors as described on page 247. While your handling has improved with experience, test-day jitters trigger handling mistakes. It is useful to simulate some typical test-day handling errors on marked tracks where you can avoid letting a big issue develop. Use high-value rewards and jackpots when your dog overcomes each instance of a handling error.
- Polish your own and your dog's skills. Review your dog's and your own performance on the last several TDX-like tracks and note any particular skill that was just "good enough" on that track but could be improved. Designate sessions that focus on improving those skills.
- Be in good physical condition (both dog and handler). Fatigue is a common issue near the end of a TDX track, which reduces the dog's drive or leads to handler errors. Conditioning your dog and yourself on days you don't track is imperative.
- Peak your own handling performance and your dog's tracking performance for the test. You want him highly motivated as you approach the start flag.
- On your test track, read your dog, trust him, and communicate your confidence in his skill.
- If he gets in trouble, keep yourself oriented in the field, organize his search, get him to circle, back up or spiral around, trust him and go with him when he finds the new leg.

The schedule on page 245 shows one good way to implement Phase X5. The first eight sessions mix proofing handler errors while at fun familiar sites with visiting the potential test site or a nearby site and working him in the terrain and conditions you will face in the test. The row labeled X5.9.a, .b, ... represents actually any number of sessions. It encourages you to do more Phase X4 sessions as you wait to get drawn into a test. Independently, set up something mentioned in "Unusual conditions" on page 232. And finally, the last 8 days you reduce the intensity, length, and difficulty of the training.

Example TDX tracks are shown on pages 176, 195, 213, 223, 226–231, 243, and 250. Also, look at tracks you saw when spectating or laying tracks at TDX tests. Use them to inspire you and your tracklayer to plot realistic TDX tracks that take advantage of the land available and the potential obstacles there.

Don't Drop the Article When Re-Scenting

Most judges consider an article dropped to the ground during re-scenting is a restart, and AKC TDX rules do not allow restarts in TDX tests.

Remember these design constraints of a TDX; feel free to "cheat" a little on these minimum distances but not too much.

AKC Design Constraints	Minimum Yards
Leg Length	50
Between Crosstrack and Corner	50
Between Article and Corner	30
Between Article and Crosstrack	30
Between Obstacle and Crosstrack	30
Between Obstacle and Article	30
Between Obstacle and Corner	0
Obstacle Along Crosstrack Path from Track	30
	Number
Corners	5–7
Crosstracks	2
Articles	4
Obstacles	At least 2

CKC rules are not as specific as AKC on these track design constraints. They do constrain the minimum leg length to 50 meters, the first article to be at least 250 meters from the start and that acute turns may be no sharper than 45°.

Proofing Handler Error Sessions. Design these tracks to be simple TDX-like tracks that contains the design elements appropriate for proofing handler errors. For these sessions (X5.1, X5.3, X5.6), look at the track map and select two or three easy corners to use for proofing. Make sure there are two food drops 30 and 35 yards past these corners or a fun article reward point. Common handler errors are:
- Unusually high tension when the dog commits to the new leg.
- The line goes slack while the dog is searching.
- Following the dog in an uncertain/disbelieving manner with a slack line or a very tight line.
- Inadvertently standing on the line as the dog first commits to the new leg.
- Standing your ground and refusing to follow the dog on the new leg the first time he tries to commit to it. Go with him on his second try.

Each session, select one or more of these common handler errors and act it out on those corners. Be as much of a ham as you need to be to put your dog off a little bit. Once your dog reacts to your acting, stop acting and return to your normal handling.

If your dog quits searching, help him with the correct track. Be very happy and upbeat about showing him the track and encouraging him to find it. If he continues to search but fails to take the new leg the next time he crosses it, help him as described above. If your dog continues to search but avoids returning to the area of the new leg for a few minutes, help him as described above.

As your dog tracks the next leg, watch his attitude. Wait to proof another handler error until his enthusiastic attitude returns to normal. It may take another leg or two for him to regain confidence in his teammate who seems to be having a very off day.

Watch your dog's general motivation level. If it drops two sessions in a row, back off the track difficulty. Reduce difficulty by reducing age, length, number of corners, hilliness of terrain, or increase the familiarity of the fields. If you have even one particularly bad day in this phase, add a fun session with a simple-marked track on a familiar field.

Distant Test Sites. I do want to emphasize the importance of training several times in the type of terrain used for the test. That typically requires a trip to the site itself, if it is public, or to a nearby similar site that is open to public dog training. For my own dogs, I go to great lengths to do this well before the test, with excellent results (see Twizzle's TDX story on page 176 and Mr. Q's story on page 212).

As a judge I frequently see teams struggle because the dog is unfamiliar with the conditions and does not track like his usual self. This causes the handler to feel lost and make handling mistakes because she is not familiar with following her dog in these conditions. If you are willing to enter a test a long drive from your home, then you should be willing to be properly prepared by traveling to that area a month before the test to give your dog and yourself an important experience.

Talk to the test secretary or someone local to the test site who is familiar with the site and get a good description of the site. Find some place near your home that approximates the site and track there several times.

If you are traveling a long distance out of your area to a test, you should make every effort to get there well before the test. In some cases, you may be unable to arrive at the test area until just a few days before the test. The earlier you can arrive, the better.

Few of us can arrive at a national specialty tracking test held across the country, two to three weeks before the event, in order to follow the Phase X5 schedule on page 245. When you do get to the test area, walk your dog around in another area similar to the test site, and then give your dog the following sequence of tracks: A 50-yard straight track 90-minute-old, a 70x50 yard single-corner "L" track 2 hours old, and a 75x75x50 zigzag track 3 hours old. Don't use the test site for these last minute tracks unless you are there more than a week before the test.

Peaking Performance for the Test. You can do a few things in the last couple of weeks before a test to make sure that your dog's skill and enthusiasm for tracking is at its peak. The general idea is to work the dog quite hard two to three weeks before a test, then back off to motivational tracks the first half of the pre-test week, followed by a layoff for 3–4 days before the test. As a procedure:
- Work diligently on X5.1–X5.8 tracks or others from Phase X4 up to 8 days before the test.
- 8-days before the test (you will know if you were drawn into the test by then), switch to shorter easier sub-TDX tracks. Avoid working on specific remaining problem areas. Stick with fun and positive tracks for your last week.
- Rest your dog for the last 4 days before a test. No more tracking and avoid working intensely on other dog sports.
- Rest and relax yourself as well. You are an important member of the team.

You want your dog to be highly enthusiastic for tracking when you take him out of your car on test day, which means he has to be under-worked for several days before.

The Day of the Test. On the day of the test, arrive early for the draw to determine the dogs' running order. The time and location of the draw are indicated on the premium list and judging schedule for the test.

If I am unfamiliar with the test site, I may drive by the site the night before the test to make sure I can find it. I typically arrive about a half-hour before the draw, so I have plenty of time to get lost, put on my boots, and exercise my dog before the draw. Typically, the dog running first will be at his start about fifteen to twenty minutes after the draw, so you should be prepared. On the other hand, the dog who runs sixth in a six-dog test may have to wait three to four hours after the draw before starting his track.

When it is your turn, you may be able to walk to your track, to drive some place near it, or you may have to ride in a stranger's truck to get to your track. However you get there, you will meet two judges who, despite their perhaps imposing demeanor, are rooting for you to pass, just as much as you are hoping to pass. They will tell you where the track starts and when you can start.

Do use your corner-communication sequence at the start, at obstacles, at crosstracks, and on every corner in the test.

If your dog gets into trouble on the track, organize his search. Recall the circling methods taught in Phase 6 and the exercise on expanding the search area on page 405. Get him to circle at several different distances from you. If he cannot find it, back up toward the last place he was definitely tracking (which is probably near the corner). If he can still not find it there, and particularly if there is some unusual scent condition in the area, circle your dog in ever-larger circles until he can reach past the unusual scent condition. Let your dog lead, move in general harmony with your dog when he is moving. If your dog is about to quit, do what you need to do to get him started again. Even if the judges fail you for guiding, I believe it is no worse to be failed for guiding than it is to be failed for quitting.

Remember to be patient and let your dog thoroughly search the area where he first indicated a change in scenting behavior. Once you do decide to move, whether backing up or expanding your dog's search area, avoid leading him as that may be interpreted as guiding. Stepping backward or side stepping as your dog is moving will allow the team to get where it might be good to search, without the handler walking some place with intent. See page 163 for additional discussion of the differences between active handling and guiding as well as page 76 for a discussion on trust.

By the time you get to the test, you and your dog are well prepared to pass. However, TDX tests are difficult, and even well-prepared teams may meet a difficulty that throws them. You can remind yourself that you need only to read your dog, trust him, communicate with him your confidence in his skill, and follow him. You know how to do all these things, so relax, and just do them.

QT's TDX Adventure — 2002.

QT had passed his TD test in October 2001 at the Westie national in Fair Hill Maryland when he was seven months old. We had worked diligently on his TDX training all year and returned to Fair Hill for his TDX test the following year. We arrived in Maryland a week before the test so we could practice in similar areas to the test for two days then rest for two days before the test. QT will tell his story first, and then Sil will continue with some training notes.

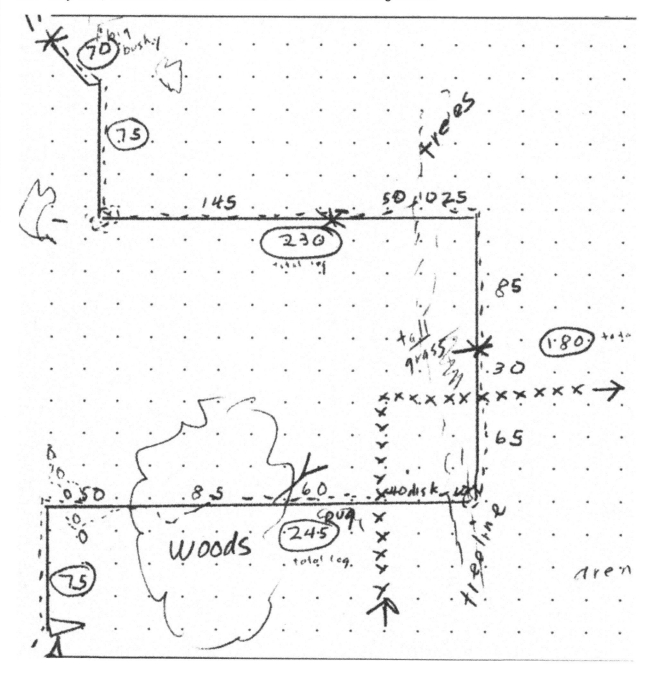

Pops is really nervous when we arrive at Fair Hill. Lots of other Westies are here with their people. We are parked right next to my TD field from last year. There is much excitement in the air as Pops draws TDX track 1 for me. After quite a while, it is time for my track, and we just walk out to a field adjacent to my TD field where a blue flag is standing all alone in the field.

It is quite hot in the sun, but I have no trouble figuring out which way the track goes as Pops holds me at the start. He finally releases me, and I trot down the first leg. The grass is quite short, and as I come alongside a group of four trees, I enter an area where some horses and people had congregated yesterday. The smell of the track changes in this area, but I know I can find it if I am careful. Something quite like it is off to the right, but it does not smell exactly right. I keep searching and circling. Pops seems to want me to check to the left, even though it is blatantly obvious to anyone with a nose that it does not cross the road, but I am a good boy and check it out anyways. This area is quite confusing, and I can't seem to find it anywhere but Pops makes me smell the start article again and asks me to continue. I circle back until I find the most similar track even though it is not quite right and follow it over to the woods.

There are brambles at the edge of the woods so I search around to see if the track turns here. I can tell it goes into the woods and so I find a good way in. Now it is cooler, and the scent is correct again. There are lots of downed branches and brush in the woods, so the track keeps changing direction, but I am too clever for such trickiness and Pops is very pleased with me.

We come out of the woods and cross some strange rubbery sand, but we are soon back on grass, and the track is easy to follow. We go through a thin line of trees, and two large pits are in front of us across a light grass road. Pops' tracks always go into pits and things like that, so I check it out, but the track is not there. I check to the right and left and find it along with a vehicle track on the grass road. The tire tracks are easier to follow than the footsteps, but when I get a little ways down the tire tracks, I notice two crosstracks and hear Pops asking is this the original track. So I swing back to the original track and soon find a gray sock in the grass. Pops is so pleased and I am so proud, but there are no hot dogs in his pack today. He offers me water, but I turn away and head back down the track.

We are soon at the intersection of two grass roads and two tree lines. I check to the right and only day-old tire tracks go that way. To the left is the track that goes up through a cluster of thin trees and hard dirt into the next field. We are on a slope above a huge riding ring and the scent is drifting up the slope. But soon I have the next article. I drink some water as it is hot out here in the sun. Right after the article, a very interesting deer track crosses the track and I check it out carefully, but Pops wants me to follow the original track, so I go back to traversing the slope until I come to the end of the riding ring.

The track disappears again right before a dirt road, and there is a set of horse tracks right here going off to the left. But the track goes to the right and is easy to follow. One more bend and then I start to smell the glove ahead. I sit on top of it and Pops comes rushing up to love me. We play with the glove, and he is so proud of me. He races me back to the car where my salmon dinner awaits the triumphant return of the newest and handsomest TDX Westie.

Sil's Training Postscript

QT was, at the time, a 19-month-old Westie who loves tracking, agility, and pretty much anything else he gets to do with his co-owners Sil and Sandy. Unlike many Westies, and particularly unlike his sire Mr. Q, he is quite interested in pleasing his person.

Fair Hill is a huge site dedicated to horse riding and hiking, but that also allows dogs and dog tests. The Westie test uses less than a quarter of the whole site.

Normally, one would visit a TDX site (or a site similar to your TDX test site) a month or more in advance of a test so the dog becomes familiar with the terrain, obstacles, and cover present in the area. But since the Specialty was 3000 miles away, I substituted tracking him in a very wide variety of places in Oregon and Washington and then arrived early to the test to track him in areas of Fair Hill that were not going to be used for the test. Had the test site been closed to the public, I would have found a similar site nearby. But whether public or private, one should not track on the actual test fields for three days before the test so your practice tracks do not interfere with the dogs entered in the test.

Normally, one will rest the dog for most of the last week before a TDX test as part of the peaking-for-the-test process. I decided that site familiarization was more important than the rest period for this very enthusiastic dog, so I reduced the pretest rest to three days before we arrived and then two days before the test.

During his two practice tracks in the area, the tracks entered and exited the woods to give him experience with the particular nature of these transitions at the site. As it turned out, his two experiences in the Fair Hill woods were important for his eventual success even though we had tracked through woods in Washington as similar as I could find to the Fair Hill woods. It turns out there were important differences to QT which required some practice on our part before we could be successful on a blind test track.

While TDX requires many separate tracking skills, one skill was very important for his success. That skill is persistence or the willingness to keep looking for the track even when the scenting is difficult or confusing. It was developed over many tracks that had difficult parts followed by rewarding parts. So I could make him search the area of the first corner where he was confused without undue fear that he would give up. When he was ready to quit in confusion after working the corner area for about 20 minutes, he was still willing to go back to work with just a soft word of encouragement from me. Then I followed him along the second leg even though he was very tentative in his commitment to the track since he had weakly indicated this direction three times before in his search. Once in the woods, his commitment returned to normal and he was successful for the remainder of his track earning his TDX.

Phase X5 Summary Log

Sesn	Site	Date	Config. & Obs.	Track Age	Evaluation
X5.1					
X5.2					
X5.3					
X5.4					
X5.5					
X5.6					
X5.7					
X5.8					
X5.9a					
X5.9b					
X5.9c					
X5.9d					

Part III — Urban Tracking Foundations: Training for the TDU

This part is primarily intended for experienced tracking dogs who have done little urban tracking. It is also appropriate for dogs who have considerable urban tracking experience in addition to their field tracking. It prepares the field-experienced less urban-experienced dog for the TDU test and builds a solid foundation for advanced urban work. For dogs with some urban experience, it completes and stabilizes their urban-skills foundation in preparation for progressing to the VST.

It is reasonable to wonder how to use this part depending on your dog's actual mix of field and urban tracking experience. Regardless of your dog's urban experience, treat this part as required reading at the very least, and recommended training for all dogs with their TD/TDX even if they have considerable urban experience. The recommended way to proceed:
- If your dog has little previous tracking experience,
  - Go to the beginning of the book, Part I, and proceed from Phase 1. If you only want to earn the TDU, you will find specific instructions in each phase on how to specialize.
- If your dog has a TD, TDX or the equivalent skills with a little urban tracking experience,
  - Proceed with Part III in its entirety.
- If your dog has a lot of urban tracking experience, do the following:
  - Study the discussion below and at the start of each of the three TDU phases.
  - To find your place, do the last 3–4 sessions in each phase of Part III to verify your dog's skill level. Use the review session to determine if and where he needs additional skill improvement in each skill area.
- When you have finished Phase U3, proceed to Part IV "Advance Urban Tracking."

If your goal is the CKC UTD, note that there are more skills required than the TDU but all TDU skills are also required. The UTD has about one-third hard surface, is at least an hour old, and at least one corner on a hard surface. Since hard surface corners are not introduced until Part IV Phase V1, specific training for the UTD is needed, which is in Part IV Phase V1S UTD, a supplemental phase done after the first VST phase. That work is all dependent on the foundations developed in this part so don't just skip ahead.

Additional Urban Skills

The recent TD dog and handler have every right to be pleased and proud of themselves. This is even truer of the recent TDX dog and handler. They still do need to step back and ask what additional skills they need to be as successful in the urban TDU and VST. In the phases of this part, we focus on urban-foundational skills with the goal of shaping a dog to be ready for his TDU.

The additional **dog skills** a TD or TDX dog needs for the TDU fall into two broad categories:
- Clear-Confident-Committed tracking on (heavily) contaminated lawns.
- Tracking across narrow hard surfaces, hard-surface transitions, and turns near to or onto hard surfaces.

The additional **handler skills**:
- Reading your dog when he is in areas of faint or confusing scent.
- Patience, patience, patience — aka letting your dog solve the problem and make the decisions.

In many parts of the country, for field tracking, one does not need to focus on contamination very much since many TD/TDX test fields are little used by the public, and where fields are public, the areas of contamination are typically small and isolated along the total length of the track. For the TDU, large parts or all of your track may be highly contaminated by the public like dog walkers, sports teams, or students walking between classes. Such activity may occur well before your track was laid, while it was being laid, while it ages, or while you and your dog are on the track.

Hoping that you will get into a test with little contamination is a fantasy that will lead to disappointment. You need to train your dog to clearly and confidently commit to tracks in the presence of heavy contamination. Certainly, some of your training can take advantage of little-used urban areas that can help the dog gain confidence and enthusiasm. Additional training will take advantage of natural contamination by choosing to train in busy parks and campuses. A significant portion of your training will use intentional contamination to put the contamination in special relationships to the track so the dog will learn and develop his needed skills.

For the AKC TDU, there is 10–30% non-vegetated surface, but there are no corners on the hard-surface areas. However, the corners can be right before or right after the hard-surface crossings so there will be plenty of scenting problems for the dog to work out. In addition, there can be lawn corners that immediately turn onto a hard surface so essentially the whole initial part of the outgoing leg is on hard surface.

The training is broken up into phases for these broad categories of required skills and set up with recommended progressions within a phase to enable the dog and handler to develop their skills.

Urban Scent Aging and Track Age — a Training Dilemma

Trainers/handlers notice that sometimes on hard surfaces their dog puts his nose down and looks like he is tracking the footprints, other times he wanders in the general vicinity of the track but prefers to be 20–50' to the side of the actual track, and sometimes he may not seem to find anything at all.

Temperature, humidity, and sunshine greatly affect the apparent age of a track on any non-vegetated surface and particularly on black asphalt. At high summertime temperatures with hot sunshine, rapid evaporation occurs so the tracklayer's scent is intense shortly after a track is laid and becomes weak quickly as the skin rafts dry out. When the track is relatively fresh, this intense scent may form a pool or puddle on the blacktop, which you can picture as a wide-low fog bank of scent. Fringing the pool or fog bank becomes the dog's tracking focus so he stays wide of the actual fresh footprints. At more comfortable tracking temperatures (35–70° F) with cloudy or damp conditions, you may see the dog paying more attention to the actual footprints regardless of the track's age. Likewise at hotter temperatures, after the pool of scent settles or dries out, the dog may again focus on the footprints.

Being able to follow the fringe on hard surface is a necessary skill for urban tracking, but dogs who stay close to the footprints when they can will be much easier to follow on a blind track. Use of scent intensifiers can help in training (see page 8). Some urban handlers have also observed that aging the track more may bring the dog back closer to the footprints. However, doing so risks aging it too much and making the scenting too hard in some places for the dog to sort out at his current level of training.

In order to facilitate the dog learning his required skills, the hard-surface tracks have three recommended ages:

- Age A is for most dogs in comfortable temperate conditions. Use for all dogs who have not done the older track age found in TDX work. Even dogs with TDX age under their belt should use these younger ages unless they consistently demonstrate no track scent recognition on the younger tracks yet consistently demonstrate they can track older hard-surface tracks close to the actual track.
- Age B is for dogs with TDX age experience who consistently wander on young tracks particularly in hot weather. It is also for dogs who have completed this phase using "Age A" and whose handler wants to repeat several hard-surface sessions to solidify her dog's skill.
- Age C is for dogs whose confidence or skill level suffers as the tracks get older under the "Age A" plan. It simply slows down the aging while working through the material to develop the skills and will step up age carefully in a later phase. Age C times are adjusted down from the Age A plan by the handler to keep the dog pretty successful with the tracks.

The progressions in this part will age the tracks so the dog becomes comfortable and confident on tracks aged appropriately to the target test: ½–2 hours for the AKC TDU. Note on intentionally or naturally-contaminated lawns, I still expect my dogs to be Clear-Confident-Committed. They will notice many of the contamination crosstracks but with training, they will efficiently reject them on their own and return quickly to the good track.

As your dog's trainer, to facilitate optimal learning, you may need to adjust the times in this section so your dog is successful on his own 75% or more of the time. While in general reducing the age will make it easier, in some conditions (hot sunshine on black asphalt) making it older may be the right thing to do. First, ask yourself "Why do I believe my dog can be successful on this scenting problem at 90 minutes old if he cannot do it at 30 minutes?" Only make it older if that makes the scenting problems easier for your dog and he becomes consistently more confident.

TDU Equipment. The same harness and line are appropriate for TDU and VST as it is for all tracking levels. Flags are typically small landscaping flags as shown in the picture on page 307. That picture also shows leather and cloth material squares that are suitable for TDU articles. TDU can also have TD-style cloth and leather objects like TD socks and gloves.

For CKC trainers who are focused on progressing to the UTD, the intermediate test article may be fabric, wood or plastic and the last one will be leather.

Both organizations' more advanced urban tests include cloth, leather, plastic, and metal with CKC also adding wood. So the trainer looking forward to the VST and UTDX should start including all materials in her article bag.

Some handlers prefer lines that are shorter than 40' (or 49' in CKC) in urban environments because the longer line gets caught in nooks and crannies. I recommend always using your full-length tracking line because you will need the length to allow your dog to search a large area while you stay rooted to your pivot point. Your dog can get used to occasionally having to wait for you to untangle the line, and you can get used to managing the tail so it only gets caught occasionally. With a shorter line, you will have to move away from your pivot point too soon in order to allow your dog to search a large enough area to solve the scenting problem.

Helping — a Most Important Balance

This section on helping repeats material also presented in the early parts (pages 59 and 99) because it is important to review as you start focusing on urban tracking. Also, it is good context for the next section on hinting.

On a blind urban track, most failures are from the handler being impatient and unconsciously suggesting to the dog where the track must go. Quite frankly, handlers are seldom good at guessing where the track goes.

Helping your dog in training offers him the opportunity to learn what is correct in this scenting situation and to develop his skills, so his tracking behavior is easy to read and follow on blind tracks.

When your dog encounters a scenting problem in training, first let him try to solve it himself. Be patient (don't rush him), but before he gets frustrated and starts to think about quitting, you should help him. Always try to help as little and as gently as possible.

Here is a hierarchy of help levels from least to most:
1. **Face in the Correct Direction** — dogs are very aware of our body posture and consistently facing down the new leg suggests to the dog what is correct.
2. **Restraint** — restrain your dog when he is at the end of his line and wanting to search farther out in the wrong direction or commit to a contamination track out there.
3. **Reel-in and Re-Scent** — by bringing the dog back to you, you have the opportunity to re-scent your dog and get him focused on what you want him to follow.
4. **Make it Easy** for your dog to follow the good track by reducing line tension or taking a few steps in the correct direction with him.
5. **Reel-in and Point** to correct track and direction.
6. **Reel-in and Love the Track** on your knees, moving forward slowing on the track talking lovingly to the footsteps until your dog moves forward in front of you focused on this interesting thing. Aka "You are Juliet, the track is Romeo, and we ignore the audience (the dog)." See page 60 for more on loving the track.

The "Be Patient" part is important to avoid some common training problems. Handler impatience leads to:
- Training your dog to grab whatever contamination track is near his nose.
- Training your dog to give up responsibility and just go wherever you want to go.

Hinting — An Important Training Technique that will be Eventually Withdrawn

When working on a marked track, it is common for handlers to give their dog hints whether consciously or unconsciously. This is a normal part of training that helps the dog learn. The dog can grow dependent on these hints to solve problem areas. That makes the later transition to blind tracks problematic as the dog's skill seems to fall apart leading the handler to blame herself for being a terrible handler or her dog for being unwilling to track as nicely as she knows he can do. Neither are good states in which to be.

When introducing a new skill or a new environment or a new type of scent challenge, use marked tracks and liberally hint to your dog as much as required. Accompany this new skill training with frequent and generous rewards by putting down multiple articles as reward points or even putting down food treats along the track if they will still be there and tasty when the dog runs the track. Small pieces of freeze-dried treats last longer than the moist treats like hot dogs for older tracks.

As the dog shows skill in this environment or challenge type, withdraw hints while still on marked tracks to make sure the skill is demonstrated by the dog without the hints. Only then should you try blind tracks.

Here is a list of common hinting techniques people use:
- Facing in the direction of the new leg before the dog searches in that area,
- Anchoring or staying on the good track when the dog tracks to the side of the footsteps,
- Quickly following the dog when he investigates the correct direction prior to his committing to it by himself,
- Taking some suggestive steps in the direction of the new leg,
- Encouraging talk when the dog is searching in the right direction,
- Increasing tension or checking the dog when he investigates an incorrect direction,
- Negative sounding talk when the dog searches in the incorrect direction,
- The tracklayer or spectators moving quickly before the dog and handler fully commit to the new direction.

So while these hints are valuable teaching techniques, they need to be extinguished gradually so your dog learns to make his own decisions before attempting blind tracks that will challenge him and you prematurely. Use hints liberally at first and then gradually reduce them on each new track until your dog has a scent issue and needs them. At that point quickly resume using them liberally. When you seldom have to give your dog hints, you'll know your dog can follow the track on his own.

In field tracking, the dog finds the track scent more obvious and avoids paying attention to the handler's hints because he is so confident in the track. In urban, with its fainter scent due to the complexity of multiple surfaces and varied micro-environmental effects, as well as the inevitable contamination by other people and dogs, few dogs acquire the same level of confidence in the track. Thus they take advantage of the hints and may become dependent on them. By gradually withdrawing the hints as your dog gains experience and confidence, you will have a dog whom you can follow confidently on a blind track.

Distractions — People, Animals, Machines and Pee Mail

There are a wide variety of distractions in urban environments that attract or repel your dog while he is on the track. By practicing at many different sites, some of which may harbor fewer or more particular distractions, preferably on marked tracks with frequent reward points (articles), we can habituate the dog to these distractions and teach him that quickly returning to the track and following it leads to great times.

As you progress through these three phases, increasingly choose sites and times of day that have more prevalent distractions, particularly when the dog is doing well in his training. If the dog has periods of difficulty or motivational issues, shift to sites with fewer distractions as well as reduce the complexity of his tracks. Almost all dogs are sensitive to urban distractions, so use the techniques described below as well as those on pages 100 and 216 to help your dog learn to acclimate to urban distractions.

The dog is not the only part of the team who may be distracted. The handler may be directly distracted by the presence of a potential dog distractor, or she may be distracted out of concern for how her dog will behave. The handler must overcome her own distraction so she can focus on the dog and the track itself.

Each type of distraction comes in many forms and intensities. Your dog will have a unique level of distraction for each type and each individual distraction. You want to provide repeated exposures to a wide variety of each type of distraction with positive outcomes after each encounter or at least, after most encounters. These experiences will habituate your dog so he can generalize and handle such instances is real test situations.

General handling advice for any of these distraction types is to remain calm and express confidence that your dog will return to the track. But you may need to take action to keep your dog safe, like when I have had to pick up my Westie as a large loose dog came bounding over with his owners a hundred yards away yelling for their dog and trying to reassure me that their ninety-pound dog is friendly. Once the other dog has been collected or loses interest, put your dog down, confidently tell him to "find it", and help him if necessary.

If safety is not an issue, then be patient to allow the dog to understand the distraction and return to the track with no more help than "No Mouses Today" encouragement. If the dog's focus does not leave the distraction, then you will need to go through the steps of help on page 258 including reeling the dog in and loving the track until the dog's focus returns to the track. And yes, you can love a hard-surface track although it may take a little more acting.

Some types of distractions require additional training beyond the general advice given above:

- For **people as distractions:** the dog's distraction issues can be trained by walking through crowded areas with the dog on leash feeding the dog cookies and otherwise teaching them that they can remain calm and focused when people are present. You can more easily control your dog's distance from the distractions when on a walk than on a track.

When you do encounter distracting people on a track, you can shorten your line and quietly reassure your dog that you are there and everything will be OK.

- For **animal distractions** like squirrels (above), birds (below), bunnies, woodchucks, gophers, or other dogs: Walk near and then through such areas with your dog on a leash or flexi while using food. Teaching a recall away from the distraction with food is useful. Controlling distance to the distraction is useful in training. Even the pee or dung of animals may be enticing for many dogs. Your focused training will make teaching them "Yuck! Back to the track" much easier and is a useful life-skill for the dog as well.

- For **machine distractions,** such a lawn mowers, cars or noisy trucks, exposure while walking on lead with your reassurance that you will keep your dog out of harm's way may help. Again, controlling the distance and then slowly reducing the spacing is important in this training.
    - Of course, tracks that have been mowed right before or after the track is laid present another training issue that is not one of distraction but rather one of scenting experience and skill. The lawns are highly disturbed by the mowing, and the track scent and article pieces may be spread quite widely from where the tracklayer walked.

- For **pee mail,** considerable training discipline needs to be added within the tracking context. This discipline is required throughout the dog's urban tracking career to enforce a rule that your dog cannot mark while tracking. In field tracking, I ignore a dog who once or twice along the length of a track goes a little off track to over-mark a pee-post and then promptly returns to the track. But in urban, there are just too many pee-posts too closely spaced, so a dog who is allowed to over-mark will drift farther and farther away from the track making sure every dog in town knows what an important dog he is.
    - I was successful teaching a dominant terrier (QT) that he was not allowed to over-mark by using my leave-it command "Yuck!" along with a quick tug back from the pee-post and a friendly "Back to the track!". The training did take time and many repetitions. One reason it was successful is the tightening of the hip muscles to lift his leg was obvious since I was watching him anyway and I could react in time to keep him off balance.
    - Increasing the value of the track by putting a freeze-dried treat every five yards whenever passing near a potential pee post can also help the dog understand that the track is worth his full attention. Slowly reduce to every 10 yards and then to occasional when a problem pee post is nearby.

Phase U1. Lawn Contamination and Hard-Surface Tracks

Purpose:
- Teach the dog to stay with the good track even when there is contamination on the track.
- Introduce the dog to hard-surface tracking.
- Maintain a high level of motivation.

Strategy:
- Fourfold:
  - On urban lawns, teach the dog that there may be contamination (crosstracks), but the best thing to do is stay with the good (original) track.
  - On urban lawns, teach the dog to stay close to the track as it serpentines across a lawn.
  - In parking lots, allow the dog to learn there is track odor along the curb and then help him discover there is tracklayer scent on the flat areas between curbs.
  - In parking lots, teach the dog to stay close to the track on large flat surfaces.

How to use this chapter:
- Read the discussion section that follows and look through the table on the next page, which summarizes the training structure of this phase.
- Do each of the 16 sessions that rotate between urban lawns and parking lots. Before each session, carefully review the detailed tracklaying and handling instructions for urban lawns on pages 266, 267, and 270, or for parking lots on page 269 and then 272.
- You may find it convenient to copy the session detail pages so your tracklayer has the details she needs to lay the desired tracks.
- Keep a detailed log of each session using a format like the one shown on page 31 and keep a summary log like the one shown on page 274.
- Finally, do the review session on page 273 to evaluate your dog's progress and your own training-skill development.

Discussion:

In Phase U1, we focus half our effort on lawn tracking challenges including contamination and half on hard-surface tracking. Try not to mix the two on the same track or at least minimize how many vegetation/non-vegetation transitions the dog has to deal with during this early stage of training.

Intentional Lawn Contamination. The goal of the lawn-contamination sessions is to teach your dog to stay on the good track even in the presence of simultaneous contamination crosstracks. Each session has two tracks, and each track is a 2-corner zigzag with articles at the start, in the middle of every leg including the first leg, and at the end; see diagram on page 264. I prefer two 2-corner zigzag tracks per session compared to a single 4-corner track as it allows the dog and handler to decompress between the two tracks and encourages the handler to have a really big party at the end of each track.

Phase U1 Session Schedule:

Sesn	Location	Config.	Age A	Age B	Track 1 Yards			Track 2 Yards		
					Leg1	Leg2	Leg3	Leg1	Leg2	Leg3
U1.1	Urban Lawn	Zigzag	15	30	75	75	25	75	75	50
U1.2	Urban Lawn	Flagged Serpentine	15	30	150			150		
U1.3	Parking Lot w/ Curbs	Beside Long Curbs	10	30	60			60		
U1.4	Parking Lot w/ Curbs	Beside Long Curbs	10	30	60			60		
U1.5	Urban Lawn	Zigzag w/ Mid-leg XT	20	45	100	75	75	100	75	75
U1.6	Urban Lawn	Flagged Serpentine	20	45	200			200		
U1.7	Parking Lot w/ Curbs	Island-to-Island Gaps	15	40	80			80		
U1.8	Parking Lot w/ Curbs	Island-to-Island Gaps	15	40	80			80		
U1.9	Urban Lawn	Zigzag w/ Mid-leg XT	25	60	100	75	75	100	75	75
U1.10	Urban Lawn	Flagged Serpentine	25	60	250			250		
U1.11	Parking Lot w/ Curbs	Island-to-Island Gaps	20	50	100			100		
U1.12	Parking Lot w/ Curbs	Island-to-Island Gaps	20	50	100			100		
U1.13	Urban Lawn	Zigzag w/ Mid-leg XT	30	90	100	75	75	100	75	75
U1.14	Urban Lawn	Flagged Serpentine	30	90	400					
U1.15	Parking Lot w/ Curbs	Island-to-Island Gaps	30	60	120			120		
U1.16	Parking Lot w/ Curbs	Island-to-Island Gaps	30	60	120			120		
U1.17		Review								

Each zigzag track should have flags at the start, 30-yard point, each corner and the end so the handler always knows where the track is actually located. Use short (about 12–18") landscaping flags. Some dogs are very visually oriented and look for the flags. For these dogs, cut an inch-long segment of a drinking straw, roll the flag up and slip into the straw. Adding a small rubber band will keep the straw in place. This makes the flag nearly invisible from a distance but quite obvious close up. You want these lawn tracks marked so you always know where the good track is when your dog investigates natural and intentional contamination. Also, the intentional-contamination tracklayer needs the flags to know where to cross the good track.

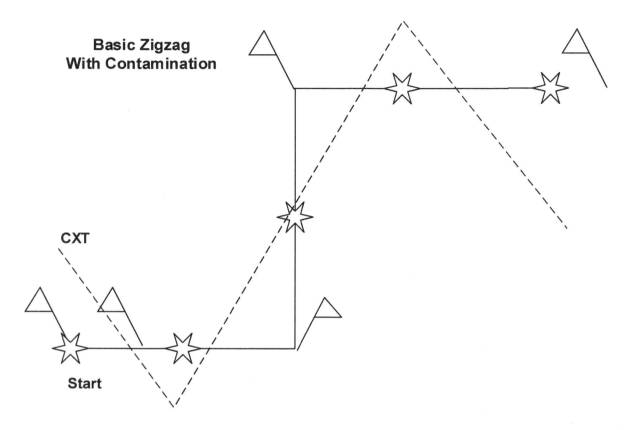

From session U1.5 onward, each zigzag track is contaminated by a contamination tracklayer as the main track is being laid. There are no crosstrack flags, the contamination layer just looks at the corner flags being left by the main tracklayer and estimates where she should cross each leg. For the first few sessions, just one or two people should cross each track. Later, when the dog gets the idea of simple contamination, the contamination layers should bring along their own dogs on leash to make the contamination realistic. It is common for TDU test sites to be on campuses where the public may walk their dogs letting them pee where they will. So it is OK for the intentional-contamination layer to let her dog pee, just don't let him pee on the flags or articles quite yet.

Throughout this phase, the contamination should be laid across each leg more than twenty yards from the corners or the start. Crossing right before, at, or after an article is fine. Cross so the angle you make with the track is roughly 45° and certainly 30° or more. Cross each leg once or twice, extending the contamination track at least 20 yards to the side of the track.

Most intentional contamination should be done at the same time as the track is laid since that minimizes the difference in age between the two tracks and encourages the dog to focus on the person-scent discrimination. Laying it at other times is OK if the contamination layer is not available when the tracklayer is laying the track.

If you don't have contamination layers available on a particular day, choose a busy park or sports field and get your contamination that way. You don't get to control the location or timing of the contamination, but it can work. Sometime you can ask passers-by to walk across that lawn and suggest a particular route, but they are not expert tracklayers, so you are still liable to get their contamination anywhere.

The handler can be the tracklayer or one of the contamination layers. Occasionally the handler should be neither the tracklayer nor the contamination layer. The only constraint is the tracklayer cannot cross her own track.

The handler needs to know how she will handle her dog when he notices and wants to commit to the contamination. Look at the help hierarchy on page 258 and use that as your guide. The four main techniques I use are Patience, Restraint, Reel-In and Re-scent, then Reel-in and Point or gesture in the correct direction. I don't expect to need the Love-the-Track step but if I do, next session I'll want to make the track age younger and the contamination level lighter.

Remember to be patient and to allow your dog plenty of time to make the correct decision for himself. Let him investigate at least 20–40' while you stay on the track.

Hard-Surface Tracking. The goal of the parking-lot tracks is to show your dog that he can find track scent on asphalt and concrete. The curbs hold the scent really well, and the gaps between islands give him opportunity to notice the track scent in the flat gaps between island curbs.

The tracklaying procedures described on page 272 are important in order to facilitate the dog learning the desired lesson and skills. Articles are placed in the middle of each island along the curb so the dog is rewarded for completing the gap. The freeze-dried treats mid-gap and where the track rejoins with a curb (the landing site) are also important to help the dog focus on the track itself. The chalk mark where the track rejoins the curb should be prominent so it can be easily spotted by the handler. I put it on the vertical surface of the curb so it is easily seen and will survive a rainstorm.

Likewise, the handling techniques described for those sessions should be understood and followed carefully. Stay close to your dog, no more than 10' to 15' behind. Do not move forward or allow your dog to move forward if he is more than a few feet to the side of the curb on the low side. Don't move forward if the dog is up on the high side. The only way for your dog to succeed is to track near the curb on its low side.

When you reach the end of the curb, stop right there and let more line out so the dog can investigate the flat gap by himself. Keep light-comfortable line tension, although it may well be lighter tension than you would use in the field. Watch for your dog noticing the track footsteps and following them for even a short distance. In the first three parking-lot sessions U1{.3, .4, .7}, encourage your dog and follow him quickly and easily when you see him notice the track on the asphalt. For the remaining sessions, stay at the end of the previous island and let him work it out by himself. When your dog gets to the next island, continue to stay right where you are and let him sort out the side of the island with the best scent and commit to the track there. If your dog struggles and starts to get frustrated, it is OK to step forward into the gap when he is near the track; but only do so if you have to.

Be very enthusiastic when your dog finds the articles. Play with your dog at each article. Have a big party at the end of each track. Make it fun for your dog.

Losing motivation is typically not an issue in this phase. Be sure to maintain a high level of motivation by using rewards your dog considers excellent and reward him lavishly with them.

Sessions U1.1 Urban-Lawn Zigzags.

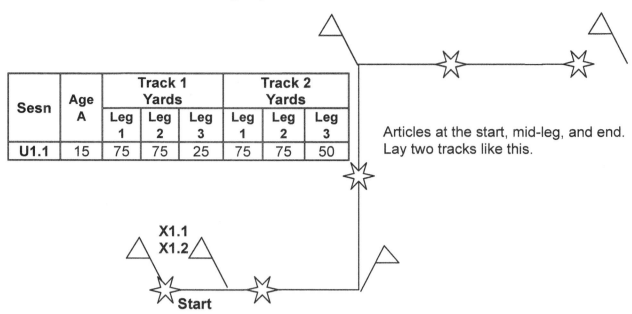

Sesn	Age A	Track 1 Yards			Track 2 Yards		
		Leg 1	Leg 2	Leg 3	Leg 1	Leg 2	Leg 3
U1.1	15	75	75	25	75	75	50

Articles at the start, mid-leg, and end. Lay two tracks like this.

Purpose:
- Familiarize the field-experienced dog with urban-lawn tracks.

Tracklayer:
- Use short landscaping flags at the start, 30 yards, each corner and 5 yards past the end.
- If the dog is highly visually oriented, roll each flag tightly and slip on a straw.
- Place an article at the start, in the middle of every leg (including the first and last), and the end.
- Lay two tracks. The exact leg lengths can vary.
- Walk behind the handler on each track.

Handler:
- These may be easy for your dog, but many dogs find the transition from field grass to lawns a challenge initially. The tracks prepare the dog and handler for the intentionally-contaminated lawn tracks to follow.
- There may be natural contamination — it is OK to let your dog investigate it. However don't let him follow it in a committed fashion more than 20-30'.
- Remember to gradually raise your arm when your dog moves off the track and increase the tension just as you did in the early TD phases. Allow your dog to investigate any natural contamination as a "corner that might go straight" expecting your dog to choose the good track. If necessary, do give him hints and help as appropriate.
- Show lots of enthusiasm when your dog finds the articles. Play with your dog at each article. Have a big party at the end of each track. Make it fun for your dog.

Evaluation:
- Note how your dog tracks, indicates the articles, how he investigates and sorts out any contamination, and his level of enthusiasm for the tracks.

Sessions U1.x Urban-Lawn Serpentines

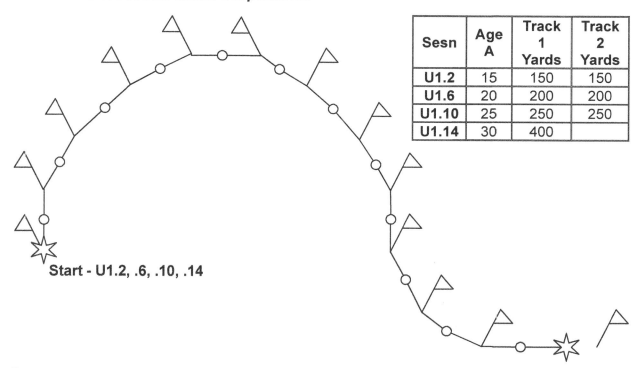

Sesn	Age A	Track 1 Yards	Track 2 Yards
U1.2	15	150	150
U1.6	20	200	200
U1.10	25	250	250
U1.14	30	400	

Start - U1.2, .6, .10, .14

Purpose:
- The curving of the track helps teach the dog that the track might not go straight ahead and that he needs to focus on it carefully.

Tracklayer:
- Laying a serpentine takes more tracklayer skill than laying a straight track. See the discussion and land marking information on page 38. Here is the technique I use:
  1. Pick a landmark directly downwind of your start, put in a flag, and place the first article.
  2. Walk 7 yards toward your landmark, drop a hot dog or freeze-dried treat, and continue on another 8 yards.
  3. Put in a flag. Then look at your landmark, scan your eyes 15–30° to the right, and pick out a new landmark.
  4. Repeat steps 2 & 3 six to twelve times. Then switch to scanning your eyes to the left instead of the right.
  5. Repeat this overall sequence of scanning your eyes to the right for several legs and then scanning to the left for several legs until you have reached the total desired length.
- Write down a sketch of each landmark. This will help you follow the track as the dog runs it and develop your urban map-making skills; the flags will do most of the work.
- Your serpentines will have many bends. As they get longer, you'll continue this undulating pattern across the lawn.
- Use hot dogs or tiny treats (¼" freeze-dried lamb lung) along the track as provided by the handler.
  - To avoid twisting while bending down to place the treat exactly in the footprint, a 3–4' length of PVC pipe is helpful. Use the pipe to guide the treat to land right in the footprint.
- Walk behind the handler on the track.

Handler:
- The handler wants her dog to stay close to the track. It is OK for the dog to investigate a little beyond the bends up to a body length. Ideally, we want him bending right by the flag. Use a combination of patience, restraint and gentle encouragement to help your dog understand how to notice these bends quickly and to bend right at the change in direction.
- Stay only 6–10' behind your dog on the line.
- On the straight sections, gradually raise your arm when your dog moves off the track and increase the tension. Keep your dog within about a body length of the track at all times.
- At the bend, tighten your tolerance to no more than a body length. We want your dog to be focused right on the track there.
- Urban lawns will have natural contamination, but this is not a contamination exercise. Do not allow your dog to investigate the contamination like you do in the intentional contamination sessions. Keep him close the track.
- Distractions are common in these urban-lawn environments. Let your dog spend a few seconds focusing on the distraction and then ask him or help him to get back to work.
- Show lots of enthusiasm when your dog finds the article. Play with your dog and article at the end of each track. Have a big party!

Evaluation:
- Note how your dog tracks, indicates the article, how he investigates and sorts out the bends, and his level of enthusiasm for the tracks.

Longer Serpentine
about 315 yards

Start

Helpful Hint — Use PVC Pipe to Place your Treats.

Placing the treats right in your footstep requires a lot of bending and twisting. Using a 3-4' long PVC pipe about 1/2" in diameter can make it easy to place tiny treats without all that bending and twisting. For larger hot dog pieces, use a larger diameter pipe.

Sessions U1.3 & U1.4 Parking-Lot Tracks along Curbs

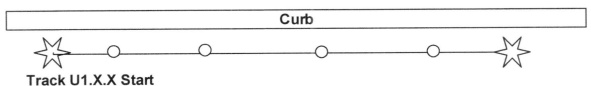

Track U1.X.X Start

Sesn	Age A	Age B	Track 1 Yards	Track 2 Yards	Treats or Inconspicuous Articles	Articles
U1.3	10	30	60	60	Every 10 yards	Start, end
U1.4	10	30	60	60	Every 15 yards	Start, end

Purpose:
- Familiarize the field-experienced dog with hard-surface tracking near curbs.

Tracklayer:
- Find fairly long curbs typically at the edge of parking lots. Avoid turns if possible, but gradual bends are fine. Avoid gaps in the curbs, if possible, or cross the smallest gap possible.
- Walk along the lower flat area beside the curb.
- Use freeze-dried treats for the younger tracks and articles for older tracks as birds learn to enjoy the treats before the track is run.
- Lay two tracks. Leg lengths can be longer if space is available.
- Walk behind the handler on each track.

Handler:
- Use track age A unless the track age conditions on pages 256-267 are satisfied.
- If the track uses a curb with lawn on the high side, your dog may be attracted to it. Let him investigate a little ways but do not move forward unless your dog is in the lower side of the curb.
- Remember to gradually raise your arm when your dog moves off the track and increase the tension just as you did in early fundamental phases.
- Show lots of enthusiasm when your dog finds the articles. Play with your dog and article at the end of each track. Have a big party!

Evaluation:
- Note how your dog tracks, indicates the articles, how he investigates and sorts out any contamination, and his level of enthusiasm for the tracks.

Phase U1. Lawn Contamination and Hard-Surface Tracks

Sessions U1.x Urban-Lawn Zigzags with Intentional Contamination.

U1.5, .9, .13

Tracklayer:
- Flags as shown.
- Articles at the start, middle of every leg, and the end.
- Leg lengths can vary.

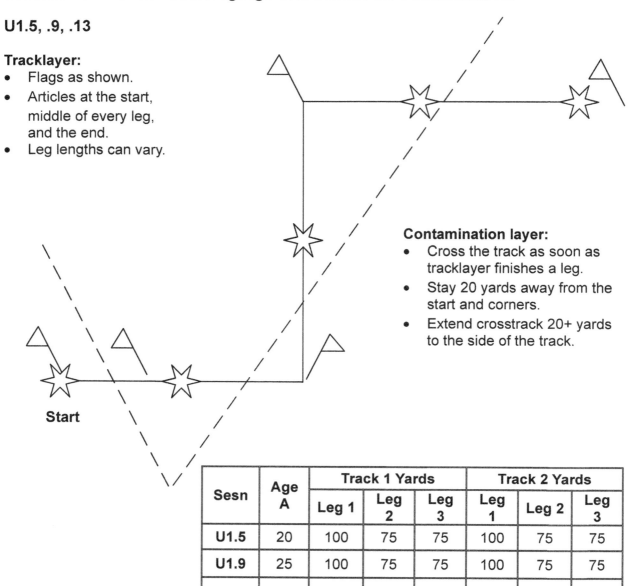

Contamination layer:
- Cross the track as soon as tracklayer finishes a leg.
- Stay 20 yards away from the start and corners.
- Extend crosstrack 20+ yards to the side of the track.

Sesn	Age A	Track 1 Yards			Track 2 Yards		
		Leg 1	Leg 2	Leg 3	Leg 1	Leg 2	Leg 3
U1.5	20	100	75	75	100	75	75
U1.9	25	100	75	75	100	75	75
U1.14	30	100	75	75	100	75	75

Purpose:
- Introduce the dog to contaminated tracks.
- Help the dog understand the best choice is to stay with the good track.

Tracklayer:
- Use short landscaping flags at the start, 30 yards, each corner, and 5 yards past the end.
- If the dog is highly visually oriented, roll each flag tightly and slip on a straw.
- Place an article at the start, in the middle of every leg, and the end.
- Lay two tracks.
- Walk behind the handler on each track.

Contamination Layer (CXT):
- Intentional contamination is optional if there is lots of natural contamination.
- Start laying the contamination track as soon as the tracklayer finishes a leg.
- Start your contamination 20–30 yards to the side and extend your crossings 20 yards to the side of the track.
- Your exact path is not critical. Avoid crossing within 20 yards of the start or a corner.

Handler:
- Your dog is likely to notice some of the contamination crosstracks and may be distracted by them or attracted to follow them. Noticing the contamination is good as that is how your dog will learn what is correct. Let your dog investigate at least 20–40' to the side before increasing the tension and stopping your dog.
- You want your dog to make the choice to return to the good track on his own. Expect your dog to be imperfect but note that each time you have to restrain him is an opportunity for him to learn which track is the good choice.
- There may be natural contamination — treat it just like the intentional contamination.
- Remember to gradually raise your arm when your dog moves off the track and increase the tension just as you did in the early fundamental training.
- Show lots of enthusiasm when your dog finds the articles. Play with your dog at each article. Have a big party at the end of each track. Make it fun for your dog.

Evaluation and Possible Adaptations:
- When your dog notices the contamination and consistently chooses the good track, you know he understands — at least in those conditions.
- Note how your dog tracks, indicates the articles, how he investigates and sorts out the contamination, and his level of enthusiasm for the tracks.
- If he is doing well and appears to understand the concept, invite the contamination layer to bring along her dog (on a leash of course).

Balancing Two Handling Techniques

When your dog is fairly close to the track focusing on it, you should raise and lower the line tension to help keep him close to the track and focused on it. When he notices the contamination, you should allow him to investigate it, reject it on his own, and return to the good track by himself. If you are unsure what he is doing when he moves to the side, prioritize letting him investigate rather than holding him close to the track.

There will be natural contamination as well as the intentional, and you will be uncertain on exactly where the intentional contamination is located. The main point of this exercise is the intentional contamination. If your dog adopts a widely casting style of tracking on minimally-contaminated lawns, do more marked zigzags like U1.1 and work just on keeping him close to the track on the lawn.

Sessions U1.x Curbed-Island Serpentines

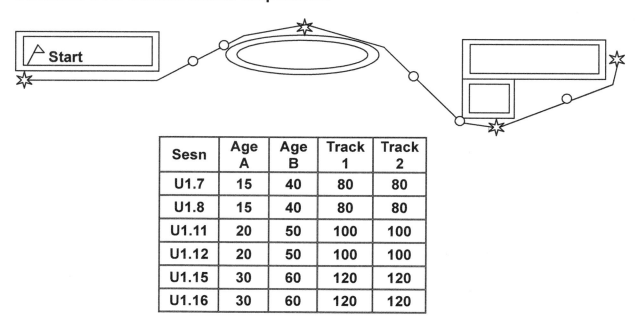

Sesn	Age A	Age B	Track 1	Track 2
U1.7	15	40	80	80
U1.8	15	40	80	80
U1.11	20	50	100	100
U1.12	20	50	100	100
U1.15	30	60	120	120
U1.16	30	60	120	120

Purpose:
- Teach the dog he can find and follow the track on flat pavement.

Tracklayer:
- Choose islands with curbs that are at the end of each double parking row so the gaps are not too wide. Avoid areas with significant traffic nearby.
- An article at the start, end, and along the side of each island.
- Randomly choose which side of the next island at each gap.
- Place freeze-dried treats mid-gap and where the track lands on the next island.
- Make a prominent chalk mark where the track lands on the next island.
- Lay two tracks. Walk behind the handler on each track.

Handler:
- Use track age A unless the track age conditions on pages 256-267 are satisfied.
- Along the curbs, only move forward behind your dog if he is focused on the track in the lower side of the curb; stay still when he investigates the high side.
- Stay 10' behind your dog when along the curbs. When you reach the end of each island:
  - For the first three sessions, stay about 10' behind your dog across the gap, raising and lowering your line to keep your dog close to the track.
  - For the remaining sessions, stop and let the line out so your dog works across on his own.
- Be patient and let your dog figure things out.
- Let your dog work out which side of the island is correct but gently restrain as necessary.
- Show lots of enthusiasm when your dog finds the articles. Play with your dog at each article. Have a big party at the end of each track. Make it fun for your dog.

Evaluation:
- Note how your dog tracks, indicates the articles, how he investigates and sorts out the track on the flat, and his level of enthusiasm for the tracks.

Sessions U1.17 Review and Evaluation.

The training in this phase begins your dog's transition from field to urban tracking. Your dog will not become fully competent in sorting out the contamination from the main track. Likewise, your dog will not become a confident hard-surface tracker in this phase; he is building his urban foundation. Hopefully, you will see he is getting the general idea even if he is far from perfect.

To review, consider the last two sessions on contaminated park lawns U1.13 & U1.14. If he noticed several of the contamination tracks and chose the good track without help more often than he needed help, move on to the next phase unless the hard surface tracks need more work.

For the hard-surface tracks in U1.15 & U1.16, if for the majority of the gaps either he notices the track in the gap or crosses the gap and efficiently chooses the correct side of the next island, move on to the next phase unless he needs more work on contaminated lawns.

Otherwise, repeat half or all of this phase at different ages, different locations, different tracklayers and different contamination layers. Build your foundation skills now before the tracks get more complicated.

Phase U1 Summary Log

Sesn	Site	Config.	Date	Actual Age	Evaluation
U1.1		Zigzag			
U1.2		Flagged Serpentine			
U1.3		Beside Long Curbs			
U1.4		Beside Long Curbs			
U1.5		Zigzag w/ Mid-leg CXT			
U1.6		Flagged Serpentine			
U1.7		Island Gaps			
U1.8		Island Gaps			
U1.9		Zigzag w/ Mid-leg CXT			
U1.10		Flagged Serpentine			
U1.11		Island Gaps			
U1.12		Island Gaps			
U1.13		Zigzag w/ Mid-leg CXT			
U1.14		Flagged Serpentine			
U1.15		Island Gaps			
U1.16		Island Gaps			

Phase U2. Contamination, Surface Transitions, and Hard Surface Skills

Purpose:
- Teach the dog to stay with the good track even when there are varied contamination and surface transitions on the track.
- Develop the dog's hard-surface tracking skill.
- Maintain a high level of motivation.

Strategy:
- Threefold:
  - On urban campuses and parks, introduce the dog to lawn tracks that cross paths, sidewalks, and narrow roads.
  - On sports field lawns, allow the dog to learn to handle tracks with intentional contamination at the start and the corners.
  - On large flat parking lots, help the dog understand he can follow close to the track even on a flat hard surface.

How to use this chapter:
- Read the discussion section that follows and look through the table on the next page, which summarizes the training structure of this phase.
- Do each of the 9 sessions that rotate between urban lawns and parking lots. Before each session, carefully review the detailed tracklaying and handling instructions for urban-lawn transitions on page 279, sports-field corner contamination on page 281, or for parking-lot straight tracks on page 283.
- Keep a detailed log of each session using a format like the one shown on page 31 and keep a summary log like the one shown on page 285.
- Finally, do the review session on page 284 to evaluate your dog's progress and your own training-skill development.

Discussion:

Phase U2 focuses on simple contamination in urban campus and park-like conditions for one-third of the sessions. The second third is similar, but with intentional contamination at the start and corners of tracks and is ideally done on sports lawn with no paths or roadways to interrupt the flow of the track. The final third focuses on straight downwind tracks on large open flat parking lots with no nearby curbs or shrubs to hold the scent for the dog.

In addition, some percentage of your tracks should be motivational tracks — perhaps a 45-minute-old zigzag on a lightly-contaminated sports field. These motivational sessions are to be just fun for your dog (and you as well). The percentage of motivational tracks you need in this phase depends on the dog: if over 2-3 sessions you see your dog is slow to commit at starts that you think should be easy, increase the percentage of tracking sessions that consist of a simple motivational track. Keep track of your target percentage motivational tracks by writing it down in the space provided on the next page or in your journal.

Phase U2 Session Schedule:

% Motivational Sessions	Range: 10–30%	Your Target:

Sesn	Location	Config.	Age A	Age B	Lengths (yards)					
U2.1	Urban Lawn w/ Path & Roads	3-Turn Lawn Zigzag	35	50	Leg1 80	Leg2 50	Leg3 50	Leg4 50		
U2.2	Urban Sports Lawn	Contaminated Zigzags	40	55	Track 1			Track 2		
					75	75	50	75	75	75
U2.3	Parking Lot	Downwind w/o curbs	20	35	Trk1 50	Trk2 75	Trk3 100			
U2.4	Urban Lawn w/ Path & Roads	3-Turn Lawn Zigzag	40	60	Leg1 100	Leg2 75	Leg3 60	Leg4 60		
U2.5	Urban Sports Lawn	Contaminated Zigzags	45	65	Track 1			Track 2		
					75	75	50	75	75	75
U2.6	Parking Lot	Downwind w/o curbs	25	40	Trk1 75	Trk2 100	Trk3 125			
U2.7	Urban Lawn w/ Path & Roads	3-Turn Lawn Zigzag	45	70	Leg1 125	Leg2 90	Leg3 75	Leg4 60		
U2.8	Urban Sports Lawn	Contaminated Zigzags	50	80	Track 1			Track 2		
					75	75	50	75	75	75
U2.9	Parking Lot	Downwind w/o curbs	30	50	Trk1 75	Trk2 100	Trk3 150			
U2.10		Review								

For the **Campus and Park Lawn Session** tracks there should be crossings of pathways or narrow driveways. Contamination should be added if there is not a lot of natural contamination. Avoid adding intentional contamination within 20 yards of the start, corners, or surface transitions. These tracks are three-turn (four leg) tracks with each leg contaminated once or twice by a person (anyone but the tracklayer) and optionally a dog on leash.

Handlers should expect their dog to go back and forth or curl off at most transitions and should be patient to let the dog work things out if possible. Help the dog happily when needed.

For the **Sports Lawn Corner-Contamination Sessions**, intentional contamination is laid near or right over the start and at every corner. This is hard to do using natural contamination so plan to do intentional contamination if at all possible. The first time we cross near the start, the crossing happens about five yards down the first leg. From then on, the contamination is right over the start article but without stepping on the start article.

The contamination layers should endeavor to cross the track at roughly a 45° angle. Once the dog consistently makes the correct choice, the contamination layer should bring along a dog to add to the contamination. Once the tracking dog is handling that level of contamination consistently, the contamination layer can narrow the angle of the contamination with the good track so the dog is in contact with the contamination longer and he is more likely to notice the contamination. Unless the dog notices the contamination, he does not have the opportunity to consciously reject it and stay with the good track.

Most intentional contamination should be done at the same time as the track is laid since that minimizes the difference in age between the two tracks and encourages the dog to focus on the person-scent discrimination. Laying it at other times is OK if the contamination layer is not available when the tracklayer is laying the track.

The **Downwind-Flat-Parking-Lot Session** tracks are all straight downwind in large flat parking lots without nearby curbs to hold the scent. Use a start article even if you are only interested in CKC tracking. Use chalk to mark the track, if necessary, but typically the articles along the track are quite obvious. Use treats on these tracks if the treats survive and are tasty until the dog runs the track. Using freeze-dried treats may be a viable option for older tracks.

The straight-track sequence on asphalt or other hard surface is similar to the straight field-track sequence from Phase 2 page 40 but this time on smooth flat asphalt. For these tracks, you can use frequent freeze-dried treats or hot dogs if the birds will not get them. Regardless, you use frequent small or inconspicuous articles as reward points — they should be inconspicuous to minimize the dog just shopping from debris to article to debris to article without using his nose to follow the track. In general, you will not need chalk to mark these tracks as the line of articles on the flat parking lot will be fairly obvious, but feel free to use it if the handler wants you to do so. For the initial few sessions, these are good tracks to lay barefoot, using Scent in a Bottle (SIAB), hydration, or other scent intensifiers (see page 8). Gradually revert to normal footwear.

The use of small articles can be troublesome to dogs and handlers who have always used articles the standard size, which is about the size of a hand or wallet. However, they are very useful in urban situations since they do not get picked up by passers-by as much as large articles. You can introduce your dog to small articles using an article circle like session 3.4 on a well-maintained urban lawn. Or, you can find regular-sized inconspicuous articles that will visually blend in with the surface where you place them.

You can start some of these track along curbs to get your dog going, but also include some unsupported flat starts to give your dog practice with those. While an urban TDU or VST test track will not start on a non-vegetated surface, the dog may find an article on a hard surface and need to restart from there.

Handlers should be quite demanding on these straight tracks that the dog works within a few feet of the track itself. This is not the time to let your dog wander to the fringe. It is very important that the dog understands that the track itself is a fun rewarding place to be.

Dogs will "shop" on flat hard surface not only for treats and articles but also for trash and debris. You cannot really stop them since some tracklayer scent may well be lying on the trash or debris. Your dog should be tracking between the articles and debris distractions. If they are just shopping and fully distracted from the track, then you need to tighten your criteria for how close to the track the dog is working and enforce it gently but firmly. Or perhaps find a parking lot with less debris for a while. Expect the dog to shop to some extent and be relaxed about it.

Two **ages** are shown in the session schedules. While many dogs can do just the Age A tracks, those handlers who want to give their dog more experience before moving to the next phase can repeat part or all of the schedule using older ages in Age B. Alternatively, if your dog lacks confidence using Age A, you can adapt these times to be shorter to maintain a reasonably high success rate for the dog learning these urban skills. See pages 256-257 for additional discussion on track ages.

Reading your Dog. You need to focus your attention on what your dog does when he tracks on a lightly-contaminated lawn, a heavily trampled lawn, at transitions to hard surfaces, and at transitions back to grass. Your light-comfortable tension may be quite a bit lighter than it was in TD or TDX, but there should still be some tension (don't let the line hang down and touch the ground between you and your dog).

When you see a change in behavior is exactly the time to stop and say "Yippee! I am on a corner that might go straight," regardless of whether you know where the track is or can see footprints in the grass.

This is a good time to use video and study what your dog looks like on the track. Your review will be without the distraction of actually doing the handling in real time.

Use your detailed log to record what you notice of his posture, head carriage, tail carriage, ear carriage, changes in sniffing patterns, changes of direction, or other behaviors.

Sessions U2.x Urban-Lawn Tracks with Path and Road Transitions

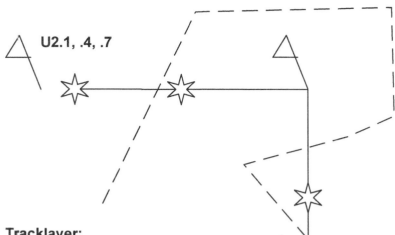
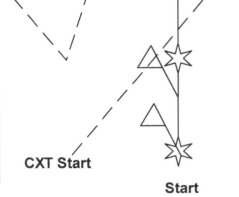

Tracklayer:
- No turns within 10 yards of a surface transition.

Contamination Layer (CXT):
- No contamination within 20 yards of the start or a corner.
- Extend contamination 20 yards to each side of track.

Sesn	Age A	Age B	Leg 1 Yards	Leg 2 Yards	Leg 3 Yards	Leg 4 Yards
U2.1	35	50	80	50	50	50
U2.4	40	60	100	75	60	60
U2.7	45	70	125	90	75	60

Purpose:
- Teach the dog the best choice is to stay with the good track.
- Introduce the dog to narrow surface transitions.

Tracklayer:
- Try to cross paths and narrow roadways in the middle of legs several times as available.
- Use short landscaping flags at the start, 30 yards, each corner and 5 yards past the end.
- If the dog is highly visually oriented, roll each flag tightly and slip on a straw.
- Place an article at the start, in the middle of every leg, and the end.
- Don't turn on a hard surface or within 10 yards of a surface transition.
- Walk behind the handler on each track.

Contamination Layer (CXT):
- Start laying the contamination track as soon as the tracklayer finishes a leg.
- Start your contamination 20–30 yards to the side and extend your crossings 20+ yards to each side of the track.
- Your exact path is not critical but avoid crossing within 20 yards of the start or a corner.

Handler:
- Your dog is likely to notice some of the contamination crosstracks and may be distracted by them or attracted to follow them. Noticing the contamination is good, as that is how your dog will learn the correct choice to make. Let your dog investigate at least 20–30' to the side before increasing the tension and stopping your dog.
- You want your dog to make the choice to return to the good track on his own. But each time you have to stop him is an opportunity for him to learn which track is the good choice.
- Prioritize letting your dog investigate and reject the contamination, see page 271.
  - There may be natural contamination — treat it just like the intentional contamination.
  - Remember to gradually raise your arm when your dog moves off the track and increase the tension just as you did in Phase 1.
- Expect your dog to go back and forth at most surface transitions — that is normal. Don't hurry your dog, let him sort it out.
- Show lots of enthusiasm when your dog finds the articles. Play with your dog at each article. Have a big party at the end of each track. Make it fun for your dog.

Evaluation and Possible Adaptations:
- When your dog notices the contamination and consistently chooses the good track without hints, you know he understands — at least in those conditions.
- Note how your dog tracks, indicates the articles, how he investigates and sorts out the contamination and surface transitions, and his level of enthusiasm for the tracks.
- If he is doing well and appears to understand the concept, invite the contamination layer to bring along her dog (on a leash of course).

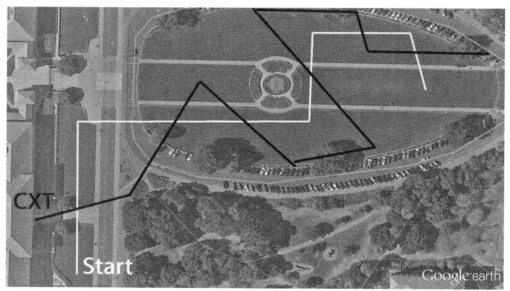

5. Images © 2016 Google

Sessions U2.x Urban Sports Lawns — Sliced and Bisected Corners

U2.2, .5 & .8

Tracklayer:
- Flags as shown.
- Articles at the start, middle of each leg including the first and last, and the end.
- Leg lengths can vary.
- Lay two separate Zig-Zags.

Contamination layer:
- Cross the track as soon as tracklayer finishes a leg.
- Cross near or at the start and slice or bisect each corner.
- Extend crosstrack 20 yards to side of track.

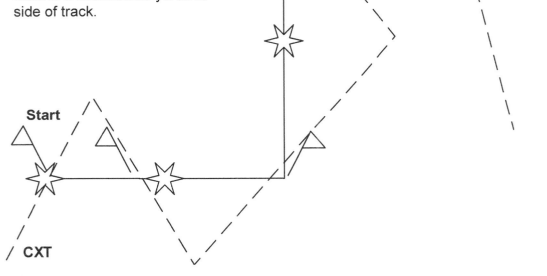

Purpose:
- Teach the dog the best choice is to stay with the good track.
- Experience contaminated start and corners as well as mid-leg.

Tracklayer:
- Choose a lawn with no or minimal surface transitions.
- Use short landscaping flags at the start, 30 yards, each corner and 5 yards past the end.
- If the dog is highly visually oriented, roll each flag tightly and slip on a straw.
- Place an article at the start, in the middle of every leg, and the end.
- Lay 2 Zigzag tracks per session.
- Walk behind the handler on each track.

Contamination Layer (CXT):
- Start laying the contamination track as soon as the tracklayer finishes a leg.
- Start your contamination 20–30 yards to the side and extend your crossings 20 yards to the side of the track.
- For U2.2, cross 5 yards from the start and for others, cross right at the start.
- Bisect half the corners and slice off 2–3 yards inside of the other corners.
- Your exact path is not critical, cross mostly at 30–60°.

Handler:
- Your dog is likely to notice some of the contamination crosstracks and may be distracted by them or attracted to follow them. That is good as that is how your dog will learn what is correct. Let your dog investigate at least 20–30' to the side before increasing the tension and stopping your dog.
- You want your dog to make the choice to return to the good track on his own. But each time you have to stop him is an opportunity for him to learn which track is the good choice.
- Remember to gradually raise your arm when your dog moves off the track and increase the tension just as you did in Phase 1.
  - There may be natural contamination — treat it just like the intentional contamination.
  - Remember to gradually raise your arm when your dog moves off the track and increase the tension just as you did in Part I. See page 271 for balancing handling techniques.
- Show lots of enthusiasm when your dog finds the articles. Play with your dog at each article. Have a big party at the end of each track. Make it fun for your dog.

Evaluation and Possible Adaptations:
- When your dog notices the contamination and consistently chooses the good track, you know he understands — at least in those conditions.
- Note how your dog tracks, indicates the articles, how he investigates and sorts out the contamination, and his level of enthusiasm for the tracks.
- If he is doing well and appears to understand the concept, invite the contamination layer to bring along her dog (on a leash of course).

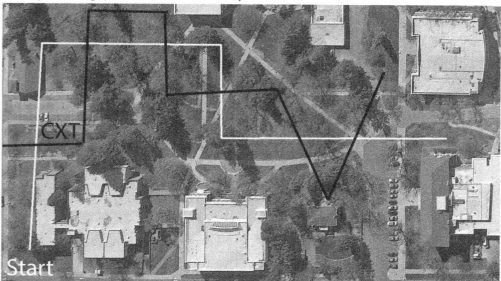

6. Images © 2016 Google

Sessions U2.x Straight Downwind Hard-Surface Tracks.

U2.3, .6, .9

Tracklayer:
- Use a wide open flat parking lot.
- Articles should be small and inconspicuous so the dog finds them by his nose.
- Hot dog or other treat every 15–20 steps.

Handler:
- Stay within 10' of your dog.
- Keep him within 3'to 10' of the track.

Sesn	Age A	Age B	Trk 1 Yards	Trk 2 Yards	Trk 3 Yards
U2.3	20	35	50	75	100
U2.6	25	40	75	100	125
U2.9	30	50	75	100	150

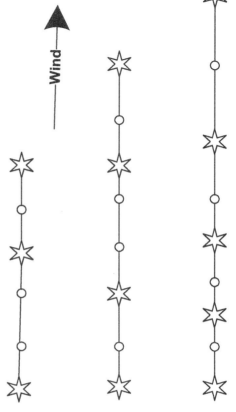

Track U2.X.1 Track U2.X.2 Track U2.X.3

Purpose:
- Teach the dog he can find and follow the track on flat pavement.

Tracklayer:
- Choose a parking lot without nearby islands or curbs. Avoid areas with heavy traffic nearby.
- Ideally, your dogs can start in the flat, but it is OK to start along a curb if necessary.
- Articles at the start, every 30-60 yards along the leg, and at the end. Use inconspicuous or small articles mid-leg.
- Tiny freeze-dried treats every 15–20 steps. Use tiny treats that birds don't tend to steal.

Handler:
- Use track age A unless the track age conditions on pages 256-267 are satisfied.
- Stay close to your dog, about 10'. Keep your dog within 3–10' of the track.
- Be patient and let your dog figure things out. Encourage only if needed.
- Show lots of enthusiasm when your dog finds the articles. Play with your dog at each article. Have a big party at the end of each track. Make it fun for your dog.

Evaluation:
- Note how your dog tracks, indicates the articles, how he investigates and sorts out the track on the flat, and his level of enthusiasm for the tracks.

Session U2.10 Review.

By the end of this phase your dog should be making most of the decisions on the zigzag lawn tracks without your help. The next phase uses blind tracks, and you need your dog making the right choices by himself before that. If you are not satisfied with the dog's confidence and commitment to the good track, redo the second half of the phase or the whole phase before going on to blind tracks. Vary the age, tracklayers, and locations for these additional sessions. For a dog who has only done the younger track ages such as Age C, repeating with older track ages is an excellent idea.

For the hard-surface tracks, your dog should be noticing the track and following it closely for much of its length, but may not be consistently committing to the tracks for their whole length. If he is, great. If he follows the hard-surface tracks fairly closely for most of their length, feel free to proceed to Phase U3. Remember if you lose that commitment later in your training, you can always redo some more of these simple straight tracks anytime. In fact, many dogs will benefit from doing many more sessions of these straight tracks on parking lots varying the location, surface, age, and length.

If you are unsatisfied with your dog's hard-surface tracking commitment, repeat the curbed-island serpentines and the straight-downwind tracks at various locations before proceeding to the next phase.

Phase U2 Summary Log

Sesn	Site	Config.	Date	Actual Age	Evaluation
U2.1		3-Turn Lawn Zigzag			
U2.2		Contaminated Zigzags			
U2.3		Downwind w/o curbs			
U2.4		3-Turn Lawn Zigzag			
U2.5		Contaminated Zigzags			
U2.6		Downwind w/o curbs			
U2.7		3-Turn Lawn Zigzag			
U2.8		Contaminated Zigzags			
U2.9		Downwind w/o curbs			

Phase U2. Contamination, Surface Transitions, and Hard Surface Skills

Phase U3. Preparing for the TDU, and Foundations of the VST Journey.

Purpose:
- Practice simple and realistic TDU-like tracks.
- Maintain and improve the dog's skill in handling contamination and hard-surface crossings.
- Maintain a high level of motivation.

Strategy:
- Practice four-corner intentionally-contaminated zigzags.
- Work marked TDU-like tracks so the handler knows what the dog is doing and can help when needed.
- Work blind TDU-like tracks so the handler gets used to not knowing where the track is and the dog gets accustomed to the handler being uncertain.
- Practice hard-surface tracks mixing curbed-island serpentines and straight downwind tracks.

How to use this chapter:
- Read the discussion section that follows and look through the table on the next page, which summarizes the training structure of this phase.
- Do each of the 16 sessions that rotate between urban lawns and parking lots. Before each session, carefully review the detailed tracklaying and handling instructions for each type of tracking session on pages 291 through 297.
- Keep a detailed log of each session using a format like the one shown on page 31 and keep a summary log like the one shown on page 300.
- Finally, do the review session on page 298 to evaluate your dog's progress and your own training-skill development.

Discussion:

Making a smooth transition from the constrained exercises of Phase U2 to being ready for a TDU test track requires a mix of simple skill exercises and realistic TDU-like tracks. The realistic marked and blind TDU tracks are important to practice, but they should not be your only training focus. Improving the dog's skills in the two critical areas of contaminated lawn tracks and hard-surface crossings is essential too.

This phase is both for people who want to earn their TDU as well as for those whose only focus is the esteemed VST. It builds important dog and handler skills before adding the many complexities of the VST.

In addition, some percentage of your tracks should be motivational tracks — perhaps a 45 minute-old zigzag on a little-contaminated sports field. They are to be just fun for your dog and you. The percentage of motivational tracks you need in this phase depends on the dog: if over 2-3 sessions you see your dog is slow to commit at starts that you think should be easy, increase the percentage of tracking sessions that consist of a simple motivational track.

Phase U3 Session Schedule:

	% Motivational Sessions	Range: 10–30%			Your Target:		
Sesn	**Location**	**Configuration**	**Age A**	**Age B**	**No. Legs**	**Turns**	**Length Yards**
U3.1	Urban Lawn	4-Corner Contaminated	45	75	4	R & L	350
U3.2	Urban Lawn Path & Roads	Marked TDU-like	40	75	4–5	R & L	400
U3.3	Urban Lawn Path & Roads	Blind TDU-like	30	60	3–5	R & L	350
U3.4	Parking Lot w/ Curbs	Island-to-Island Gaps	35	60	1	N/A	200
U3.5	Urban Lawn	4-Corner Contaminated	50	45	4	R & L	400
U3.6	Urban Lawn Path & Roads	Marked TDU-like	45	90	5–6	R & L	450
U3.7	Urban Lawn Path & Roads	Blind TDU-like	35	45	3–5	R & L	400
U3.8	Parking Lot	Downwind w/o curbs	40	60	1	N/A	150
U3.9	Urban Lawn	4-Corner Contaminated	60	90	4	R & L	450
U3.10	Urban Lawn Path & Roads	Marked TDU-like	50	45	4–6	R & L	500
U3.11	Urban Lawn Path & Roads	Blind TDU-like	40	60	4–6	R & L	450
U3.12	Parking Lot w/ Curbs	Island-to-Island Gaps	45	75	1	N/A	250
U3.13	Urban Lawn	4-Corner Contaminated	75	120	4	R & L	500
U3.14	Urban Lawn Path & Roads	Marked TDU-like	60	120	4–6	R & L	450
U3.15	Urban Lawn Path & Roads	Blind TDU-like	50	75	4–6	R & L	450
U3.16	Parking Lot	Downwind w/o curbs	50	75	1	N/A	200
U3.17		Review					

Contaminated Four-Corner Tracks should have a simple shape with the corners marked and not too many surface transitions. They are a straightforward extension of the 2-corner zigzags with intentional contamination done in Phase U2 but now strung end-to-end into a single track.

Most intentional contamination should be done at the same time as the track is laid since that minimizes the difference in age between the two tracks and encourages the dog to focus on the person-scent discrimination. Occasionally, some intentional contamination can be laid right before the dog runs the track to make it more attractive. Laying it at other times is OK if the contamination layer is not available when the tracklayer is laying the track.

**Urban Lawn
Intentional Contamination**

**Zigzag or
Linear Track**

Chair

Start

Hat

Start

Start

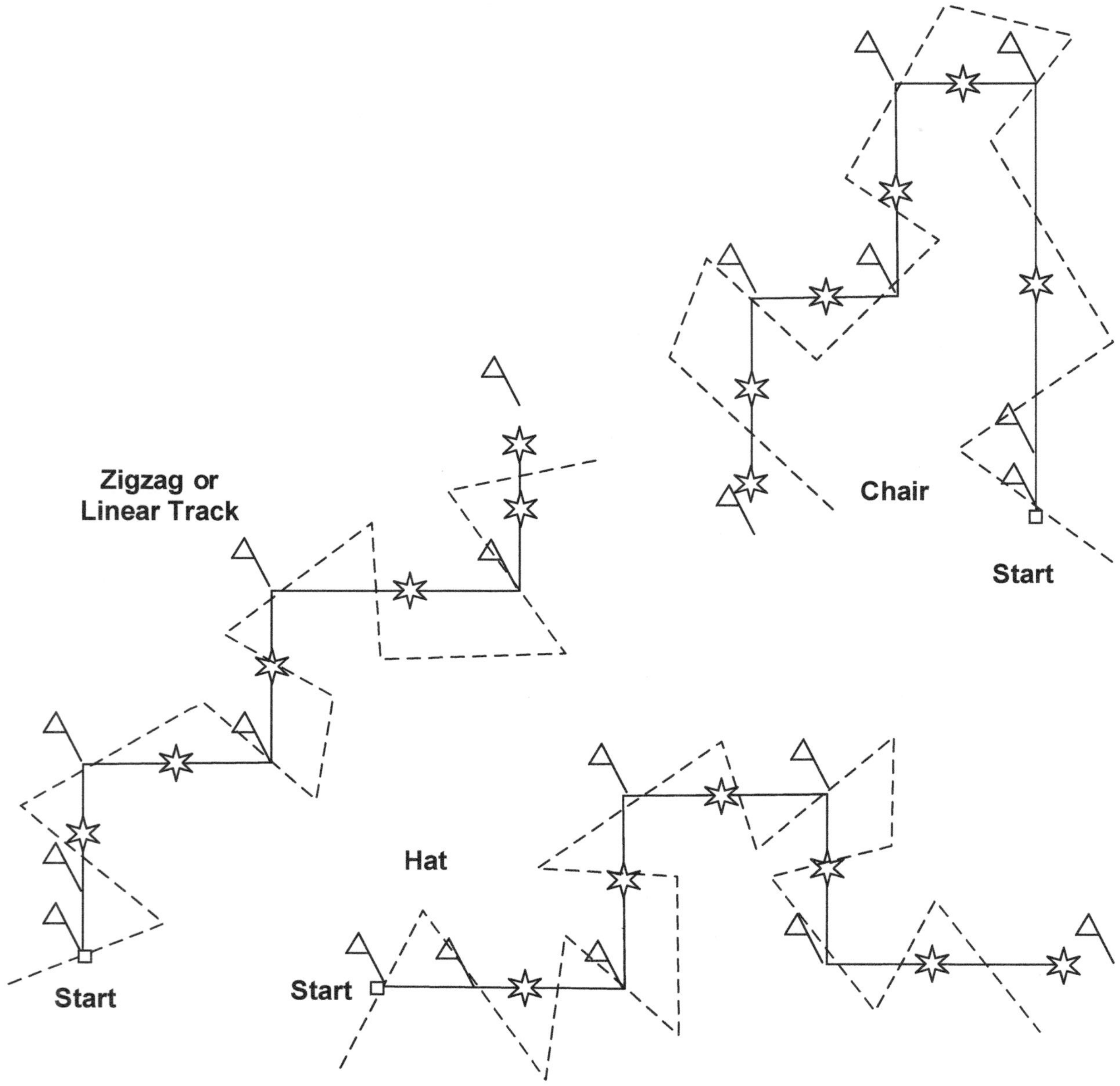

Your goal for your dog is that he chooses the good track even when he notices and investigates the contamination out to the full 40' of your line without any checking or restraint to hint or help him. And your goal for yourself is to let him investigate the contamination and when he chooses the good track, let the line out to 35–40' before following him and immediately climbing up the line to 15–20'. Use these simple-marked tracks to allow your dog to learn and accept the responsibility to make his own good choices.

Designing TDU-like Tracks. Phase U3 introduces simple TDU-like tracks with half of them blind so the handler can get used to following a blind urban track.

The table below is replicated from Phase 7 and shows the essential design parameters for the TDU as well as the UTD tracks.

Comparison of AKC TDU and CKC UTD Test Tracks

Essential Parameters	AKC TDU	CKC UTD
Length	400–500 yards	300–400 meters
Age (hours)	½–2	1–2
Corners	3–5	3–5
Hard-Surface Corners	None	1 or more
Ratio Non-Veg to Total	10–30%	About 33%
Non-Veg Surface Types	At least 1	At least 1
Start Article	Leather or Cloth	Scent pad only
Start Surface	30+ yards veg	25+ meters veg
Other Articles	Leather or Cloth	AKC-like or wood

The handler should remember her blind tracking skills from the TD work, but urban environments with heavy contamination pose their own unique challenges for the handler. Contamination can create dozens of 'corners that might go straight' along each leg. Each one is an opportunity for the dog to sort things out and choose the good track. Don't suggest where to go next before the dog has a chance to solve the challenge.

The TDU-like tracks should be 3–5 corner tracks without turns right on a hard surface. Also, avoid turning on grass adjacent to a hard surface so the first step is onto the hard surface. While a real TDU track has only a single intermediate article, I recommend at least one article in the middle of each leg as reward points. Use chalk and flags to mark the non-blind tracks and don't for the blind ones.

The tracks on the next page show realistic shapes although a TDU track can have 3–5 corners. It is easy to reduce the number of corners or to add another corner to the shown shapes. See page 116 for more TDU track shapes. Note that TDU tracks have 40 to 150 yards of non-vegetated surface without any corners directly on those surfaces. Typically, the track will incorporate sidewalk, driveway and small parking-lot crossings. They may also follow a segment of a sidewalk or end by finishing out in the middle of a large parking lot.

The track designs also show only one intermediate article, which is like the test itself. In training, add additional articles like an article in the middle of each leg to provide additional reward points.

Real TDU test track shapes are typically heavily influenced by buildings and driveway locations. See pages 113–115 for three real test track examples.

In training add contamination if there is little natural contamination — be gentle with the contamination on the blind tracks in this phase. Add more natural or intentional contamination if the dog is doing well with light contamination.

Video. Recording most of the tracks in this phase with a video using either an action camera showing only your dog or a tracklayer-carried device will allow you to review your dog's performance and your own performance as well. You need to understand how your dog acts when he encounters contamination, transitions, and distractions. You will see more by reviewing the video when you are not completely focused on your handling. If over time your dog does a similar track to one he did some time ago, you can compare the two and see how much he and you have improved.

Simple TDU Track Designs

TDU tracks have 40–150 yards of non-vegetated surface without any corners right on them.

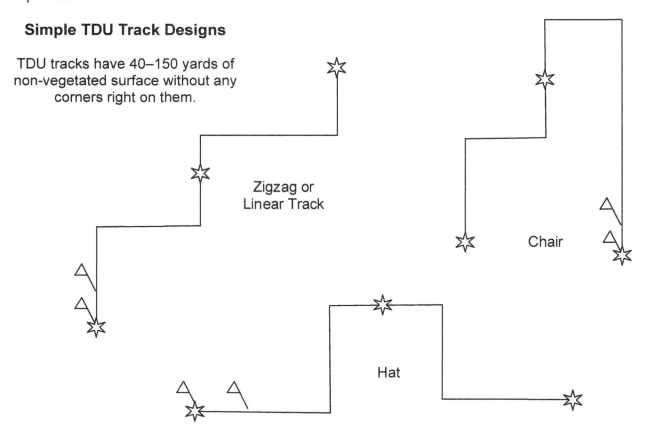

Zigzag or Linear Track

Chair

Hat

Polishing Skills. Review your own and your dog's performance on the last 3–5 tracks. Identify any skills that could use improvement, even if they were good enough to get you through that particular track. Focus one or more sessions on improving those skills one at a time.

Peaking Performance for the Test. You can do a few things in the last couple of weeks before a test to make sure your dog's skill and enthusiasm for tracking are at its peak. The general idea is to work your dog quite hard two to three weeks before a test, then back off to motivational tracks the first half of the pre-test week, followed by a layoff for 3–4 days before the test. You want your dog to be highly enthusiastic for tracking when you take him out of your car on test day, which means he has to be under-worked for several days before. In addition to avoiding tracking training for 3–4 days, I avoid other types of training for 2–3 days. See page 152 for the final preparation schedule for TDU.

Test Day. Review the Part I section on test day, page 154.

Sessions U3.x Four-Corner-Contaminated Zigzag

Tracklayer:
- Flags as shown.
- Articles at the start, middle of each leg, and the end.
- Leg lengths can vary.

Contamination layer:
- Cross the track as soon as the tracklayer finishes a leg.
- Cross at the start
- Extend the crosstrack 20 yards to the side of the track.
- Slice or bisect each corner.

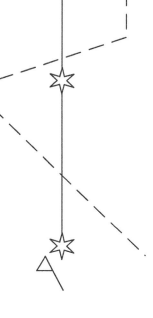

Sesn	Age A	Age B	Total Yards
U3.1	45	75	350
U3.5	50	45	400
U3.9	60	90	450
U3.13	75	120	500

CXT   Start   U3.1, .5, .9, .13

Purpose:
- Teach the dog the best choice is to stay with the good track.
- Practice contaminated starts and corners as well as mid-leg contamination.

Tracklayer:
- Choose the track shape as shown above or one of the ones on page 288.
- It is OK to cross non-vegetated paths and roads but make no turns on non-vegetated surfaces.
- Use short landscaping flags at the start, 30 yards, each corner and 5 yards past the end.
- If the dog is highly visually oriented, roll each flag tightly and slip on a straw.
- Place an article at the start, in the middle of every leg, and the end.
- Walk behind the handler on each track.

Contamination Layer (CXT):
- Start laying the contamination track as soon as the tracklayer finishes a leg or lay it shortly before the track is run if requested by the handler.
- Start your contamination 20–30 yards to the side and extend your crossings 20 yards to the side of the track.
- Bisect half the corners and slice off 2–3 yards inside of the other corners.
- Your exact path is not critical, cross mostly at 30–60°.

Handler:
- Your dog is likely to notice some of the contamination crosstracks and may be distracted by them or attracted to follow them. That is good, as that is how your dog will learn what is correct. Let your dog investigate at least 20–30' to the side before increasing the tension and stopping your dog.
- You want your dog to make the choice to return to the good track on his own. But each time you have to stop him is an opportunity for him to learn which track is the good choice.
- Prioritize letting your dog investigate and reject the contamination, see page 271.
  - There may be natural contamination — treat it just like the intentional contamination.
  - Remember to gradually raise your arm when your dog moves off the track and increase the tension just as you did in Phase 1.
- Show lots of enthusiasm when your dog finds the articles. Play with your dog at each article. Have a big party at the end of each track. Make it fun for your dog.

Evaluation and Possible Adaptations:
- When your dog notices the contamination and consistently chooses the good track, you know he understands — at least in those conditions.
- Note how your dog tracks, indicates the articles, how he investigates and sorts out the contamination, and his level of enthusiasm for the tracks.
- If he is doing well and appears to understand the concept:
  - Invite the contamination layer to bring along her dog (on a leash of course).
  - If contamination at the same age as the track is handled consistently, consider adding the contamination shortly before the track is run or perhaps at both times. You can get varying age random natural contamination by choosing a site which sees a good deal of public use.
  - If your dog is not experiencing being greeted by strangers as he tracks, consider having your contamination layer come by in the middle of a track to greet you both and pet your dog.

Sessions U3.x Marked TDU-like

U3.2, .6, .10, .14

Tracklayer:
- Flags as shown.
- Articles at the start, middle of each leg
- Shape and leg lengths can vary.

Sesn	Age A	Age B	Turns	Total Yards
U3.2	40	75	3–4	400
U3.6	45	90	4–5	450
U3.10	50	45	3–5	500
U3.14	60	120	3–5	450

Purpose:
- Familiarize both the dog and the handler with TDU-complexity tracks.
- Allow the handler to help her dog as needed to improve the dog's skills.

Tracklayer:
- Choose the track shape as shown above or one of the ones on page 290.
- It is OK to cross non-vegetated paths and roads, but no turns on non-vegetated surfaces.
- Use short landscaping flags at the start, 30 yards, mid-way along each leg about 6–10 steps apart. Use chalk on and off hard-surface transitions.
- If the dog is highly visually oriented, roll each flag tightly and slip on a straw.
- Place an article at the start, in the middle of every leg, and the end.
- Walk behind the handler on each track.

Contamination Layer (CXT):
- Only add contamination if the site is not much used and there is little contamination.

Phase U3. Preparing for the TDU, and Foundations of the VST Journey.

Handler:
- Remember "Yippee! We're at a corner that might go straight" to help keep your handling neutral and allow your dog to be fully responsible for choosing the right track.
- There may be natural contamination — treat it just like the intentional contamination.
- If your dog is doing well and his motivation is high, consider occasionally doing some intentional handler errors as described on pages 153 and 247 to proof your dog and help him understand that he is responsible for taking you down the good track.
- Show lots of enthusiasm when your dog finds the articles. Play with your dog at each article. Have a big party at the end of each track. Make it fun for your dog.

Evaluation and Possible Adaptations:
- When your dog notices the contamination and consistently chooses the good track, you know he understands — at least in those conditions.
- Note how your dog tracks, indicates the articles, how he investigates and sorts out the contamination, and his level of enthusiasm for the tracks.
- If he is doing well and appears to understand the concept, invite the contamination layer to bring along her dog (on a leash of course).

Sessions U3.x Blind TDU-like

U3.3, .7, .11, .15

Tracklayer:
- Flags as shown.
- Articles at the start & middle of each leg.
- Articles should be inconspicuous.
- Shape and leg lengths can vary.

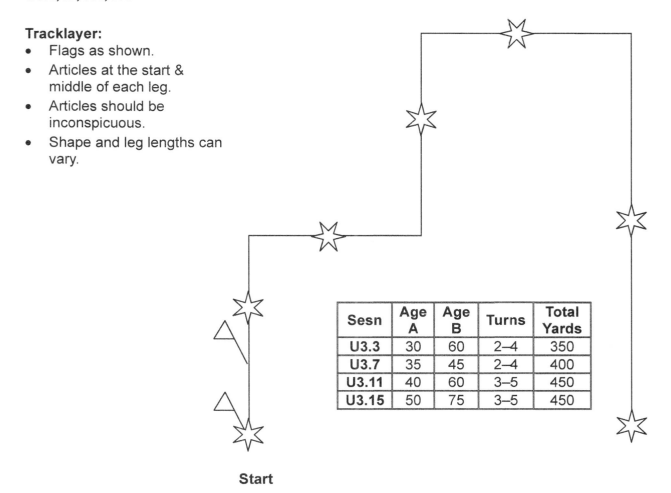

Sesn	Age A	Age B	Turns	Total Yards
U3.3	30	60	2–4	350
U3.7	35	45	2–4	400
U3.11	40	60	3–5	450
U3.15	50	75	3–5	450

Start

Purpose:
- Familiarize the dog and handler with TDU-complexity tracks.
- Allow the handler to improve her skills on blind tracks.

Tracklayer:
- Choose the track shape as shown above, one of the ones on page 290 or 116, or create your own to fit the site.
- OK to cross non-vegetated paths and roads but no turns on non-vegetated surfaces.
- Place an article at the start, in the middle of every leg, and the end.
- Walk behind the handler on each track.

Contamination Layer (CXT):
- Only add contamination if the site is not much used and there is little contamination.

Handler:
- Remember "Yippee! We're at a corner that might go straight" to help keep your handling neutral and allow your dog to be fully responsible for choosing the right track.
- There may be natural contamination — treat it just like the intentional contamination.
- Show lots of enthusiasm when your dog finds the articles. Play with your dog at each article. Have a big party at the end of each track. Make it fun for your dog.

Evaluation and Possible Adaptations:
- In your log, note the first two or three times you needed to help or significantly hint to your dog the correct choice. Note where on the track it happened, the nature of any nearby surface transitions, contamination, or distractions that might have influenced your dog or handler.
- If you are tempted to think your dog is lying to you when he commits to something that is not the track, please see the text box on page 366.
- Note how your dog tracks, indicates the articles, how he investigates and sorts out the contamination, and his level of enthusiasm for the tracks.
- If he is doing well and appears to understand the concept, invite the contamination layer to bring along her dog (on a leash of course).

Sessions U3.x Hard-Surface Tracks

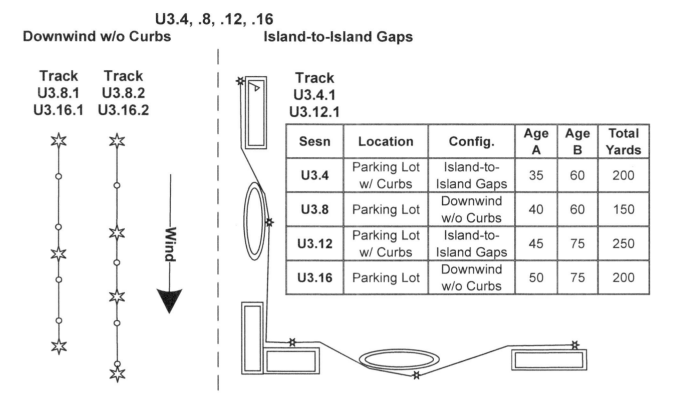

U3.4, .8, .12, .16

Downwind w/o Curbs — Island-to-Island Gaps

Track U3.8.1 Track U3.8.2
U3.16.1 U3.16.2

Track U3.4.1
U3.12.1

Sesn	Location	Config.	Age A	Age B	Total Yards
U3.4	Parking Lot w/ Curbs	Island-to-Island Gaps	35	60	200
U3.8	Parking Lot	Downwind w/o Curbs	40	60	150
U3.12	Parking Lot w/ Curbs	Island-to-Island Gaps	45	75	250
U3.16	Parking Lot	Downwind w/o Curbs	50	75	200

Purpose:
- Develop the dog's hard-surface tracking skills.

Tracklayer:
- Do either two straight downwind tracks out in a flat parking lot (U3.8, .16) or a curbed-island serpentine (U3.4, .12) but not both in the same session.
- Use small or inconspicuous articles along the leg every 40-60 yards so the dog finds them using his nose.
- Walk behind the handler on each track.

Handler:
- Use track age A unless the track age conditions on pages 256-267 are satisfied.
- Stay close to your dog, about 10'. Keep your dog within 3–10' of the track.
- Be patient and let your dog figure things out. Encourage only if needed.
- Show lots of enthusiasm when your dog finds the articles. Play with your dog at each article. Have a big party at the end of each track. Make it fun for your dog.

Evaluation:
- Note how your dog tracks, indicates the articles, how he investigates and sorts out the track on the flat hard surfaces, and his level of enthusiasm for the tracks.

Session U3.17 Review.

Review and summarize how your dog progressed on each of the four session types.

The key on how to proceed is whether you and your dog are passing the blind TDU-like tracks within the ½ hour to 2 hour age of the test. If you passed one or more of them without any tracklayer help, you are ready to enter a TDU test. If you don't already have an AKC TD, you will need to get certified by a judge. Once certified, find the next test in your area and enter it. While you wait to get into a test, either repeat some of this material or move right along to the next part that is preparing you for the VST as well as the CKC UTD & UTDX.

On the other hand, if you and your dog have not completed a blind TDU-like track without help yet, you will want to analyze the team's strengths and weaknesses based on all four session types.

Blind TDU	Marked TDU	Contamination	Hard Surface	Recommendation
Passed 1+	N/A	N/A	N/A	Enter a TDU and Proceed to Part IV VST.
Not Yet	Passed	N/A	N/A	Repeat half or all this phase becoming a less helpful handler while shifting the responsibility to your dog. Keep the reward schedule for success high.
"	Failing on lawns	Sometimes Takes	N/A	Repeat this phase doing more intentional and natural contamination tracks.
"	Failing near Non-Veg	N/A	Not fully focused	Repeat this phase doing extra hard-surface tracks and extra marked TDU tracks with lots of surface transitions.

Issues commonly arise at the transition from marked to blind tracks (e.g., this phase). While this is primarily a handler/trainer issue, it can also be a dog confidence issue. One approach is to slowly withdraw the flags and chalk marks. Start out marking the first part of the track but leave the last corner and last leg unmarked. Once that is successful, leave the last two corners and legs unmarked. When that is successful, mark only up to the first corner and then finally drop the first corner marking.

Evaluate if your dog has one or more weak skills. Also, evaluate if some of your skills need improvement. Select specific exercises or design tracks to focus on thee issues one at a time.

It is a good idea to review the material on Hinting and Helping on pages 258-259. Consistently hinting or helping your dog causes him to be dependent on your continuing to do so. You have to wean him off this extra support so he learns to rely on his own nose.

And review the descriptions of peaking for a test (page 150) and test day (page 154). These procedures are highly recommended for every tracking test including the TDU.

Sample Journal Log Entry — TDU-like

Session: *U3.6*
Dog: *Twizzle*
Date: *7/22/2014*
Layer: *Sil*
Location: *Legion Park*
Weather: *Sunny, warm*
Wind: *1-4*
Length: *435*
Age: *45*

Evaluation: Very good

Mild to severe contamination, lots of kids playing, distractions near playground.

Articles 2 & 7 missing.

She had trouble staying with the track near the building. Cat Pee perhaps, so I helped.

Very good elsewhere.
Investigated areas of heavy contamination. Made good choice but choices seemed fragile.

Handled bus turning around on roadway and kids playing distractions well.

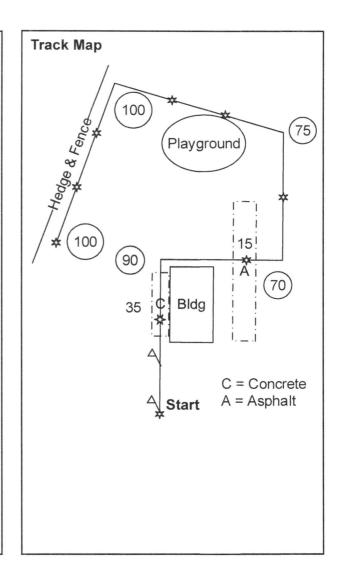

Track Map

Twizzle's TDU test is described in some detail on page 156.

Phase U3. Preparing for the TDU, and Foundations of the VST Journey.

Phase U3 Summary Log

Sesn	Site	Configuration	Date	Actual Age	Evaluation
U3.1		4-Corner Contaminated			
U3.2		Marked TDU-like			
U3.3		Blind TDU-like			
U3.4		Island-to-Island Gaps			
U3.5		4-Corner Contaminated			
U3.6		Marked TDU-like			
U3.7		Blind TDU-like			
U3.8		Downwind w/o curbs			
U3.9		4-Corner Contaminated			
U3.10		Marked TDU-like			
U3.11		Blind TDU-like			
U3.12		Island-to-Island Gaps			
U3.13		4-Corner Contaminated			
U3.14		Marked TDU-like			
U3.15		Blind TDU-like			
U3.16		Downwind w/o curbs			

Part IV — Advanced Urban Training for the VST, UTD, and UTDX

This part is for dogs who have already earned their TDU and are preparing for the more difficult CKC UTD or the much more difficult VST or UTDX tests. It is also suitable for a dog who has not been formally tested on a TDU but who has passed several informal TDU-like blind tracks, preferably in new locations where the dog and handler have not been training. Other dog/handler teams not meeting these prerequisites should use Part III TDU (page 255) to develop their urban foundation skills before commencing this more advanced training regimen.

For CKC tracking enthusiasts, their first urban test is the UTD, which can be entered after the dog earns his CKC TD. The UTD-hopeful dog will need to handle contamination and surface transitions just like the AKC TDU. In addition, the dog will need to handle corners on hard surface, non-vegetative surfaces accounting for about one-third of the track, and track age between one and two hours. The Phase V1S UTD Supplement on page 329 is a special phase designed to prepare the dog-handler team for the CKC UTD test after completing Phase V1. Since the CKC UTD is a prerequisite for the CKC UTDX, the supplement is a necessary phase for handlers focused on the Canadian tests. The supplement is optional for those focused only on the AKC VST.

The CKC UTDX and the AKC VST tests are virtually identical except for a few details: The scent-pad at the start instead of an article, and the use of wooden articles. Anyone entering UTDX training has to be familiar with scent-pad starts, so that is straightforward although the lack of an article to use for re-scenting can be problematic. The use of wooden articles turns out to be surprisingly easy for the dog to understand. So I will not include separate material for the UTDX. CKC participants can substitute UTDX for VST in any of the remaining text below.

Additional VST Handler and Dog Skills. The optimistic handler might say "Wow, I just passed my TDU! I just need to add a little age and additional work on hard-surface turns, and we'll be ready for the VST." Such a handler needs to be incredibly lucky with one of the best natural tracking dogs in the world to avoid disappointment. My advice is to control your goal seeking and focus on skills development and refinement before even thinking about being tested. If you rush to VST test-taking, you will neglect to build important fundamental skills and waste a lot of time miss-training your dog.

VST tracks are very complex for the dog and handler to negotiate even when they are plotted as the simplest track meeting the requirements of the test. This is because the test uses campus-like environments that interact with the tracklayer scent and create highly complex scenting situations. From the urban training earlier in this book, you have a good start on many of the necessary skills. Now you need to develop and refine them to handle the wide variety of conditions you will face in a VST test.

Here is a list of the important skills required for VST success:

Dog Skills:
1. Clear-Confident-Committed tracking on heavily-contaminated lawns including well-contaminated starts.
2. From "Cross the road and find it on the other side" (TDX & TDU) to "Clear-Confident-Committed tracking on large flat hard surfaces".
3. Turns on non-vegetated surfaces constrained by buildings and barriers.
4. Turning onto and off of narrow hard surfaces — sidewalks and driveways — with nearby vegetation.
5. Turning in the middle of large, flat hard-surface area (Moment of Truth turns).
6. Turning off scent-trapping channels like sidewalks with nearby buildings and alternative pathways.
7. Returning to lawns after lots of hard surface.
8. Being comfortable tracking in highly distracting urban environments with people and other dogs nearby, squirrels scampering from tree to tree, and pee-posts everywhere.
9. Staying focused for a whole track.
10. Clear-Confident-Committed tracking on 4–5 hour-old tracks in warm, dry weather.
11. Tracking and finding varied articles in many weather conditions.
12. Finding articles to the side of the dog's path.

Handler Skills:
A. Subtle encouragement and restraint to teach your dog his required skills.
B. Reading very fragile signals from your dog.
C. Shifting responsibility for "Staying with the good track" to your dog.
D. Learning how far off the footprints your dog might work tracklayer scent in different environments.
E. Accepting that your dog may move well off the track to investigate scent pools and scent distractions like doorways, loading docks, and storm drains.
F. Recovering from being off track. Specifically, helping your dog search a large area without taking responsibility away from your dog.
G. Safe tracking in parking lots full of cars and on lightly traveled roads.

The four VST phases will help you develop these dog skills and handling skills in a step-by-step fashion. Phase V1 develops the dog's hard-surface turns and continues to improve his understanding of contamination. Phase V2 continues that development to include MOT turns (unconstrained hard-surface turns) while adding age as well. Phase V3 brings those separately developed skills together and prepares the handler for blind tracks. Phase V4 completes the preparation of the dog-handler team for this most challenging test.

Microclimatology — Scent Movement and Distribution. The VST track scent component that is most useful to the dog is the volatile chemicals evaporating off the tracklayer's skin rafts. The scent of crushed vegetation and disturbed dirt is unreliable because so much of the vegetation and dirt have been crushed by others who happen to have walked across the track both before and after it was laid.

The motion of people and vehicles causes turbulence that moves scent around. VST tracks use heavily-traveled pathways and lightly-traveled roads and parking lots, so there is a lot of potential scent movement.

The differing albedo, or reflective properties, of urban surfaces causes them to be at quite different temperatures in the sunshine. You may find the sunlit asphalt is 20–30°F hotter than sunlit concrete that is 20–30°F hotter than shaded surfaces. These thermal differences cause air to move and scent to flow with it. They also cause the track to age differently in warm, dry places than in cooler ones.

Wind interacting with man-made structures creates vortexes and eddies at ground level out to three to eight-times the height of the buildings. These vortexes act like miniature tornadoes and can move the track scent substantially away from where it was first shed by the tracklayer

Typical campus architecture creates spaces with a high potential for turbulence and scent movement, like these tall buildings with an archway creating a "wind tunnel":

A smaller scale narrow passage has its own unique potential for scent movement:

A wide open plaza presents many mechanisms for scent to move:

The sun hitting the side of a building will heat it causing air to rise next to the building and eventually cool and fall some distance from the wall. The track scent will circulate with the air flow. You may notice your dog working a track 5–20 yards or more from the face of a sunlit building where the track had been laid quite close to the building. Or, the track scent may be close to the building when the tracklayer had walked well to the side. The best track scent may not be right over the footprints.

Man-made buildings are not the only things that cause wind turbulence to move scent. Natural trees interact with the wind as well, but their smoother shape and more porous nature mean the wind-tree interaction is not as strong. Fences, in particular chain-link fences, are famous for pushing or pulling the scent considerable distances. Passing cars will move scent in their turbulence. Even pedestrians will move scent in their wake.

Wind interacting with undulating slopes causes turbulence that moves scent around:

Man-made berms along roadways provide long stretches of lawn suitable for legs of tracks where the track scent is likely to flow down the slopes of the berm and settle some distance to the side.

Storm drains have distracting smells themselves as well as affecting the flow of air and scent nearby. As your dog investigates a storm drain, remember the line he was tracking before he diverted to the storm drain and look around for a possible article placed nearby.

Models of Scent Movement

The wind farm pictured here was inspired by Terri Everwine's use of a similar apparatus at her seminar. It is a matrix of little flags at four different heights with a wooden building somewhat higher than the main layer of flags. A large fan on the left blows steadily to the right.

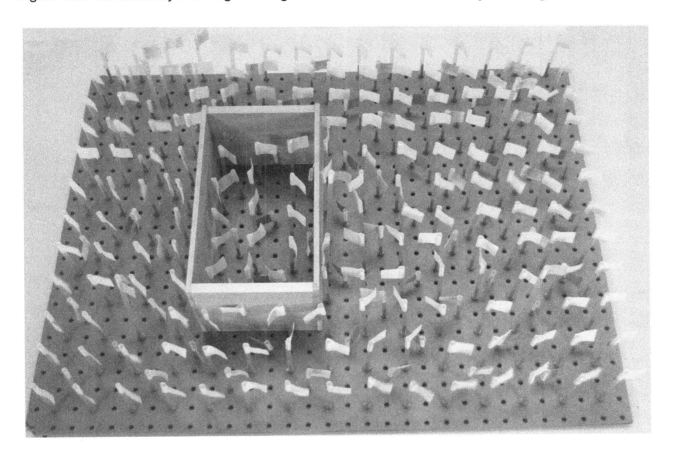

To the left (upwind) of the building, the flags are pointing in a variety of directions. The flags in the lower-left corner of the picture are generally indicating airflow around the near side of the building where a good deal of turbulence is indicated by some flags pointing to the left. The flow on the upper side of the building is far from uniform but not so obviously turbulent. To the right (downwind) of the building, there appear to be irregular turbulent flows out some distance. The flags at the far right of the wind farm indicate the flow has mostly straightened out at 2½ times the height of the building. The shorter flags, which are more difficult to see in this picture, do show ongoing turbulence near the ground at the far right side of the wind farm.

Even the simplest rectangular building has this effect as shown in the rough sketch on the right. The curving arcs of the dashed lines should be interpreted figuratively as both horizontal and vertical spinning and mixing of the air and scent particles. The interested reader should see the relevant texts by Conover (2007), Foken (2008), Oke (1978), Pagen (1993), and Syrotuck (1972) that include a variety of diagrams and illustrations to help you understand turbulence and wind flow near natural and man-made flow obstructions.

The idea of looking at the wind diagram to the right and the wind farm on the previous page is not to suggest you need to become a fluid-flow engineer to handle a tracking dog. It is to sensitize you to the potential for scent moving widely so you can accept that sometimes your dog will track well to the side of the tracklayer's footsteps.

You will learn a lot more by watching your dog work even if the way he works does not match the way you would like the best scent to be located. Go back to a particular area after the track and use a Smoke Pencil or other airflow visualization tool — see www.smokepencil.com.

Choice Points and Complexity. Any place along a track where a dog has to make a decision because of contamination, surface transition, scent movement due to wind vortexes, or corners, is called a choice point. Full VST tracks will have dozens to hundreds of choice points — that is one reason the test is so difficult. In our early VST training, we are going to try to limit track complexity somewhat so the dog can be mostly successful, and then very gradually increase it to realistic VST levels over the course of the four phases. So learning to recognize the choice points your dog notices will help you learn to maintain track complexity at an appropriate level for your dog's current skill level. See page 384 for additional discussion of choice points.

Handling. Most handlers became very good at handling their dogs in TD, TDU, and TDX because their dogs became very skilled and as a result were Clear-Confident-Committed to each leg along the track. Due to the very fragile nature of scent in urban environments, the high levels of contamination, and the frequent surface changes, dogs will not be as clear, confident, or strongly committed on a VST track as they were on other test tracks. That means the handler will have to become much more skilled at reading her dog's subtle signs while following the track. Relax; get used to it; you need to become a fully-contributing member of your tracking team.

Key handling concepts are discussed in further detail starting on page 362 in Phase V3. While your early VST tracks will be marked, you may want to look ahead and get an image of how your handling is going to need to evolve to become an expert VST handler.

Motivation. Like TDX, VST training can be stressful for the dog if progress is made too quickly, the weather becomes warm and dry, the handler does not express her deep appreciation for the dog's work even when imperfect, or an intact bitch's hormones affect her mood. Do your best to maintain motivation at a very high level. Use freeze-dried tiny-treats on your tracks, particularly on hard surfaces, throughout your VST training. Watch for a lack of excitement approaching the start flag, messing around at the start, and slow commitment to each leg as signs of reduced motivation. If you find your dog has become demotivated, consider the re-motivation plan in the supplement on page 408.

Be Aware — Better Safe than Sorry. You will be tracking your dog in a wide variety of situations where some diligence can protect your dog from danger. Oil, coolant, and other toxic liquids can dribble out of parked cars and pool on the asphalt. If you notice any as you are laying a track, just stop laying the track; it can still be used up to the previous article. Typically these puddles are washed away in a heavy rain.

Chemical fertilizers, herbicides and pesticides that may have been recently applied to lawns and landscaping should be avoided as well. It is safest to track where dandelions and other wide- leaf weeds grow in the lawn. Sometimes the landscape people put up little signs saying what they have applied, but that is the exception rather than the rule. Generally, most herbicide warning labels suggest that they are safe for pets as soon as they are dry, but one wonders if the chemical company considers the intense nose-down sniffing that many tracking dogs use when following difficult tracks. QT was well known to finish a track with a black beard and tongue because he would lick the asphalt when struggling to take advantage of his vomeronasal organ to complement his nasal olfactory system. His licking may have also dissolved chemicals that used back-channel flow to reach the main olfactory system in his nose.

Traffic presents a problem even in low-volume driveways and parking lots. When tracking through a lot of parked cars, visibility is hampered requiring even more diligence on the handler's part. Typically the tracklayer acts as a second set of eyes and ears to warn the handler that a car is coming. But the handler must be responsible for her dog and herself and be watchful of moving cars or even people getting into a parked vehicle and about to drive away.

VST Equipment. The same harness and 40' or 49' line is appropriate for VST as it is for all tracking levels. Management of the forty-foot line takes some care to avoid it getting caught on the variety of nooks and crannies that all seem to want to grab it as it drags behind you. The flags you use will typically be small landscaping flags, and the articles are pieces of material rather than personal objects.

The picture to the right shows typical VST articles. Starting from the middle of the top: a metal lid, a piece of denim, a plastic switch plate cover, a square of leather, a square of rug, and a half an insole are all full-sized articles. Below those are a plastic lid, and a half sock of intermediate size. Below those are a small piece of sock, a fruit juice lid, a spice jar lid, and a small piece of leather – all are good for practice but too small for test articles. At the bottom is a field book for keeping your session-by-session track details. On the left are two small landscaping flags and above them are two with the flagging rolled up in a straw so they will be invisible from a distance.

Varieties of Non-Vegetated Surfaces. Much of your non-vegetated training will be on concrete, asphalt or brick, but many different types of non-vegetated surfaces are used in tests so should be included with some frequency in your training. Dirt, mud, gravel, sand, stone, mulch, and tree litter are all common even on neat college campuses and business parks. Strips of carpet, wooden walkways, or areas of artificial grass are also possible. So make sure you include enough practice using all of them in a variety of ways so your dog is comfortable tracking on them.

This segment of forest litter next to a campus building is quite suitable for a VST leg even though it also looks like it could be part of a TDX track.

Become a VST Test Spectator or Tracklayer. Attending VST tests as a spectator, tracklayer, or worker will greatly enhance your understanding of the test. As you go through the phases of VST training, take the time to visit tests at all the sites you might consider entering once you are ready. Watch all the tracks you can, watch the more successful dogs and handlers even if they don't happen to pass that day, sketch the tracks in your notebook to have a better idea what realistic VST tracks are like, take pictures of the areas used and talk to others who are also in training for new ideas that might help you and your dog. It is useful to collect a library of VST tracks plotted on Google Earth so you will be able to refer to them later in your training when you want to plot some realistic test-like training tracks. Spend more than a year watching VST tests before you think about entering a test yourself.

As you follow along on a VST test track, take time to observe the changes in wind direction and speed as you approach buildings and groups of buildings. Pay attention to the changes in temperature as the track transitions from sun to shade and back again. Feel the heat radiated off sunlit walls. In warm weather, stoop down and feel the temperature of each of the surfaces along the track. All these micro-environmental changes influence the aging of the scent and the location of the strongest scent relative to the track itself.

Phase V1. VST Hard-Surface Corners

Purpose:
- Develop the dog's understanding of hard-surface turns to expand his skill in working them successfully.
- Maintain a high level of motivation.

Strategy:
- Systematically introduce hard-surface turns using open angles against barriers.
- Then sharpen the corners to 90° while aging and reducing barriers.
- Continue to enrich the dog's experience with intentional contamination.

How to use this chapter:
- Read the discussion section that follows and look through the table on the next page, which summarizes the training structure of this phase.
- Do each of the 20 sessions that rotate between campuses, urban lawns, and parking lots. Before each session, carefully review the detailed tracklaying and handling instructions for each type of tracking session on pages 317 through 326.
- You may find it convenient to copy the session detail pages so your tracklayer has the details she needs to lay the desired tracks.
- Keep a detailed log of each session using a format like the one shown on page 31 and keep a summary log like the one shown on page 328.
- Finally, do the review session on page 327 to evaluate your dog's progress and your own training-skill development.

Discussion:

This phase will weave together sessions to develop and improve the first four dog skills from page 302:
- Clear-Confident-Committed Tracking on Heavily-contaminated Lawns.
- Clear-Confident-Committed Tracking on Flat Hard Surfaces.
- Constrained Turning on Non-vegetated Surfaces.
- Turning from vegetation onto hard surfaces and from hard surfaces onto vegetation.

It presumes the dog has the skills developed in Part III Phases U1–U3, so review that material before proceeding.

One-half of this phase's sessions are at schools, campuses, and parks with sidewalks and paved areas that can be used for teaching hard-surface turns at barriers. One-quarter of these sessions are on similar sites with minimal sidewalk crossings where the training focus is on intentional contamination. The remaining sessions are on parking lots or large plazas with curbed islands separated by some narrow and wide gaps. It is fine to adjust the order of the sessions to suit your ability to use different tracking sites on particular days of the week. Do try to get all the work done in roughly the indicated order.

Phase V1 Session Schedule:

% Motivational Sessions	Range: 10–30%	Your Target:

Sesn	Location	Configuration	Age A	Track 1 HS Turn	Track 1 Leg Yards	Track 2 HS Turn	Track 2 Leg Yard	Track A Gap Size	Track A Trk Yard
V1.1	Urban Lawn w/ Path & Roads	Zigzags with HS Turn at barrier	30	150° (30°)	50–100	135° (45°)	50–100		
V1.2		4-Turn Track with Slices & Bisects	45						300–500
V1.3		Zigzags with HS Turn at barrier	35	135° (45°)	50–100	120° (60°)	50–100		
V1.4	Parking Lot w/ Curbs	Island-to-Island Gaps	20					15–40	150–350
V1.5	Urban Lawn w/ Path & Roads	Zigzags with HS Turn at barrier	40	120° (60°)	50–100	90°	50–100		
V1.6		4-Turn Track with Slices & Bisects	60						350–500
V1.7		Zigzags with HS Turn at Curb	45	135° (45°)	50–100	120° (60°)	50–100		
V1.8	Parking Lot w/ Curbs	Island-to-Island Gaps	30					15–50	200–400
V1.9	Urban Lawn w/ Path & Roads	Zigzags with HS Turn at Curb	50	120° (60°)	50–100	90°	50–100		
V1.10		4-Turn Track with Slices & Bisects	75						350–500
V1.11		Zigzags with HS Turn at Curb	55	90°	50–100	90°	50–100		
V1.12	Parking Lot w/ Curbs	Island-to-Island Gaps	40					15–75	300–400
V1.13		Evaluate to Proceed or Repeat V1.1-V1.12							
V1.14	Park Lawn w/ Path & Roads	Zigzags with HS Turn on Driveway	30	135° (45°)	50–100	120° (60°)	50–100		
V1.15			45	120° (60°)	50–100	90°	50–100		
V1.16			60	90°	50–100	90°	50–100		
V1.17		4-Turn Track with Slices & Bisects	90						350–500
V1.18		Zigzags with HS Turn on Flat Parking Lot	30	135° (45°)	50–100	120° (60°)	50–100		
V1.19			45	120° (60°)	50–100	90°	50–100		
V1.20			60	90°	50–100	90°	50–100		
V1.21	Parking Lot w/ Curbs	Island-to-Island Gaps	50					15–75	300–400
		Evaluate to Proceed							

- See pages 256 and 313 for descriptions of the alternative track-age plans: Age B and C.

In addition, some percentage of your tracks should be motivational tracks — perhaps an hour-old zigzag on a little-contaminated sports field. They are to be just fun for your dog and you. The percentage of motivational tracks you need in this phase depends on your dog: if over 2-3 sessions you see your dog is slow to commit at starts that you think should be easy, increase the percentage of tracking sessions that consist of a simple motivational track.

V1 Track Designs. In each of the schedule's four-session training stages, we use the training pattern of two sessions of zigzag tracks with one hard-surface turn interspersed with a session on contamination and a session of curbed-island serpentines. The zigzags open hard-surface turns and progress to 90°; then the size of the barrier is reduced, and the process is repeated from open to 90°. This helps your dog understand the need to search and find the new leg while the barrier prevents or discourages overshooting the turn. At the end of these twelve sessions, we evaluate and decide if your dog is confident enough to start doing corners without barriers. If not, we repeat some of the recent exercises in different locations and at different ages.

- Hard-surface-turn tracks V1.1, .3, .5, .7, .9, .11 can use the track design shown on page 317 adjusted to the actual site configuration. The barrier is to limit the dog's choices to just left-right. As the sessions progress, the angle is sharpened to 90°, and the barrier is reduced in size until it is just a curb. In the picture below, track #1 shows a typical open turn against a building as an example of V1.5.1. The photographs on page 341 show other sites with similar opportunities.

- Hard-surface-turn tracks V1.14–.16, .18–.20 are similar but remove the barrier at the turn. The first three sessions turn in the middle of a driveway and the second set turn well out in a parking lot. In the picture below, track #2 shows an open turn on a driveway as an example of V1.14.2 or V1.15.1.

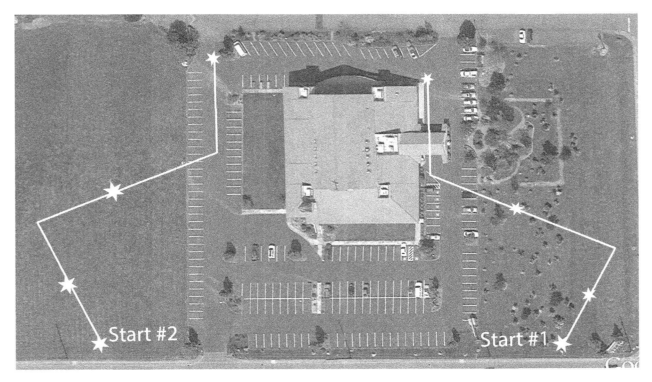

7. *Image © 2016 Google*

- Intentional contamination tracks V1.2, .6, .10, .17 should be kept simple like the design shown on page 319, but any three- or four-corner track shape can be used like those shown on page 290. Of course, the actual track shape should vary each time as well as the details of the intentional contamination. As your dog becomes confident in choosing the correct track, the contamination layer should bring along another dog to make the contamination more interesting and then make the angle of crossing shallower to further challenge your dog.

- Curbed-Island tracks with large gaps V1.4, .8, .12, .21 can use the design shown below as an example but adapted to your local parking lot. You may also find some shopping center parking lots have islands at the end of every other double row of parking spaces; that configuration works well for this exercise. To minimize your dog's tendency to just run to visible articles, use very small or inconspicuous flat articles mid-gap in place of food drops or omit the mid-gap rewards.

Finding good parking-lot islands requires some investigation. You are looking for islands at the end of each row or double row of parking spaces so the gaps are not too wide. In the picture below, the total length is 250 yards, the narrow gaps are 8 yards, and the wide gaps vary from 20–40 yards.

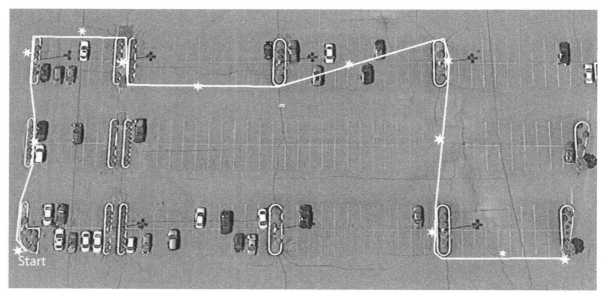

8. Image © 2016 Google

Once your dog is lowering his nose while tracking across the small gaps (see Part III exercises on page 297), you can progress to using wide gaps. Typical narrow gaps are about 5-10 yards wide. Medium gaps created by mall-type every other double-row islands are about 15-30 yards wide. Really wide gaps can be almost any length.

In this hard-surface training:
- Don't expect your dog's nose to be flat against the asphalt; most dogs will track with a higher nose carriage than on grass.
- Don't expect your dog to be as close to the footsteps on asphalt or concrete as he is on lawn; accept your dog is tracking even though he is paralleling the track several feet to several yards to the side.
- If your dog's nose is low and right over the footsteps, enjoy your clever dog.

VST Training Track Age. This phase has three recommended "Track Ages" much like the TDU phases (see pages 256-267).

A. "Age A" is for dogs who have done most of their urban work at 30 minutes to 1½ hours. For the mixed surface tracks, it carefully steps up age during this phase to 90 minutes in small increments. For the hard-surface-only tracks, it steps up age more slowly.

B. "Age B" is for dogs with extensive experience with older tracks, or for dogs who have completed this sequence once with the careful age stepping and the handler wishes to improve the dog's fundamental skills by repeating this phase. Rather than prescribe particular times, this choice asks you to vary the times between one hour and 4 hours on each session. It does not mean to keep all sessions in a narrow range of times that happen to be convenient for you; it means to vary the time so the dog is exposed to all age conditions on an ongoing basis.

C. "Age C" is for dogs whose confidence or skill level suffers as the tracks get older under "Age A." It simply slows down the aging while working through the material to develop the skills and will later step up age carefully in a later phase. Try half or two-thirds the Age A times and adjust to keep your dog fairly successful. Increase the age gradually over the next 2-3 phases.

The careful stepping up of age is a powerful tool to improve the dog's skill and confidence on older tracks. Simply doing all your tracks at 3–5 hours is not very effective but slowly stepping up in age once, twice or three times will really improve your dog's confidence on older tracks. So I recommend Age A for most dogs, or Age C for dogs who show a lack of confidence on older tracks (regardless of their experience with older tracks).

Individualizing the V1 Schedule. This phase is substantial and will take the typical team more than a couple of months to complete. You may well experience a seasonal weather change during this time that will also affect your dog's tracking acumen and confidence. Regardless of whether you follow Age A, B, or C, work through the seasonal change adjusting the times up or down as appropriate to keep the sessions positive and productive.

Some dogs with really good fundamentals, combined with great natural tracking talent, may zip through this material while others may need to repeat sections of it, or the whole sequence, to fully develop the needed skills. Your eventual success in a VST test depends on your dog strongly developing these skills regardless of whether he does so quickly or more slowly. You, as the trainer, need to evaluate his actual skill in these exercises and choose to repeat some material or push forward. Be patient, be willing to repeat (but don't get stuck for too long). Be willing to push ahead and come back if pushing ahead does not work.

While your dog does not need to fully meet the following criteria, he should be close before progressing to MOT turns in Phase V2:

- For intentional contamination tracks V1.2, .6, .10, .17: without any help from you, is he making the right choice three out of the four times he notices the contamination? If he commits to the contamination more than 25% of the time, contamination will interfere with learning by keeping you off kilter and your dog under-rewarded for his cleverness. Do more contamination exercises at different tracking sites, with various contamination layers crossing at difficult locations along the tracks like corners, transitions and starts, and at various delays relative to the track age. Simplify the track shape and the contamination and then progressively make the track more complicated and the contamination more devious.

- For hard-surface tracks, most of the time, is his nose lowered toward the surface, close to the track, and is he moving parallel to the actual track? When he fails to stay close to the track, is he using the scent pooling against vertical surfaces like curbs, walls or bushes? Or do you

need to help him by constraining his movement for him to get back to the track? If he needs help much of the time, he won't be able to solve MOT turns without help or luck, so you are better off doing Phase V1 material again, with variations, so he gains experience and skill.
- For turns on narrow hard surfaces like sidewalks, is he making the right choice without any help almost all the time for 90º corners? It is OK if he makes the choice by fringing the turn by sniffing the grass or bushes at the edge of the sidewalk, although ideally, he would solve it by putting his nose down on the footprints in the middle of the sidewalk.
- As a handler, have you developed your subtle encouragement and restraint skills so you can help him when he needs help and let him work things out by himself most of the time?

Shifting Responsibility to the Dog. In your VST-level training, you will need to help your dog several times a track. Use the smallest assistance necessary to allow him to make the decisions, if at all possible. Use hints as needed (page 259) and use the hierarchy of help described on page 258 to guide the type of help you offer your dog.

Regardless of how little and how well you offer help, your dog will learn it is useful to pay attention to your posture and behavior, particularly when he is unsure. In fact, he has been spending his whole life becoming an expert in your behaviors so he can get the best deal for himself from you. So whenever your dog is doing well on a track or a track segment, you can gently misdirect with your posture and behavior to reduce your dog's reliance on your signals.

Many of your training tracks in this phase and future phases will be known because the tracklayer used flags and chalk to mark the track, because you laid the track yourself, or because your tracklayer is actively saying things to indicate where the track goes. Having knowledge of the track is important so you can develop your dog's skills to the high level needed to be successful on blind test tracks of VST complexity. However, you do need to try to avoid communicating everything you know to your dog.

Some typical conscious or unconscious handler behaviors that hint or help the dog are listed below, along with substitute behaviors you can use to extinguish your dog's dependency on your knowing where the track goes:
- Turning your body in the direction of the next leg before your dog commits to the leg. Instead, keep your body facing the heading of the incoming leg until you need to pivot to watch your dog circle in his search pattern; and make sure these pivots are in response to the dog rather than because the next leg goes in a particular direction.
- Stopping at a corner when your dog overshoots. Instead, note the corner position to yourself but continue behind your dog another 30–50' or so to give your dog the opportunity to signal he is out of scent. If the dog struggles well past the corner, you can always back up to the corner; but first try to let your dog search back there, giving you the opportunity to follow him back to the area of the corner.
- Checking, restraining or stopping your dog every time he investigates a little bit in the wrong direction. Instead, let the line out so your dog has the time and distance to sort things out for himself.
- Following your dog on a new leg just as soon as he heads in generally the correct direction. Instead, stand in place and let the line slide between your fingers until he gets to the end of the line. Once you do start to follow, climb back up the line to 15' or to your normal following distance.

For dogs early in their VST training, you can use any of the handling behaviors listed above to make it easy for your dog to gain confidence in the complex scenting conditions in a positive way. For a more complete list of helping and hinting behaviors, see pages 258 and 259.

A helpful training technique when a dog is tentative about committing to a leg is to sidestep out behind your dog while giving your dog more line to make it easy for him to commit. You can also say encouraging words. These are teaching moments, not testing.

However, later in your VST training, you will need to reduce and withdraw hints and help to fully shift responsibility to your dog. Your eventual goal is for your dog to be Clear-Confident-Committed so you can let the line out to 35–40' on every corner or choice point as the dog commits and then immediately climb up the line to 15–20'. Only do this when your dog is confident; to build his confidence, support him by following more quickly or helping him as necessary.

Reading your Dog. You need to focus your attention on what your dog does when he tracks on lightly-contaminated lawn, heavily trampled lawn, at transitions to hard surfaces, extended segments of hard surfaces, at transitions back to grass, near buildings, fences, and hedges. Wind, sun, temperature, and humidity will all affect what the scent is doing and determine how your dog behaves as he follows it.

You also should learn to tell when he starts to focus on pee mail. I use a sharp "Yuck! Back to the track." I do this when I see my dog focusing on pee mail even when the pee mail is right on the track. You might get by on field tracks with a dog you have to plead with to leave pee mail, but there is just too much of it in urban test sites to hope your track does not go near it. Also, see the acclimation discussion on the next page concerning other distractions.

Your light-comfortable tension is likely to be quite a bit lighter than it was in the field, but there should continue to be some tension (don't let the line hang down and touch the ground between you and your dog).

When you see a change in behavior, that is the time to stop, say "Yippee! I am on a corner that might go straight" regardless of whether you know where the track is or can see footprints in the grass. Your stop may be brief if he quickly recognizes it as contamination and returns to the good track. But stop you should.

This is a good time to use video and study what your dog looks like when reviewing it without the stress of actually doing the handling in real time. Use your detailed log to record what you notice about his posture, head carriage, tail carriage, ear carriage, changes in sniffing patterns, changes of direction, or other behaviors.

Acclimation. Typical VST test sites contain many challenging distractions. To be successful, both you and your dog need to learn to be comfortable and able to focus with many distractions all vying for your attention.

Tracklayer to the handler: "Honest. No one was around when I laid the track 3 hours ago!"

Acclimation is for both the dog and the handler. Review the previous discussions on acclimation and distractions on pages 100, 216, and in particular 260 where people, animal, machine and pee mail are all discussed in some detail.

- Spend some quality time with your dog working on acclimation independently of your main tracking training.
- Remain aware in your practice sessions when distractions affect your dog's tracking focus or your ability to concentrate on your dog. These are the kinds of distractions that need more targeted acclimation work separate from your tracking training.
- Also, evaluate how well you are able to be aware of moving cars, people and dogs walking in the vicinity, or machines moving, while also keeping your dog in focus. This can be a safety issue where, for example, you have to restrain your dog from moving between parked cars into a roadway when a car is coming along beyond the parked cars.
- Handlers who can enter a Zen State (page 388) when on a blind track will be less likely to mess up their dog due to their own distractions.

Sessions V1.x Two Zigzags with One Hard-Surface Turn Against a Barrier.

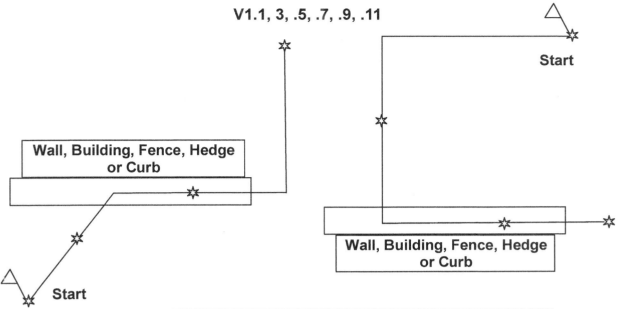

Session	Age A	Track 1 HS Turn	Track 1 Leg Yards	Track 2 HS Turn	Track 2 Leg Yards
V1.1	30	150° (30°)	50–100	135° (45°)	50–100
V1.3	35	135° (45°)	50–100	120° (60°)	50–100
V1.5	40	120° (60°)	50–100	90°	50–100
V1.7	45	135° (45°)	50–100	120° (60°)	50–100
V1.9	50	120° (60°)	50–100	90°	50–100
V1.11	55	90°	50–100	90°	50–100

Purpose:
- Teach your dog to indicate loss of scent and search for the new leg on the hard surface.
- Teach him that he can find the new leg on the hard surface.

Tracklayer:
- V1.1, .3, .5, require a hard surface with lawn on one side for the incoming leg and some sort of barrier on the other like a building, fence, or hedge. The outgoing leg runs alongside the barrier.
- V1.7, .9, .11 require a hard surface with lawn on one side for the incoming leg and a curb on the other side. The outgoing leg runs alongside the barrier.
- You make the appropriate open-angle turn near the barrier, and the next leg stays on the hard surface for 30 or more yards.
- Each track has an open turn that steadily sharpens to 90° over several sessions. Remember the angles listed describe the corner angle, not your change in direction. So for the 150° corner, you will turn 30°. In the schedule, I show the corner angle first, and the angle the tracklayer turns herself in parenthesis. See the compass diagram on page 72.
- Use right and left hard-surface turns. It can be either the first or second turn.

- Use chalk on the hard surface to mark the corner and the direction of the new leg.
- Set a reward point 30–40 yards down the hard-surface leg by placing a small or inconspicuous article there. Or place a tiny treat at 20–25 yards with the small or inconspicuous article about 10-20 yards beyond that.

Handler:
- Be patient at each hard-surface corner; don't rush your dog to make a decision.
- Ideally, use your whole line to allow your dog to make the choice before you move forward. Until your dog gains confidence, it is OK to make it easy for him to follow the track there.
- If your dog chooses the wrong direction, let him investigate at least 30' before restraining him.
  - Ask him if this is the good track.
  - Re-scent him if you need to reel him in to you.
  - Use the steps of help on page 258.
- Give lots of treats and praise at each article.

Evaluation and Possible Adaptations:
- Note in your journal and your summary log (page 328) details of each track, how your dog worked the track, and how you handled him.
- If he needs help on most hard-surface corners:
  - Use scent intensifiers like bare feet or SIAB (see page 8).
  - Try younger age (fresher scent) and then age more slowly.
  - Repeat these sessions several times.
- If he lacks confidence on many hard-surface turns:
  - Add very small freeze-dried treats at 5, 10 & 15 yards past the hard-surface turn for a while. Then just use a small freeze-dried treat at 20 yards and a small or inconspicuous article at 30–40 yards past the corner. Then remove the treat but continue with the inconspicuous reward article.
  - Repeat several sessions in different locations with less natural contamination.

Tracklaying Tips

Three of these session types require specific angles for the hard-surface turns. See the corner angle diagram on page 72 that shows the required angles and can help the tracklayer lay the proper track angles.

A plastic protractor can also be a helpful tracklayer tool. But none of these angles need to be exact so long as the tracks provide angles that get progressively smaller towards 90°.

Sessions V1.x Four-Turn Track with Slices and Bisects

V1.2, .6, .10, .17

Tracklayer:
- Flags as shown.
- Articles at the start, middle of each leg and end.
- Leg lengths can vary.

Contamination layer:
- Cross the track as soon as the tracklayer finishes a leg.
- Cross at the start, gradually reduce your crossing angle from 45°, 30°, to 15°.
- Slice or bisect each corner.
- Extend crosstracks 20+ yards to the side of track

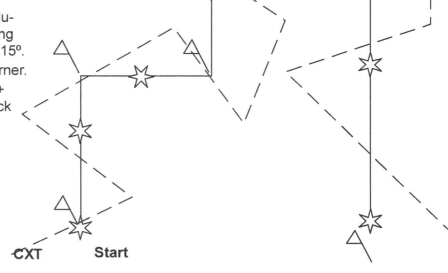

Sesn	Age A	Total Yards
V1.2	45	
V1.6	60	300–
V1.10	75	500
V1.17	90	

Purpose:
- Improve and maintain focus on the good track in the presence of contamination.

Tracklayer:
- Lay a simple TD-like track with four corners like shown above, or a hat or zigzag as shown on page 288.
- Make a scent pad at the start even for AKC trackers. A scent pad is made by trampling a one-meter square close to the start flag.
- Flag the start, each corner and the end (6 flags).
- Place an article at the start, in the middle of every leg, and the end.
- Optionally, add a tiny treat between each article and corner.

Contamination Layer:
- Lay the contamination just as the tracklayer finishes a leg or any time thereafter.
- If the dog is doing well sorting out the contamination, bring along your own dog on leash.
- Cross the start at 45°. If the dog is confident, reduce the angle to 30° and then 15°.
- Dashed line above shows one contamination path but vary it. Cross mid-leg once or twice.
- At corners, slice half of them and bisect the other half.

Handler:
- Approach the start flag first on the opposite side from the contamination layer.
  - When your dog is confident, approach from midway between the lines of approach of the tracklayer and contamination layer.
- Be patient as your dog sorts out the scent discrimination required by the contamination.
- Don't rush your dog to make a decision.
- Ideally, use your whole line to allow your dog to make the choice before you move forward along the good track or restrain him on the contamination.
- If your dog chooses the wrong direction, let him investigate at least 30' before restraining him.
  - Ask him "is this the good track?" when he is well out along on the contamination.
  - Remember this is a question, not a correction.
  - Restrain if he commits to the contamination.
  - See steps of hinting on page 259 and helping on page 258.
- Give lots of treats and praise at each article.

Evaluation:
- Each time your dog notices the contamination, he has a learning opportunity.
- You want to see your dog notice the contamination several times along each track, and consistently choose, without assistance, to return to the good track.
- In training, be happy to help your dog by restraining him or even showing him the good track — this is a learning opportunity you both have in practice rather than at a test.
- Note in your journal and your summary log (page 328) details of each track.

Proofing for Contamination

This is one of my favorite exercises. Use it all through your more advanced urban training.
- Once your dog is really solid on a single contamination layer, have the contamination layer take along her own dog on leash.
- Once the dog is reliable on dog walkers, let multiple people (and dogs) contaminate the track walking side-by-side, taking different paths, or at different times as you age the track.
- Have someone contaminate right before or as you start your dog on the track. They can also come up to the two of you and want to pet your dog. This is something that will happen several times in your dog's tracking career, so practice it in a controlled way.

Sessions V1.x Curbed-Island Serpentines with Big Gaps

V1.x.4, .8, .12, .21

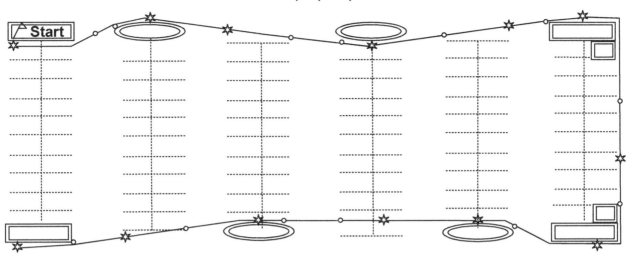

Sesn	Age A	Gap Size	Total Yards
V1.4	20	15–40	150–350
V1.8	30	15–50	200–400
V1.12	40	15–75	300–400
V1.20	50	15–75	300–400

Purpose:
- Help the dog focus on following the track on flat hard surfaces.
- Practice 90° corners on hard surface supported by curbs.

Tracklayer:
- These tracks require a sequence of islands often found at the end of parking rows. Try to find a sequence of islands with one or more wide gaps of the approximate size indicated in the chart above.
  - Typical every double row islands are 5-10 yards apart. Every other double row islands are 15-30 yards apart.
- Start along a curb and use an article.
- At the end of that island, randomly choose the side of the next island. If the dog is doing well, you can turn up to 90° at the end of an island.
- Use chalk on the hard surface to mark the angle you leave one island and the curb where you join the next island.
- Mid-gap and where the track rejoins the curb, put down a small piece of freeze-dried treat unless the handler asks for no food.
- For gaps over 15 yards wide, place an inconspicuous or small article midway across instead of the treat. The article should be inconspicuous so the dog can find it with its nose before he finds it with his eyes.
- Halfway down each island, place an article.
- Repeat for the sequence of islands for the distance indicated.

Handler:
- Be patient at the gaps, don't rush your dog to make a decision.
- Ideally, use your whole line to allow your dog to get across the gap before you move forward. Until your dog gains confidence, it is OK to make it easy for him to follow the track there.
- If your dog chooses the wrong side of the next island, let him investigate at least 30' before restraining him.
  - There will be tracklayer scent over on the opposite curb. Your dog is not wrong, just not as right as we want him to be.
  - The correct side has an article, so we hope your dog chooses to cross the island to indicate the article. Any attempt to do so should be encouraged.
  - If he insists on staying on the wrong side, back up into the gap. Let your dog sort it out and find the other side by himself.
- Give lots of treats and praise at each article.

Evaluation:
- It is more important for your dog to learn to track across the gap than to skip across and find the right side of the island.
- Note any lowering of the head as your dog crosses the gap even if it is to the side of the actual footsteps.

You are looking for your dog to lower his nose in the flat gaps between islands and track across the gaps rather than run across and look for it on one curb or the other. The nose does not need to be plastered to the asphalt, but it should be lowered with your dog paying attention to and following the scent on the smooth hard surface. If not, repeat these sessions several times as your dog needs to attend to the track on the hard surface — this is critical to your dog's long-term confidence and success in urban tracking. Also, consider repeating some of the straight down-wind tracks on flat parking lots described on page 283.

If your dog mostly skips across the gap to the curbs on the next island, find wider gaps like mall-type parking lots that typically have islands only on every other double parking row. Use a very small or inconspicuous article or freeze-dried treats mid-gap.

Sessions V1.x Zigzags with a Hard-Surface Turn on a Driveway.

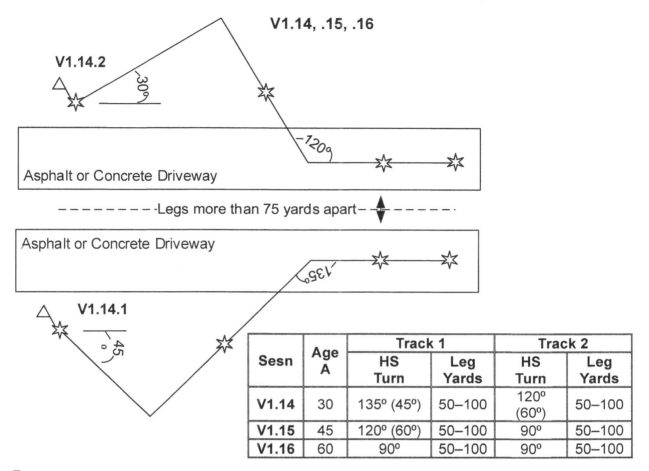

Sesn	Age A	Track 1		Track 2	
		HS Turn	Leg Yards	HS Turn	Leg Yards
V1.14	30	135° (45°)	50–100	120° (60°)	50–100
V1.15	45	120° (60°)	50–100	90°	50–100
V1.16	60	90°	50–100	90°	50–100

Purpose:
- Teach your dog to indicate loss of scent and search for the new leg on the hard surface.
- Teach him that he can find the new leg on the hard surface.

Tracklayer:
- Choose a campus-like setting with driveways or quiet roadways next to lawns.
- V1.14–.16 require a driveway with lawn on one side for the incoming leg. The turn and outgoing leg runs down the middle of the driveway and will typically be at least 5 yards from the edge of the driveway.
- Lay 2 two-corner zigzags with one corner on hard surface down a quiet roadway.
  ◦ Keep each hard-surface turn at least 75 yards from any other track laid by the tracklayer.
- Each track has an open turn that steadily sharpens to 90° over several sessions. Remember the angles listed describe the corner angle, not your change in direction. So for the 150° corner, you will turn 30°. In the table above, I show the corner angle first, and the angle the tracklayer turns herself in parenthesis.
- Use right and left hard-surface turns (typically the second turn).
- Use chalk on the hard surface to mark the corner and the direction of the new leg.
- Set a reward point 30–40 yards down the hard-surface leg by placing a small freeze-dried treat or an inconspicuous article there.

Phase V1. VST Hard-Surface Corners

Handler:
- Be patient at each hard-surface corner; don't rush your dog to make a decision.
- Ideally, use your whole line to allow your dog to make the choice before you move forward.
- Feel free in this phase to make it easy for your dog to commit down the hard-surface leg by sidestepping behind him fairly quickly when he notices the correct direction.
   - Be willing to follow him if he chooses the correct direction well to the side of the next leg.
- If your dog chooses the wrong direction, let him investigate 30' before restraining him.
   - Ask him if this is the good track.
   - Re-scent him if you need to reel him in to you.
   - Use the steps of help on page 258.
- Give lots of treats and praise at each article.

Evaluation and Possible Adaptations:
- Note in your journal and your summary log (page 328) details of each track.
- If he needs help on most hard-surface corners:
   - Use scent intensifiers like bare feet or SIAB (see page 8).
   - Try younger age (fresher scent) and then age more slowly.
   - Repeat these sessions several times.
- If he lacks confidence on several hard-surface turns:
   - Add very small freeze-dried treats at 5, 10 & 15 yards past the hard-surface turn for a while. Then use a small freeze-dried treat at 20 yards and an inconspicuous or small article at 30–40 yards past the corner. Then remove the treat but continue with the inconspicuous article.
   - Repeat several sessions in different locations with less natural contamination.

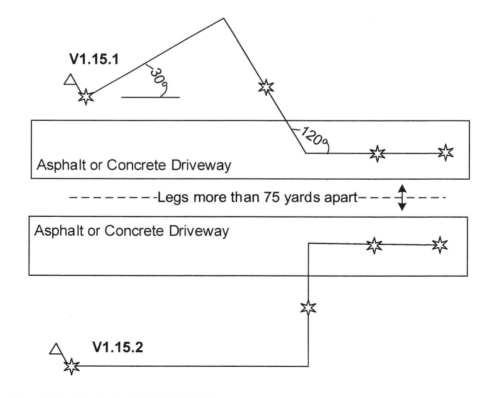

Sessions V1.x Zigzags with a Hard-Surface Turn in a Parking Lot or Plaza.

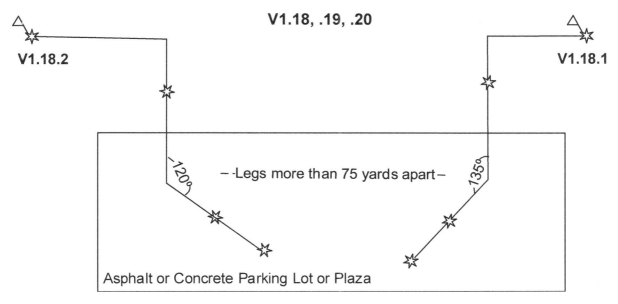

Session	Age A	Track 1		Track 2	
		HS Turn	Leg Yards	HS Turn	Leg Yards
V1.18	30	135° (45°)	50–100	120° (60°)	50–100
V1.19	45	120° (60°)	50–100	90°	50–100
V1.20	60	90°	50–100	90°	50–100

Purpose:
- Teach your dog to indicate loss of scent and search for the new leg on the hard surface.
- Teach him that he can find the new leg on the hard surface.

Tracklayer:
- V1.18–.20 require a parking lot at least 30 yards wide with the turn and outgoing leg at least 15 yards from the edge of the parking lot.
- See page 341 for a discussion of these tracks. The start can be on lawn and transition onto asphalt or concrete — be sure to approach the transition perpendicularly. Or, the start can be on hard surface along a curb so the start is not difficult for the dog.
- Lay 2 two-corner zigzags with the second corner out in a plaza or parking lot.
  - Keep each hard-surface turn at least 75 yards from any other track laid by the tracklayer.
  - Having each zigzag be U-shaped with their corners in the same direction can save space.
- Each track has an open turn that steadily sharpens to 90° over several sessions. Remember the angles listed describe the corner angle, not your change in direction. So for the 150° corner, you will turn 30°. In the table above, I show the corner angle first, and the angle the tracklayer herself turns in parenthesis.
- Use right and left hard-surface turns.
- Use chalk on the hard surface to mark the corner and the direction of the new leg.
- Set a reward point 30–40 yards down the hard-surface leg by placing a small freeze-dried treat or an inconspicuous or small article there.

Phase V1. VST Hard-Surface Corners

Handler:
- Avoid squaring up the lawn to hard surface transition, see page 340.
- Be patient at each hard-surface corner; don't rush your dog to make a decision.
- Ideally, use your whole line to allow your dog to make the choice before you move forward.
- Feel free in this phase to make it easy for your dog to commit down the hard-surface leg by sidestepping behind him fairly quickly when he notices the correct direction. Turning your body and sidestepping behind your dog can make it easy for your dog to continue to investigate the track without your confirming body language of face-on following him.
- If your dog chooses the wrong direction, let him investigate at least 30' before restraining him.
    - Ask him if this is the good track.
    - Re-scent him if you need to reel him in to you.
    - Use the steps of help on page 258.
- Give lots of treats and praise at each article.

Evaluation and Possible Adaptations:
- Note in your journal and your summary log (page 328) details of each track.
- If he needs help on most hard-surface corners:
    - Use scent intensifiers like bare feet or SIAB (see page 8).
    - Try younger age (fresher scent) and then age more slowly.
    - Repeat these sessions several times.
- If he lacks confidence on many hard-surface turns:
    - Add very small freeze-dried treats at 5, 10 & 15 yards past the hard-surface turn for a while. Then use a small freeze-dried treat at 20 yards and an inconspicuous or small article at 30–40 yards past the corner. Then remove the treat but continue with the inconspicuous reward article.
    - Repeat several sessions in different locations with less natural contamination.

Session V1.13 & V1.21. Review and Evaluate.

You may have noticed that your dog does not always track as nicely on asphalt or concrete as he did through a natural field for his TD or even his TDX. Dogs typically need multiple skills to follow a hard-surface track segment, and handlers need to understand and follow them regardless of which skill they need to use for any particular track segment. A great deal of time and frustration occurs when handlers feel their dog must always track in a particular way.

Your dog can learn to use several tactical skills for hard-surface tracking:
- Use curbs and other vertical surfaces to follow scent pooled there.
- Follow the footsteps themselves.
- Follow the edge of the puddle of scent on flat hard surface.
- Follow the vegetative fringe.

Three of these four tactical skills or styles of hard-surface tracking lead the dog much farther from the actual track than is ideal for the handler. Articles will be missed unless our dogs learn to go over to the article when they smell it in the distance. Plus, turns away from the side of the track that the dog is working will require searching a large area.

The more your dog learns to follow the footsteps themselves regardless of the surface, the better. But you and your dog can be successful by using all four of these styles. Few dogs succeed in passing their VST test without being a considerable distance from the track several places along the track.

V1.13 Proceed to the remainder of this phase or repeat V1.1-V1.12?

This mid-phase review session is to evaluate whether your dog is confident on hard surface turns yet. He needs to show pretty good directional choices at the hard surface turns although he does not need to be perfect by any means. For many dogs, repeating this material at ages about 60 minutes older than you did them in your previous pass will allow the dog to better understand the scent complexities near buildings, barriers, and curbs so he develops the confidence he needs to do these corners in flat driveways and open parking lots.

If he is pretty good, continue on to V1.14-V1.20, and you will do another review in V1.21.

V1.21 Proceed to the UTD Supplement, Phase V2 or Do More V1?

See page 313 for a list of criteria for repeating V1 material or progressing to Phase V1S UTD or Phase V2. Review the list now and make sure your dog and you significantly fulfill these criteria.

Phase V2 is a fairly natural extension of V1. So if your dog is fairly accurate on the V1 skills, you can move on to V2 or the UTD Supplement. If your dog is struggling with some skills at some of the older V1 tracks, consider repeating parts of V1 before moving on to the next step. The tracks in higher phases get older and more complex fairly fast, so be sure of your dog's fundamentals before adding those factors.

Phase V1 Summary Log

Sesn	Location	Config.	Date	Age	Evaluation
V1.1		ZZ with Barrier Turn			
V1.2		Slices & Bisects			
V1.3		ZZ with Barrier Turn			
V1.4		Island Big Gaps			
V1.5		ZZ with Barrier Turn			
V1.6		Slices & Bisects			
V1.7		ZZ with Curb Turn			
V1.8		Island Big Gaps			
V1.9		ZZ with Curb Turn			
V1.10		Slices & Bisects			
V1.11		ZZ with Curb Turn			
V1.12		Island Big Gaps			
V1.14		Zigzag with Driveway Turn			
V1.15					
V1.16					
V1.17		Slices & Bisects			
V1.18		Zigzags with Parking Lot Turn			
V1.19					
V1.20					
V1.21		Island Big Gaps			

Phase V1S UTD Supplement — Preparing for the CKC UTD.

Purpose:
- Polishing UTD skills, which are hard-surface turns, one-to-two hour age, and 33% hard surface.
- Maintain a high level of motivation.

Strategy:
- Work progressively more difficult UTD-like tracks in a variety of locations with one-quarter of them blind to the handler while varying age from one to two hours.
- Intermix four-turn zigzag with intentional contamination and island-to-island wide-gap tracks while varying age from ½ hour to 2 hours.
- Evaluate your performance on blind UTD-like tracks to decide whether to start entering UTD tests or to repeat the sequence using different locations and ages.

How to use this chapter:
- Read the discussion section that follows and look through the table below, which summarizes the training structure of this phase.
- Before each session, carefully review the detailed tracklaying and handling instructions for each type of tracking session on pages 319, 321, and 333.
- Keep a detailed log of each session using a format like the one shown on page 31 and keep a summary log like the one shown on page 335.
- Finally, do the review session on page 334.

Phase V1S UTD Session Schedule:

% Motivational Sessions	Range: 10–30%	Your Target:

Session	Location	Configuration	Age	HS Turn Angle	Leg Yards	Page
V1S.UTD1	Urban Lawn w/ Path & Roads	4-Turn Track with Slices & Bisects	30–120			319
V1S.UTD2	Park Lawn w/ Path & Roads	UTD-like with HS Turn at Curb	60–120	90°	50–100	333
V1S.UTD3	Park Lawn w/ Path & Roads	UTD-like with HS Turn on Driveway	60–120	90°	50–100	333
V1S.UTD4	Parking Lot w/ Curbs	Island-to-Island Gaps	30–120			321
V1S.UTD5	Park Lawn w/ Path & Roads	UTD-like with HS Turn in Parking Lot	60–120	90°	50–100	333
V1S.UTD6	Park Lawn w/ Path & Roads	Blind UTD-like	60–120	90°	50–150	333
V1S Review	Review and Evaluate					

Discussion:

For CKC tracking enthusiasts, the first urban test is the UTD, which can be attempted after the dog earns his CKC TD, or you can wait until he also earns his TDX. The CKC UTD has more non-vegetated surfaces than an AKC TDU, a hard-surface turn, and a minimum age of 60 minutes.

The CKC UTD Test Track

Essential Parameters	CKC UTD
Length	300–400 meters
Age	1–2 hours
Corners	3–5, both right & left, at least 2 will be 90°
Hard-Surface Corners	1 or more
Vegetated Surfaces	200–270 meters
Non-vegetated Surfaces	100–140 meters
Start Article	Scent pad only
Start Surface	30+ meters vegetated
First Article Location	At least 100 meters from start.
Other Articles	Cloth, wood, plastic or leather

This is a short phase to prepare the dog and handler for the UTD test after they have completed both TDU Part III and Phase V1. It is composed of sets of six sessions, four that are UTD-like, one for lawn contamination, and one for hard-surface tracking. The set may be repeated as appropriate for your dog and is typically repeated several times.

In addition to the schedule of sessions shown, some percentage of your tracks should be motivational tracks — perhaps a 30–45 minute-old zigzag on a little-contaminated sports field. They are just fun for your dog. The percentage of motivational tracks you need in this phase depends on the dog: if over 2-3 sessions you see your dog is slow to commit on starts that you think should be easy, increase the percentage of tracking sessions that consist of a simple motivational track.

One of the UTD-like tracks should have its hard-surface turn against a curb or other barrier to make it easy, another should have its hard-surface turn in a driveway, and another should have its hard-surface turn out in an open flat parking lot. The fourth UTD-like track should be blind, and the hard-surface turn can be anywhere. In addition to these variations, incorporate the following within the context of this phase, to be well prepared for the test.

- Turns on narrow sidewalks are often handled by the dog fringing on the grass. It is hard to break this because the dog may find the scent a lot more obvious there than on the contaminated sidewalk. Practice narrow sidewalk turns as well as wide walkways, plazas, or driveways, where the dog should solve the corner on the hard surface.
- Distraction training should have occurred naturally by your use of urban parks and campuses. If you have been avoiding some situations, like loose dogs, dogs playing in the distance, or friendly people who want to come up to your dog, consider working through these issues in a controlled fashion.
- Your test-like UTD tracks should have about 100–140 meters of hard surface. If it all comes in a single segment and then returns to grass, your dog may have difficulty finding and committing to the track on the lawn. Once you have your dog doing hard surface well, consider designing tracks with a segment of about 100 meters of hard surface, which then returns to lawn with an article just 30-50 meters out on the lawn. Try adding tiny treats 10 yards past the transition.

UTD track shapes are similar to TD and TDU track shapes.

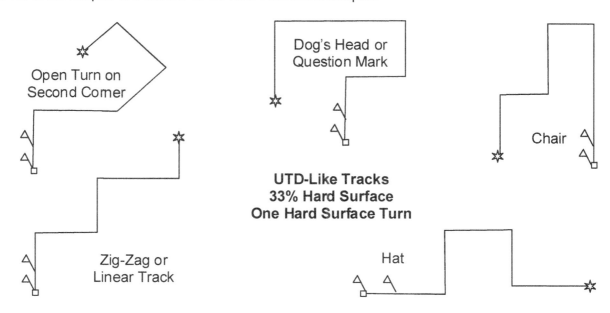

UTD-Like Tracks
33% Hard Surface
One Hard Surface Turn

The above designs work well when plotting a UTD in a park or sports field if you can get the required hard surface. Many UTD tracks are plotted around elementary or middle schools, and the tracks have to adapt to the reality of the structures and available hard surface.

Below are several UTD tracks within the context of actual school grounds. The two tracks in the left photo have constrained hard-surface turns while the other track has a turn well out on the hard surface. All these happen to be three-corner tracks; some school sites require four or five turns.

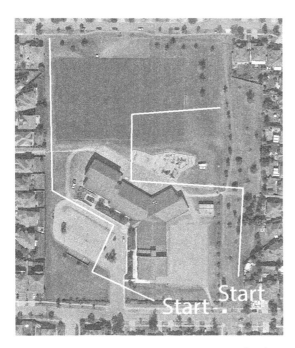 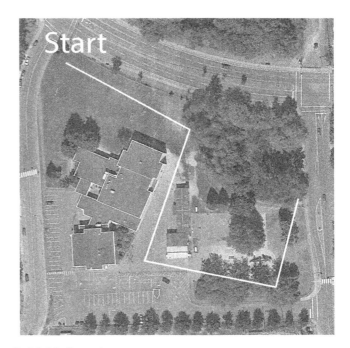

9. Images © 2016 Google

V1S.UTD1 is identical to V1.x Four-Turn Track with Slices and Bisects on page 319. See the procedure details there. Age can be between 30 minutes and two hours.

V1S.UTD1

Tracklayer:
- Flags as shown.
- Articles at the start, middle of each leg, and end.
- Leg lengths can vary.
- Age 30–120 minutes.
- Optionally, add a tiny treat between each article and corner.

Contamination layer:
- Cross the track as soon as the tracklayer finishes a leg.
- Cross at the start; over several sessions reduce the crossing angle from 45° to 30° to 15°.
- Slice or bisect each corner.
- Extend the crosstracks 20+ yards to the side of track.

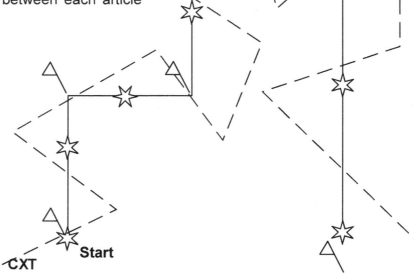

V1S.UTD4 is identical to V1.x Curbed-Island Serpentines with Big Gaps on page 321. See the procedure there. Use big gaps between 15 and 75 yards wide, age between 30 minutes and 2 hours.

Tracklayer:
- Randomly choose the next side of the island.
- If the dog is doing well, you can turn up to 90° at the end of an island.
- Chalk marks in the gap and on the curb where the track rejoins an island.
- Articles in the middle of wide gaps; treats optional.

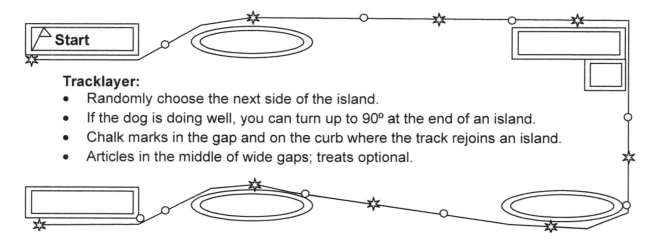

Sessions V1S.UTD.x UTD-like Tracks

Session	Configuration	Age
V1S.UTD2	UTD-like with HS Turn at Curb	60–120
V1S.UTD3	UTD-like with HS Turn on Driveway	60–120
V1S.UTD5	UTD-like with HS Turn in Parking Lot	60–120
V1S.UTD6	Blind UTD-like	60–120

Purpose:
- Teach the handler to read her dog on a blind track with a hard-surface turn.

Tracklayer:
- These tracks require typical urban parks or campuses with sidewalks, driveways and parking lots. They should have some natural contamination.
- See sample shapes on page 331 and examples also on that page. Flip all rights and lefts for variation. Use a shape suitable for your particular site constraints.
- Plan the hard-surface turn appropriate to the session configuration:
  - V1S.UTD2 against a curb or other barrier,
  - V1S.UTD3 on a sidewalk or driveway,
  - V1S.UTD5 out in a large flat parking lot.
  - V1S.UTD6 choose a barrier, sidewalk or driveway turn for this track.
- If the handler requests chalk at the corners, mark the corner and the new leg.
- Set a reward point 30–40 meters down the hard-surface leg by placing an inconspicuous article there.
- For any long legs, place an article down about every 30–60 meters to help maintain motivation.
- Place a mid-leg article on 1–2 of the other legs as reward points.

Handler:
- Be patient and let your dog sort out the natural contamination and the hard-surface turn.
- Ask for chalk marks on the hard-surface corner(s) and optionally two flags mid-leg on grass legs. Remove these markings once you gain confidence reading your dog so you will be able to follow your dog on blind tracks.
- Ideally, use your whole line to allow your dog to make the choice before you move forward.
- If your dog chooses the wrong direction, let him investigate at least 30' before restraining him.
- Give lots of treats and praise at each article.

Evaluation and Possible Adaptations:
- Note in your journal and your summary log (page 335) details of each track.
- Note your dog's confidence when he chooses the good outgoing leg.
- If he needs help at most hard-surface corners, repeat sessions from Phase U3 (page 297) and hard-surface corner exercises in Phase V1 such as Curbed-Island Serpentines with Big Gaps, page 321.
- If he lacks confidence on these tracks but does well on the hard-surface exercises in Phase U3 and V1, then repeat several of these sessions first at familiar locations and then at different locations.

Session V1S.UTD Review and Evaluation

After each set of six tracks, evaluate if you are ready to enter a UTD test, need to repeat more sessions from this phase, or are ready to proceed to Phase V2. If you have had the legs or corners marked or you laid them yourself, you should do several blind UTD tracks so you can evaluate your handling on test-like UTD tracks. Repeat the six-session sequence with several of the tracks blind.

Once you and your dog have passed a truly blind UTD practice track (V1.UTD6), then you may be ready to enter a test. Be sure to peak your dog for your UTD as described on pages 150 and 152. Of course, once you are ready to enter a UTD test, you can proceed to Phase V2 while you wait to get into a test.

Evaluate your dog's skill and your own skill:
- Is my dog consistently choosing the good track over the contamination at least 90% of the times he notices the contamination (natural or intended)?
    - If not, do more intentional-contamination exercises at different ages and new locations.
- Is my dog showing loss of track consistently on hard-surface turns within 50' of the actual corner?
    - Many times, it is the handler who fails to see the dog's change of behavior. But assume it is the dog unless your video review shows the change or your friend can see the change.
    - Use a chest- or head-mounted sports camera or have someone video the track from behind. Review in detail, noting changes of behavior missed in real time.
    - If there are no changes of behavior, mark the corners, the legs (two flags in the middle) or both, so you can restrain him when he overshoots substantially.
- Is my dog diligently searching the hard surface for the new leg or does he always seek any nearby grass?
    - If he seeks grass rather than search the hard surface, adapt Phase 8 Plan C to hard-surface turns. Start with the hard-surface turn out in the open and gradually bring it closer to the lawn over several sessions.
- Does my dog consistently commit to the new leg on the hard surface?
    - If not, adapt Phase 8 Plan C to hard-surface turns. Make sure to mark the corners with chalk.
- Can you read his "loss of scent" or "change of behavior" at both lawn and hard-surface turns?
    - If not, mark the corners or legs so you can watch his behavior and restrain him when he overshoots substantially.
    - Use a sports camera or have someone video the track from behind and review.
- Are you being patient and letting him sort out the scent issues as he searches for the new leg?
    - Patience is required for urban tracks. There is no reason to rush and every reason to take your time.
- Can you read his commitment to the new leg?
    - Use a sports camera or have someone video the track from behind and review.
    - Have a trusted friend watch your track and give you feedback.
- Do you let him out to nearly the full length of your line before following him or are you giving him immediate feedback that he is correct by moving after him or praising him?
    - Dogs learn to read their handlers when they are uncertain.
    - You need to shift the responsibility to your dog.

Phase V1S UTD Summary Log

Session	Site	Configuration	Date	Age	Evaluation
V1S.UTD1		4-Turn Track with Slices & Bisects			
V1S.UTD2		UTD-like with HS Turn at Curb			
V1S.UTD3		UTD-like with HS Turn on Driveway			
V1S.UTD4		Island-to-Island Gaps			
V1S.UTD5		UTD-like with HS Turn in Parking Lot			
V1S.UTD6		Blind UTD-like			
		Review			
V1S.UTD1		4-Turn Track with Slices & Bisects			
V1S.UTD2		UTD-like with HS Turn at Curb			
V1S.UTD3		UTD-like with HS Turn on Driveway			
V1S.UTD4		Island-to-Island Gaps			
V1S.UTD5		UTD-like with HS Turn in Parking Lot			
V1S.UTD6		Blind UTD-like			
		Review			

QT's UTD Test, May 2012

QT and I traveled to Armstrong, BC to test his skill in Canadian Urban Tracking in 2012.

The draw is at A&W where I drew track 3. While the day was warm and due to get into the low eighties, at 10:00 when his track starts, it is warm and dry but not hot. He starts confidently on the front lawn of a school and crosses the property efficiently in a straight line. Twice he indicates others had crossed his track, but he returns and pulls me straight alongside a bark playground on our right with the street somewhat to the left. When he indicates loss of scent, he searches to the left but refuses to circle around to the right, which is the only logical place the track could go. I keep talking to him confidently, telling him he can find it and maneuver him back to the front of the bark playground.

That was the area he had found contamination crosstracks, so he investigates them again and finally works his way to the right alongside the playground. When he gets to the far end of the playground, he searches along the front of the school beyond the playground until he scents the plume of an article back in the bark playground. He follows the plume and indicates the article nicely.

Of course, we had approached the article backward, so I just release him to search. Again he searches beyond the playground and in front of the school before going straight along the side of the school for its whole length. At the building's far corner, he indicates loss of scent and searches and finds it along the back of the school, so another right turn. That leg is short and mostly concrete with a left turn across another bark playground and out across a soccer field.

He searches beyond the corner and circles out past the playground and farther out into the soccer field. The field is littered with old plastic bags, and he visits most of them before finding another plume and following it back to where the track exits the second playground. He then follows that track well out into the soccer field before investigating more contamination crosstracks and a few more plastic bags. Finally, he fringes forward into some taller grass and searches it until he smells the final article and zeros in on it.

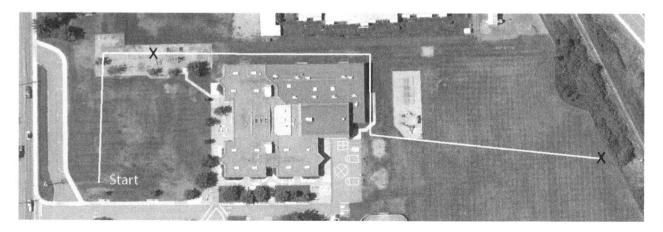

10. Image RDNO, © 2016 Google

Phase V2. Non-Vegetated Corners Developed.

Purpose:
- Improve the dog's skill working all sorts of hard-surface turns.
- Prepare the handler to read her dog in these varied situations.
- Maintain a high level of motivation.

Strategy:
- Systematically develop hard-surface turns using open angles against barriers, open angles along sidewalks, out in open flat parking lots, and near surrounding buildings.
- Progressively sharpen the corners to 90° while aging, reducing barriers, and constraints.
- While seemingly repetitive of Phase V1, this strategy of repeating the progression from young-to-old is a powerful learning technique. It is important for all dogs and handlers to follow the whole sequence of exercises.

How to use this chapter:
- Read the discussion section that follows and look through the table on the next page, which summarizes the training structure of this phase.
- Do each of the 24 sessions that rotate between urban campuses and parking lots. Before each session, carefully review the detailed tracklaying and handling instructions for each type of tracking session on pages 346 through 353.
- Keep a detailed log of each session using a format like the one shown on page 31 and keep a summary log like the one shown on page 355.
- Finally, do the review session on page 354 to evaluate your dog's progress and your own training-skill development.

Discussion:

A **Moment of Truth** (MOT) turn is a track design concept where a turn is placed out in the open with little except the track scent to suggest the direction of the next leg to the dog and hopefully nothing to suggest the direction to the handler. It is a concept that applies equally well to TD/TDX field tracks as it does to urban tracks. However, it is often used to refer specifically to a hard-surface turn with no nearby vegetation to support a dog trying to fringe the corner and new leg, and for VST this is its usual meaning. It is also called a non-fringeable corner.

The AKC VST rules specify there will be at least one 90° MOT turn in an area devoid of vegetation and where the outgoing leg does not return to vegetation within 30 yards. Often in tests, MOT turns are well out into a flat, featureless parking lot or plaza with vegetation much further away than 30 yards. And often the track ends up with more than one MOT turn due to the constraints of the test mapped onto the reality of the campus topology.

Phase V2 Session Schedule:

% Motivational Sessions	Range: 10–30%	Your Target:

Session	Location	Configuration	Age A	Track 1 Angle	Track 2 Angle	Track 3 Angle	
V2.1	Campus-like with Buildings	Turns at Buildings	1:15	150º (30º)	135º (45º)	120º (60º)	Group A
V2.2		Turns on Sidewalks	1:15	150º (30º)	135º (45º)	120º (60º)	
V2.3	P. Lot or Plaza	Open Angle HS Corner	:30	150º (30º)	135º (45º)	120º (60º)	
V2.4		Zigzag Buildings	1:00	3–4 turns, HS turns 150º			
V2.5	Campus-like with Buildings	Turns Buildings	1:45	135º (45º)	120º (60º)	90º	Group B
V2.6		Open Turns Sidewalks	1:45	135º (45º)	120º (60º)	90º	
V2.7	P. Lot or Plaza	Open Angle HS Corner	1:00	135º (45º)	120º (60º)	90º	
V2.8		Zigzag Buildings	1:30	3–4 turns, HS turns 135º			
V2.9	Campus-like with Buildings	Open Turns Buildings	2:00	135º (45º)	120º (60º)	90º	Group C
V2.10		Open Turns Sidewalks	2:00	135º (45º)	120º (60º)	90º	
V2.11	P. Lot or Plaza	Open Angle HS Corner	1:15	135º (45º)	120º (60º)	90º	
V2.12		Zigzag Buildings	2:00	3–4 turns, HS Turns 120º			
V2.13	Campus-like with Buildings	Open Turns Buildings	2:30	120º (60º)	90º	90º	Group D
V2.14		Open Turns Sidewalks	2:30	120º (60º)	90º	90º	
V2.15	P. Lot or Plaza	Open Angle HS Corner	1:30	120º (60º)	90º	90º	
V2.16		Zigzag Buildings	2:30	3–4 turns, HS Turns 90º			
V2.17	Campus-like with Buildings	Open Turns Buildings	3:00	120º (60º)	90º	90º	Group E
V2.18		Open Turns Sidewalks	3:00	120º (60º)	90º	90º	
V2.19	P. Lot or Plaza	Open Angle HS Corner	1:45	120º (60º)	90º	90º	
V2.20	Campus-like with Buildings	Zigzag Buildings	3:00	3–4 turns, 90º HS Turn			
V2.21		Open Turns Buildings	3:30	90º	90º	90º	Group F
V2.22		Open Turns Sidewalks	3:30	90º	90º	90º	
V2.23	P. Lot or Plaza	HS Corner	2:00	90º	90º	90º	
V2.24	Campus-like	Zigzag Buildings	3:30	3–4 turns, 90º HS Turn			
V2.25		Evaluate to Proceed					

Sometimes VST test tracks have another type of hard-surface turn that may not be classified as a true non-fringeable MOT turn because there is some vegetation nearby or there are only limited choices of direction. These are typified by the track coming down a channel like a sidewalk with a narrow garden and a building or wall on one side and an open hard-surface area like a parking lot on the other side. The track turns into the parking lot while the sidewalk-channel continues straight ahead. These turns can be tricky if the tracklayer's scent pools along the landscaping or a building past the corner causing the dog to overshoot the turn significantly. Another example is when the track comes to the intersection of two walkways with buildings on all corners of the intersection and some of the walkways have landscaping. Depending on the wind direction, scent may pool down one of the wrong channels drawing the dog far off the actual track.

In this phase, we will develop hard-surface turns in four contexts:
1. Turns against buildings.
2. Turns down sidewalks.
3. Turns out in flat parking lots.
4. Turns that are part of simple multi-corner zigzags through campus building walkways.

Each of the four strands of skill development has their own "Age A" track-age progression to help develop the dog's confidence on older tracks. Handlers can choose to use "Age B" that widely varies the age of these tracks from one to four hours. Or handlers can choose "Age C" for dogs whose skill drops off rapidly with age (see page 313).

The **Open Turns Against a Building** sessions help develop skill with dealing with the multitude of complex environmental issues occurring against buildings using simple track shapes so that the dog and handler will not be overwhelmed. They are essentially an extension of the Phase V1 zigzags with one hard-surface turn against a barrier. Now we use three single-corner tracks to focus exclusively on these turns while extending the age. Both right and left turns should be used, chosen randomly. Tracklayers may notice that due to physical constraints, some building approaches mandate a turn in one direction or the other. This is fine so long as the right-left balance is maintained over several sessions. Ideally, three tracks will be laid and run each session but doing just the first two may work well also.

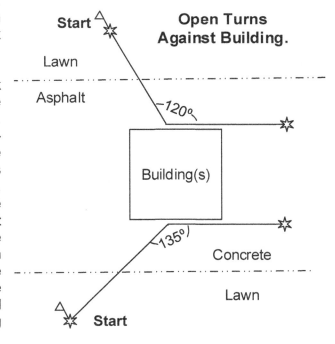

The adjacent diagram shows a two track session against opposite sides of a large building, for example V2.9.1 and V2.9.2. Adjust the angles per the Phase V2 schedule shown on page 338. Avoid getting the tracks close together. This diagram shows a typical configuration for this type of track. It is good to start on some lawn to allow the dog to settle into the track, but it is OK to start on hard surface near a curb if that is all the site provides. The diagram shows the lawn transitioning to asphalt or concrete as the building is approached. The point of these exercises is to allow the dog to learn to deal with all the swirling scent that may be lying

Phase V2. Non-Vegetated Corners Developed.

close to the building or pushed well away from the building by the vortexes near the building. Also, vary the surface compositions near the building as they are available; make sure you have some asphalt, some concrete, and some gravel.

Both dogs and handlers tend to **square up a transition** from lawn to hard surface by bending to make their path perpendicular to the transition line. This leads them away from the leg they are on and away from the next corner (the MOT) as shown below. The tracklayer should make sure she has a good landmark as she approaches a lawn to broad hard-surface transition. She should use chalk as necessary to mark the correct angle on the hard surface.

Handlers should be cognizant of their dog or themselves squaring off the transition at any lawn to hard-surface transition. Having a good landmark as the dog approaches the transition can help the team make a straight-ahead transition. If the team squares up the transition, they will end up approaching the corner search area well to the side of the corner.

Regardless of whether the team squared-up the transition, the dog should be given considerable freedom to sort out the scent-situation at the building and commit to the correct direction, even if it is closer to the building or well out from the building, so long as it is in the correct general direction. This requires the handler to be patient and observe the dog carefully.

Squaring-up a Transition

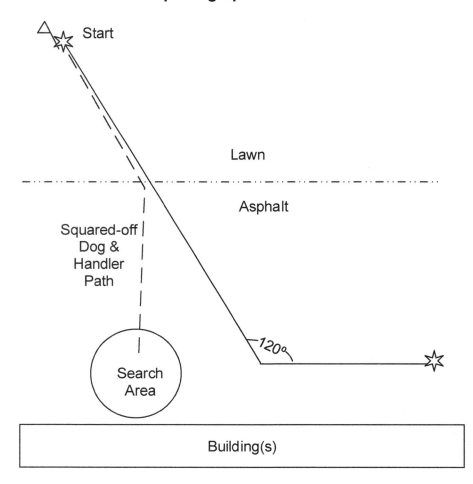

The aerial views below show two schools whose topologies allow laying corners at the side of buildings. Your site with buildings will be different, but these offer ideas about places that provide opportunities to lay these open-turn tracks against buildings.

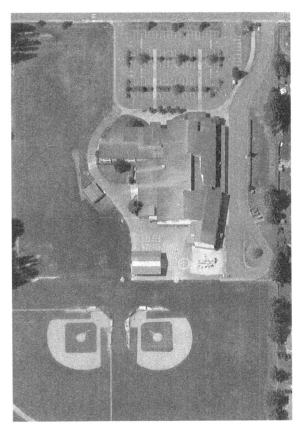
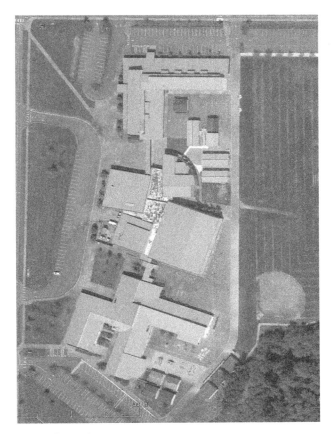

11. Images © 2016 Google

The **Open Turns onto Sidewalks** require normal width sidewalks with lawn on one or both sides. The opposite side of the sidewalk may have a low wall, fence, landscaped garden, or an open lawn. Over these sessions and individual tracks, a wide variety of opposite sides should be used, particularly open lawns, which give the dog the opportunity to overshoot the corner. Use sites with natural contamination on the lawns or add light, intentional contamination in the vicinity of the sidewalk turn.

The **Open-Angle Hard-Surface Corner** sessions introduce the prototypical non-fringeable MOT turn by being out in a flat parking lot or plaza with no nearby vegetation, curbs, or walls to help pool the scent. The track may be started on lawn and transition out into a large plaza or parking lot, or be started on hard surface — design about half the tracks with a lawn start and the other half with a hard-surface start. Regardless of the start surface, bring the dog to the start article at an angle to the first leg making the start a corner-not-tracked-into. Laying these and handling the dog are both similar to the open turns against a building discussed in the previous pages. All legs of these tracks should be at least 75 yards away from the other tracks if laid by the same tracklayer to avoid scent plumes from one track drawing your dog off to another track.

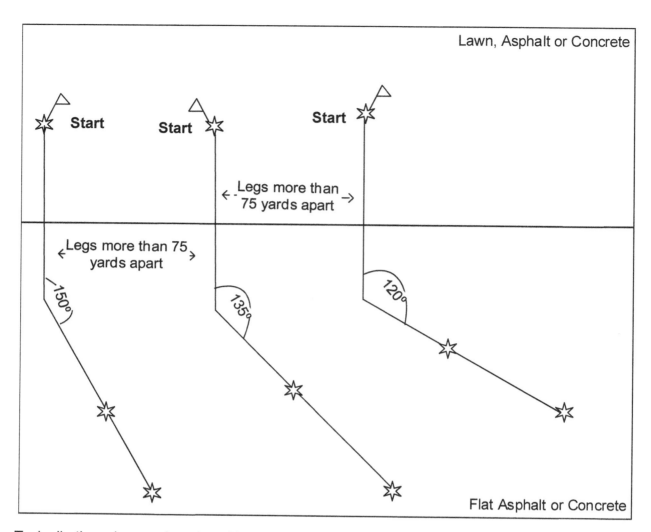

Typically there is a surface transition before the corner, so approach the transition perpendicularly to avoid handlers and dogs squaring up the transition. Diagonal transitions from surface to surface can be tricky for the dog and handler alike. We typically have to make them when approaching a building, but we don't when using an open parking lot. While appropriate in this phase, this constraint will be relaxed in V3 and particularly V4 so the team is prepared to navigate all types of transition angles. See the first leg of a VST test track on page 395 for an example of where the track squared up at the transition.

We introduce mini-VST tracks by trying to make the turns go in alternating directions or having a long leg and barrier between any sequential turns that do go in the same direction. I call these simple tracks **Zigzags Between Buildings.** The tracks have 3-4 turns. Through v2.12, hard surface turns should be an open angle as indicated or against a barrier so the choices are limited.

A fairly simple zigzag track is shown on the next page. While the first and second corners go in the same direction, the second leg is 90 yards, and there is a big building separating the first and third legs. It is considered simple because there is a lot of grass and few choices at each corner: specifically there is a pond boundary beyond the first corner, building G beyond the second corner, building S blocking a turn to the left at the third corner, and the jog between buildings F and G is supported by lawn grass.

12. Images © 2016 Google

The aerial view below shows a more challenging three-corner zigzag that starts in the center of the picture in an area of the University of Washington Quad on highly-contaminated grass, turns left on a sidewalk between two buildings then right at a full sidewalk intersection and then left again along the front of another building. A ground-level view of the quad is pictured on page 316 from the left-hand side of the quad.

13. Image © 2016 Google

Phase V2. Non-Vegetated Corners Developed.

The tracks you plot should start out being easier than the second track if possible. It is a good technique to use chalk and to lay these yourself so you know where the track goes while you are handling. Doing these tracks blind is great, but first, you need to get your dog accustomed to these conditions and develop your own handling skills so when you do blind tracks, they are mostly or all successful for both you and your dog.

Laying Zigzags Between Buildings is fairly easy if you are on a familiar campus. For less familiar sites, plan your track on satellite imagery applications like Google Earth (Pro). When you get to campus, you may have to adapt to current conditions.

Handling. Handlers should review the subsection on helping your dog on page 258. To quickly review, the hierarchy or steps from minor help to substantial help are:
1. Face in the correct direction.
2. Restraint.
3. Reel-in and Re-Scent.
4. Reel-in and point to the correct track and direction.
5. Reel-in and love the track.

Following this hierarchy is critical for teaching your dog the skills he needs to be successful. Most important, the need for handler patience cannot be over-emphasized. The handler should be patient and avoid pushing or rushing the dog. Doing so will train the dog to pay attention to the handler's expectation, as described on page 314, regarding shifting responsibility to the dog.

Handling Hard-Surface Turns. Being the best partner to your dog when faced with any difficult corner or choice point requires considerable skill that is developed over time. If you and your dog have worked on advanced TDX skills, you will remember the need to organize a dog's search over a wide area. Similar techniques are needed at difficult urban choice points. See Appendix A (ATE 2) on page 405 for a handling exercise to improve your search skill as a handler.

You will have noticed that many times on urban tracks your dog is better able to track several feet or yards to the side of a track than right on the track itself. This can be due to the complex urban environment moving scent around, or it can be due to contamination that just happens to be parallel to your track. You will need to accept that sometimes your dog will work to the side of the footprints and you need to be able to follow him so long as he moves in a roughly parallel direction to the actual footprints.

For the turns themselves, start out remembering "Yippee! I am at a corner that might go straight" to avoid telling your dog what to do (see page 92). Stay still in your pivot location, encourage your dog to search in all directions until he finds and commits to the new leg, and only follow your dog once he has committed to the full length of your line. If your dog cannot find it within the length of your line, expand his area of search by spiraling out from your pivot point. Sidestep and back up so you are not leading your dog some place but rather allowing your dog to search a large area.

You may have noticed that your dog often bobs his head briefly in the direction of the new leg as his behavior changes from tracking a leg to loss of scent at a corner. It is good to notice this direction and remember it. Your dog also bobs his head at many scent phenomena along a leg like contamination and transitions, both of which may or may not co-exist with the real corner.

In this phase, you are still teaching your dog to be reliable on hard-surface turns, and so your tracks should be marked. Regardless of whether he head-bobs in the correct direction or not, let him search and make the decision himself. If he is very slow to commit to the new leg, feel free to sidestep out behind your dog in the correct direction while giving the dog more line and gently saying encouraging words. These are teaching moments, not testing.

However, as the dog gains experience and confidence, you do need to slowly reduce and gradually withdraw hints to shift responsibility to the dog. In the next phase, you will start doing blind tracks with your dog, and you want your dog fairly reliable in committing to the new legs on hard surface by then.

Shopping. The more hard-surface tracking your dog does, the more he visually notices nearby debris and wanders off track to investigate whether it is something that will pay off with treats. You will pretty much have to let the dog do so unless he gets fully distracted from the track and fails to return to it.

Video. Recording almost all tracks with a video, using either an action camera showing only your dog or a tracklayer-carried device, will allow you to review your dog's performance and your own performance as well. You need to understand how your dog acts when he encounters contamination, transitions, and distractions and you will learn better by reviewing the video when you are not completely focused on your handling. If your dog does a similar track to one he did some time ago, you can compare the two and see how much he and you have improved.

Scheduling. The order of the Phase V2 sessions can be rearranged to suit the locations available to you for tracking on any particular day. Try to keep generally in balance between the four styles of exercises interweaved here. Of course, you may feel the need to repeat material to improve your dog's understanding of the desired skills.

Motivational Tracks. As your training tracks become more complex, the dog may experience stress and start to lose motivation. Some percentage of your tracks should be motivational tracks — perhaps a 60–90 minute-old zigzag on a little-contaminated sports field. They are just fun for your dog. The percentage of motivational tracks you need in this phase depends on the dog: if over 2-3 sessions you see your dog is slow to commit on starts that you think should be easy, increase the percentage of tracking sessions that consist of a simple motivational track.

Sessions V2.x Open Turns against a Building.

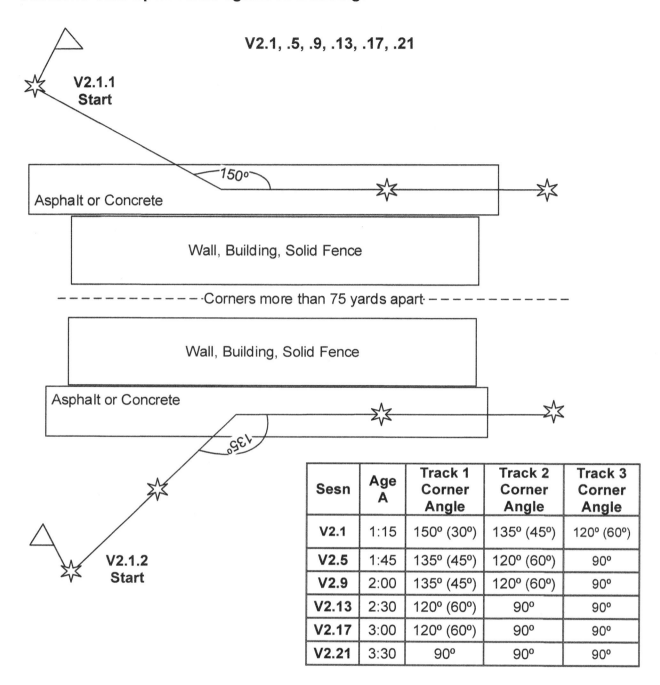

Sesn	Age A	Track 1 Corner Angle	Track 2 Corner Angle	Track 3 Corner Angle
V2.1	1:15	150° (30°)	135° (45°)	120° (60°)
V2.5	1:45	135° (45°)	120° (60°)	90°
V2.9	2:00	135° (45°)	120° (60°)	90°
V2.13	2:30	120° (60°)	90°	90°
V2.17	3:00	120° (60°)	90°	90°
V2.21	3:30	90°	90°	90°

Purpose:
- Let the dog learn how scent changes at transitions.
- Encourage him to search for the new leg on the hard surface.
- Let him learn that he can find the new leg on the hard surface.

Tracklayer:
- See page 339 for a descriptive discussion of these tracks. Choose a campus-like setting with suitable features to do the turns against walls, buildings, or solid fences. School buildings may have hard-surface areas right up against the building with surrounding lawns beyond.
- Lay 3 separate hard-surface single-corner tracks or 2 two-corner zigzags with one corner on hard surface against a barrier.
    - Ensure the hard-surface turn is at least 75 yards from other tracks laid by the same tracklayer.
    - If doing two zigzag tracks, use the angles of Track 1 and Track 2.
- Plan the track with the appropriate open-angle turn near the barrier so the next leg stays on the hard surface for 30 or more yards. Vary the distance to the building from adjacent to as much as 5 to 10 yards before the building.
- Each track has an open turn that steadily sharpens to 90° over several sessions. Remember the angles listed describe the corner angle, not your change in direction. So for the 150° corner, you will turn 30°. In the schedule, I show the corner angle first, and the angle the tracklayer herself turns in parentheses.
- Use right and left hard-surface turns.
- Use chalk on the hard surface to mark the corner and the direction of the new leg.
- Set a reward point 30–40 yards down the hard-surface leg by placing an inconspicuous or small article there.

Handler:
- Avoid squaring up the lawn to hard-surface transition. Find a good landmark before your dog reaches the transition.
- Be patient at each hard-surface corner; don't rush your dog to make a decision.
- Ideally, use your whole line to allow your dog to make the choice before you move forward.
- If your dog chooses the wrong direction, let him investigate at least 30' before restraining him.
    - Ask him if this is the good track.
    - Re-scent him if you need to reel him in to you.
    - Use the steps of help on page 258.
- Give lots of treats and praise at each article.

Evaluation and Possible Adaptations:
- Note in your journal and your summary log (page 355) details of each track.
- If he needs help on most hard-surface corners:
    - Use scent intensifiers like bare feet or SIAB (see page 8).
    - Try younger age (fresher scent) and then age more slowly.
- Repeat these sessions several times.
- If he lacks confidence on many hard-surface turns:
    - Add very small freeze-dried treats at 10, 15 & 20 yards past the hard-surface turn for a while. Later, use a small freeze-dried treat at 20 yards and an inconspicuous or small article at 30–40 yards past the corner. Then remove the treat but continue with the inconspicuous reward article.
    - Repeat several sessions in different locations with less natural contamination.

Sessions V2.x Open Turns on Sidewalks.

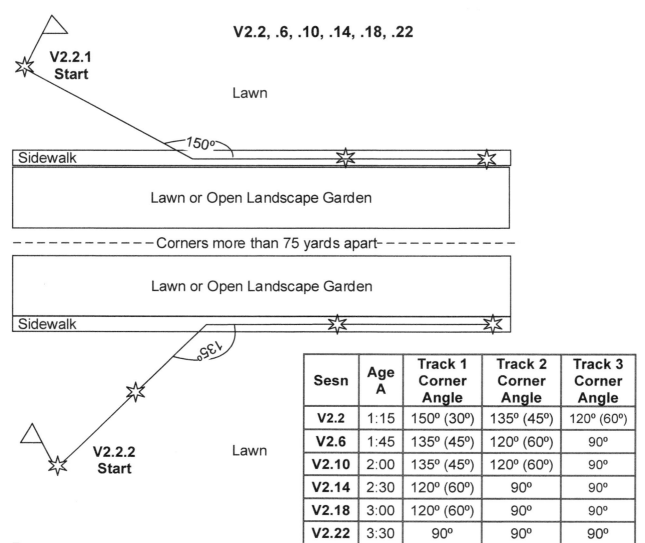

Sesn	Age A	Track 1 Corner Angle	Track 2 Corner Angle	Track 3 Corner Angle
V2.2	1:15	150° (30°)	135° (45°)	120° (60°)
V2.6	1:45	135° (45°)	120° (60°)	90°
V2.10	2:00	135° (45°)	120° (60°)	90°
V2.14	2:30	120° (60°)	90°	90°
V2.18	3:00	120° (60°)	90°	90°
V2.22	3:30	90°	90°	90°

Purpose:
- Teach your dog to indicate loss of scent and search for the new leg on the hard surface.
- Teach him that he can find the new leg on the hard surface.

Tracklayer:
- Choose a campus-like setting with sidewalks with lawns on both sides if possible. It is OK if the opposite side has some sparse landscaping so long as the dog can get through it to investigate the area beyond the corner.
- Lay 3 separate hard-surface single-corner tracks or 2 two-corner zigzags with one corner on hard surface down a sidewalk.
  - Keep each hard-surface turn at least 75 yards from any other track laid by the same tracklayer.
  - If doing two zigzag tracks, use the angle of Track 1 and Track 2.

- Plan the track so you will make the appropriate open-angle turn near the barrier and so that the next leg stays on the hard-surface sidewalk for 30 yards or more.
- Each track has an open turn that steadily sharpens to 90° over several sessions. Remember the angles listed describe the corner angle, not your change in direction. So for the 150° corner, you will turn 30°. In the table above, I show the corner angle first and the angle the tracklayer herself turns in parenthesis.
- Use right and left hard-surface turns.
  - If you lay zigzags, ideally the hard-surface turn is the second.
- Use chalk on the hard surface to mark the corner and the direction of the new leg.
- Set a reward point 30–40 yards down the hard-surface leg by placing an inconspicuous or small article there.

Handler:
- Be patient at each hard-surface corner; don't rush your dog to make a decision.
- Ideally, use your whole line to allow your dog to make the choice before you move forward.
- If your dog chooses the wrong direction, let him investigate at least 30' before restraining him.
  - Ask him if this is the good track.
  - Re-scent him if you need to reel him in to you.
  - Use the steps of help on page 258.
- Give lots of treats and praise at each article.

Evaluation and Possible Adaptations:
- Note in your journal and your summary log (page 355) details of each track.
- If he needs help on most hard-surface corners:
  - Use scent intensifiers like bare feet or SIAB (see page 8).
  - Try younger age (fresher scent) and then age more slowly.
  - Repeat these sessions several times.
- If he lacks confidence on many hard-surface turns:
  - Add very small freeze-dried treats at 10, 15 & 20 yards past the hard-surface turn for a while. Later, use a small freeze-dried treat at 20 yards and an inconspicuous or small article at 30–40 yards past the corner. Then remove the treat but continue with the inconspicuous reward article.
  - Repeat several sessions in different locations with less natural contamination.

Sessions V2.x Open Turns on Parking Lots or Plazas.

V2.3, .7, .11, .15, .19, .23

Sesn	Age A	Track 1 Angle	Track 2 Angle	Track 3 Angle
V2.3	:30	150° (30°)	135° (45°)	120° (60°)
V2.7	1:00	135° (45°)	120° (60°)	90°
V2.11	1:15	135° (45°)	120° (60°)	90°
V2.15	1:30	120° (60°)	90°	90°
V2.19	1:45	120° (60°)	90°	90°
V2.23	2:00	90°	90°	90°

Purpose:
- Teach your dog to indicate loss of scent and search for the new leg on the hard surface.
- Teach him that he can find the new leg on the hard surface.

Tracklayer:
- See page 341 for a discussion of these tracks. The start can be on lawn and transition onto asphalt or concrete. Or the start can be along a hard-surface curb, which should not be as difficult for the dog as a start out in the flat.
- Lay 3 separate hard-surface single-corner tracks or 2 two-corner zigzags with one corner on hard surface down a sidewalk.
    - Keep each hard-surface turn at least 75 yards from any other track laid by the same tracklayer.
    - If doing two zigzag tracks, use the angle of Track 1 and Track 2.

Modern Enthusiastic Tracking, The New Step-by-step Training Handbook

- Approach the hard-surface transition perpendicular to the line of the transition as shown in the diagram.
- Each track has an open turn that steadily sharpens to 90° over several sessions. Remember the angles listed describe the corner angle, not your change in direction. So for the 150° corner, you will turn 30°. In the table above, I show the corner angle first, and the angle the tracklayer herself turns in parenthesis.
- Use right and left hard-surface turns.
  ◦ If you lay zigzags, ideally the hard-surface turn is the second.
- Use chalk on the hard surface to mark the corner and the direction of the new leg.
- Set a reward point 30–40 yards down the hard-surface leg by placing a small freeze-dried treat or an inconspicuous or small article there.

Handler:
- Be patient at each hard-surface corner; don't rush your dog to make a decision.
- Ideally, use your whole line to allow your dog to make the choice before you move forward.
- If your dog chooses the wrong direction, let him investigate at least 30' before restraining him.
  ◦ Ask him if this is the good track.
  ◦ Re-scent him if you need to reel him in to you.
  ◦ See handling tips on page 344.
  ◦ Use the steps of help on page 258.
- Give lots of treats and praise at each article.

Evaluation and Possible Adaptations:
- Note in your journal and your summary log (page 355) details of each track.
- If he needs help on most hard-surface corners:
  ◦ Use scent intensifiers like bare feet or SIAB (see page 8).
  ◦ Try younger age (fresher scent) and then age more slowly.
  ◦ Repeat these sessions several times.
- If he lacks confidence on many hard-surface turns:
  ◦ Add very small freeze-dried treats at 10, 15 & 20 yards past the hard-surface turn for a while. Later, use a small freeze-dried treat at 20 yards and an inconspicuous or small article at 30–40 yards past the corner. Then remove the treat but continue with the inconspicuous reward article.
  ◦ Repeat several sessions in different locations with less natural contamination.

Phase V2. Non-Vegetated Corners Developed.

Sessions V2.x Zigzag Between Buildings.

V2.4, .8, .12, .16, .20, .24

Sesn	Age A	Corner Angle
V2.4	1:00	3–4 turns Hard surface turns 150°
V2.8	1:30	3–4 turns Hard surface turns 135°
V2.12	2:00	3–4 turns Hard surface turns 120°
V2.16	2:30	3–4 turns Hard surface turns 90°
V2.20	3:00	3–4 turns Hard surface turns 90°
V2.24	3:30	3–4 turns Hard surface turns 90°

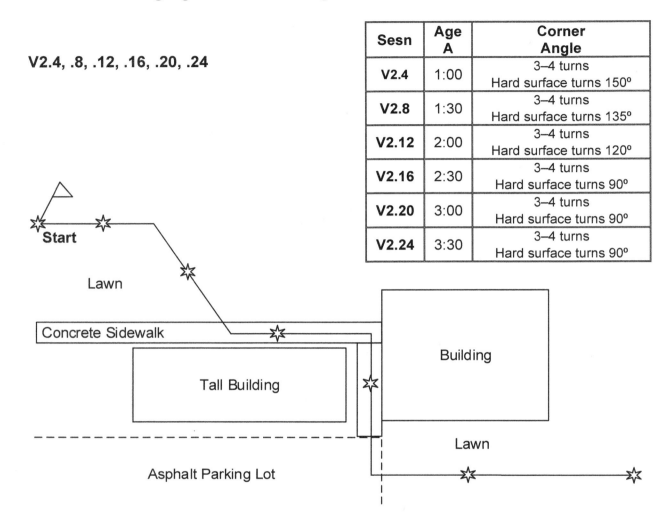

Purpose:
- Teach your dog to indicate loss of scent and search for the new leg on the hard surface.
- Teach him that he can find the new leg on the hard surface.

Tracklayer:
- See the discussion of designing zigzags through buildings on page 342.
- The diagram above is a single example; use the campus site you have available as best as you can. The diagram on the next page is more difficult because the third and fourth corners are both 90° hard-surface corners.
- Lay a single 3–4-turn zigzag that uses lawns, sidewalks, and/or parking lots.
- Alternate turn direction to avoid parallel legs getting too close.
- If you have to make two sequential turns in the same direction, make the intervening leg at least 75 yards, if possible.
- Your hard-surface turns should be open, if possible, for the first three sessions. The diagram above includes three hard-surface turns, so it is a quite advanced track suitable for the later sessions in this phase.

- Use chalk on the hard surface to mark the corner and the direction of the new leg.
- Use an inconspicuous or small article 25–35 yards down each leg to reward the dog for taking the corner.

Handler:
- Be patient at each hard-surface corner; don't rush your dog to make a decision.
- Ideally, use your whole line to allow your dog to make the choice before you move forward.
- If your dog chooses the wrong direction, let him investigate at least 30' before restraining him.
    - Ask him if this is the good track.
    - Re-scent him if you need to reel him in to you.
    - Use the steps of help on page 258.
- Give lots of treats and praise at each article.

Evaluation and Possible Adaptations:
- Note in your journal and your summary log (page 355) details of each track.
- If he needs help on most hard-surface corners:
    - Use scent intensifiers like bare feet or SIAB (see page 8).
    - Try younger age (fresher scent) and then age more slowly.
    - Repeat these sessions several times.
- If he lacks confidence on many hard-surface turns:
    - Add very small freeze-dried treats at 10, 15 & 20 yards past the hard-surface turn for a while. Later, use a small freeze-dried treat at 20 yards and an inconspicuous or small article at 30–40 yards past the corner. Then remove the treat but continue with the inconspicuous reward article.
    - Repeat several sessions in different locations with less natural contamination.

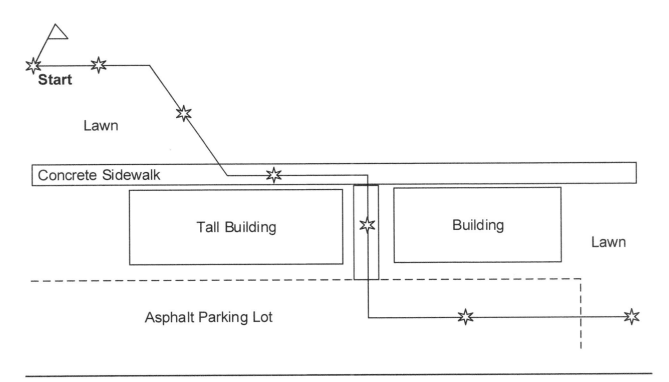

Phase V2. Non-Vegetated Corners Developed.

Session V2.25. Review and Evaluate.

You most likely have noticed that your dog does not always track as nicely on asphalt or concrete as he did tracking through a natural field for his TD or even his TDX. Dogs typically need multiple skills to follow a hard-surface track, and handlers need to understand and follow them regardless of which skill they need to use for any particular track segment. A great deal of time and frustration occurs when handlers feel their dog must always track in a particular way.

Your dog can learn to use several tactical skills for hard-surface tracking:
- Use curbs and other vertical surfaces to follow scent pooled there.
- Follow the footsteps themselves.
- Follow the edge of the scent puddle on a flat hard surface.
- Follow the vegetative fringe.
- Follow to the side when the track scent has been moved by wind vortexes.

Four of these five tactical skills or styles of hard-surface tracking lead the dog much farther from the actual track than is ideal. Articles will be missed unless our dogs learn to go over to the article when they smell it in the distance. Also, turns away from the side of the track that the dog is working will require searching a large area.

The more your dog learns to follow the footsteps themselves regardless of the surface, the better. You and your dog can still be successful by using all five of these styles. Few dogs succeed in passing their VST test without being a considerable distance from the track at several places on the track.

Proceed to V3 or continue to repeat material in V2?

The next phase emphasizes more VST-like tracks, some of which will be blind to the handler. Before proceeding, your dog should be solid on his VST skills (page 302) but not necessarily perfect. You as a handler should be ready to trust your dog on blind tracks at least some of the time.

To judge how solid is solid enough, consider his skills on tracks older than two and a half hours:
- Is he Clear-Confident-Committed on contaminated lawn tracks and self-reliant concerning the contamination?
- Is he quite reliable on constrained hard-surface turns and quite good on MOT turns?
- Is he pretty comfortable tracking in highly distracting urban environments?
- As a handler, have you mostly shifted the responsibility for making decisions to your dog and has he accepted that responsibility when he understands the scent issues?

If any of the answers are "No, not yet," then you will make faster progress by repeating V2 material focusing on these issues.

If all the answers are "He is pretty good, but there is room for improvement," then you can proceed to V3 with confidence. In Phases V3 and V4, you will continue to do many skill-building tracks and problem-solving tracks.

Phase V2 Summary Log

Sesn	Site	Config.	Date	Age	Evaluation
V2.1		Turns at Buildings			
V2.2		Turns on Sidewalks			
V2.3		HS Corners			
V2.4		Zigzag Buildings			
V2.5		Turns Buildings			
V2.6		Open Turns Sidewalks			
V2.7		Open Angle HS Corner			
V2.8		Zigzag Buildings			
V2.9		Open Turns Buildings			
V2.10		Open Turns Sidewalks			
V2.11		Open Angle HS Corner			
V2.12		Zigzag Buildings			

Phase V2. Non-Vegetated Corners Developed.

Sesn	Site	Config.	Date	Age	Evaluation
V2.13		Open Turns Buildings			
V2.14		Open Turns Sidewalks			
V2.15		Open Angle HS Corner			
V2.16		Zigzag Buildings			
V2.17		Open Turns Buildings			
V2.18		Open Turns Sidewalks			
V2.19		Open Angle HS Corner			
V2.20		Zigzag Buildings			
V2.21		Open Turns Buildings			
V2.22		Open Turns Sidewalks			
V2.23		Open Angle HS Corner			
V2.24		Zigzag Buildings			

Phase V3. Putting the Pieces Together.

Purpose:
- Develop the dog's skill handling full-complexity full-age tracks.
- Develop the handler's skill on blind full-complexity tracks.
- Maintain a high level of motivation.

Strategy:
- Mix complex VST-like tracks with tracks focused on a single issue and specific skill exercises.
- Gradually reduce the marking on VST-like tracks so the tracks become blind.
- Develop the handler's skill on blind full-complexity tracks.

How to use this chapter:
- Read the discussion section that follows and look through the table on the next page, which summarizes the training structure of this phase.
- Do each of the 18 sessions and review your team's progress about every nine sessions. Before each session, carefully review the detailed tracklaying and handling instructions for each type of tracking session on pages 365 through 375.
- Keep a detailed log of each session using a format like the one shown on page 31 and keep a summary log like the one shown on page 377.
- Finally, do the review session on page 376 to evaluate your dog's progress and your own training-skill development.

Discussion:

It is great that you and your dog have developed all the basic urban skills and you are now starting to put the pieces together, including learning to read and follow your dog on blind VST-like tracks. It is a significant transition, even if some of your tracks in previous phases were not well marked.

In this phase, one-third of the tracks are VST-like zigzags, one-third are short tracks focused on a single issue, and one-third are skill exercises from earlier phases. In addition, some percentage of your tracks should be motivational tracks — perhaps an hour-old zigzag on a little-contaminated sports field. They are just fun for your dog and for you. The percentage of motivational tracks you need in this phase depends on the dog: if over 2-3 sessions you see your dog is slow to commit at starts that you think should be easy, increase the percentage of tracking sessions that consist of a simple motivational track.

In the previous phase, one-quarter of your tracks were on campus-like settings weaving through complexes of buildings. They were marked with chalk and flags so you knew right where the track was located. In this phase, we will continue this theme of realistic mini-VST-like tracks while gradually weaning you off chalk and flags. It is important to specify to your tracklayer exactly how you want the track marked and how much should be marked. There is no reason to rush to fully blind tracks as doing too many blind tracks too soon may ingrain confusion in your handling style, slowing down your dog's progress as well as your own. One technique I use is to ask for the first leg and corner to be unmarked and then the rest marked, so I can see how we do on a blind segment. Once confident for a blind first leg, I can ask for two or more legs to be unmarked. See also page 298.

Phase V3 Session Schedule:

% Motivational Sessions	Range: 10–30%	Your Target:

Sesn	Location	Configuration	Marked	Age	Yards
V3.1	Campus-like	VST-like Zigzag with Lawns, Buildings & Parking Lots	As needed		300–600
V3.2	Campus-like	Short Track Focused on a Single Issue	Yes		150–300
V3.3	As Required	Choose a skill exercise from Phase V1, V2	Yes		
V3.4	Campus-like	VST-like Zigzag with Lawns, Buildings & Parking Lots	As needed		300–600
V3.5	Campus-like	Short Track Focused on a Single Issue	Yes	1:30–5:00	150–300
V3.6	As Required	Choose a skill exercise from Phase V1, V2	Yes		
V3.7	Campus-like	VST-like Zigzag with Lawns, Buildings & Parking Lots	As needed		300–600
V3.8	Campus-like	Short Track Focused on a Single Issue	Yes		150–300
V3.9	As Required	Choose a skill exercise from Phase V1, V2	Yes		
		Evaluate to Proceed			
V3.10	Campus-like	VST-like Zigzag with Lawns, Buildings & Parking Lots	As needed		300–600
V3.11	Campus-like	Short Track Focused on a Single Issue	Yes		150–300
V3.12	As Required	Choose a skill exercise from Phase V1, V2	Yes		
V3.13	Campus-like	VST-like Zigzag with Lawns, Buildings & Parking Lots	As needed		300–600
V3.14	Campus-like	Short Track Focused on a Single Issue	Yes	1:30–5:00	150–300
V3.15	As Required	Choose a skill exercise from Phase V1, V2	Yes		
V3.16	Campus-like	VST-like Zigzag with Lawns, Buildings & Parking Lots	As needed		300–600
V3.17	Campus-like	Short Track Focused on a Single Issue	Yes		150–300
V3.18	As Required	Choose a skill exercise from Phase V1, V2	Yes		
		Evaluate to Proceed			

For the **VST-like Zigzag with Lawns, Buildings, and Parking Lots** sessions, each track should incorporate a mix of lawn, asphalt, concrete, and other non-vegetated surfaces as the site allows. Have the track pass alongside buildings, turn at a building, or turn away from a building as your creativity suggests. Try to control overall complexity and avoid the really tricky problems (we will do them on the short tracks). Use chalk and flags as appropriate for this dog and handler. If the tracklayer forgets to put a chalk mark where appropriate, quietly tell the handler as she approaches the area what the track is doing. Vary the age between 90 minutes and five hours.

Novice VST tracklayers may have a tendency to bring the track back close to itself particularly since the buildings create constraints. I like to keep from coming back within 75 yards of an earlier point to avoid tempting the dog to jump across the gap. The buildings and wind vortexes can move scent a long way but allowing 75 yards has proven adequate for most dogs in most situations. Of course, the simplest way to keep this from happening is to always alternate the turns to the right and then the left. Often you will have to come back toward the earlier track, just make sure there is a big gap when you do.

Here is the kind of track that can tempt the dog to jump the gap (the track is shown in black):
- On the first leg at the transition to asphalt and concrete, wind currents could draw the dog up toward the third corner 60 yards away.
- On the second corner, the dog only needs to overshoot 45 yards to reach the last leg.

A better plan would be to extend the second leg and finish the track in the upper right area.

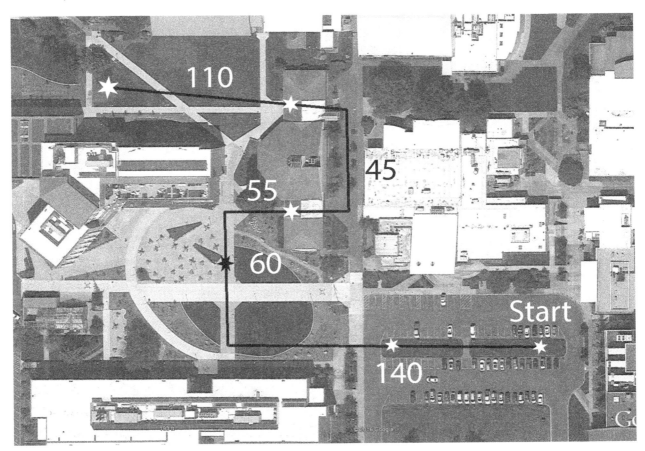

14. Images © 2016 Google

Phase V3. *Putting the Pieces Together.*

Short Tracks Focused on a Single Issue constitutes the middle third of your sessions. They will be marked tracks and will set up a particularly tricky track design component within the otherwise simplest track possible. This way, your dog can gain experience dealing with these tricky problems while you help him as needed. As he gains skill and acumen, you will also be able to learn to handle him without helping or hinting him.

For these tracks focused on a single issue, try to limit the track to 2–4 legs and try to make the track quite easy leading up to the tricky spot and again quite easy once past the tricky spot. Ideally, both the dog and the handler should find everything about the track easy except the one tricky spot. The handler should suggest several tricky issues she wants, and the tracklayer should choose one that she can find on this site with good areas leading up to it and past it.

Review your last several VST-like tracks to identify a specific issue your dog is having, or a handling issue you are experiencing. Any of these issues can be the focus of one of these sessions.

Alternatively, there are a lot of things that different dogs will find tricky. Here is a list of **Tricky Situations** to get you started but add to it as you find tricky things on your other tracks.

A. MOT turn in a large parking lot.
B. MOT turn in a concrete or brick plaza.
C. Unusual non-vegetated surfaces like large areas of dirt, sand, mulch or gravel.
D. Unpredictable turn at the intersection of two sidewalks without nearby buildings.
E. Unpredictable turn at the intersection of two sidewalks with nearby buildings.
F. Turn away from a scent trap just beyond the corner.
G. Turn away from following a curb, a hedge, a wall, or a building out into a large parking lot.
H. Turn away from a curb, a hedge, a wall, or a building onto a lawn.
I. Track or turn toward a noisy crowd, basketball game, or busy playground.
J. Track through a windy courtyard or gap between buildings.
K. Turn near a busy pedestrian crossing.
L. Turn in or near a bowl-like depression in a lawn or courtyard.
M. Turn on a sidewalk crossing with lawn ahead (particularly a down-sloping lawn ahead).
N. Turn on a sidewalk crossing with lawn ahead just 40 yards from the start.
O. Returning to lawn after more than 150 yards of hard surface.
P. Up or down long stairways; turns away from the stairways.
Q. Attractive scent pools and scent distractions like doorways, loading docks, and storm drains well to the side of the track luring the dog off-track for a distracting investigation.
R. Starts and first legs right along a pee-post alley.
S. Tracking across sloped parking lots in heavy rain.
T. Add other problematic issues as you notice them on your own and your friends' dogs' tracks.

Attractive scent pools and scent distractions can be particularly problematic for the handler on marked tracks because she can see that the dog is going well off the track to investigate. However, until you are willing to allow your dog to satisfy his curiosity about the attractive issue, he is unlikely to be comfortable proceeding on the track itself. Accept that you as a handler may need to expand the dog's search after the investigation so he gets back close to the main track.

The images below show examples of four tracks focused on a single issue. In the upper left, the second turn is away from a curb into a parking lot. In the upper right, the second turn is a MOT in an asphalt plaza. In the lower right, in white, is a turn onto a sidewalk just 40 yards from the start. In the lower-left is a track through a windy gap between buildings.

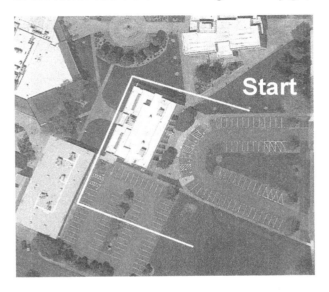

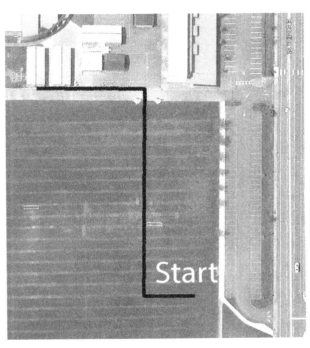

15. Images © 2016 Google

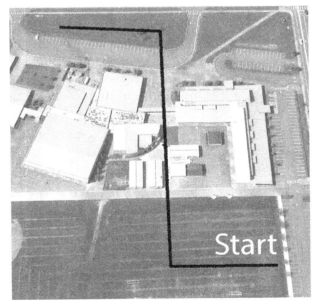

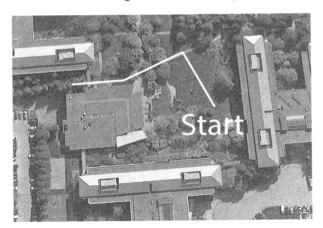

Skill Exercises from V1 and V2 constitute the last third of your sessions. They should be focused exercises chosen from phases V1, V2 or Part III TDU to practice and tune up your dog's specific skills, as well as your own. An additional skill exercise introduced in this phase helps the dog understand the need to follow the tracklayer even when there is parallel contamination anywhere on the track and in particular at the start. This is surprisingly common at tests where the start flag seems to attract curious passers-by.

The dog can tell which tracklayer to follow on AKC tracks by the scent on the start article. For the CKC scent pad, the scent of the tracklayer is heavier at the scent pad than the contamination layer who in these exercises does not stop at the start flag.

Choose a skill exercise from V1 or V2 on which you and your dog could do better. Two zigzags with intentional contamination is always a good choice if you are at a loss for what to do. If your dog is perfect on contaminated lawns, do intentional contamination on tracks with lots of transitions between surfaces or in broad areas of hard surface.

Enjoy your Practice Tracks and Have Fun with your Dog. How many Phase V3 tracks are enough? This phase's schedule (page 358) shows 18 sessions or 6 sets of the three track types. Blocks of six sets is arbitrary and may be enough for some very good dogs and handlers, but many dogs and handlers will need to stay in Phase V3 longer to reach the skill level appropriate for Phase V4. For example, I list 17 different tricky situations, so you really should do lots of tracks focused on a single issue to develop skills in these common situations. In addition, all dogs need problem-solving exercises to correct issues that have cropped up in their training.

In your session evaluations, give your dog an overall rating as was recommended in TDX Phase X4 on page 223. I use Excellent, Very Good, Good, Needs-Work, or Flawed. Periodically assess how you and your dog are doing on the blind zigzag tracks through campuses and the marked tracks focused on a single issue.
- Is your dog consistently making the right choices, and needs no help or at most a little help once per track?
- On the hard-surface segments of the track, is he close to the track moving in a straight line, or at least fairly close to the track, bracketing the track via the fringe?
- Are you consistently reading him correctly — no more than one mistake a track?

Stay in Phase V3 until you can answer "Yes" to all these questions. The schedule suggests it is appropriate to evaluate and review your dog's skills and your own handling skills about every nine sessions, although you may do so more often if you like.

VST Handling — Key Issues. There are several handling issues which, while not unique to VST, certainly need review when following your dog on blind tracks or really, on any urban track.
- During your training in the first two VST phases, you should have started to develop some sensitivity to your dog's **subtle signals** when he is following 3–5 hour-old scent in urban environments. Keep watching your dog carefully on marked tracks to see how he works out contamination, surface transitions, and swirling scent near structures and roads. Review your videos of him working. Noticing any of these same behaviors on the blind track may give you an idea of what is happening. Remember, these signals are fragile and not 100% reliable. They give you hints of what might be happening, not what surely is happening to the track.
- When a track exits a narrow alley onto a roadway, or passes between parked cars and crosses a driveway, handlers need to be vigilant for the **safety** of their dog and themselves.

Remember what you were told as a child about playing in traffic. Look both ways, be ready to hold your dog back until one or more cars pass, reel the tail of your line up so it does not get caught by a tire, and when it is safe, let your dog work the area normally.

- When a dog is struggling to sort things out anywhere on a VST track, **don't rush** the dog to make a decision or push the dog in a direction you think it might go. Be patient and let the dog sort things out and make his own decision.
- While a VST track has 4–8 turns, it has dozens to hundreds of **choice points** where the scent has been disturbed by passers-by, animals, vehicles, wind vortexes, surface transitions, or other distractions. Be prepared to say "Yippee! We're at a corner that might go straight" hundreds of times on a full-length full-complexity blind VST track. Have confidence in your dog and his training and you will get through.
- In some urban situations, particularly near buildings, tall fences, or active roadways, the **swirling airflow** may move the scent some distance while sweeping it clean from the 40' search area. Don't rush to move but be willing to follow your dog out one or more channels to allow the dog to either find the track with confidence or reject the channel. When you follow a dog who is still searching (not committed), turn your body and sidestep behind him rather than following full front on. He may interpret the latter as a confirmation that the scent he is investigating right now is a good one to follow regardless of whether it is the original track or not.
- When your dog is fixated by a particular **distraction**, be patient and first let him have time to get used to it or for it to go away. Then calmly and quietly ask the dog to go back to work. When that does not work, reel him in or go up to him and re-scent him and ask him to work again. Keep working at it until the dog finally decides to go back to work.
- When your dog has thoroughly searched all the possible choices in an area and cannot find the track, you will need to **expand his search,** which may involve backing up or spiraling out, or just blindly choosing a direction and hoping for the best. If you do need to move the search, don't take control – move slowly so the area he is able to search gradually changes. He still needs to be responsible for sorting out the scent and making the decision to commit in the direction of the good track.
- Learn to read his **out-of-scent behavior**. Track scent can be moved by the wind and turbulence a considerable distance down the wrong channel from a choice point. Eventually, the dog recognizes he cannot find the track anywhere in this direction. By learning to read his out-of-scent behavior, you will be able to back up to the prior choice point and let him check out the alternative channels.
- The handler must **remain neutral** to avoid pushing the dog in the wrong direction. That is why it is best to use "Yippee! ..." at every choice point. Even the good handler may occasionally feel they know something about the site, and that the track could not go down one of the alternative channels at a choice point. On blind test tracks, the handler may be ignorant of all the site possibilities, and that "impossible direction" is just where the track goes. Unfortunately, if she does not let her dog fully investigate that alternative path, the dog may not be able to commit to it. The good handler must be skeptical of her own hunches about where the track goes and does not go.
- The transition to **blind tracks** can expose dog and handler skill issues. Evaluate both performances on blind tracks and make those issues the focus of tracks focused on a single issue.

Attending VST Tests. Hopefully, you have been to several VST tests in your area and developed a sense of what VST tests look like and the kind of challenges that confront the dog and handler. Review your notes and memory of these tests and ask what happened on those tracks that your dog has not faced recently. If there are test sites you have not seen, it is worthwhile to visit them and walk around to see what kind of things might present novel challenges to you and your dog. See page 308 for additional discussion about tracklaying and spectating at VST tests.

Often the novel things are quite common everyday things that your training has not encountered recently. Three personal examples:
- I went to a campus in Eastern Washington to practice some months before a test was to be held there. I saw their sprinklers were going. Gosh, in wet coastal Washington, few places have sprinklers. So I laid the track right through the sprinklers, but they were not going when I ran the dog. Luckily, they came on in another area and QT got to experience getting this high-velocity water sprayed at him.
- I was thinking about entering a test in Oregon and realized that many of the tracks could be dramatically 3-D going up stairs and along cantilevered walkways on the second story. So I found a local community college with similar 3-D opportunities.
- That same Oregon campus had terraced parking lots where scent can spill down the steep slopes between the terraces. Again, I found a similar parking lot locally and gave my dog valuable experiences to be properly prepared.

Whether by spectating at tests or practicing at test sites, you will be surprised by the physical challenges and scenting issues that you don't encounter in your local tracking haunts.

Use of Video. If you have not used video to record your dog's tracks up until now, this is a great time to start doing so. Reviewing these videos after your tracking session will help you see things you did not realize in real time. I use a chest-mounted action camera to record my dog since its wide-angle lens keeps the dog in view, and all that is required to operate it is my remembering to push the record button at the start of the track. While I use a GoPro, there are a wide variety of brands to choose from, and some are quite inexpensive. I do recommend wide-angle high-definition at 60 frames per second so you will be able to see what is happening.

In addition to, or instead of, the action camera, have the tracklayer video you and the dog with a smartphone, tablet or old-fashioned camcorder. By having both you and the dog in the frame, you can review what you are doing that might be unconsciously helping your dog or sending him in inappropriate directions. You'll see less detail of the dog, which is why I like the chest-mounted action camera for learning to read my dog. Still, the view of both of us is valuable since it helps me see and subsequently correct handling issues I miss while I am handling the dog in real time.

Track Age. All these tracks, except the motivational tracks, should be run somewhere between 90 minutes and five hours with a pretty even distribution of all track ages. If you used the "Age A" or "Age B" sequences in Phases V1 and V2, this just means varying the age uniformly from an hour and a half to five hours. Scent ages more quickly in hot, dry weather, so be aware of the scent age as well as the by-the-watch age.

If you used the "Age C" sequence, you will need to build the age of these tracks. Say you have done almost all the Phase V1 and V2 work between 45 and 90 minutes, and your dog skills are solid at the 90 minute age. Then for half of these Phase V3 tracks, keep the age between 60 and 90 minutes for a while and for the other half, start increasing the age by 15 minutes at a time. Watch for your dog's confidence to drop and if it does, vary the track age below and near where the confidence dropped until the dog regains confidence.

Motivation. Continue to monitor your dog's enthusiasm and adjust his schedule accordingly.

Sessions V3.x VST-like Zigzag with Lawns, Buildings, and Parking Lots.

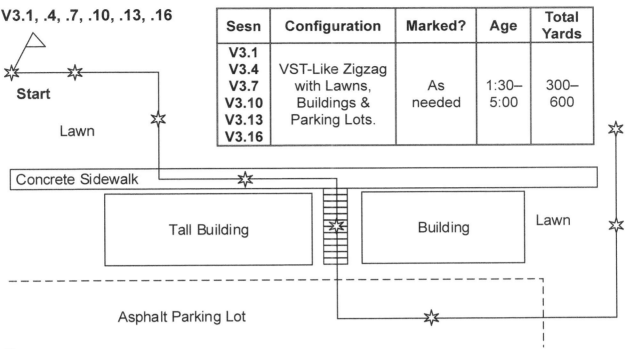

Sesn	Configuration	Marked?	Age	Total Yards
V3.1 V3.4 V3.7 V3.10 V3.13 V3.16	VST-Like Zigzag with Lawns, Buildings & Parking Lots.	As needed	1:30–5:00	300–600

Purpose:
- Develop the dog's skill in handling complex tracks in a realistic context.
- Develop the handler's skill in reading her dog, organizing the dog's search and avoiding interfering or helping the dog unless absolutely needed.

Tracklayer:
- Make these tracks sub-VST level of complexity or at most simple VST-like.
    - See the discussion of designing zigzags through buildings on page 359.
    - Avoid the complexity that many real VST test tracks have as we will practice those in the tracks focused on a single issue.
- The diagram above is a single example; use the campus site you have available as well as you can.
- Lay a single 3–6 turn zigzag that uses lawns, sidewalks, and/or parking lots.
    - Alternate turn direction to avoid parallel legs getting too close.
    - If you make two sequential turns in the same direction, the intervening leg should be at least 75 yards, if possible.
- If requested by the handler, use chalk on the hard surface to mark the corners and surface transitions.
    - If you forgot to put a chalk mark or the handler does not notice it, quietly tell the handler she is at a corner.
- Leave an inconspicuous or small article 30–45 yards down each leg to reward the dog for taking the corner.

Phase V3. Putting the Pieces Together.

Handler:
- Be patient at each hard-surface corner; don't rush your dog to make a decision.
- Ideally, use your whole line to allow your dog to make the choice before you move forward.
- If your dog chooses the wrong direction, let him investigate at least 30' before restraining him.
    - Ask him if this is the good track.
    - Re-scent him if you need to reel him in to you.
    - Use the steps of help on page 258.
- Give lots of treats and praise at each article.

Evaluation and Possible Adaptations:
- Note in your journal and your summary log (page 377) details of each track.
- Give your dog an overall rating as described on pages 223-224 in TDX Part II.
- The transition to **blind tracks** can expose dog and handler skill issues. Evaluate both your own and your dog's performance on blind tracks and make those issues the focus of tracks focused on a single issue.
- If he needs help on most hard-surface corners:
    - Use scent intensifiers like bare feet or SIAB (see page 8).
    - Try younger age (fresher scent) and then age more slowly.
    - Repeat these sessions several times.
- If he lacks confidence on many hard-surface turns:
    - Add very small freeze-dried treats at 15 & 25 yards past the hard-surface turn for a while. Later, use a small freeze-dried treat at 25 yards and an inconspicuous or small article at 35–50 yards past the corner. Then remove the treat but continue with the inconspicuous reward article.
    - Repeat several sessions in different locations with less natural contamination.

Do Tracking Dogs Lie?

This question is here because you are starting to handle your dog on blind VST-like tracks. You will find your dog makes mistakes, occasionally or pretty frequently, and you may be tempted to think that your dog is lying to you.

My simple answer is "No", he may make mistakes, but when he commits to something that is not part of the track, he doesn't intend to deceive you.

Regardless of whether you agree or not, it is a training issue. As a trainer, you need both to develop your dog's skill to follow the original track and to build his motivation to choose to stay with the good track in all cases.

Sessions V3.x Short Track Focused on a Single Issue.

V3.2, .5, .8, .11, .14, .17

Shown: "Turn away from a scent trap just beyond the corner"

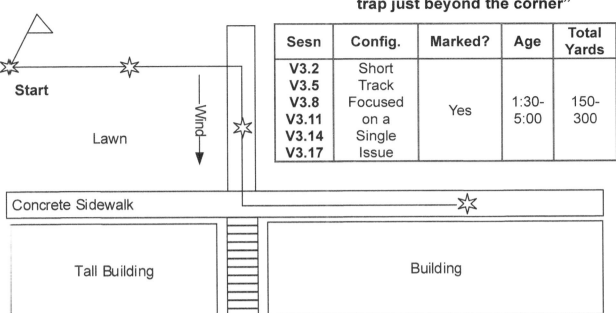

Sesn	Config.	Marked?	Age	Total Yards
V3.2	Short			
V3.5	Track			
V3.8	Focused	Yes	1:30-	150-
V3.11	on a		5:00	300
V3.14	Single			
V3.17	Issue			

Purpose:
- Develop the dog's skill in handling tricky situations.
- Develop the handler's skill in reading her dog, organizing the dog's search, and avoiding interfering or helping the dog unless absolutely needed.

Tracklayer:
- See the discussion on tracks focused on a single issue on page 360 including the list of tricky situations.
   A. MOT turn in a large parking lot.
   B. MOT turn in a concrete or brick plaza.
   C. Unusual non-vegetated surfaces like large areas of dirt, sand, mulch or gravel.
   D. Unpredictable turn at the intersection of two sidewalks without nearby buildings.
   E. Unpredictable turn at the intersection of two sidewalks with nearby buildings (diagram on page 369).
   F. Turn away from a scent trap just beyond the corner (above diagram).
   G. Turn away from a curb, a hedge, a wall, or a building out into a large parking lot.
   H. Turn away from following a curb, a hedge, a wall, or a building onto a lawn.
   I. Turn toward or beside a noisy crowd, basketball game, or busy playground.
   J. Track through a windy courtyard or gap between buildings (diagram on page 369).
   K. Turn near a busy pedestrian crossing.
   L. Turn in or near a bowl-like depression in a lawn or courtyard.
   M. Turn on a sidewalk crossing with lawn ahead (particularly a down-sloping lawn ahead).
   N. Turn on a sidewalk crossing with lawn ahead just 40 yards from the start (see page 370).
   O. Returning to lawn after more than 150 yards on hard surface.

Phase V3. Putting the Pieces Together.

P. Up or down long stairways; turns away from the stairways.
Q. Attractive scent pools and scent distractions like doorways, loading docks, and storm drains, well to the side of the track, luring the dog off-track for a distracting investigation.
R. Starts and first legs right along a pee-post alley.
S. Tracking across sloped parking lots in the heavy rain (a sloped lot is pictured on page 370).
T. Other issues as you notice them on your own and your friends' dogs' tracks.

- Alternatively, review the dog's last several VST-like tracks to identify a specific issue he is having, or an issue the handler is experiencing. Any of these issues can be the focus of one of these sessions.
- Also, review the TDX problem-solving suggestions starting on page 236 for ideas. Most of those exercise suggestions can be adapted to urban environments.
- Try to design a track with an easy segment, the chosen tricky situation, and end with an easy segment.
- If you make two sequential turns in the same direction, the intervening leg should be at least 75 yards, if possible.
- Use chalk on the hard surface to mark the corners and surface transitions, unless requested otherwise.
- Leave an inconspicuous or small article 30–45 yards down each leg to reward the dog for taking the corner.

Handler:
- Choose several issues from the list above from which the tracklayer can choose. Her selection will depend on the configuration of the tracking site and the activity going on when she lays it.
- Be patient at each tricky situation and elsewhere; don't rush your dog to make a decision.
- Ideally, use your whole line to allow your dog to make the choice before you move forward.
- If your dog chooses the wrong direction, let him investigate at least 30' before restraining him.
  ◦ Ask him if this is the good track.
  ◦ Re-scent him if you need to reel him in to you.
  ◦ Use the steps of help on page 258.
- Give lots of treats and praise at each article.

Evaluation and Possible Adaptations:
- Note in your journal and your summary log (page 377) details of each track.
- Give your dog an overall rating as described on page 223 in TDX Part II.
- If the track turns out to be easy for the dog, you can count it as a motivational session as well.
  ◦ Consider what made it easy and if necessary, select the issue again at a site that will be more challenging for the dog and handler.
- If he needs help on most hard-surface corners, you should consider using scent intensifiers, running it at a younger age, and repeating the session several times in different locations.
- If he lacks confidence at the tricky situation:
  ◦ Add very small freeze-dried treats at 15 & 25 yards past the hard-surface turn for a while. Later, use a small freeze-dried treat at 25 yards and an inconspicuous or small article at 35–50 yards past the corner.
  ◦ Repeat several sessions in different locations with less natural contamination.

Other tricky-situation examples:

Unpredictable turn at the intersection of two sidewalks with nearby buildings.

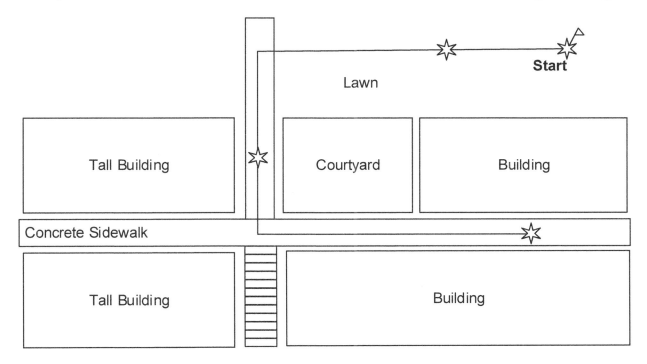

Track through a windy courtyard or gap between buildings.

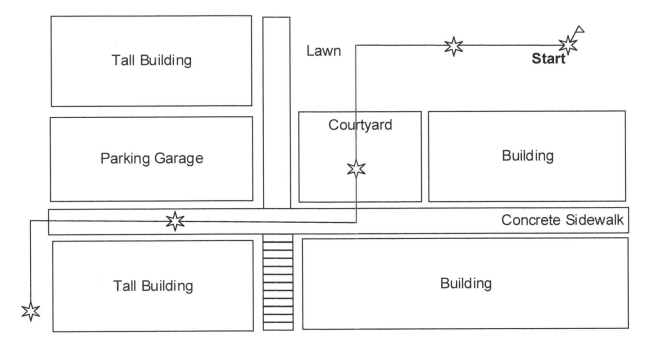

Phase V3. Putting the Pieces Together.

Turn on a sidewalk with lawn ahead just 40 yards from the start.

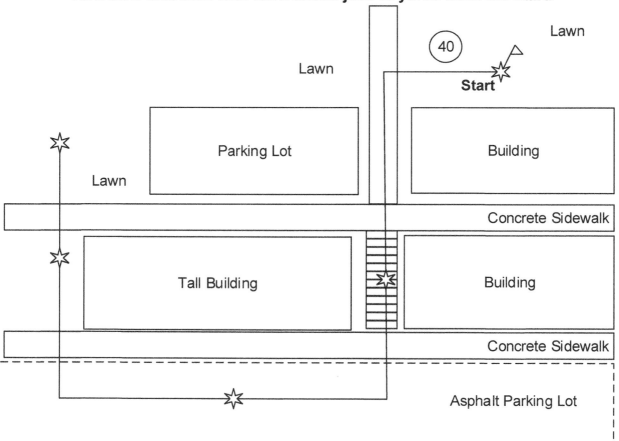

VST Track Using a Sloped Parking Lot

This full-complexity VST includes a MOT on the second leg, a steep leg up across a terraced parking lot, and a number of transitions that will challenge most dogs and handlers.

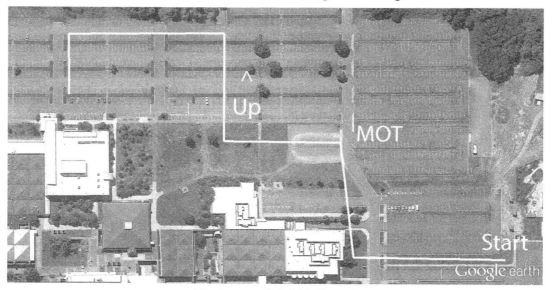

16. Image © 2016 Google

Sessions V3.x Select a Skill Exercise from Phase V1 or V2.

Sesn	Configuration	Marked?	Age	Total Yards
V3.3 V3.6 V3.9 V3.12 V3.15 V3.18	Choose a Skill Exercise from V1 or V3	Yes	1:30 - 5:00	As Appropriate

Purpose:
- Maintain and improve your dog's skills and your own handling skills.

Skill Exercises:

For each of these sessions, choose a skill exercise from this list:
- Four-turn track with slices and bisects — see page 319.
- Parallel contamination at the start or elsewhere — see page 372.
- Curbed-Island serpentines with big gaps — see page 321.
- Hard-surface turns at barriers — see page 346 or 317.
- Hard-surface turns onto and off of sidewalks — see page 348.
- Hard-surface turn on a parking lot or plaza — see page 350.
- Lawn serpentines to refocus the dog onto the track on the grass while aging appropriately for your dog's current skill level — see page 267.
- An urban downwind-downhill acute to improve his circling on corners — see page 102.
- A simple short motivational track with lots of articles.
- A simple all-lawn track or all-parking-lot curbed-island track with articles tossed 5 to 15' to the side of the track.
- A simple short VST-like track in a heavily distracting area.
- 4–5 hour-old simple short VST-like track on a warm, dry day.
- Specific problem issues can be addressed in these sessions. Review the TDX problem-solving suggestions starting on page 236. Most of those exercise suggestions can be adapted to urban environments.

Handler:
- See the relevant procedure for the chosen exercise on the page referenced above.
- Make sure your dog is having fun.

Evaluation:
- Note in your journal and your summary log (page 377) details of each track.
- Give your dog an overall rating as described on page 223 in TDX Part II.
- If the track turns out to be easy for the dog, you can count it as a motivational session as well.
- Evaluate based on the evaluation section of the chosen session referenced above.

Session V3.x. Parallel Contamination.

Purpose:
- Help the dog understand to stay with the tracklayer's track even when contamination parallels the track at the start or elsewhere.

Notes:
- Parallel or nearly parallel contamination at the start is surprisingly common at tests due to the start flag attracting passers-by.
- These exercises assume you and your dog are nearly perfect on the intentional contamination with slices and bisects from Phase V1 (page 319).
- Each of these six exercises should be done in sequence to allow the dog to develop the experience and skill to handle these situations.
    - Do the sequence of exercises first at 30-60 minutes and then repeat at 2–3 hours old.
    - For exercises 3–6, do two tracks per session.

Tracklayer:
- Lay the parallel contamination exercise 1-6 as chosen by the handler.
- Avoid placing an article in segments with parallel contamination. Treats are optional.
- For first 2 patterns, pause at points A and B for the contamination layer to catch up with you, then walk shoulder-to-shoulder.
- For the third pattern, pause at point A for the contamination layer to catch up with you, then walk shoulder-to-shoulder about 1' apart.
- For the remaining patterns at the start, put down your flag and start article (or scent pad) and signal to the contamination layer to come up beside you. Walk shoulder-to-shoulder.

Contamination Layer:
- Lay at the same time as the tracklayer.
- For exercises 1-3, wait 20 yards behind and to the side of the start. For exercises 4-6, wait 10 yards behind the tracklayer. Come up and join her when and where she is ready.
- On parallel segments, walk shoulder-to-shoulder with tracklayer about 1' apart.
- Do not step on the tracklayer's footprints, walk just to the side of her.
- Optionally, place a flag or clippie where the contamination layer joins and leaves the track.

Handler:
- For designs 1–3, approach the start halfway between tracklayer and contamination layer.
- Be patient as your dog sorts out the scent discrimination required by the contamination.
- Don't rush your dog to make a decision.
- Ideally, use your whole line to allow your dog to make the choice before you move forward along the good track or restrain him on the contamination.
- If your dog chooses the wrong direction, let him investigate at least 30' before restraining him.
- See steps of hinting on page 259 and helping on page 258.
- Give lots of treats and praise at each article.

Evaluation:
- Note in your journal and your summary log (page 377) details of each track and whether your dog needed help or hints to avoid committing to the contamination.

V3.x Parallel Contamination 1

Tracklayer:
- Keep parallel CXT 30 yards from corners.
- Pause at points A & B for the contamination layer to catch up with you.
- Flags as shown; treats are optional.
- Articles at the start & where shown.
- Leg lengths can vary.

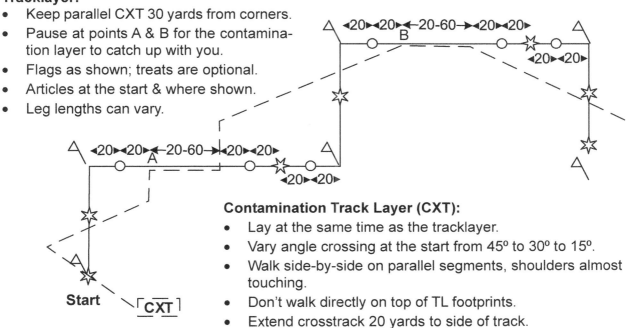

Contamination Track Layer (CXT):
- Lay at the same time as the tracklayer.
- Vary angle crossing at the start from 45° to 30° to 15°.
- Walk side-by-side on parallel segments, shoulders almost touching.
- Don't walk directly on top of TL footprints.
- Extend crosstrack 20 yards to side of track.

V3.x Parallel Contamination 2

Contamination Track Layer (CXT):
- Lay at the same time as the tracklayer.
- Vary angle crossing the start from 45° to 30° to 15° over several sessions.
- Walk shoulder-to-shoulder on parallel segments.
- Approximately 45° departing & re-joining tracklayer

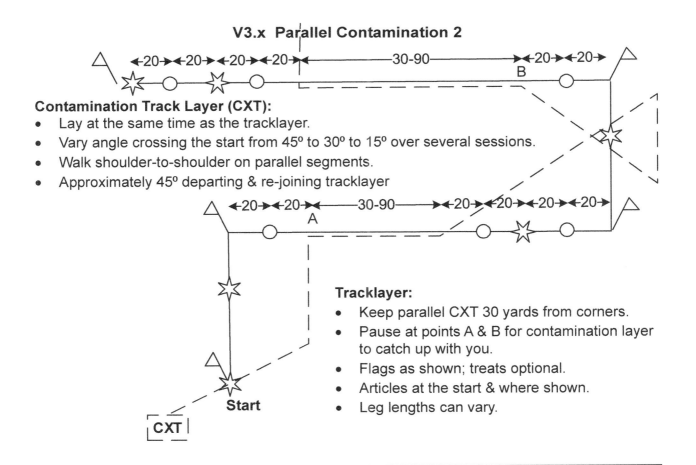

Tracklayer:
- Keep parallel CXT 30 yards from corners.
- Pause at points A & B for contamination layer to catch up with you.
- Flags as shown; treats optional.
- Articles at the start & where shown.
- Leg lengths can vary.

Phase V3. Putting the Pieces Together.

V3.x Parallel Contamination 3

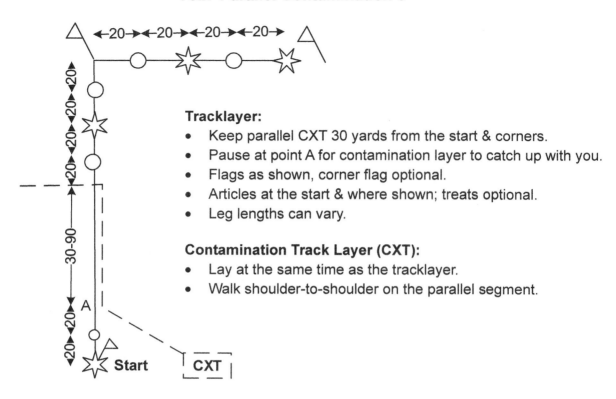

Tracklayer:
- Keep parallel CXT 30 yards from the start & corners.
- Pause at point A for contamination layer to catch up with you.
- Flags as shown, corner flag optional.
- Articles at the start & where shown; treats optional.
- Leg lengths can vary.

Contamination Track Layer (CXT):
- Lay at the same time as the tracklayer.
- Walk shoulder-to-shoulder on the parallel segment.

V3.x Parallel Contamination 4

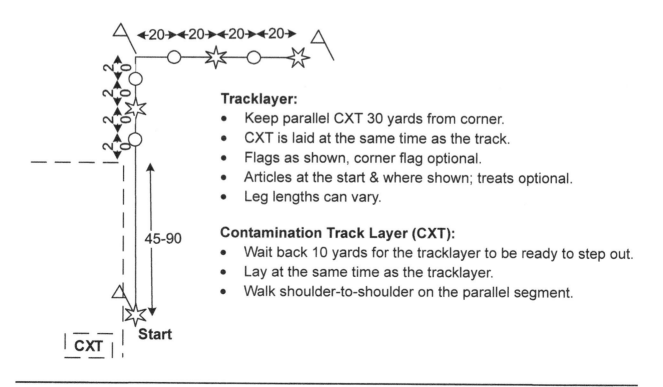

Tracklayer:
- Keep parallel CXT 30 yards from corner.
- CXT is laid at the same time as the track.
- Flags as shown, corner flag optional.
- Articles at the start & where shown; treats optional.
- Leg lengths can vary.

Contamination Track Layer (CXT):
- Wait back 10 yards for the tracklayer to be ready to step out.
- Lay at the same time as the tracklayer.
- Walk shoulder-to-shoulder on the parallel segment.

V3.x Parallel Contamination 5

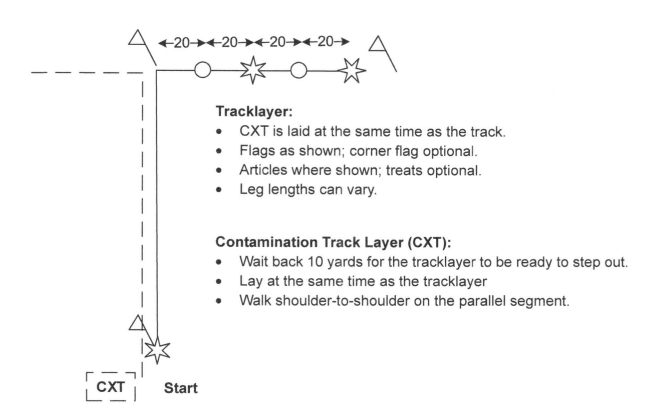

Tracklayer:
- CXT is laid at the same time as the track.
- Flags as shown; corner flag optional.
- Articles where shown; treats optional.
- Leg lengths can vary.

Contamination Track Layer (CXT):
- Wait back 10 yards for the tracklayer to be ready to step out.
- Lay at the same time as the tracklayer
- Walk shoulder-to-shoulder on the parallel segment.

V3.x Parallel Contamination 6

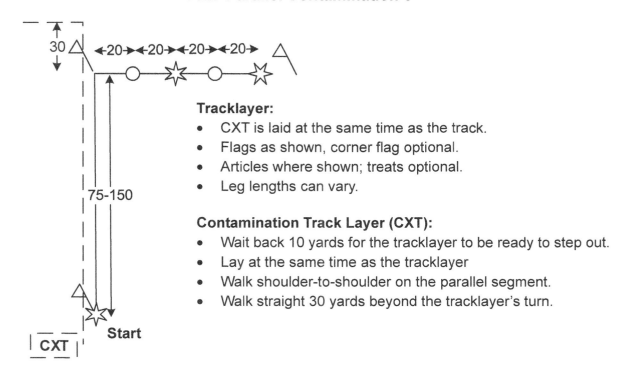

Tracklayer:
- CXT is laid at the same time as the track.
- Flags as shown, corner flag optional.
- Articles where shown; treats optional.
- Leg lengths can vary.

Contamination Track Layer (CXT):
- Wait back 10 yards for the tracklayer to be ready to step out.
- Lay at the same time as the tracklayer
- Walk shoulder-to-shoulder on the parallel segment.
- Walk straight 30 yards beyond the tracklayer's turn.

Phase V3. Putting the Pieces Together.

Session V3.9+ and V3.18+. Review, Evaluate, and Decide How to Proceed.

Do a periodic assessment about every 9 sessions. Evaluate how you and your dog are doing on the blind zigzag tracks through campuses and the short tracks focused on a single issue. Consider only the tracks that are two hours old or older. Use the following questions to decide how to proceed.

- Is your dog making the right choices and needs no help, or at most a little help, once per track?
- On the hard-surface segments of the track, is he close to the track moving in a straight line or at least fairly close to the track, bracketing the track via the nearby fringe?
    - Have a wider notion of "close to the track" on large hard surfaces than you have on either field grass or lawns. He should be roughly paralleling the footsteps when to the side.
- Are you consistently reading him correctly — no more than one mistake a track?
- Review the list of **Dog Skills** from page 302 and evaluate his required skills:
    - Clear-Confident-Committed tracking on heavily-contaminated lawns including well-contaminated starts.
    - Clear-Confident-Committed tracking on flat hard surfaces.
    - Turns on non-vegetated surfaces constrained by buildings and barriers.
    - Turning onto and off of narrow hard surfaces — sidewalks and driveways — with nearby vegetation.
    - Turning in the middle of flat hard surfaces (Moment of Truth Turns).
    - Turning off scent-trapping channels like sidewalks with nearby buildings and alternative pathways.
    - Returning to lawns after lots of hard surface.
    - Being comfortable tracking in highly distracting urban environments with people and other dogs nearby, squirrels scampering from tree to tree, and pee-posts everywhere.
    - Staying focused for a whole track.
    - Clear-Confident-Committed tracking on 4–5 hour-old tracks in warm, dry weather.
    - Tracking and finding varied articles in many weather conditions.
    - Finding articles to the side of the dog's path.
- Review the list of **Handler Skills** from page 302 and evaluate your required skills:
    - Subtle encouragement and restraint to reinforce your dog's required skills.
    - Reading very fragile signals from your dog.
    - Shifting responsibility for "Staying with the good track" to your dog.
    - Understanding how far off the footprints the dog might work tracklayer scent in different environments.
    - Accepting that the dog may move well off the track to investigate scent pools and scent distractions like doorways, loading docks, and storm drains.
    - Recovering from being off track. Specifically, helping your dog search a large area without taking responsibility away from the dog.
    - Safe tracking in parking lots full of cars and on lightly traveled roads.

Stay in Phase V3 until you can answer yes to the first three questions and give good-to-excellent ratings for all the dog and handler skills. Until then, adjust your training schedule to include more exercises that develop and improve those needed skills. The schedule shows it is appropriate to evaluate and review your dog's skills and your own handling skills about every 9 sessions, although you may do so more or less often if you like.

Phase V3 Summary Log

Sesn	Site	Config.	Date	Age	Evaluation
V3.1		VST-like Zigzag			
V3.2		Single Issue			
V3.3		Choose a skill			
V3.4		VST-like Zigzag			
V3.5		Single Issue			
V3.6		Choose a skill			
V3.7		VST-like Zigzag			
V3.8		Single Issue			
V3.9		Choose a skill			
V3.10		VST-like Zigzag			
V3.11		Single Issue			
V3.12		Choose a skill			
V3.13		VST-like Zigzag			
V3.14		Single Issue			
V3.15		Choose a skill			
V3.16		VST-like Zigzag			
V3.17		Single Issue			
V3.18		Choose a skill			

Phase V3. Putting the Pieces Together.

Phase V4. Preparing for the VST Test — Special Situations & Blind Tracks.

Purpose:
- Develop and refine your dog's skill and handler's skill working full-complexity full-age blind tracks in a variety of environments.
- Maintain a high level of motivation.

Strategy:
- Mix complex VST-like tracks with tracks focused on a single issue and specific skill exercises.
- Mark the VST-like tracks as little as possible and continue to reduce any marking so the tracks are blind.
- Develop the handler's skill on blind full-complexity tracks.

How to use this chapter:
- Read the discussion section that follows and look through the table on the next page, which summarizes the training structure of this phase.
- Do each of the 18 sessions and review your team's progress about every nine sessions. Before each session, carefully review the detailed tracklaying and handling instructions for the session type starting on page 389.
- Keep a detailed log of each session using a format like the one shown on page 31 and keep a summary log like the one shown on page 400.
- Finally, do the review session on page 394 to evaluate your dog's progress and your own training-skill development.

Discussion:

This phase will prepare you and your dog for the VST and UTDX tests by mixing blind VST test-like tracks with sessions focused on a single issue, and specific skill development sessions. Of course, some 10–30% of the sessions should be fun, motivational sessions to maintain the dog's enthusiasm.

This phase is structured similarly to Phase V3. In that phase, you and the dog were working on developing your skills in handling a full-complexity test-like VST track by starting with partially-marked mini-VST tracks and steadily developing the team's ability as well as their trust in each other. Proceeding to this phase implies you both have mastered most of the required skills, and they just need to be refined and polished to test-ready status.

While the schedule on the next page shows six stages of three session types, the actual number of sessions to be ready to enter a VST and to be successful when you get into a test is highly variable. Use the schedule on the next page or individualize for your dog using the basic schedule stage shown on page 387, repeated as appropriate.

Rushing or ignoring important issues is not the way to success. Don't be reluctant to try techniques and session types you learn from friends or at classes or seminars. Continue to use them if they seem to work for your dog. There is no one magic bullet way to prepare for this difficult, but rewarding test.

Phase V4 Session Schedule:

% Motivational Sessions	Range: 10–30%	Your Target:

Session	Location	Configuration	Marked?	Age	Length Yards
V4.1	Campus-like	VST-like Track with Lawns, Buildings & Parking Lots.	No		500–800
V4.2	Campus-like	Short Track Focused on a Single Issue	Optional		150–400
V4.3	As Required	Choose a skill exercise from Phase V1, V2 or V3.	Optional		
V4.4	Campus-like	VST-like Track with Lawns, Buildings & Parking Lots.	No		500–800
V4.5	Campus-like	Short Track Focused on a Single Issue	Optional		150–400
V4.6	As Required	Choose a skill exercise from Phase V1, V2 or V3.	Optional		
V4.7	Campus-like	VST-like Track with Lawns, Buildings & Parking Lots.	No		500–800
V4.8	Campus-like	Short Track Focused on a Single Issue	Optional		150–400
V4.9	As Required	Choose a skill exercise from Phase V1, V2 or V3.	Optional	1:30–5:00	
V4.10	Campus-like	VST-like Track with Lawns, Buildings & Parking Lots.	No		500–800
V4.11	Campus-like	Short Track Focused on a Single Issue	Optional		150–400
V4.12	As Required	Choose a skill exercise from Phase V1, V2 or V3.	Optional		
V4.13	Campus-like	VST-like Track with Lawns, Buildings & Parking Lots.	No		500–800
V4.14	Campus-like	Short Track Focused on a Single Issue	Optional		150–400
V4.15	As Required	Choose a skill exercise from Phase V1, V2 or V3.	Optional		
V4.16	Campus-like	VST-like Track with Lawns, Buildings & Parking Lots.	No		500–800
V4.17	Campus-like	Short Track Focused on a Single Issue	Optional		150–400
V4.18	As Required	Choose a skill exercise from Phase V1, V2 or V3.	Optional		
V4.19		Review and Evaluate			
V4…	Vary Locations	Repeat the above			

As you know from tracklaying or spectating at local VST tests, special VST track situations are pretty common at most VST tracking sites. You may already have incorporated some of them in your Phase V3 zigzags through campuses.

Here is an ad hoc list of some **common situations** where a little practice may greatly improve your dog's ability to follow a track near or through these features:

A. **Open Stairways.** Since the scent falls down to the ground or floor below, the dog may spend a lot of time below the stairs before trying to go up the stairs where the tracklayer went. Also, your dog may be stressed by the visually open nature of these stairways.

B. **Second-story Cantilevered Open-Deck Walkways.** The tracklayer scent spills over the railing and falls to the ground below. So the dog may track that scent on the ground in preference to going up the stairs to the walkway.

C. **Loading Docks.** These are great scent pools, particularly the kind with a driveway ramp down to the dock.

D. **Building Doorways.** Pedestrian traffic in and out the door pushes and pulls the tracklayer scent as well as creating an interesting scent distraction.

E. **Parking Garages.** Many parking garages have openings that allow a track to go through them. In addition to the extensive car traffic, they never get rained on so they are much drier than outside parking lots. In addition, their open-sided construction creates strange vortexes moving and pooling the scent away from the track.

F. **Open Barns and Sheds** in fairgrounds. These are similar to garages except they may have a dirt floor instead of concrete and lingering animal smells for potential distraction opportunities.

G. **Returning to Grass** after hundreds of yards of concrete and asphalt. Dogs seem to have a lot of trouble transitioning back to vegetation after spending a long time on hard surface. On campuses where this happens, the judges often have to end on vegetation to have enough vegetated surfaces.

H. **Mirrored Glass-sided Buildings.** One issue is the track can get quite hot in the sun. Also, handlers and dogs can get disoriented in areas with mirrored glass because they see themselves and they see other landmarks multiple times.

I. **Outdoor Amphitheaters.** Amphitheaters or similar stepped areas can cause the scent to pool well away from the track. Watch your dog's handling of articles on stairs or stepped areas like amphitheaters since the scent plumes of the article may waterfall down the steps or over the sides.

J. **Outdoor Cafeteria** eating areas. Large numbers of tables and chairs can catch your line and pool the scent.

K. **Large Fountains and Pools.** They affect temperature and humidity locally, enhance vortexes and scent pools, and attract large numbers of people adding contamination to your track.

L. **Unusually Shaped Architectural Features.** For example, buildings with cantilevered sections under which one might track.

M. **Terraced Parking Lots.** Scent flows downhill and may pool against the next terrace. In the rain, the scent may be washed down a considerable distance. See example on page 370.

Hopefully, you have been going to VST tests in your area as a tracklayer or spectator and have seen the kinds of architectural features, building configurations, and landscaping styles that are found near the test tracks. Add to the list of "interesting" features in your area and prioritize the kinds of things you see being used in your local VST tests.

Six of these common situations are illustrated in photos below:

Open Stairs

Stairs & 2nd Story Walkways

Open-sided Garage

Terraced Amphitheater

Splashing Sunlit Fountain

Outdoor Cafeteria Area

One-third to one-half of your tracks should be blind tracks laid by trusted tracklayer friends who will listen to your directions about what you want today and lay good unpredictable tracks for your dog. The remainder of your training tracks should be shorter and simpler tracks, focused on a single issue or skill that needs improvement.

The satellite views below show a number of representative VST test tracks. Although these pictures show the track configuration and the track's relationship to large features like buildings, parking lots, fountains, and sidewalks, there is neither the detail nor the 3-D perspective to fully appreciate the way these features influence the scent. You must walk behind a tracking dog to see what the dog tells you about where the scent lingers in these environments.

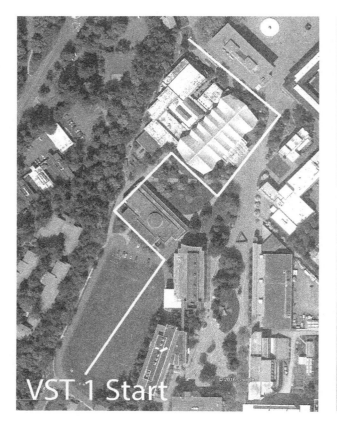

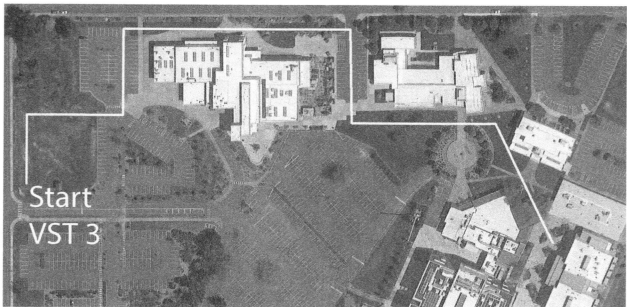

17. Images © 2016 Google

It is important to review the requirements for VST or UTDX tracks by rereading the AKC or CKC rules in detail. They both contain a specific section on the test and the test requirements. The AKC rules also include extensive guidelines for designing VST tracks. As you study the rules, consider the test tracks you have seen as a spectator and try to understand why the judges designed the track that particular way. Most judges are trying to plot good test tracks. Perhaps they will be your judge when you enter a test yourself, so knowing what they typically do can be useful.

Comparison of AKC VST and CKC UTDX Test Tracks

	AKC	CKC
Age:	3–5 hours	3–5 hours
Length:	600–800 yards	600–750 meters
Start:	Start flag with article. First 20 yards vegetated.	Start flag with scent pad. First 25 meters vegetated.
Surfaces:	1+ vegetated, 2+ non-vegetated. Must utilize buildings.	Vegetated & non-vegetated. Must utilize buildings.
Ratio:	1/3–2/3 vegetated & 1/3–2/3 non-vegetated.	1/2–2/3 vegetated & 1/3–1/2 non-vegetated.
Articles:	Cloth, leather, metal & plastic. Cloth or leather at the start.	Intermediate: fabric, wood, plastic. The last article is leather.
	1+ article on non-vegetated.	1+ article on non-vegetated.
Corners:	4–8, rights & lefts.	5–7, rights & lefts, acutes ≥ 45°.
MOT	1 or more 90° on hard surface. Next leg, at least 30 yards on non-vegetated before returning to vegetated.	1 or more 90° on hard surface. Next leg, at least 25 meters on non-vegetated before returning to vegetated.
Crosstracks:	None plotted.	None plotted.
Obstacles:	Only stairs are OK, other types of physical obstacles are not.	Only guardrails, fences, stairs & open buildings are OK.
Line:	20–40', Handler may work as close as 10'.	16–49', Handler may work as close as 10'.

I won't repeat the complete AKC or CKC rules here. As a training aid, I do include a list of the essential AKC VST-test design elements that I like to incorporate in blind training tracks for this phase.

- 600–800 yards, more likely to be at the lower end of the range.
- Several different surfaces with a fair amount of asphalt and concrete.
- 3–5 hours old with 4–8 turns. Vary age and vary the number of turns.
- Good start on lawn.
- Unpredictable MOT on hard surface with no fringeable vegetation nearby. Perhaps more than one.
- Buildings and groups of buildings; e.g., tracks must go near buildings so the dog and handler experience the wind vortex driven scent movement, and the constrained movement of people coming and going to the buildings.
- Maintain sufficient spacing between legs to avoid encouraging the dog to jump across.

I add the following training elements so the blind track can be good for training my dog when he struggles, as well as a fun experience for him.

- Use inconspicuous or small articles that are unlikely to be picked up by a passerby. Place them about 25–50 yards past each area of difficulty as reward points.
- Try to find easy segments between the difficult ones if possible — it is not always possible.
- Sometimes use very active sites to maximize contamination and sometimes use less active sites to make it easier on the dog.
- Go out of my way to use a wide variety of different training sites, including some that mimic test sites I am likely to enter.

Avoid using the same location more than once every other week, if possible, and certainly no more frequently than once a week. Regardless of whether or not your dog will be drawn off by a several-day-old previous track, he may be drawn off by memory (down that alley was an article and a party). Avoid using a tracklayer who works in a building complex nearby unless she can use another part of the building complex where she does not normally roam.

On blind tracks, the tracklayer should hang back 50 or so yards behind the handler to avoid inadvertently signaling to the handler or dog which choice is correct. Of course, the tracklayer must come closer if the dog and handler go out of sight around a corner or behind landscaping. Don't tell the handler she is off until the dog is so far off the team cannot recover; 50–75 yards off is an OK rule of thumb at this point in their training. If the handler requests information on the track, move forward and explain what is going on. Try to be very clear, as the handler is trying to focus on her dog and get directions from you at the same time. For the remainder of the track, you can stay closer to the handler so you can offer track information as needed by the handler.

Putting in your own Blind Tracks. Well, of course they are not really blind, but as the tracklayer-handler you will need to act as if you did not know where the track is going. We all have times when we can go tracking and don't have a trusted tracking friend to lay a blind track for our dog. While this will never be as good as a true blind track, if you handle as if it were blind, you can get valuable opportunities to read your dog, and he can get valuable lessons in making the right choices on his own. If he struggles too much, you can just turn to yourself rather than the tracklayer and shift into help mode as needed.

When I put in my own "blind" tracks, I find it takes quite a lot of mental discipline to avoid using my actual knowledge of the track when handling my dog. It helps to focus on your dog 100% of your attention and suppress your natural tendency to think about what the track is doing. It means following your dog well off the track if he needs to do so to sort out a scent problem.

Track Complexity — Choice Points and Corners. Once a skilled dog finds and commits to a leg, it is relatively easy for the dog to continue on that leg until something interrupts the scent picture. Places where the scent picture changes can be called choice points as the dog must make a decision there. Corners are obvious choice points, but there are many more, like contamination, surface transitions, nearby roads with vehicle traffic, and physical structures that affect the air flow and thus the scent distribution. In addition, distractions present while the track is being run provide more choice points that can break the dog's and handler's concentration. It is hard to plot realistic VST tracks and predict where all the choice points are located until you follow along behind the dog and see where he has to investigate scent issues. While accurately predicting track complexity is impossible, having a general sense of the nature of the campus being used and particular local issues seen before can be used to adapt the designed complexity of the track.

Let's examine the choice points (CP) along the representative VST track in the picture below, that is labeled VST 4.

1. The direction of the first leg at the start is a CP.
2. CPs include the sun-to-shade transitions along the first leg under the trees.
3. The first corner is a CP.
4. The transition to asphalt on the second leg is a CP.
5. The second corner just under the solar panel is a MOT CP.
6. The transition out from under the solar panel into full sun is a CP.
7. The transition over the curb and onto grass is a CP.
8. The third corner is a CP.
9. The sun-to-shade transitions under the trees and the transitions crossing the curving sidewalk are several CPs.
10. The transition to cross the road is a CP to cross and a CP to continue onto the lawn on the other side.
11. The corner of the first building (on the right) is a CP.
12. Entering the corridor formed by the second building (on the left) and the first is a CP.
13. The end of the first building is a CP as is the continuation straight between the third building and the second.
14. The fourth turn is a CP.
15. Continuing along the fourth building is a CP.
16. Turning at the end of the fourth building is a CP.
17. The many transitions across concrete sidewalks are CPs, as are the gaps between the buildings (on the right) or turning out into the parking lot (on the left).

18. Image © 2016 Google

In total, there are about 30 critical decisions the dog needs to make. In addition, contamination adds many more choice points. The dog is the best-equipped team member to make those decisions, so train him thoroughly, and then trust him to make them in the test itself.

Phase V4. Preparing for the VST Test — Special Situations & Blind Tracks.

Two more VST test tracks are shown below as examples of appropriate VST-like complexity. Identify some of the choice points in the maps below.

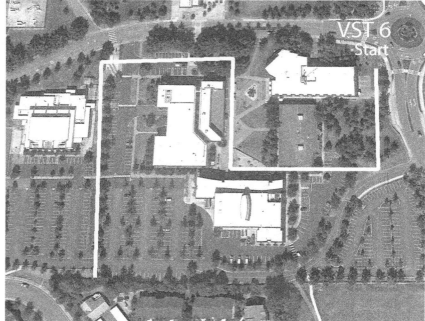

19. Images © 2016 Google

Handlers and Tracklayers Beware. Handlers, in particular, should monitor the appropriate complexity of the "VST-like" tracks their tracklayers are laying to make sure they are of appropriate complexity. Based on the recent performance of the dog, the handler may ask for an "easy" or "motivational" VST-like track. If multiple tracks end up being super-difficult, she needs to help the tracklayer know what is inappropriately difficult about them so the tracklayer can do better. Likewise, if the handler asks the tracklayer for challenging "VST-like" tracks and several such tracks are all easy, the handler may need to communicate with the tracklayer so she understands what she could have done differently to make the track challenging. Finally, when the handler is also the tracklayer, these conversations still need to occur, even if they are with yourself.

If all the tracks you are doing are too easy, then you and your dog will not be ready for your track when you get into a test. If all your tracks are too hard, your dog will get frustrated and lose motivation; a demotivated dog will not get you any closer to passing a test. Adapt the complexity up and down so your dog is exposed to challenges while still maintaining a high level of motivation. Some actual VST test tracks are shown on pages 382, 385, and 386 to exemplify appropriate VST-like complexity.

Tracklayers laying blind tracks should strive to be unpredictable without making the track inappropriately complex for the dog and handler. Both dogs and handlers get habituated to the kinds of things you do in a particular area or situation and may be predisposed to investigate that alternative. VST judges may be less predictable.

Individualize the Session Schedule for your Dog. You can think of customizing the schedule freely within the percentage range shown in the table below or follow the recommended schedule on page 379 with one-third of your tracks of each type.

Sesn	Location	% of Sessions	Configuration	Marked	Age	Len
V4.1	Campus-like	33–50%	VST-like Tracks with Lawns, Buildings & Parking Lots	No	1:30–5:00	500–800
V4.2	Campus-like	25–33%	Short Track Focused on a Single Issue	Optional		150–300
V4.3	As Required	25–33%	Choose a skill exercise from Phase V1, V2 or V3	Optional		
V4…	Vary Locations		Repeat the above			

In addition to the scheduled sessions, some percentage of your tracks should be motivational tracks — perhaps an hour-old zigzag on a little-contaminated sports field. They are just fun for your dog. The percentage of motivational tracks you need in this phase depends on the dog: if over 2-3 sessions you see your dog is slow to commit at starts that you think should be easy, increase the percentage of tracking sessions that consist of a simple motivational track and shorten and simplify all practice tracks for a while.

As you progress through numerous repetitions of Phase V4, you will find your dog gaining confidence and completing the blind test-like tracks successfully without any help from you or the tracklayer. Review the track design to make sure it meets all the requirements of a VST track, with the minor exception of something like using more than two intermediate articles. You are ready to enter a VST or UTDX test. While waiting to get in, continue doing blind tracks, tracks focused on a single issue, and skill exercises so you and your dog will continue to get better.

Jerry Lewis' 2008 book ***VST — A Journey Worth Pursuing*** describes his training methods. It is a good book and should be in everyone's library who seriously trains for the VST or UTDX. One interesting characteristic of his training is to tracklay or spectate at VST tests and then return over subsequent weeks and months to lay the same test tracks he had seen the judges plot. He would run these tracks repeatedly over several sessions until his dog would track them correctly. Feel free to train like Jerry for a while as you prepare for your dog's successful VST test; I recommend mixing in the focused tracks and skill exercises throughout this period. Note: I prefer not to use the same site for VST training tracks within 2 weeks of the tracklayer having been on the site before.

Polishing Skills. Regularly review your own and your dog's performance on the last 3–5 tracks. Identify any skills that could use improvement even if they were good enough to get you through that particular track. Focus one or more sessions on improving those skills, one at a time.

Peaking Performance for the Test. You can do a few things in the last couple of weeks before a test to make sure that your dog's skill and enthusiasm for tracking is at its peak. The general idea is to work your dog quite hard two to three weeks before a test, then back off to motivational tracks the first half of the pre-test week, followed by a layoff for 3–4 days before the test. You want your dog to be highly enthusiastic for tracking when you take him out of your car on test day, which means he should be under-worked for several days before. As well as avoiding tracking training for 3–4 days, I avoid other types of training for 2–3 days. Adapting a schedule like the one on page 152 to your current VST training can be helpful.

Stormy Weather. I have judged several VST tests where the weather was extremely unkind to the dog and exhibitor. High winds and driving cold rain make for an unpleasant experience for the team, the judges, and the spectators. This is one reason I used to skip out of work early any day when the weather was extreme — so my dog and I were used to those conditions. It is very difficult to get into VST/UTDX tests; you certainly want to take advantage of every one you do get into. So don't let the test be the first day you try to track over asphalt with flowing water and cold driving rain making your hands shake.

Adopting a Zen State as a Test Handler. Without getting metaphysical, think of this kind of Zen as a total state of focus incorporating the togetherness of handler and dog. As the handler member of the team, you need to be aware of the environment around you but not distracted by it. You certainly need to avoid being distracted by counterproductive speculations about where the track might go. Relax, enjoy your dog and how well he tracks, and, at each choice point, keep saying "Yippee! I'm on a corner that might go straight".

Entering VST Tests. Review the discussion on trust on page 76 as well as the test day discussion on page 249. While the latter is for TDX, it is easy to apply for the VST as well. The complexity of the AKC VST test and the CKC UTDX test should not be underestimated. They are very difficult tests for both the dog and the handler. The frequent areas of contamination make the dog's job very difficult to sort out the correct track to follow. The dog's behavior is complex as he studies the constantly changing scent-complex along the track, which can confuse the handler, who subsequently mishandles the dog.

Sadly, I cannot offer you one or two training or handling tricks to give you a 90% chance of passing on your next try. I don't believe there are such magic tricks to offer. What I have shared is a large number of training and handling techniques as well as training progressions for both you and your dog that will enable you both to get better and better. Enjoy the training and testing process. Have fun with your dog every time you track him, whether it is a simple single-leg starter track or a real test track.

Despite the complexity or perhaps because of it, the test is incredibly fun for both the dog and handler. So it is worth all the training hours required to reach a skill level where passing becomes possible.

Sessions V4.x VST-like Tracks with Lawns, Buildings, and Parking Lots.

V4.1, .4, .7, .10, .13, .16

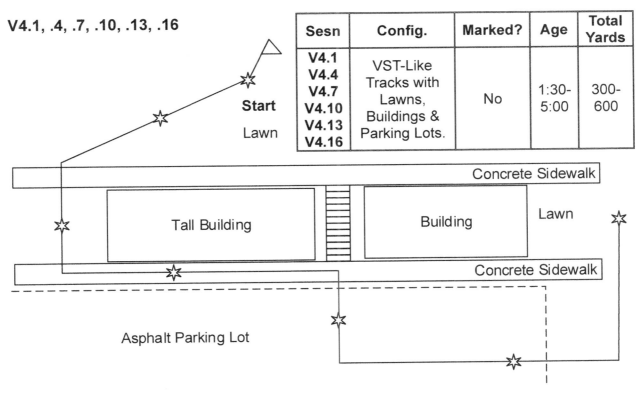

Sesn	Config.	Marked?	Age	Total Yards
V4.1	VST-Like Tracks with Lawns, Buildings & Parking Lots.	No	1:30–5:00	300–600
V4.4				
V4.7				
V4.10				
V4.13				
V4.16				

Purpose:
- Develop your dog's skill and handler's skill in solving complex tracks in a realistic context.

Tracklayer:
- See the discussion of Phase V3 designing VST-like tracks through lawns, buildings and parking lots on page 359 and the examples shown in the discussion section of this phase.
- In particular, design these tracks with VST test-like complexity unless the handler asks for something simpler.
- Avoid having more than once per track the "common situations" listed on page 380 or the tricky situations listed on page 360. It is best to practice each situation in its own track focused on a single issue.
- The diagram above is just an example; use the campus site you have available as best as you can. See similar diagrams on pages 367-370 for additional ideas.
- Lay a single 3–8 turn zigzag that uses lawns, sidewalks, and/or parking lots.
- Prefer to alternate turn direction to avoid parallel legs getting too close.
- If you make two sequential turns in the same direction, the intervening leg should be at least 50 yards but preferably 75 yards. If a barrier is between the legs, shorter separation is OK.
- If requested by the handler, use chalk on the hard surface to mark the corners and surface transitions.
- Leave an inconspicuous or small article 30–60 yards down each leg to reward the dog for taking the corner. Do so after obvious choice points as well.

Phase V4. Preparing for the VST Test — Special Situations & Blind Tracks.

Handler:

- Be patient whenever your dog spends time sorting out the scent; don't rush your dog to make a decision.
- Ideally, use your whole line to allow your dog to make his choice before you move forward.
- If your dog chooses the wrong direction, let him investigate at least 30' before restraining him.
  - Ask him if this is the good track.
  - Re-scent him if you need to reel him in to you.
  - Use the steps of help on page 258.
- If your dog is doing well and his motivation is high, consider occasionally doing some intentional handler errors as described on pages 153 and 247 to proof your dog and help him understand that he is responsible for taking you down the good track.
- Give lots of treats and praise at each article.

Evaluation and Possible Adaptations:

- Note in your journal and your summary log (page 400) details of each track, how your dog tracked, and how you handled.
- Give your dog an overall rating as described on page 223 in TDX Part II.
- The transition to **blind tracks** can expose dog and handler skill issues. Evaluate both performances on blind tracks and make those issues the focus of tracks focused on a single issue.
- If he needs help on most hard-surface corners:
  - Use scent intensifiers like bare feet or SIAB (see page 8).
  - Try younger age (fresher scent) and then age more slowly.
  - Repeat these sessions several times.
- If he lacks confidence on many hard-surface turns:
  - Use a small freeze-dried treat at 30 yards and an inconspicuous or small article at 35–50 yards past the corner. Then remove the treat but continue with the inconspicuous reward article.
  - Repeat several sessions in different locations with less natural contamination.

VST-Like Example Track.

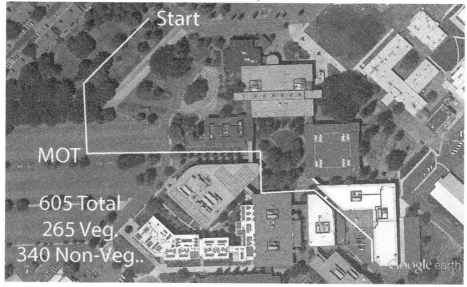

20. Image © Google

Sessions V4.x Short Track Focused on a Single Issue.

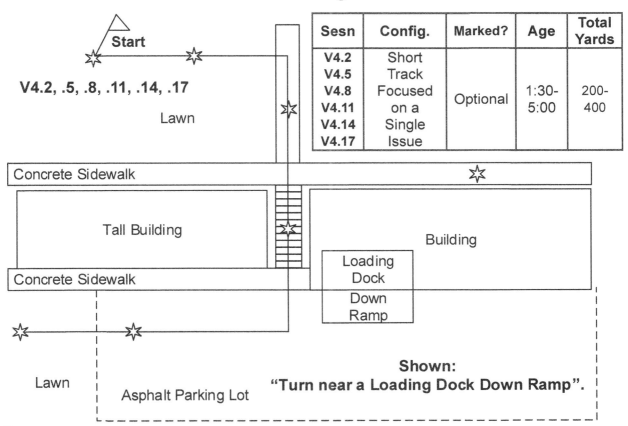

Shown: "Turn near a Loading Dock Down Ramp".

Purpose:
- Develop your dog's skill in handling tricky situations.
- Develop the handler's skill in reading her dog, organizing your dog's search, and avoiding interfering with or helping him unless absolutely needed.

Tracklayer:
- See the discussion on focused tracks on page 380 including the list of "common situations":
  - Open stairways — see picture on page 381.
  - Second-story open deck walkways — see picture on page 381.
  - Loading docks (see diagram above).
  - Building doorways.
  - Parking garages — see picture on page 381.
  - Returning to grass after hundreds of yards of concrete and asphalt.
  - Mirrored glass-sided buildings.
  - Outdoor amphitheaters or similar wide-stepped areas — see picture on page 381.
  - Outdoor cafeteria eating areas — see picture on page 381.
  - Large fountains and pools — see picture on page 381.
  - Unusually shaped architectural features on buildings like cantilevered sections.
  - Terraced parking lots.
  - Parallel contamination on the track or at the start and first leg — see page 372.

- Or see the Phase V3 list of tricky situations on page 360.
- Alternatively, review the dog's last several VST-like tracks to identify a specific issue he is having, or an issue the handler is experiencing. Any of these issues can be the focus of one of these sessions.
- Try to design a track with an easy segment, the tricky situation, and ending with an easy segment.
- If you make two sequential turns in the same direction, the intervening leg should be at least 50 yards but preferably 75 yards. If a barrier is between the legs, shorter separation is OK.
- If requested, use chalk on the hard surface to mark the corners and surface transitions.
- Leave an inconspicuous or small article 30–60 yards down each leg to reward the dog for taking the corner.

Handler:
- Choose several issues from the list above for the tracklayer to choose from. Her selection will depend on the configuration of the tracking site and the activity going on when she lays it.
- Be patient at each tricky situation and elsewhere; don't rush your dog to make a decision.
- Ideally, use your whole line to allow your dog to make the choice before you move forward.
- If your dog chooses the wrong direction, let him investigate at least 30' before restraining him.
  - Ask him if this is the good track.
  - Re-scent him if you need to reel him in to you.
  - Use the steps of help on page 258.
- Give lots of treats and praise at each article.

Evaluation and Possible Adaptations:
- Note in your journal and your summary log (page 400) details of each track, how your dog tracked, and how you handled.
- Give your dog an overall rating as described on page 223 in TDX Part II.
- If the track turns out to be really easy for the dog, you can count it as a motivational session as well.
  - Consider what made it easy and if necessary, select the issue again at a site that will be more challenging for the dog and handler.
- If he needs help on most hard-surface corners:
  - Use scent intensifiers like bare feet or SIAB (see page 8).
  - Try younger age (fresher scent) and then age more slowly.
  - Repeat these sessions several times.
- If he lacks confidence at the tricky or common situation:
  - Add very small freeze-dried treats at 25 & 30 yards past the hard-surface turn for a while. Then use a small freeze-dried treat at 30 yards and an inconspicuous or small article at 35–50 yards past the corner. Then remove the treat but continue with the inconspicuous article.
  - Repeat several sessions in different locations with less natural contamination.

Sessions V4.x Select a Skill Exercise from Phase V1, V2 or V3.

Sesn	Configuration	Marked?	Age	Total Yards
V4.3 V4.6 V4.9 V4.12 V4.15 V4.18	Skill Exercise from Phase V1, V2 or V3.	Optional	1:30 - 5:00	

Purpose:
- Maintain and improve your dog's skills and your own handling skills.

Skill Exercises:
For each of these sessions, choose a skill exercise from this list:
- Four-turn track with slices and bisects — see page 319.
- Parallel contamination at the start or elsewhere — see page 372.
- Island-to-island wide gaps — see page 321.
- Hard-surface turns at barriers — see page 346 or 317.
- Hard-surface turns onto and off of sidewalks — see page 348.
- Hard-surface turn on a parking lot or plaza — see page 350.
- Any of the tricky situations from Phase V3 — see page 367.
- A simple short motivational track with lots of articles.
- Lawn serpentines to refocus the dog onto the track on the grass while aging appropriately for your dog's current skill level — see page 267.
- An urban downwind-downhill acute to improve his circling on corners — see page 102.
- A simple track with articles tossed 5 to 15' to the side of the track.
- A simple short VST-like track in a heavily distracting area.
- 4–5 hour-old simple short VST-like track on a warm, dry day.
- Specific problem issues can be addressed in these sessions. Review the TDX problem-solving suggestions starting on page 236. Most of those problem-solving exercises can be adapted to urban environments. Also, use relevant exercises from earlier TDU and VST phases as appropriate.

Handler:
- See the relevant procedure for the chosen exercise on the page referenced above.
- Make sure the dog is having fun.

Evaluation:
- Note in your journal and your summary log (page 400) details of each track, how your dog tracked, and how you handled.
- Give your dog an overall rating as described on page 223 in TDX Part II.
- If the track turns out to be easy for the dog, you can count it as a motivational session as well.
- Evaluate based on the evaluation section of the chosen session referenced above.

Session V4.x. Review and Evaluate.

Periodically assess how you and your dog are doing in the blind VST-like tracks through campuses, the tracks focused on a single issue and the skill exercises.

Do you need to go back to Phase V3, repeat more V4 material, or are you ready to enter a VST or UTDX test?

1. Is your dog confident committing at the start?
2. Is your dog consistently making the right choices and needs no help, or at most a little help, once per track?
3. On the hard-surface segments of the track, is he close to the track moving in a straight line, or at least fairly close to the track bracketing the track via the fringe?
4. If he is tracking to the side of a track, will he come in and indicate articles right on the track?
5. Are you consistently reading him correctly — no more than one mistake per track?
6. Can you organize his search over a large area when he is well off the track?

Stay in Phase V4 until you can answer "Yes" to all these questions. The schedule shows it is appropriate to evaluate and review your dog's skills and your own handling skills about every 9 sessions, although you may do so more often if you like.

If you find the complexity of these tracks too difficult for your dog, step back into Phase V3, or even Phase V2, working your dog at younger track ages and simpler track complexity.

When you can answer "Yes" to all of five questions, particularly when at least one of the last five blind VST-like tracks was completed without any help, you are as prepared as anyone else entering these tests. In fact, you will be more prepared than most since many people tend to enter prematurely.

If you do enter a test and get in, remember to follow the peaking procedure described on page 388. If you are successful, fantastic! Have a party for all your tracking friends who helped you along the way. If you are not successful, don't be discouraged. It is a very difficult test, and you will have learned from the experience so you will be better prepared for your next try.

Avoid Premature Test Entry

When you optimistically enter any test before you have a reasonable chance of passing, you end up disrupting your training and falling behind in building your dog's skills and your own skills. In the weeks leading up to the test, you will inevitably shift your training focus from developing fundamental skills to trying to polish skills which are still missing a firm foundation.

The VST and UTDX tests are very difficult; avoid entering before you pass one or more full-complexity blind tracks in a new location.

If you do enter and end up going astray in the test, learn from the experience, and don't rush to enter another test until you pass one or more full-complexity blind tracks laid in a new location.

Sample Journal Log Entry — VST-like

Session: _V4.4_
Dog: _Twizzle_
Date: _6/23/2016_
Layer: _Sil_
Location: _Clark College_
Weather: _Rain showers, cool_
Wind: _1-4_
Length: _525_
Age: _120_

Evaluation: _Quite good_

+ Nice start on berm.
+ Nice turn 1 onto concrete (rabbits).
+ Good leg 2 & turn 2 with rabbits.
+ Good transition to Asphalt.
Weak/vague commitment on leg 4.
Vague MOT but OK.
Return to grass lacked confidence.
Corner 4 onto concrete needed help.
Wants to track on the grass beside the sidewalk.
+ Good turn onto grass
Vague transition onto mulch
Weak article indication.
+ Other articles good to excellent.

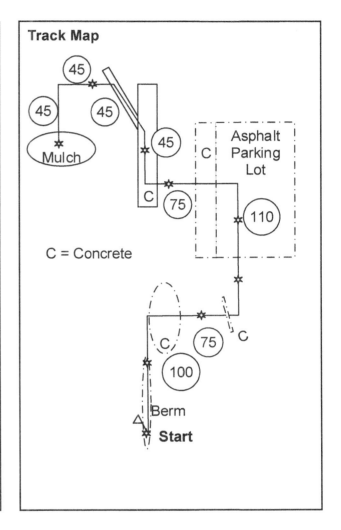

Track Map

QT's VST

Success after Many Tests of Having Fun but Coming Up Short.

After many years of training including a lot of experimentation, I entered QT in his first VST test. He did great and got to the last corner, a second MOT, before going off track. We kept entering tests at a slow but steady rate for the next two years because QT kept doing so well but not quite doing everything needed to pass. Finally, in the summer of 2009, we headed over to Missoula, Montana where we had missed the last corner two years earlier.

3:00 a.m. sharp, August 9th, 2009, at the base of a mountain just where its steep descent levels out into the groomed landscape of the University of Montana, volunteer tracklayer Mary-Ann Bowman steps off to lay her very first VST test track. She is watched walking through the dark shadows and under the stark street-lamps by judges Anne Hershey and Tannis Witherspoon. They all rose so many hours before dawn to lay a test with the faint hope that one or more of the six dogs might pass today.

4:00 a.m. — across town in a small motel two alarms blare out to wake me up. QT is curled up on the bed and just moves his paw over his eyes as the lights go on. He knows I will stumble around knocking things over for quite a while before it is time to go out to the car.

5:19 a.m. — QT and I drive away from the motel for the short trip across the river to the University. I find the partially lit parking lot with several cars and a card table topped with orange juice, coffee, and bagels. I first check in with the secretary to make sure she knows QT is here, then walk QT and arrange my fanny pack with two water bottles, a water dish on a zip cord, and no food or tennis balls.

5:45 a.m. — time for the draw. QT is catalog number 3 and I draw track 1, so we will get to run the first track. QT's TDX was on track 1, so perhaps this will be our lucky day.

6:05 a.m. — QT and I walk up the stairs that start the path to the top of the mountain and turn off onto a well-groomed lawn just to the right of the path and approach the starting flag. The start article is cloth, and I lay QT down in the wet lawn with his nose right over the cloth. He struggles to smell to the right, left and in front, then settles down to wait out my slow count to 20 while he breathes in and memorizes the scent.

6:09 a.m. — "Find it!" and QT is off, quickly focusing on and committing to a straight line across the grass. As the line slips through my hands, QT is perfectly committed to a line that will exit this lawn area in a gap between some trees.

At the gap, QT puts his nose down on the concrete sidewalk and roadway but veers off slightly to the right making a more perpendicular angle across the road than the angle of the incoming leg. His nose is low, and he is fully focused and committed, so I follow him across. At the far side of the road, he goes back and forth along the curved curb before crossing the sidewalk and checking out the grass beyond. He indicates no track there and moves back to the curb, checking more to the left, which would better match the incoming angle. He searches over to the grass, back out to the street, over to a bus-stop shelter, back out to the street. Finally he commits just to the left of the bus-stop shelter (the tracklayer had passed to the right of the bus-stop shelter, but I did not know it, and QT follows scent where he finds it.

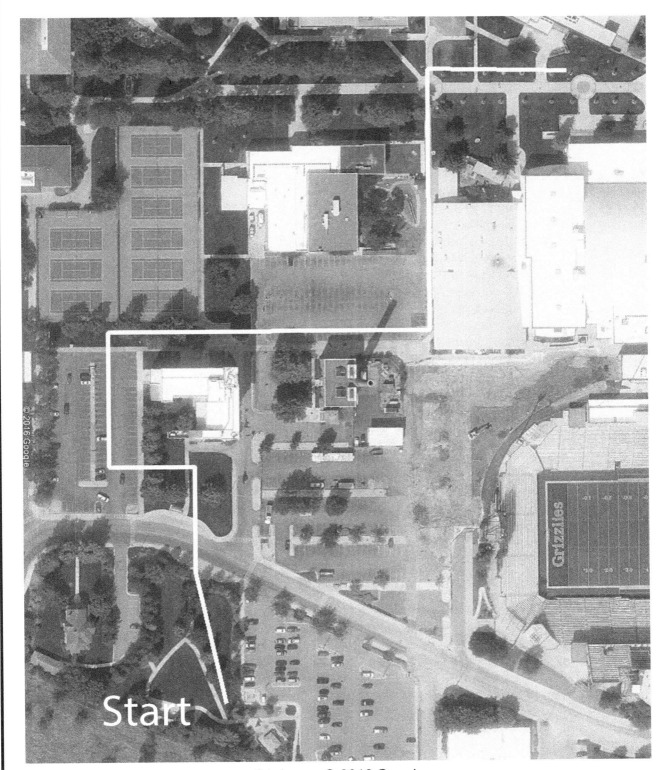

21. Image © 2016 Google

Phase V4. Preparing for the VST Test — Special Situations & Blind Tracks.

He takes me with weak commitment across a small lawn at an angle so he is probably on a fringe. Then he crosses into a parking lot; at the transition, he moves along the curb to the right and then picks up leg 2 but goes only a few yards with commitment before lifting his head. He searches to the left, ahead, to the left again, and as he comes back to me, I bring him in to re-scent him. We are right where he had run out of scent before. He puts his nose down on the blacktop and commits to the right down the ends of the empty parking spaces. I follow him, and in a short distance, he stops at a plastic article. I praise him, try to give him water, re-scent him with the start article, and he heads off down the parking lot.

At the end of the lot, he crosses a walkway and then enters a narrow strip of grass bounded by the high chain-link fence of a group of tennis courts. He starts to commit to the left, breaks off, and then he commits strongly to the right. At the end of the fence line, he transitions onto a concrete walkway. Ahead I see more grass and another parking lot; to the right is the door of a building, and to the left the sidewalk hugs the tennis courts. QT first checks out the door on the right and then commits confidently to the left staying right on the sidewalk rather than fringing it in the grass as he often does. I happily follow him perhaps 40 yards when he turns to the right out onto the lawn at an angle that would put him into a dead-end corner in an L-shaped building. He circles back across the lawn, steadily circling back the full 40 yards until we get in line with the previous leg. Here he circles a metal plate down in the grass, picks up the track and tracks the last 5' to the article. Cool, I think, we just recovered from a major diversion, we have both intermediate articles, and we are clearly heading out into this next big parking lot.

QT commits down the track, quickly makes the transition to blacktop, and with a deep nose holds a straight line along the ends of the parking stalls only a few of which are occupied. Another thirty yards out into the parking lot, he indicates loss of scent, circles right and commits down a sidewalk at the edge of a brick building. A man sits on the steps of the building drinking his early morning coffee. QT looks up, is startled by the man's sudden appearance, and freezes. The man senses that something is going on, walks back inside the door, and watches QT continue to work. QT checks out the steps where the man had been sitting, searches the area and the grass nearby, and circles back to the parking lot. He finds the track again but rejects the straight-ahead direction where it really went, choosing instead to angle over to the top of some stairs along the left side of the parking lot. But he rejected the stairs with a single sniff and also rejected the handicap ramp next to it, choosing to follow scent along the curb to the far left-hand corner of the parking lot. Here he finds the next leg and strongly commits to the track down a sidewalk.

QT stays committed to the track on the sidewalk and once past the surrounding buildings, he traverses a couple of crosswalks and comes alongside a chain-link construction fence where he indicates loss of scent. He starts to commit to the left, then circles back and searches onto a lawn to the right. He starts to line out nicely, and as I look up, I realize he is headed to the Adams Center where a huge gun show has attracted thousands of people. As the line runs through my hand, I think the judges would not have gone down there into that crowd, but QT is firmly committed. Wisely, I tell myself to not second guess my dog at this late stage in the track and step off at the end of the 40-foot line. He is strongly committed to this leg just the way he had been committed to the first 60 yards of the first leg.

6:45 am — after 96 easy yards on the lawn, he noses up a small square of leather and earns his VST and CT.

Here is a blurry picture of QT committing onto the final leg of his successful VST track in 2009. Thanks to Sally Zimmerman, a driver for the test, who saw us coming towards them and pulled out her brand-new camera to catch this moment just 50 yards from the number 4 as the end article is known.

And one of QT licking his lips once he got back to my car and his treats.

Phase V4 Summary Log

Sesn	Site	Config.	Date	Track Age	Evaluation
V4.1		VST-like			
V4.2		Single Issue			
V4.3		Choose a skill			
V4.4		VST-like			
V4.5		Single Issue			
V4.6		Choose a skill			
V4.7		VST-like			
V4.8		Single Issue			
V4.9		Choose a skill			
V4.10		VST-like			
V4.11		Single Issue			
V4.12		Choose a skill			
V4.13		VST-like			
V4.14		Single Issue			
V4.15		Choose a skill			
V4.16		VST-like			
V4.17		Single Issue			
V4.18		Choose a skill			

Appendix A — Advanced Training Exercises

This appendix describes optional field and urban tracking exercises that can help you and your dog learn specific and useful skills. They are here because they are optional, but many people find them useful, particularly if they have some extra training time before getting into a test or have seen a particular issue that may be helped by a particular exercise.

	Exercise	Location	Page
ATE 1	Track Direction	Sports or Natural Field	402
ATE 2	Expanding the Search Area	Sports or Natural Field	405
ATE 3	Fringing instead of Tracking	Sports or Natural Field	406
ATE 4	Re-motivating a Demotivated Dog	Sports or Natural Field	408
ATE 5	Crazy Contaminated One Corner Tracks	Sports Lawn	410
ATE 6	Crazy Contaminated Zigzags	Sports Lawn	412
ATE 7	Crazy Contaminated Field Track	Natural Field	415
ATE 8	Group Curbed-Island Serpentines	Parking Lot	417

The Crazy-Contaminated exercises, as well as the Group Curbed-Island Serpentines, are meant for a group tracking together as in a class or seminar setting. The others are intended for individuals although "Expanding the Search Area" can also be used by a group.

- **ATE 1 Track Direction** can be used as remediation or simply to teach or improve the skill.
- **ATE 2 Expanding the Search Area** is an important handler skill, and this exercise helps people understand how they can do it.
- **ATE 3 Fringing Instead of Tracking** is a remediation set of exercises intended for dogs who primarily use air scent to wander near the track instead of focusing on the track itself.
- **ATE 4 Re-motivating a Demotivated Dog** is a remediation exercise for the dog who has lost all or most his motivation to track, not the dog who has just had one or two difficult experiences.
- **ATE 5 Crazy Contaminated One Corner Tracks** is a good exercise for a group of students who all want to be introduced to or practice intentional contamination.
- **ATE 6 Crazy Contaminated Zigzags** is another good exercise for a group of a little more advanced students.
- **ATE 7 Crazy Contaminated Field Track** is a game that lets TDX hopeful dogs experience a combination of group contamination and crosstracks in the field without the overhead of doing individual U-over-U or X-over-U tracks for each member of the group. This group exercise is not a substitute for regular U-over-U, X-over-U, and M-over-U crosstrack training.
- **ATE 8 Group Curbed-Island Serpentines** is a good way to let a group of students all work curbed-island serpentines when there are not enough curbed islands for everyone to work in isolation.

ATE 1 — Track Direction

Purpose:
- Help your dog learn to determine track direction when re-finding the track. We do so by repeatedly bringing him into short starter tracks in the middle of the leg.
- This is a skill useful in TDX where obstacles can cause a dog to search well away from the track and have to determine its direction when he re-finds the track
- Likewise, it is a skill useful in VST where surface transition, contamination, and wind vortexes can cause a dog to search well off the track and have to determine its direction when re-finding it.
- Suitable for a single dog per set with a large natural or sports field available.
- Dogs may need to do this separately during their TDX and again during their VST training using natural fields for the TDX and sports lawns for the VST.

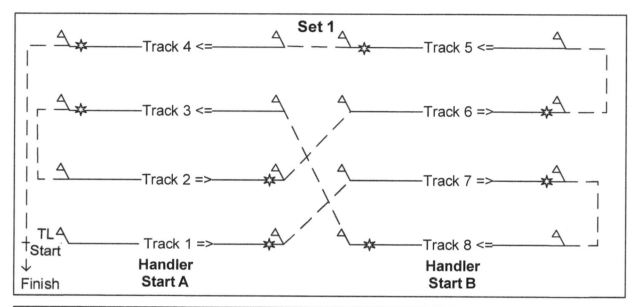

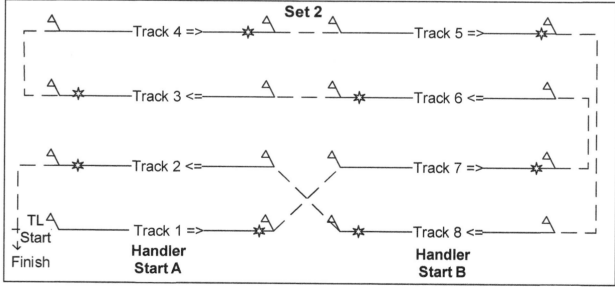

Tracklayer (TL):

- Choose one from the selection of Sets 1–4 (see the next page for sets 3 & 4) or make up your own to fit the field you have available. Do not tell the handler which set you are laying.
- You need 8 gloves or other friendly articles and 16 flags. Do not put down start articles.
- Put in each track in turn following the dashed lines between tracks. This will create a "random" direction for the handler.
- Each track should be about 60 yards long. Optionally you can put another flag in the middle where you will start the dog.
- The ends of the tracks should be separated by about 30 yards, and the parallel tracks should be 50 yards from each other.
- Once you are done, age an appropriate amount of time for the dog.
- If there is room and you are unfamiliar to the dog, lay a starter track between base camp and the start so the dog can warm up on you as a tracklayer. In a test situation, the dog will have followed you for some time before searching away from the track and needing to re-find it.
- When ready, bring the handler to the middle of either Track 1 or Track 8.
- The tracklayer should let the handler know if the dog is incorrect when the handler has committed behind the dog in the wrong direction 40' or more.

Handler:

- The purpose of this exercise is to help your dog understand track direction. There will be a glove and a party 30 yards in the correct direction from where you start.
- You should do this blind unless your dog has demonstrated a strong tendency to backtrack when he has re-found the track after being off on a search.
- Even if you know the direction of the track, give your dog the full 40' of line to make his decision. Don't rush him or check him early.
- This is a shaping exercise, give your dog the chance to work it out before you hint or help him. Make it worth his while to go in the correct direction by having a big fun party at every glove.

Evaluation and Possible Adaptations:

- Some dogs never seem to figure out track direction, although others are able to do so within two or three footsteps or even within a single footprint.
  - I speculate the 2–3 footstep dogs are using scent intensity.
  - I speculate the single-footprint dogs are using the crushed vegetation and disturbed dirt scent that may be different between the heavy heel and the broad toe area.
- If your dog makes several mistakes in the eight-track set, then you should do this exercise multiple times.
  - Do one session with the direction marked by different color flags at the start and the end; Help your dog so he understands there is a fun party in the good direction.
  - Then do a blind session, but once your dog makes two mistakes, have the tracklayer tell you the correct direction for the remainder of the tracks in the set.
  - If your dog does it correctly when you know the direction, make sure you are not checking or otherwise hinting your dog when he searches.
- If you have a really good direction-finding dog, you can use this exercise as a test. He needs to do it perfectly 20 tracks in a row without any errors to "prove" he is 95% reliable. Once he makes even a single mistake, it becomes really hard to "prove" his reliability to the 95% level. Perhaps the 20-track test will be fun if you have the time.

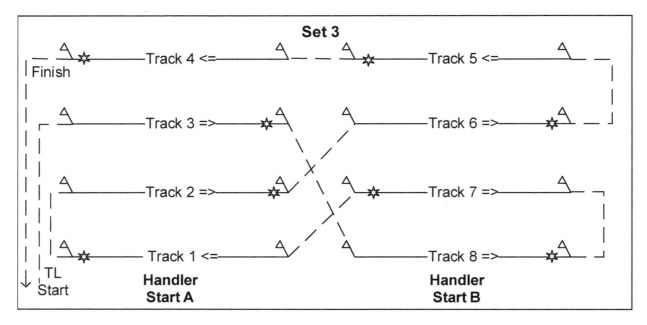
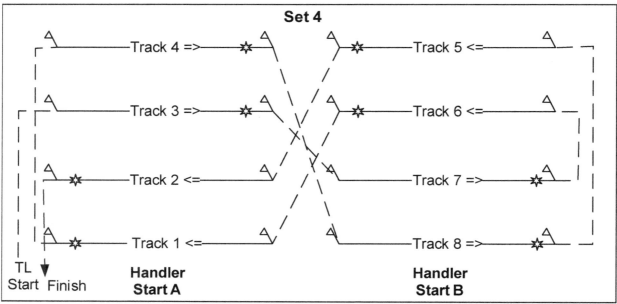

ATE 2 — Expanding the Search Area

Purpose:
- Teach the handler to expand the search area or move the dog's search to a new area.

Description:
- Place a flag in each corner of a square about 30 yards to the side.
- Get a friend to play dog, hook her up to your tracking line, and ask her to act like a willing dog.
- The "dog" should track nicely into the center of the square where she loses the scent. She will willingly circle whenever the handler has light-comfortable tension on the line and otherwise respond to her handler's line handling.
- The "dog" can stop at any time to give the handler feedback.

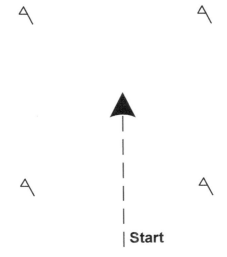

Handler:
- You need to encourage the "dog" to circle a full 360° at 2–3 different radii from your initial pivot point until you are sure the "dog" cannot find the track within the radius of your line.
- Then you should move slowly so the "dog" is able to circle beyond the four corners of the track without forcing the "dog" anywhere intentionally, which may be interpreted as guiding. See page 163 for a discussion of the differences between training, handling, and guiding.
- The key to allowing your "dog" to move to a new area without "guiding" is to sidestep or back up as your "dog" is moving in that direction as part of his circling.
  - You are organizing the "dog's" search to visit new areas, not telling your "dog" the location or direction of the track.
  - In this exercise, you are done when your "dog" is able to go beyond the four flags.
- In a real test, you may need to continue to spiral out from the point of initial loss-of-scent. Or you may decide that you have overshot the corner, so you would choose to allow and encourage your dog to keep circling backward.

ATE 3 — Fringing Instead of Tracking

When fringing, the dog primarily wanders well to the side of the track typically with his head fairly high. If your dog consistently spends most of the track 15–40' to the side of a blind track going back and forth, I'd consider the dog has learned to be a fringing dog rather than a tracking dog. While these dogs may have excellent air-scenting capabilities, they need to learn to be more committed to the track itself, instead of the highly irregular wind-driven scent-fringe. Often these dogs did not learn to track following the step-by-step methods of this book and need significant remediation to adopt the more successful tracking style. Sometimes the dog had a good tracking foundation but was subsequently allowed to wander too widely. This issue may seem related to Shortcuts to Upwind Articles (page 135), but in this case, the dog does not need an upwind article to pull it off the track.

Remediation consists of doing field or lawn serpentines where every footstep has a tiny treat like a ⅛" to ¼" piece of freeze-dried lamb lung right in each and every footprint. When working in a natural field, use large ½" pieces or hot dogs. Diligently try to drop the treat right in a footprint. I find using a 3–4' piece of PVC pipe allows more treats to hit the footprint while requiring a lot less twisting and bending of my body. Use a flag at each open turn with straight legs of 15–20 yards each. Stay just 10' behind your dog and do not let his nose move more than 2–3' to the side of the track or beyond each open corner.

Close-to-the-Track Remediation Serpentines with Tiny Treats

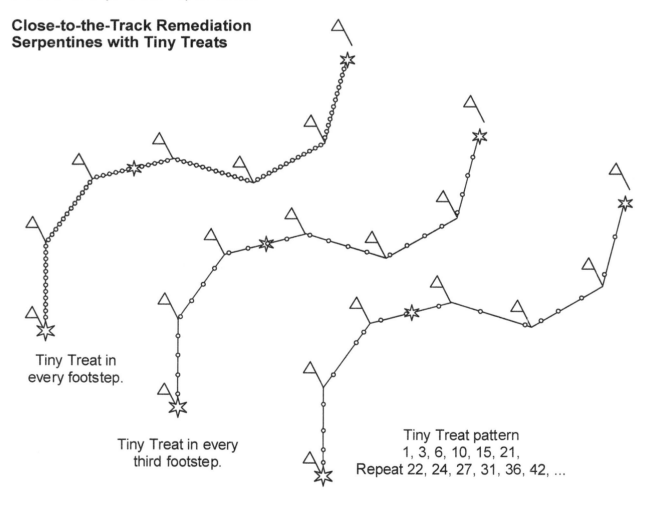

Tiny Treat in every footstep.

Tiny Treat in every third footstep.

Tiny Treat pattern 1, 3, 6, 10, 15, 21, Repeat 22, 24, 27, 31, 36, 42, ...

As your dog gets good at staying focused on the track without your restraint, spread the tiny treats out to every other footstep, e.g. footsteps 1, 3, 5, 7 ... Then every third footstep, e.g. footsteps 1, 4, 7, 10... Finally, start placing tiny treats in a variable rotating pattern like placing the tiny treat of footstep 1, 3, 6, 10, 15, 21, (repeat) 22, 24, 27, 31, 36, 42... Also, place a small intermediate article every third leg, and play happily with your dog there, even if he wants to get right back to collecting all these delicious tiny treats.

The length of these tracks depends on your dog, but 120–300 yards should work for most dogs. Make sure you eventually include all wind directions over several sessions so your dog becomes used to this tracking style regardless of the wind.

For a dog who mostly stays close to the track and only occasionally becomes an air-scenting wanderer, a few of these sessions should suffice to refocus your dog onto the track. For a dog who typically "tracks" most of the time well-wide of the track itself, expect to spend many sessions building his behavior to favor the close-to-the-track style. You will find it a worthwhile training investment.

If ants or insects make the treats less than a reward for your dog, keep to younger-aged tracks for a while. Then resume normal tracks but have them well marked so you can continue to keep your dog close to 30–60-minute-old tracks most of the length of the track.

This kind of remediation requires considerable training judgment on how to adapt the exercise and the sequence of rewards for your particular dog. Adjust track age and length, the spacing of the tiny treats as well as their type, and the sites that you use can help keep your dog interested in motivated in doing what you need him to do along the track. Don't rush to get through this, take your time so your dog truly learns how much fun it is to be a tracking dog. And become a good tracking dog does not preclude his remaining an excellent air scenting dog - he can be both as the task requires.

ATE 4 — Re-Motivating a Demotivated Dog

The following steps have been helpful in re-motivating dogs who have become demotivated. Demotivation can occur because of a series of too difficult or badly planned training sessions, tracking in unusually hot-dry weather, not enough reward along the track, boring parties at articles, handlers becoming unhappy with their dog when he struggles, or hormonal changes due to an intact bitch's season or false pregnancy. Typically you see it as a lack of excitement as you approach the start, or when your dog searches aimlessly at the start or fails to start an otherwise quite doable track. You also see it as poor ongoing focus on the track and being more easily distracted than normal for that dog.

Some dogs become demotivated but not very deeply. If given a break of a couple of weeks followed by a simple motivation track, they will bounce back and be good as new. Other dogs become deeply demotivated and require a bigger break followed by a much slower restart to training.

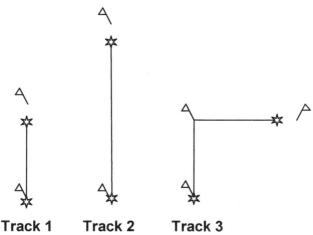

Track 1   Track 2   Track 3

Deeply Demotivated Dogs:

1. First, give your dog a break of six weeks. No tracking whatsoever. If your dog does other sports, also stop any of them where his motivation is low. Except for exercise walks, complete inactivity is the kind of break he needs.
2. Then try a session of three simple tracks laid one after the other in an area where your dog has tracked well in the past. The first is 50 yards straight, the second is 100 yards straight, and the third is 50 yards to a corner and 50 yards to the glove. Place tiny freeze-dried treats every 10–15 yards along each track. After running each track, evaluate your dog's excitement and motivation level.
    - Run the first track as soon as you get back and get your dog.
    - If that goes well, wait another 15 minutes for TD-level dogs or 20 minutes for more advanced dogs and run the second track. If the first track is just OK, go right on to the next track without waiting. If the first track does not go well at all, just take your dog back to the car, and go pick up the rest of the articles yourself.
    - If the second track goes well, wait another 15–30 minutes and run the third track. But if track 2 was just OK, go right on to the next track without waiting. If track 2 does not go well, just take your dog back to the car and go pick up the rest of the articles yourself.

3. If the three tracks went well, look at the kinds of tracks you were doing recently, the complexity and age difference between the three-track session you just did and the kind of tracks you had done before he became demotivated.
    - If the three-track session did not go well, take another 2-week break and try again making sure you choose a fun place where your dog likes to track.
4. Plan five sessions, called your bridge sessions, which gradually bridge the complexity of the three-track session and the kind of sessions he was doing enthusiastically before he became demotivated.
5. Proceed to do each bridge session in turn making sure each goes well. Use more articles and treats on the track than you were using before. When you see a drop in motivation, no matter how small, stop and consider the previous session your re-entry level.
6. Look through the phases of your current training level and decide where this re-entry level fits in terms of age and general track complexity.
7. Restart at that place in the schedule, keeping up the fun, and reward lavishly. Keep your own attitude very up beat as you progress forward.
8. Very gradually progress to the kinds of tracks you were doing when he became demotivated, making sure his motivation does not drop this time. Progress gradually, don't rush.

Shallowly Demotivated Dogs:
1. First, give your dog a break of two weeks. No tracking whatsoever. If your dog does other sports, also stop any of them where his motivation is low. Complete inactivity, except for exercise walks, is the break he needs.
2. Then lay a short motivational marked track in a nice field and run it about half the age you were working before the break. Evaluate primarily your dog's excitement and motivation level. Use hot dogs in the field or tiny freeze-dried treats for urban tracks, several per leg.
    - A motivational track for a TD or TDU level dog is 2 corners similar to Plan 8C tracks on page 142.
    - A motivational track for a TDX level dog is a 45–90-minute-old 3-corner track about 400 yards long with no complex obstacles, for example, see page 240.
    - A motivational track for a VST level dog is a 45–90-minute-old 3-corner track about 400 yards long with long stretches of only slightly-contaminated grass and simple transitions to hard surfaces.
3. If the motivational session went well, divide the age difference and complexity difference between the motivational track and the tracks you were doing just before he became demotivated into four parts. The next four sessions will be your bridge sessions. Do each of the steps in these bridge sessions in turn, staying in fun places where your dog likes to track. Continue to use more treats on each leg than normal.
    - If the motivational session did not go well, take another one-to-two-week break and then do an even simpler motivational track in a fun place your dog likes to track.
4. Proceed to do each bridge session in turn, making sure each goes well. When you see a drop in motivation no matter how small, stop and consider the previous session your re-entry level.
5. Look through the phases of your current training level and decide where this re-entry level fits in terms of age and general track complexity.
6. Restart at that place in the schedule, keeping up the fun, and reward lavishly. Keep your own enthusiasm very high as your dog progresses through the sessions.
7. Very gradually progress to the kinds of tracks you were doing when he became demotivated, making sure his motivation does not drop this time.

ATE 5 — Crazy Contaminated One Corner Tracks

Purpose:
- Provide controlled experience with contaminated one-corner tracks with other dogs nearby.
- Suitable for a class or seminar setting if very large natural or sports fields are available.
- Handlers can lay tracks for another pair's one-corner tracks but preferably not their own.

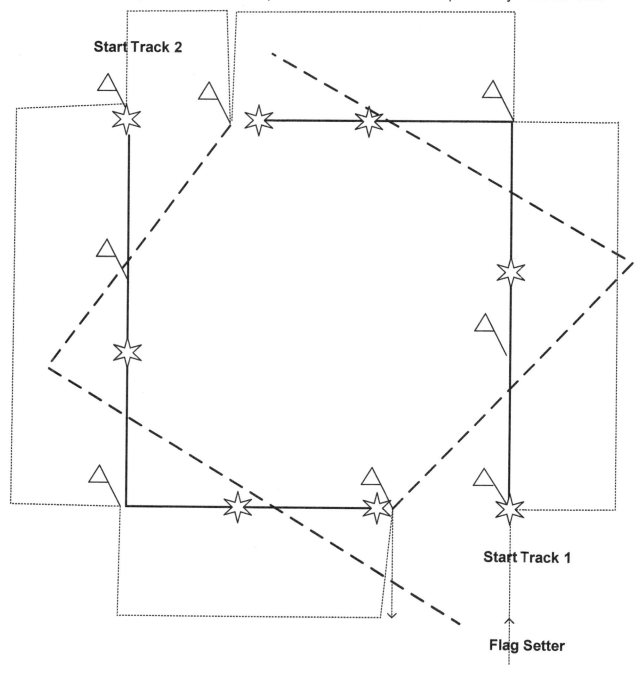

Flag Setter:
- The flag setter is someone who will not be a tracklayer or handler in this exercise. I generally do the flag setting in my role as instructor. The flag setter is laying contamination that the dog may notice, but that is OK as this is a contamination exercise.
- The flag setter sets all the flags first except the 30-yard direction flags. There should be two different color flags for each pair of tracks, and those colors should not be reused on adjacent tracks.
- Place the start flag for track 1, turn 90° to your right and walk 25 yards (facing "right").
  - Directions "right", "left", "up", and "down" are relative to the diagram on the previous page.
- Turn 90° to your left (facing "up") and walk 70 yards in that direction.
- Turn 90° to your left (facing "left") and walk 25 yards to the corner where you place a flag.
- Turn 90° to your right (facing "up") and walk 25 yards. Turn 90° to your left (facing "left") and walk 50 yards.
- Turn 90° to your left (facing "down") and walk 25 yards to place the end flag for track 1.
- Turn 180° (facing "up"), walk 25 yards, then 90° to your left ("left") and walk 25 yards, then 90° to your left again ("down") and walk 25 yards. Place the start of track 2 there.
- Turn 90° to your right (facing "left"), walk 25 yards, turn 90° to your left (facing "down"), walk 70 yards, turn 90° to your left (facing "right") walk 25 yards and place the corner flag.
- Turn "right" (facing "down"), walk 25 yards, turn left (facing "left") and walk 50 yards.
- Turn right (facing "up"), walk 25 yards, place the second track's end flag, turn 180° (facing "down"), and exit the field.

Tracklayer:
- Tracklayers will need 4 articles and a directional flag of the same color as the track being laid. The two intermediate articles should be inconspicuous and/or small. If the handler has given you treats to place down in addition to the articles, bring them along.
- Get in the vicinity of the start flag and wait for the other tracklayer to get into position as well.
- Start laying both tracks at the same time. Place your articles, the direction flag, and any treats as directed. Place the final article about 5 yards before the end flag.
- Continue to the end flag, then turn an open left to cross the other track roughly as shown, twice on the first leg and once on the second.
- If you are also running your dog on a track in another pair, go get your dog. Otherwise, walk behind the handler and make sure she understands where the good track is located.

Handler:
- Get your dog in the vicinity of your start, harness up, and wait for the signal to start as we want both dogs tracking at the same time to work our dog with distractions.
- When everyone is ready, move up to the start and handle like normal. Of course, don't let your dog go all the way over to contact another dog.

Spectators:
- If you are not working a dog when these dogs run their tracks, take a position in the middle of the square and watch both dogs and handlers. If a handler gets confused, help them locate their track and its direction.

ATE 6 — Crazy Contaminated Zigzags

Purpose:
- Provide controlled experience with contaminated zigzags and other dogs tracking nearby.
- Suitable for a class or seminar setting if very large natural or sports fields are available.
- Participants can lay a track for another, but the Flag Setter and the CXT layers cannot be a main tracklayer since they contaminate all the tracks.

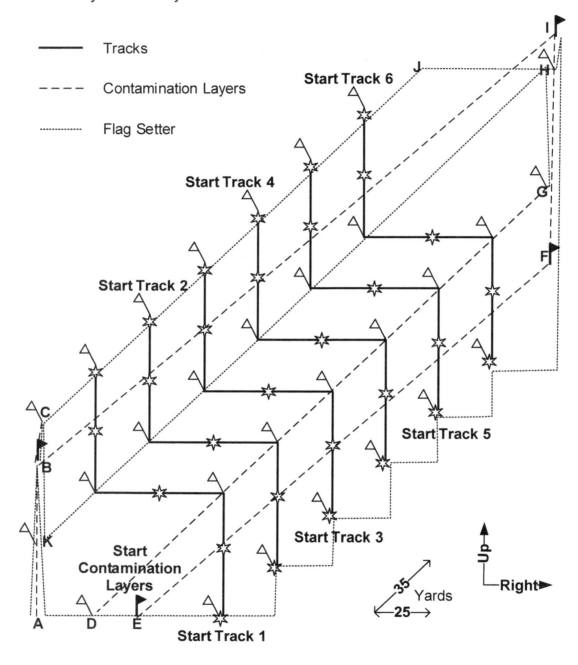

Description and Tracklaying:
Each of the legs of the tracks is *intended* to be 60 yards, and each track is separated by 25 yards. Dogs will start on both sides of the field so each dog will see other dogs on adjacent tracks.

Flag Setter:
- Sets all the flags first. There should be at least four different color flags for the main tracks, flags of a fifth color for the CXT, and flags of a sixth color for the setter's sighting flags.
  - The flag setter needs to use good landmarks.
- Starting at Point A where she leaves a temporary flag, walk 35 yards in direction "up" to point K and put in a setter's flag. Continue on 35 yards to point B and put in a CXT flag. Go on another 20 yards to point C and lay a setter's sighting flag. Retrace your steps to point A.
- Turn 90° to your left (facing "right") and go 25 yards to point D where you place another setter's flag. Proceed another 25 yards and put in a CXT flag. Then proceed 35 yards to put in the flag to start Track 1. Continue in the same direction 25 yards, turn 90° to your left (facing "up"), find a good landmark and walk 25 yards where you put the flag at the end of track 2.
- Continue in this 25 "right" then 25 "up" pattern for each desired track. Six are shown.
- Once you have done all the alternating start and end flags, turn 90° to your right (facing "right") and walk 25 yards, then 90° to your left (facing "up") walk 50 yards where you place a CXT flag at point F.
- Continue in the "up" direction for 40 more yards to point G and place a Setter's flag. Then 60 more yards to point H for another Setter's flag. Then 35 more yards to point I and a CXT flag.
- Return to flag H and turn 90 to your right (facing "left"). Walk 50 yards to point J (No flag is needed there). Turn 45° to your "left" (facing diagonally "left" and "down") and look for flag "C" in the distance.
- Walk 35 yards towards flag C where you put the start flag for track 6 (or whatever your last track may be). Make sure the color of this flag matches the flag at the other end of the track. Continue on another 35 yards to place the end flag of track 5. Repeat this procedure until you put in the end flag for track 1. Continue on to point C.
- Turn another 45° to your left (facing "down") and walk 55 yards to point K. Turn 135° to your left (facing diagonally "up" and to the "right") where you will see flag H. Walk 35 yards to the second corner of track 1 and place track 1 colored flag. Make sure it is the correct color for that track. Repeat walking 35 yards for each additional track.
- When you get to flag H, turn 135° to your right (facing "down") and walk to flag G.
- Now turn 45° to your right (facing diagonally to the "down" and "left") and look for flag D. Walk 35 yards to place the second corner flag for track 6. Make sure it the correct color for that track. Then continue walking 35 yards and place a corner flag. Repeat until you have placed the first corner flag for track 1. Continue on to flag D.
- Organize the tracklayers and CXT layers, making sure they see their flags. See the tracklayer instructions on the next page.
- Later, when the handlers are lining up to start their track, pick one or two teams to watch like 1 & 3. Walk behind one of them but watch both. If a handler gets disoriented, help her figure out where the track is located. Solicit other people to assist with this helper role.

Tracklayer:
- Tracklayers need five articles. The 3 intermediate articles should be inconspicuous if the grass is short like on a sports field. Bring the handler's treats along, if requested.
- Tracklayers should line up about 5 yards before their start and wait for all tracklayers to get in place.

- The setter should blow a whistle or otherwise indicate when the tracklayers should start laying each track; ideally, all tracks are laid at the same time.
- Once done, return without crossing any of the tracks, get your dog, and go to within about 5 yards of the start of your dog's track (which is not the one you laid).

Contamination Layers (CXT):
- At the same time the tracklayers are lining up to lay their tracks, or shortly thereafter, one or two contamination layers start at point E and walk diagonally "up" and to the "right" to point F, then "up" to point I, then diagonally "down" and to the "left" to point B.
- When the handlers are lining up to start their track, pick one or two to watch. Walk behind one of them. If a handler gets disoriented, help her figure out where the track is located.

Handler:
- Line up about 5 yards before your start flag, get your dog harnessed and ready.
- When everyone is ready, move up to the start and handle normally. Of course, don't let your dog go all the way over to contact another dog.

Track Assignments (Example):

Track	Tracklayer	Handler
1	Abby	Dot
2	Betty	Eileen
3	Carol	Frank
4	Dot	Abby
5	Eileen	Betty
6	Frank	Carol

How a seven track version looks on a large sports field.

22. Image © 2016 Google

ATE 7 — Crazy Contaminated Field Track

Purpose:
- A fun game with plenty of contamination in the field, suitable for a group of 6 or more participants.

Description:
- This is one of the few exercises I recommend where more than one dog tracks the same track (the other one is article ovals in Phase 3). Designate half the participants into Group A and the other half into Group B. One person in each group will be designated as the tracklayer and all the others will be crosstrack layers. The Group-A tracklayer lays the Group-B track and the Group-A crosstrack layers cross the Group-B track just after that track is laid. Vice versa for the Group-A track. Then each Group-A dog will run track-A while the Group-B dogs run track-B. Each handler will drop the article in place once her dog heads off down the track so the article is there for the next dog.

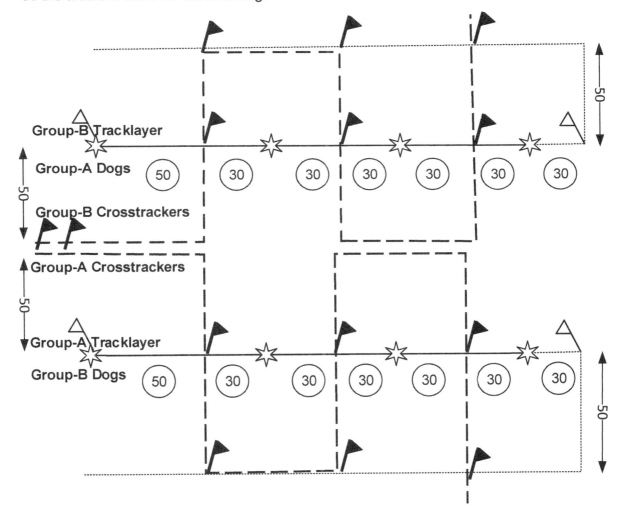

Appendix A — Advanced Training Exercises

Tracklayers and Crosstrack Layers:
- The tracklayer who is a member of Group-B lays Track-A, and the tracklayer who is a member of Group-A lays Track-B.
- Each tracklayer needs four cloth or leather articles, two track flags of one color and six crosstrack flags of another color.
- The Group-A tracklayer lays her track with flags and articles as shown in the diagram, placing the end flag about 20–30 yards past the glove. She turns 90° to her left and walks 50 yards "up" then 90° left again and parallels her track placing the outer crosstrack flags to align with the crosstrack flags on the track.
- The Group-B tracklayer lays her track 100 yards to the right of the first track and parallel to it placing the end flag about 20–30 yards past the glove. She turns 90° to her right and walks 50 yards "down" then 90° right again and parallels her track on the outside placing the outer crosstrack flags to align with the crosstrack flags on the track.
- The crosstrack layers from each group cross the track laid by their group's tracklayer.
- Then everyone gets their dogs and congregates at their own dog's track start.
- One or two non-working coordinators should stand out between the two tracks aligned with the first or second intermediate articles when the dogs are ready to run. They watch the working dog and remind the handler to drop the article behind them for the next dog. And they signal the next dog when to start (when the previous dog has left the second intermediate article).

Handler:
- The first dog starts and the handler makes sure to drop each article behind her once her dog commits on the track ahead.
- Handlers need to be aware of your dog before them on the track so they don't overrun a slower team. Each handler can start their dog once your dog before them has left the second intermediate article.
- When your dog notices a crosstrack, let him investigate it even to the end of your 40' line. If he wants to commit farther, stop him, pull or call him back to be re-scented, and tell him "Find the good track." The second time, re-scent and gesture down the track taking a few steps with him to make it easy for him to commit to the good track.
- If your dog repeatedly tries to commit to a crosstrack, you will need to pull him in, put him at your side firmly but neutrally, and lean down and love the track yourself until he gets interested and moves forward (page 60).
- Give lots of treats and praise at each article.

Variations:
- Leave one non-participant where the middle crosstrack intersects the track. She should stand just to the side of the track for confident dogs and move to the side for less-confident dogs. The handler can direct her to move more to the side as they approach.
- Leave two non-participants near where the middle crosstrack intersects the track. They should be sitting on the ground having a picnic with real food. They should be ready to move farther to the side if asked by the handler.
- Leave one non-participant with a well-behaved on-lead dog where the middle crosstrack intersects the track. She should stand just to the side of the track for confident dogs and move to the side for less-confident or reactive dogs. The handler can direct her to move farther to the side as they approach.

ATE 8 — Group Curbed-Island Serpentines

Purpose:
- Introduce or practice curbed-island serpentines in a group setting.

Description:
The usefulness of curbed-island serpentines is emphasized in several areas of this book including Phases 2–4, U1–U3, and V1. For groups, the issue is finding a large enough parking lot with many series of curbed islands. When you find one, you can re-use a set of islands by putting a tracklayer and handler pair on it in the opposite direction who had not been part of the first pair to use that series of islands.

23. Image © 2016 Google

The A–E letters designate long curbs where beginner dogs can get some simple curb work. The 1–12 numerals show series of curbed islands where participants can practice in pairs (tracklayer & handler). Although the same pair with roles reversed cannot re-use an island sequence, they can start at the opposite end of another island series using a different color of chalk

---

Appendix A — Advanced Training Exercises 417

Bibliography

AKC, *A Beginner's Guide to Tracking*, www.AKC.org.

AKC, *Tracking Regulations*, www.AKC.org.

Alex, Richard, "The molecular logic of scent", *Scientific American*, v. 273, no. 4, pp. 154, Oct. 1995.

Brown, Wentworth, *Bring Your Nose Over Here*, ASAP Printing, Albuquerque, NM, 1984.

Budgett, H. M., *Hunting by Scent*, Eyre and Spottiswoode, London, 1937 ~ An interesting historic look at dog tracking for animal hunting as well as man tracking.

Button, Lou, *Practical Scent Dog Training*, Alpine Publications, Loveland, CO, 1990.

Chadwick, Derek, Joan Marsh & Jamie Goode, eds., *The Molecular Basis of Smell and Taste Transduction*, Wiley, Chichester, NY, 1993.

CKC, *Tracking Test Rules & Regulations*, www.ckc.ca.

Conover, Michael R., *Predator-Prey Dynamics, The Role of Olfaction*, CRC Press, Boco Raton, 2007 ~ A modern scientific book including many topics of interests to dog tracking enthusiasts.

Davis, L. Wilson, *Go Find!*, Howell Book House, New York, NY, 1974.

Dold, Catherine, "For rescue dogs nothing is better than a live find", *Smithsonian*, v. 28, no. 5, pp. 72–82, August 1997.

Foken, Thomas, *Micrometeorology*, Springer, Berlin, 2008 ~ A scientific-mathematical book on boundary layer turbulence.

Ganz, Sandy & Susan Boyd, *Tracking From the Ground Up*, Show-Me Publications, St. Louis, 1989.

Hammond, Shirley, *Training the Disaster Search Dog*, Dogwise Publications, Wenatchee, WA, 2005.

Horowitz, Alexandra, *Being a Dog: Following the Dog into a World of Smell*, Scribner, New York, 2016 ~ An interesting and detailed look at canine and human olfaction.

Hunter, Roy, *Fun Nosework for Dogs*, Howln Moon Press, Eliot, ME, 1994.

Johnson, Glen R., *Tracking Dog — Theory And Methods*, Arner Publications, Inc., Canastota, NY, 1977 ~ The original step-by-step tracking training book that significantly influenced my own training methods. Be wary of demotivating your dog if you follow his training schedule literally.

Kearney, Jack, *Tracking — A Blueprint for Learning How*, Pathways Press, El Cajon, CA 1986.

Koehler, William R., *Training Tracking Dogs*, Howell Book House, New York, 1984.

Krause, Carolyn, *The Puppy Tracking Primer*, Firedog Enterprises, Springfield, MO, 1992.

Lewis, Jerry, *VST — A Journey Worth Pursuing*, 2008 ~ An interesting short book on how he learned to train his dog for the VST.

Mueller, Betty A., *About Tracklaying, Guidelines for Dog Tracking Enthusiasts*, Howln Moon Press, Franklin, NY, 2001.

Oke, T. R., *Boundary Layer Climates, 2nd Ed.*, Routlege, London, 1978 ~ A good textbook for anyone interesting in digging deeper into understanding scent movement.

Pagen, Dennis, *Performance Flying, Hang Gliding Techniques for Intermediate and Advanced Pilots*, Sports Aviation Publications, Spring Mills, PA, 1993 ~ Another good book about airflow with interesting diagrams for the tracking enthusiast.

Palo Alto Foothill Tracking Association, *Guidelines for Tracklayers by PAFTA*, PAFTA.org, 2010 ~ a good explanation of what is needed to lay tracks at AKC tracking tests.

Presnall, Ed, *Mastering Variable Surface Tracking Book and Workbook*, Dogwise, Wenatchee, 2004 ~ many people find this catalog of VST components useful.

Pearsall, Milo D. & Hugo Verbruggen, M.D., *Scent — Training to Track, Search, and Rescue*, Alpine Publications, Loveland, CO, 1982 ~ A well respected book on olfaction, scent and training.

Pollard, Hugh B. C., *The Mystery of Scent,* Eyre and Spottiswoode, London, 1937 ~ Another interesting historical book on hunting by scent published the same year as Budgett (1937).

Ripley, Steve, *Making Scents of the Urban Jungle, 2nd ed.*, self-published, 2011 ~ A good book on VST training focusing on specific issues and training techniques.

Sanders, William (Sil), *Enthusiastic Tracking, The Step-by-Step Training Handbook*, 2nd Ed., Rime Publications, Stanwood, WA, 1998 ~ Popular predecessor to this book.

Syrotuck, William G., *Scent and the Scenting Dog*, Arner Publications, Westmoreland, NY, 1972 ~ A well respected book about dog olfaction for search and tracking dog, although newer research on olfaction has updated some of his concepts.

Theses, A., Steen, J. B., Doving, K. B., "Behavior of dogs during olfactory tracking", *Journal of Experimental Biology*, Vol. 180, 247–251, July 1993.

Index

acclimation 100, 216, 260, 316
acute 87, 102, 105, 173
advanced basics 162
age .. 107, 109, 151, 166, 179, 256, 313, 364
anchor 259
animal tracks 134, 237
article indication 16, 133, 167, 237
asphalt 8, 265, 337
backtracking .... *See* track direction
basics skills 162
blacktop .... see asphalt
birds 134, 237
blind tracks ... 89-91, 214-215, 286, 357, 384
casting 4
certification 117
checking 183, 237, 259, 314
choice point 306, 363, 384
clear-confident-commitment .37, 46, 85, 105, 200, 208, 234, 241, 257, 302, 306, 376
clippie 92, 163, 168
commitment to the track 237
communication 75, 79, 89, 119, 121, 128, 162
complexity 115, 170, 225, 384
compound obstacles 170, 180, 217
concrete 8, 265, 337
conditioning 51, 161, 175, 194, 246
confidence (dog) 68, 91, 139, 313
confidence (handler) 17, 76, 89, 125, 162
contamination .. 19, 80, 112, 258, 262, 264, 277, 410, 412
contamination, corner .. 112, 120, 281, 288, 291, 319
contamination, mid-leg 25, 83, 103, 270, 279
contamination, parallel 372
corner handling 75-76, 79, 81, 89, 91
crittering 134, 237, 261
crosswind 19, 77
crosstrack laying 182
crosstracks 160, 179, 181, 199, 220, 225, 237
cupcakes 164
curbs 43, 66, 265, 272
customizing 18, 257, 313, 387
detailed log 31

distractions 134, 237, 260
distrust, disbelief 76
dog skills 1, 13, 128, 163, 255, 302
downwind 19, 77
equipment 5, 163, 257, 307
expanding the search 363, 405
fast dogs 29
following distance 23
food .... *See* rewards
fooling around 60
freeze-dried treat 6
fringing 4, 77, 237, 238, 406
frustration 5, 17, 99, 132, 258
glove game 36, 53, 133, 162
gradual turns 70
grab & go 6, 9, 167, 238
ground animals 134, 237
ground covers 170, 217
guiding 163, 405
handler errors 150, 247, 294, 390
handler skills 1, 255, 302
handling. 16, 36, 80, 89, 117, 181, 183, 265, 294, 306, 344, 362, 405
handling (active) 163, 175, 405
hard surface 8, 265, 337
haystack 92
helping 59, 99, 258, 314
hinting 259, 314
invisible flags 57, 263, 308
jargon 4
journal 7, 31, 32
land 7
light-comfortable tension 30, 278, 315
line length 5, 23
line tracking 60
love the track 17, 59, 99, 258
make it easy .... see helping, hinting
mapping skills 41, 96, 169
moment of truth .... *See* MOT
MOT 302, 337, 339, 361
motivation .. 5, 110, 128, 134, 142, 150, 159, 161, 162, 174, 215, 223, 236, 240, 248, 275, 290, 306, 345, 388, 408
motivational track ... 150, 161, 240, 286, 311, 330, 345

mulch 8, 308
non-vegetated .... See hard surface
obstacles 160, 170, 180, 217, 225
overshooting 60, 133
parallel contamination 362
parking lots 7, 39, 265, 312
party 5, 17, 162
peaking performance 150, 248, 290, 388
pee mail 261
pivoting 58, 89-92, 181, 344
playing .... See fooling around
polishing skills 136, 246, 290, 388
poor starts 133, 237, 307, 345
praise 5, 23, 164, 191
problem solving . 51, 60, 132, 174, 216, 236, 360, 368, 371, 392, 393
proofing 150, 153, 247, 294, 390
puppies 18, 24, 37, 44, 51
quartering 4
quitting 17, 61, 91, 134, 181
reading skills 75, 87, 97, 200, 255, 278, 315, 362
re-scent 37, 99, 189, 258, 318
restarts 167
restraint .... see helping
rewards .5, 6, 35, 57, 98, 111, 129, 162, 164, 265, 307
scent 2, 78, 256, 302
scent cone 4
scent distractions ... 261, 302, 315, 360, 380
scent intensifiers 8
search area .. 89-90, 225, 238, 340, 363, 405
serpentines 38, 41, 43, 66, 267, 272, 297, 321, 406, 417
shifting responsibility 164, 175, 258, 314
shopping 278, 345
sidestep 181, 225, 315, 363, 405
site familiarity 149, 246, 248, 387
spiraling 181, 225, 344, 363, 405
square up transitions 340
starts 80, 133, 180, 237
storm drains 306, 360
stories .... see tracking stories
straw flags 57, 263, 308
stride length 51
summary log .... 7, end of each phase
suitable sites 7, 16, 39, 165
surface transitions 117, 275

TD test 110
TD-like 110
TD & TDX on urban sites 8, 79, 165, 203
TDU skills 255
TDU test 112
TDU-like 112, 289
TDX skills 160
TDX test 160
TDX-like 225, 233, 247
tension 16, 30, 36, 58, 183, 265
test day 154, 249, 290, 388
toy breeds 18, 37, 51
toys 6, 129, 162
track design ... 110, 112, 216, 225, 289, 330, 359, 383
track direction 8, 164, 238, 402
track rating 224
track scent 3
track shapes 116, 289, 331
tracking stories 20, 155, 156, 176, 194, 212, 242, 250, 336, 396
tracklayer scent 3
tracklaying ..19, 38, 48, 51, 57, 92, 111, 171, 182, 224, 386
training alone 16, 182
training philosophy 5, 132, 159
treats .... See rewards
trust *1, 76, 87, 154*
unusual conditions 231, 380
upwind 19, 77
upwind articles 135
UTD skills 329
UTD test 330
UTD-like 333
UTDX test 383, 388
UTDX-like 357
video ... 75, 85, 98, 201, 225, 239, 290, 345, 364
visual dogs 57, 263
vomeronasal organ 3, 307
VST skills 302
VST test 378, 383, 388
VST-like 357
weather 11, 117, 169, 388
wind 18, 50, 77
withdrawing treats 98, 111
yippee 80, 92, 175, 278, 344
zigzag 74